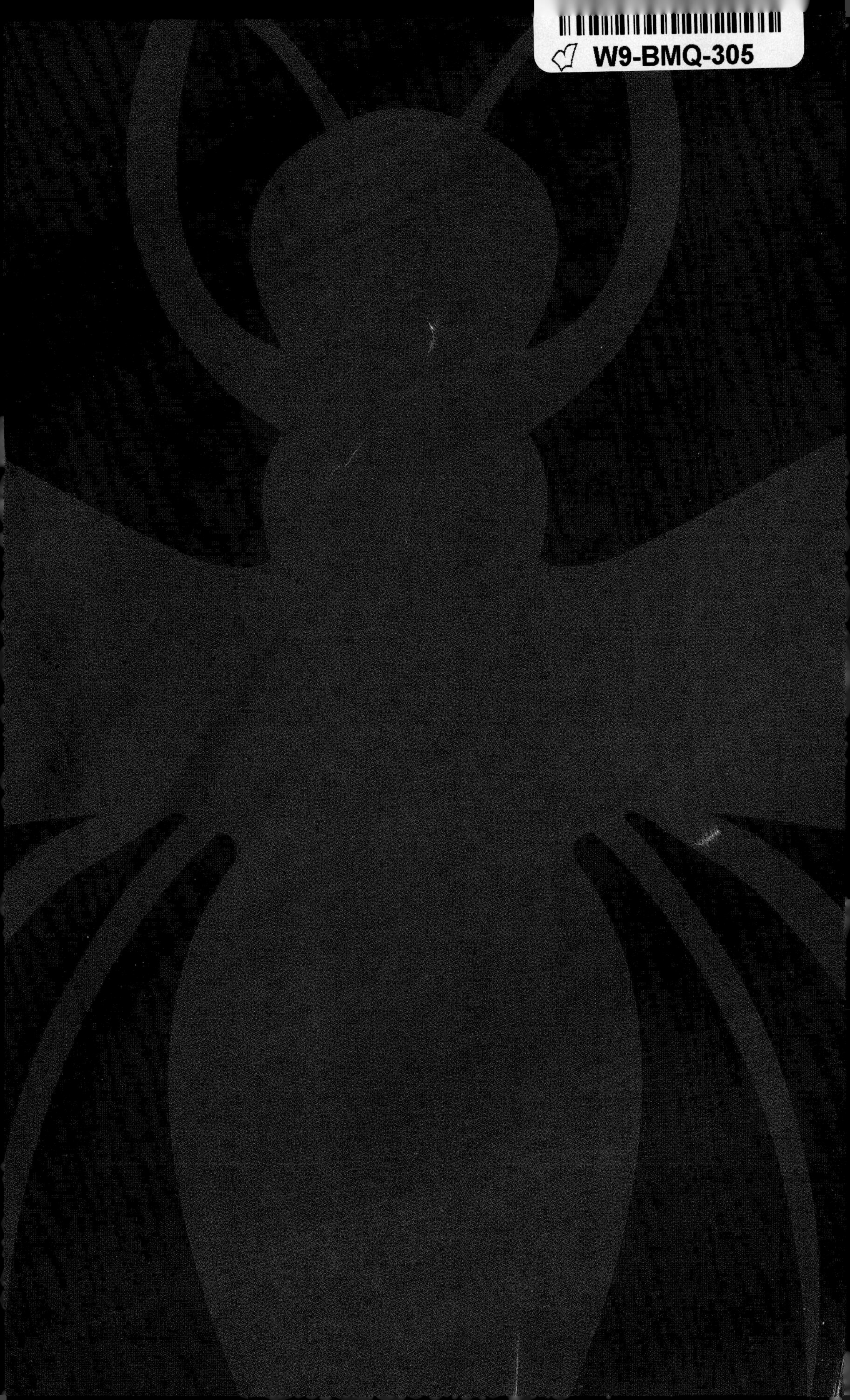

Dynamite Entertainment Presents:

The Green Hornet™ Year One

Volume One: THE STING OF JUSTICE

Script and Art Direction by MATT WAGNER

Pencils and Inks by AARON CAMPBELL

Colors by FRANCESCO FRANCAVILLA

Letters by SIMON BOWLAND

Collection Cover by ALEX ROSS

Collection design by JASON ULLMEYER

Special thanks to DAVID GRACE at Green Hornet Inc.

This volume collects issues one through six of The Green Hornet: Year One originally published by Dynamite Entertainment.

ISBN-10: 1-60690-149-4 ISBN-13: 978-1-60690-149-6 First Printing 10 9 8 7 6 5 4 3 2 1

DYNAMITE® ENTERTAINMENT

WWW.DYNAMITEENTERTAINMENT.COM

NICK BARRUCCI • PRESIDENT
JUAN COLLADO • CHIEF OPERATING OFFICER
JOSEPH RYBANDT • EDITOR
JOSH JOHNSON • CREATIVE DIRECTOR
RICH YOUNG • DIRECTOR OF BUSINESS DEVELOPMENT
JASON ULLMEYER • GRAPHIC DESIGNER

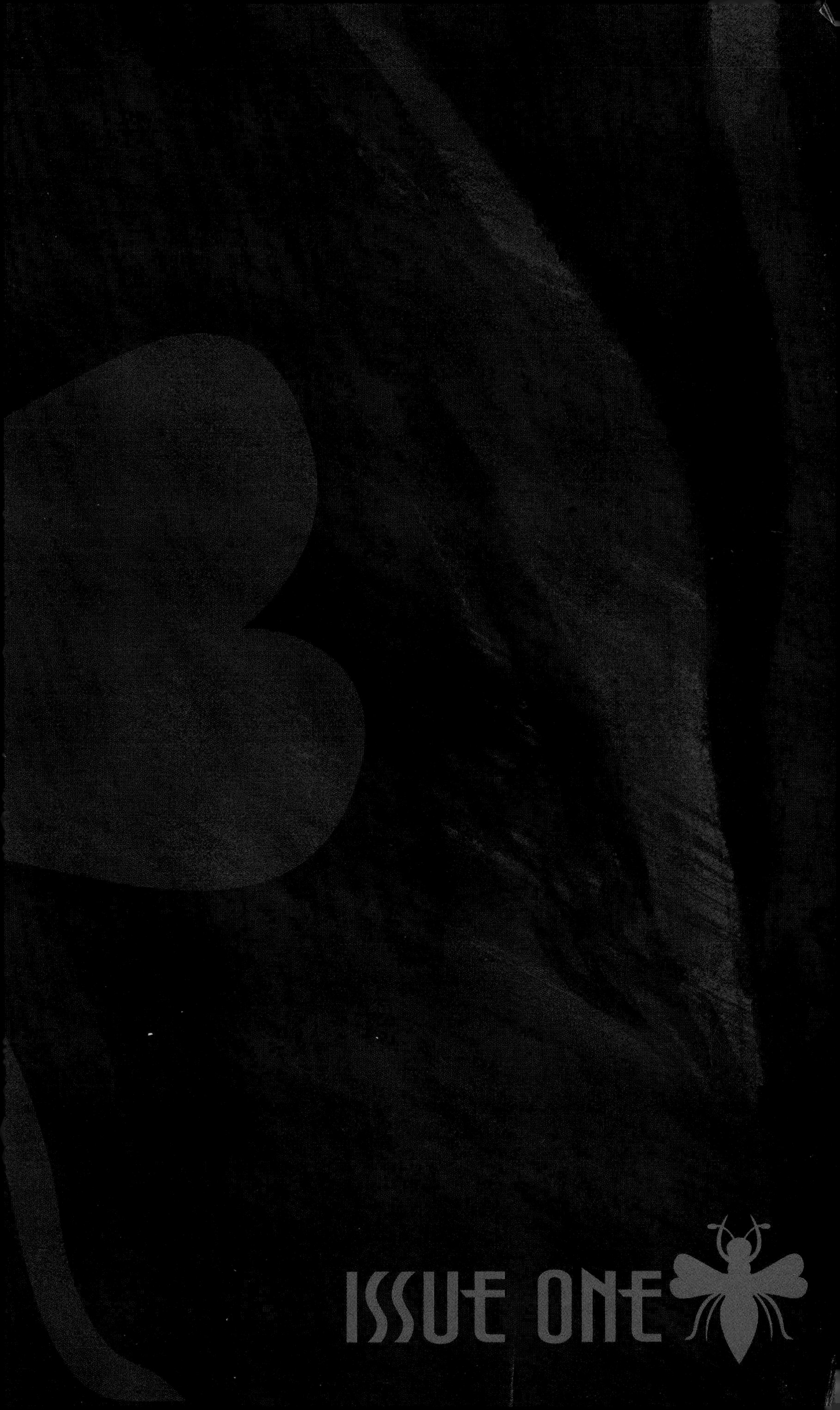
ISSUE ONE

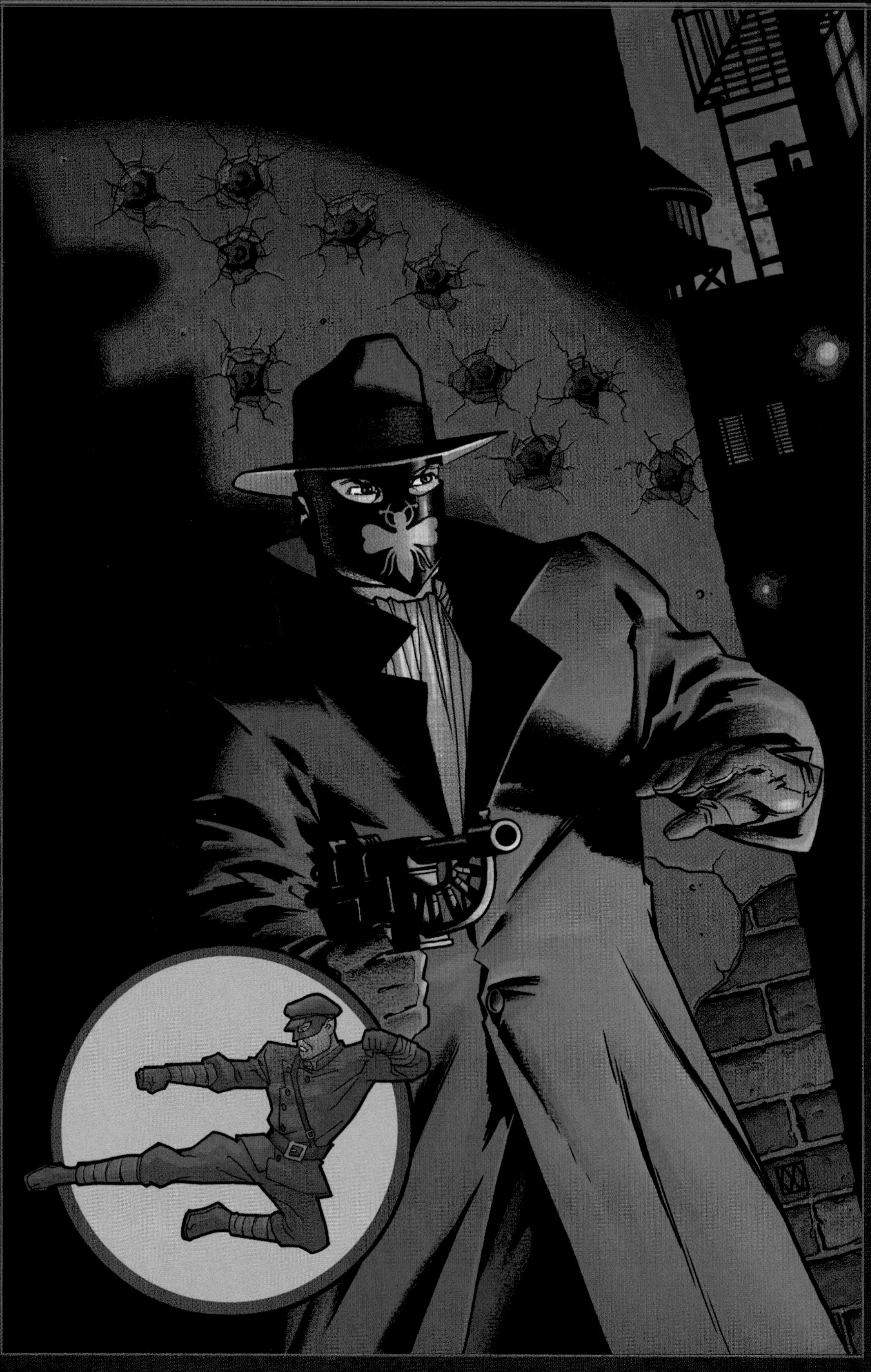

Issue one cover by MATT WAGNER

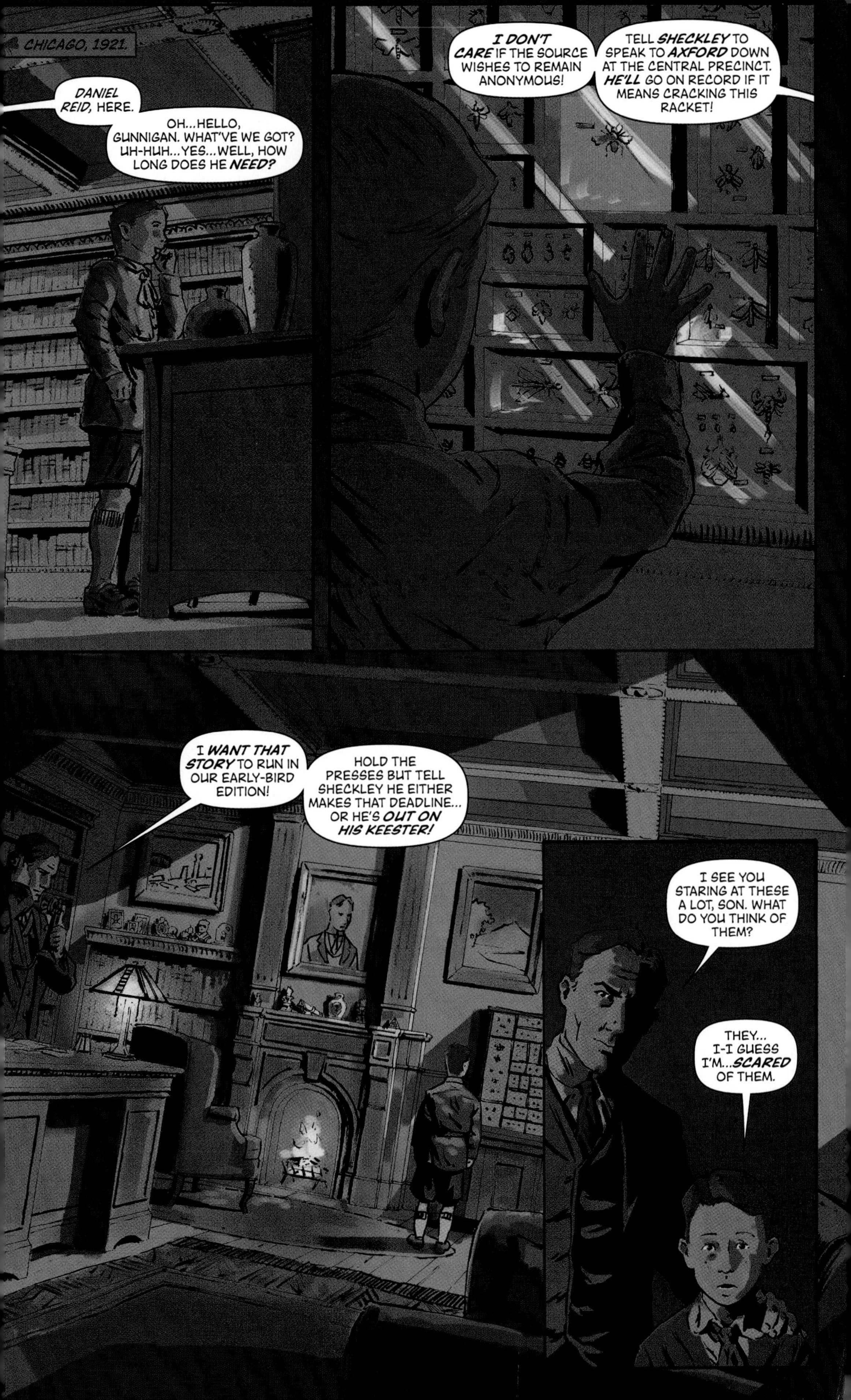
CHICAGO, 1921.
DANIEL REID, HERE.
OH...HELLO, GUNNIGAN. WHAT'VE WE GOT? UH-HUH...YES...WELL, HOW LONG DOES HE NEED?
I DON'T CARE IF THE SOURCE WISHES TO REMAIN ANONYMOUS!
TELL SHECKLEY TO SPEAK TO AXFORD DOWN AT THE CENTRAL PRECINCT. HE'LL GO ON RECORD IF IT MEANS CRACKING THIS RACKET!
I WANT THAT STORY TO RUN IN OUR EARLY-BIRD EDITION!
HOLD THE PRESSES BUT TELL SHECKLEY HE EITHER MAKES THAT DEADLINE... OR HE'S OUT ON HIS KEESTER!
I SEE YOU STARING AT THESE A LOT, SON. WHAT DO YOU THINK OF THEM?
THEY... I-I GUESS I'M...SCARED OF THEM.

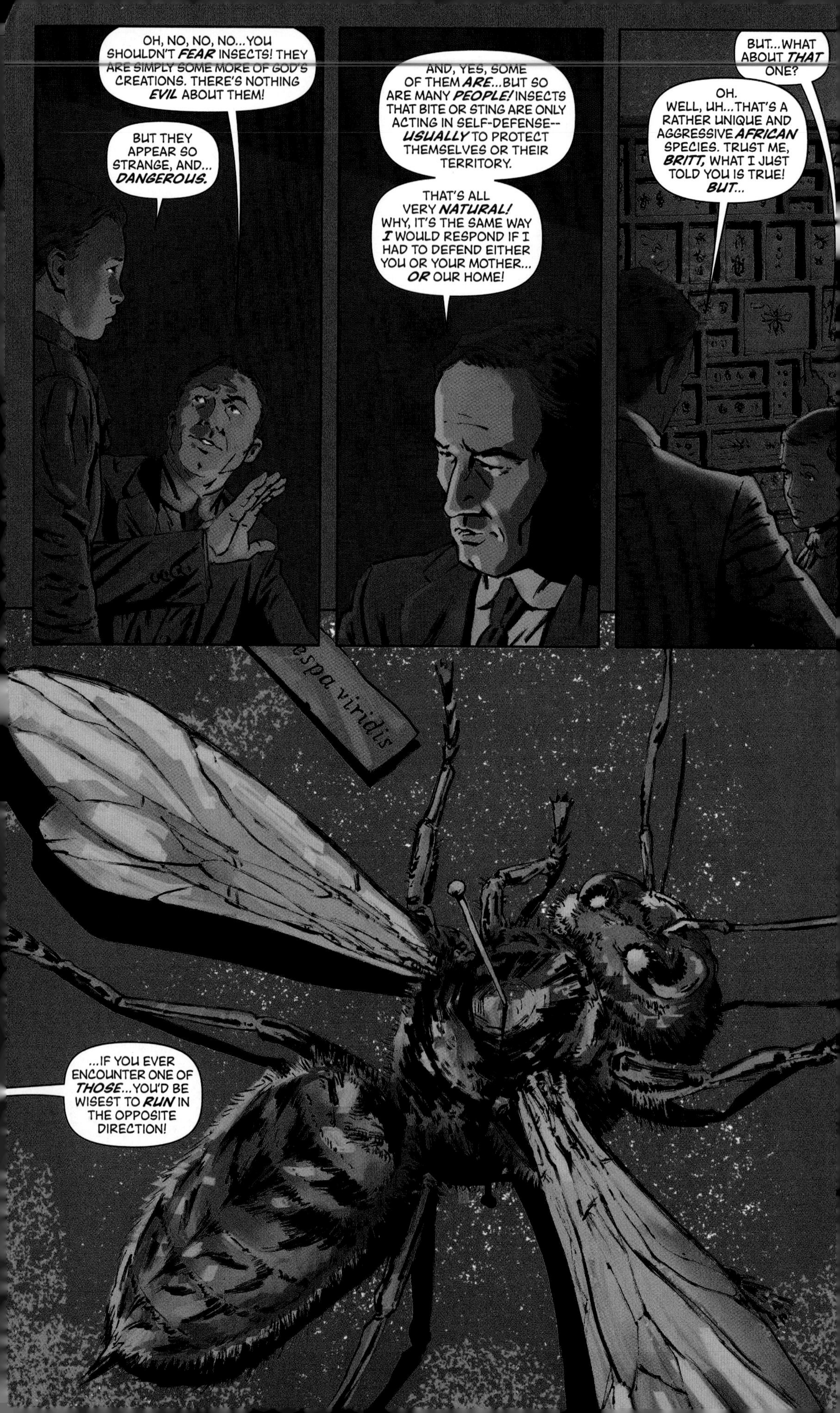
OH, NO, NO, NO...YOU SHOULDN'T FEAR INSECTS! THEY ARE SIMPLY SOME MORE OF GOD'S CREATIONS. THERE'S NOTHING EVIL ABOUT THEM!
BUT THEY APPEAR SO STRANGE, AND... DANGEROUS.
AND, YES, SOME OF THEM ARE...BUT SO ARE MANY PEOPLE! INSECTS THAT BITE OR STING ARE ONLY ACTING IN SELF-DEFENSE-- USUALLY TO PROTECT THEMSELVES OR THEIR TERRITORY.
THAT'S ALL VERY NATURAL! WHY, IT'S THE SAME WAY I WOULD RESPOND IF I HAD TO DEFEND EITHER YOU OR YOUR MOTHER... OR OUR HOME!
BUT...WHAT ABOUT THAT ONE?
OH. WELL, UH...THAT'S A RATHER UNIQUE AND AGGRESSIVE AFRICAN SPECIES. TRUST ME, BRITT, WHAT I JUST TOLD YOU IS TRUE! BUT...
espa viridis
...IF YOU EVER ENCOUNTER ONE OF THOSE...YOU'D BE WISEST TO RUN IN THE OPPOSITE DIRECTION!

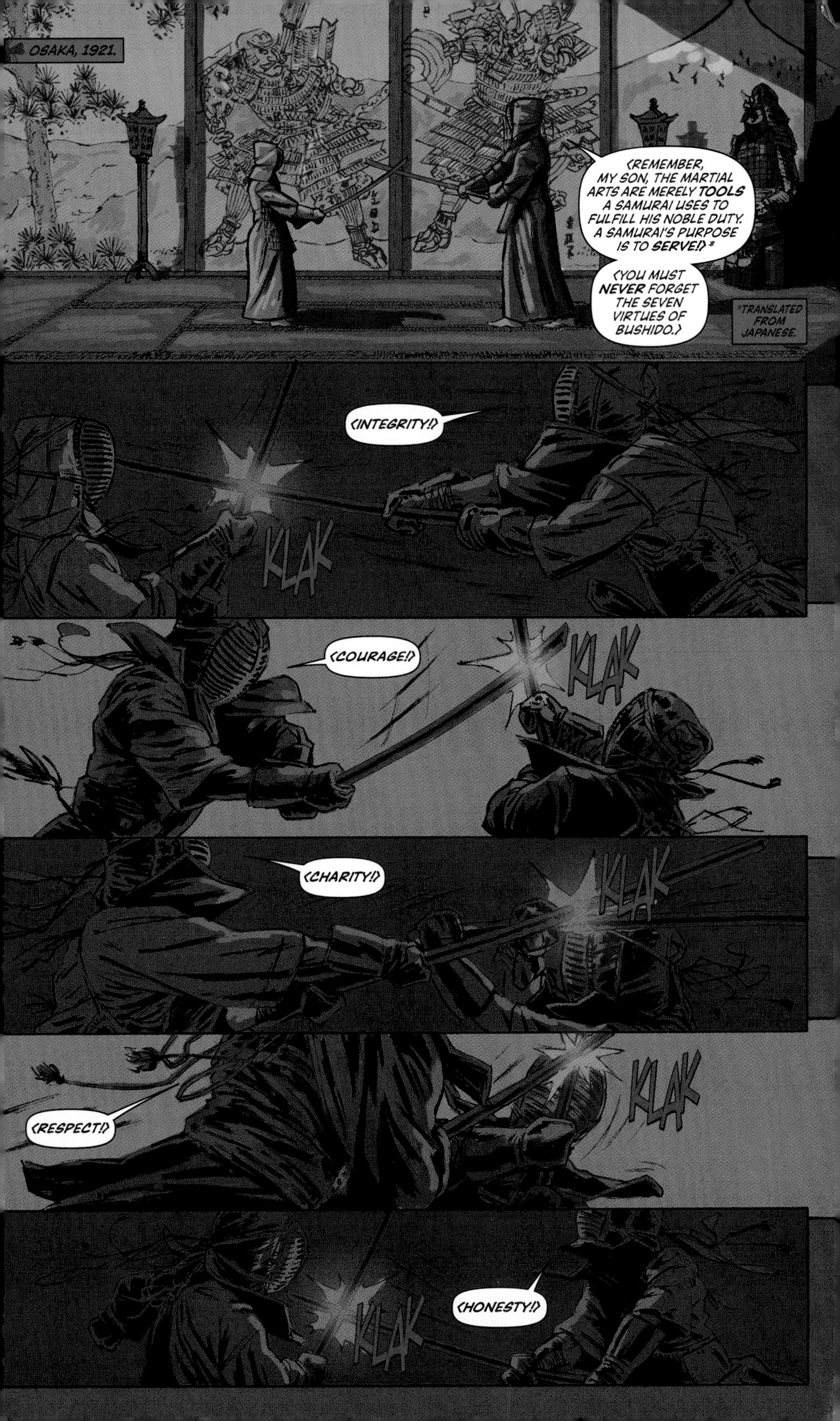
OSAKA, 1921.
<REMEMBER, MY SON, THE MARTIAL ARTS ARE MERELY TOOLS A SAMURAI USES TO FULFILL HIS NOBLE DUTY. A SAMURAI'S PURPOSE IS TO SERVE!> *
<YOU MUST NEVER FORGET THE SEVEN VIRTUES OF BUSHIDO.>
*TRANSLATED FROM JAPANESE.
<INTEGRITY!>
KLAK
<COURAGE!>
KLAK
<CHARITY!>
KLAK
<RESPECT!>
KLAK
<HONESTY!>
KLAK

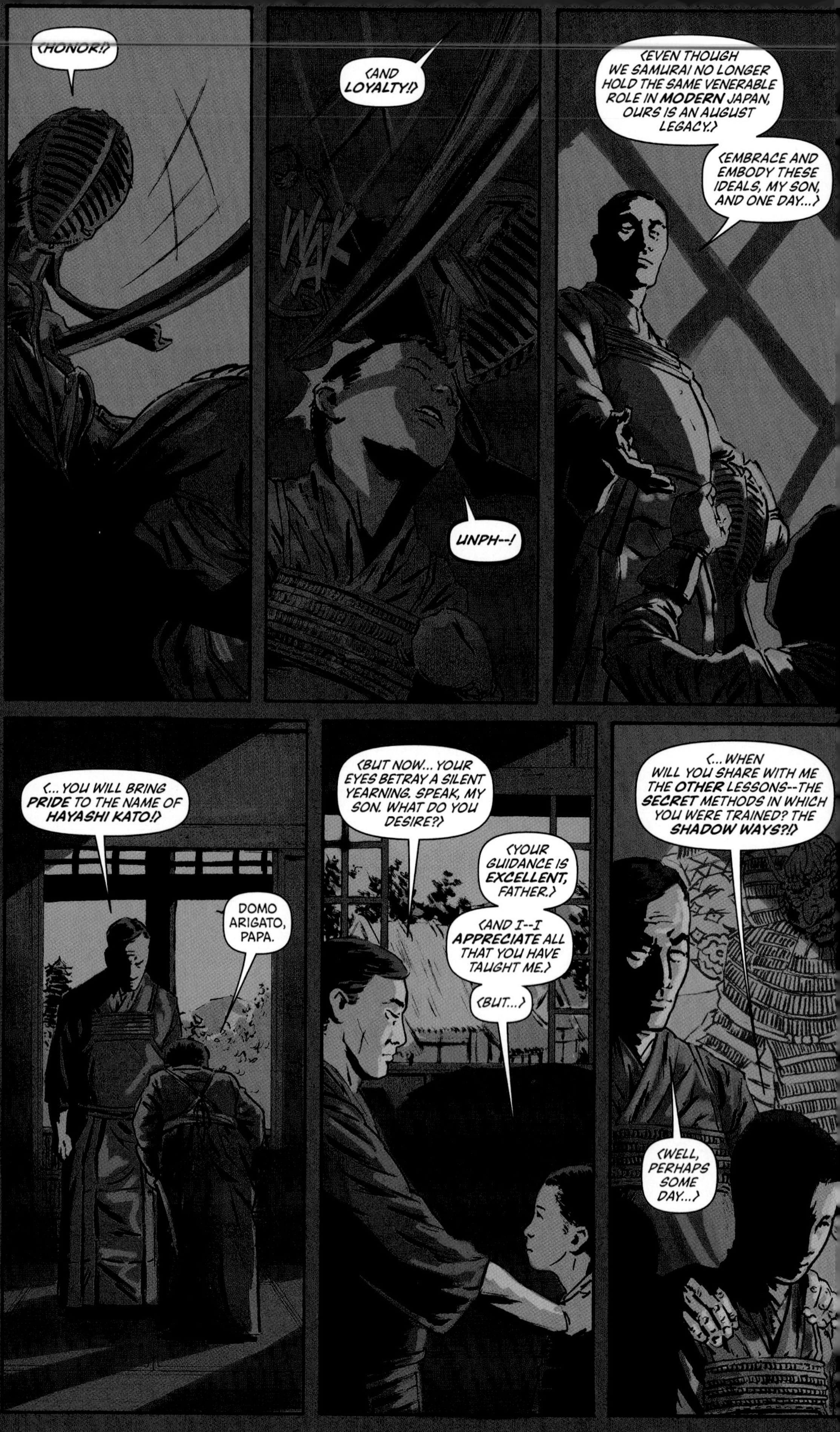

‹HONOR!›
‹AND LOYALTY!›
WAK
UNPH--!
‹EVEN THOUGH WE SAMURAI NO LONGER HOLD THE SAME VENERABLE ROLE IN MODERN JAPAN, OURS IS AN AUGUST LEGACY.›
‹EMBRACE AND EMBODY THESE IDEALS, MY SON, AND ONE DAY...›
‹...YOU WILL BRING PRIDE TO THE NAME OF HAYASHI KATO!›
DOMO ARIGATO, PAPA.
‹BUT NOW... YOUR EYES BETRAY A SILENT YEARNING. SPEAK, MY SON. WHAT DO YOU DESIRE?›
‹YOUR GUIDANCE IS EXCELLENT, FATHER.›
‹AND I--I APPRECIATE ALL THAT YOU HAVE TAUGHT ME.›
‹BUT...›
‹...WHEN WILL YOU SHARE WITH ME THE OTHER LESSONS--THE SECRET METHODS IN WHICH YOU WERE TRAINED? THE SHADOW WAYS?!›
‹WELL, PERHAPS SOME DAY...›

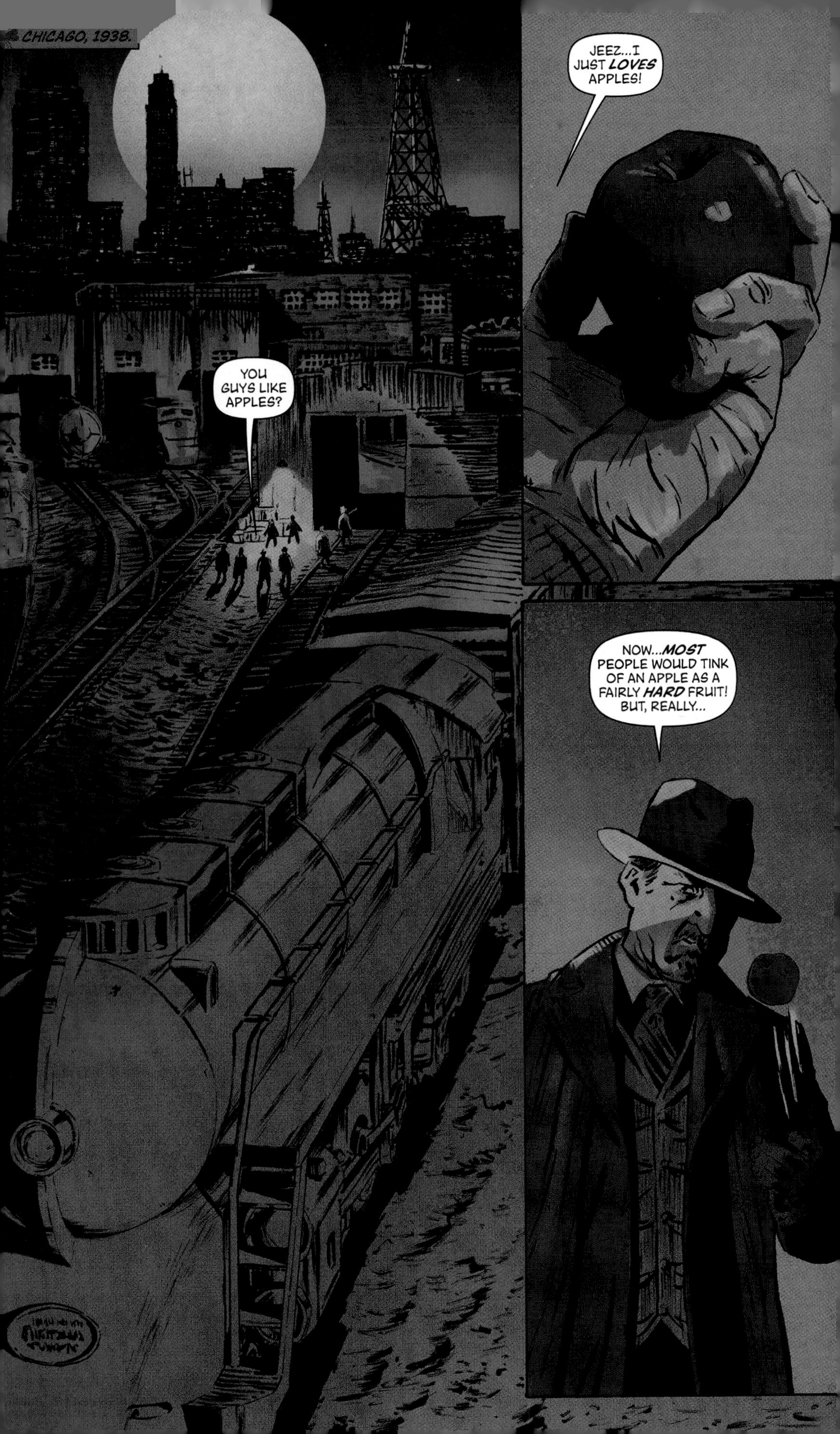
CHICAGO, 1938.
YOU GUYS LIKE APPLES?
JEEZ...I JUST LOVES APPLES!
NOW...MOST PEOPLE WOULD TINK OF AN APPLE AS A FAIRLY HARD FRUIT! BUT, REALLY...

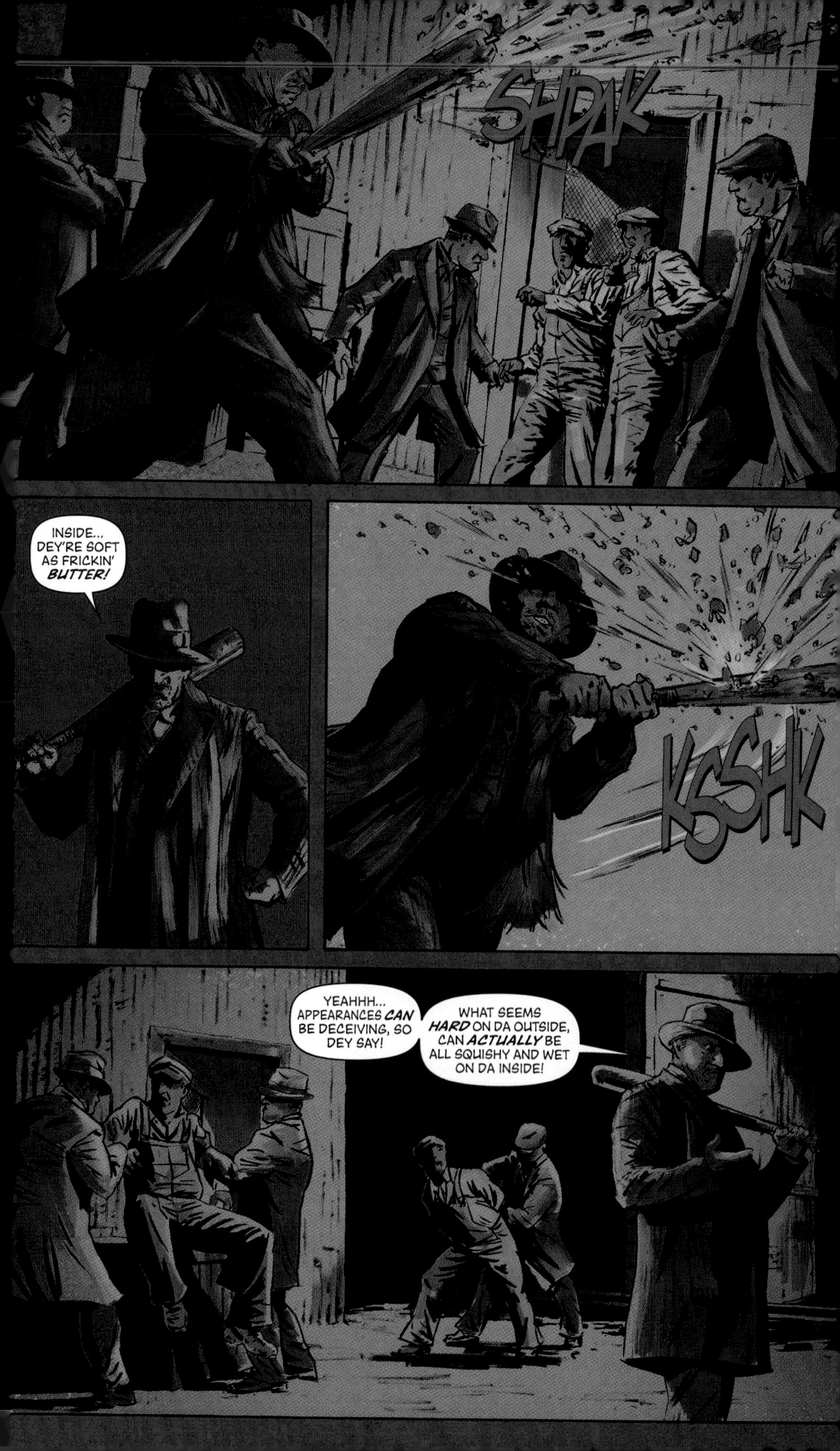
SHPAK
INSIDE... DEY'RE SOFT AS FRICKIN' BUTTER!
KSSHK
YEAHHH... APPEARANCES CAN BE DECEIVING, SO DEY SAY!
WHAT SEEMS HARD ON DA OUTSIDE, CAN ACTUALLY BE ALL SQUISHY AND WET ON DA INSIDE!

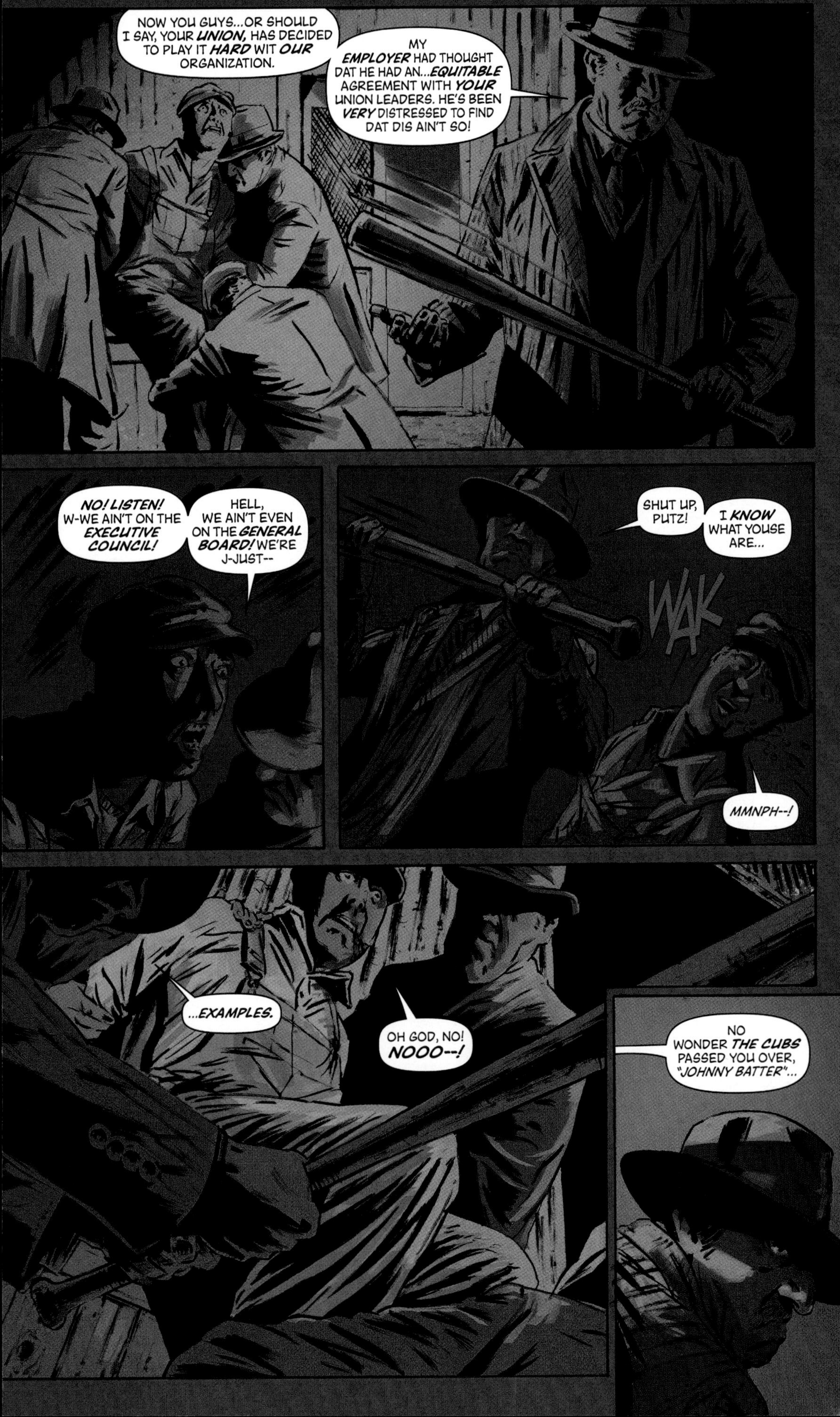
NOW YOU GUYS...OR SHOULD I SAY, YOUR UNION, HAS DECIDED TO PLAY IT HARD WIT OUR ORGANIZATION.
MY EMPLOYER HAD THOUGHT DAT HE HAD AN...EQUITABLE AGREEMENT WITH YOUR UNION LEADERS. HE'S BEEN VERY DISTRESSED TO FIND DAT DIS AIN'T SO!
NO! LISTEN! W-WE AIN'T ON THE EXECUTIVE COUNCIL!
HELL, WE AIN'T EVEN ON THE GENERAL BOARD! WE'RE J-JUST--
SHUT UP, PUTZ!
I KNOW WHAT YOUSE ARE...
WAK
MMNPH--!
...EXAMPLES.
OH GOD, NO! NOOO--!
NO WONDER THE CUBS PASSED YOU OVER, "JOHNNY BATTER"...

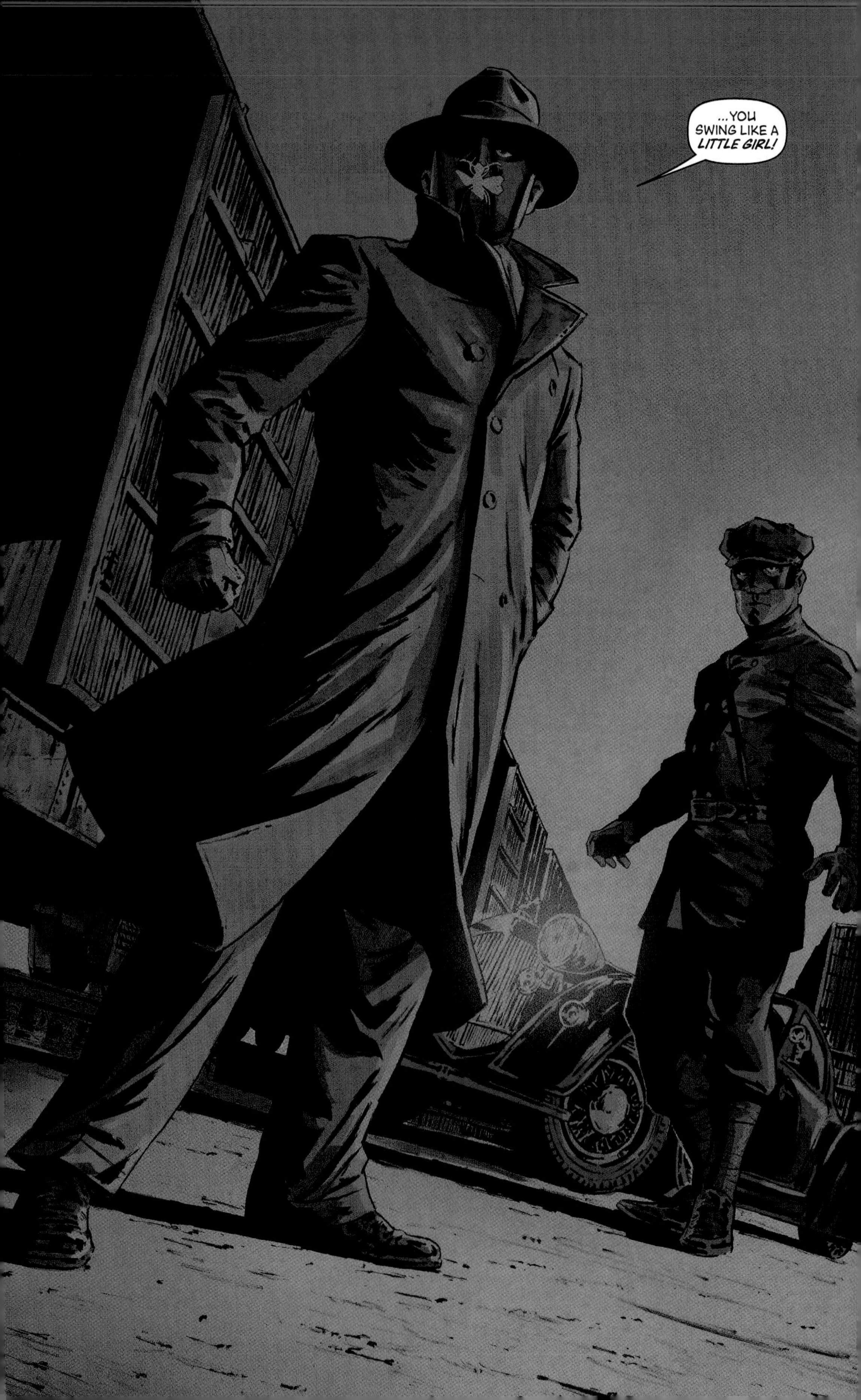
...YOU SWING LIKE A LITTLE GIRL!

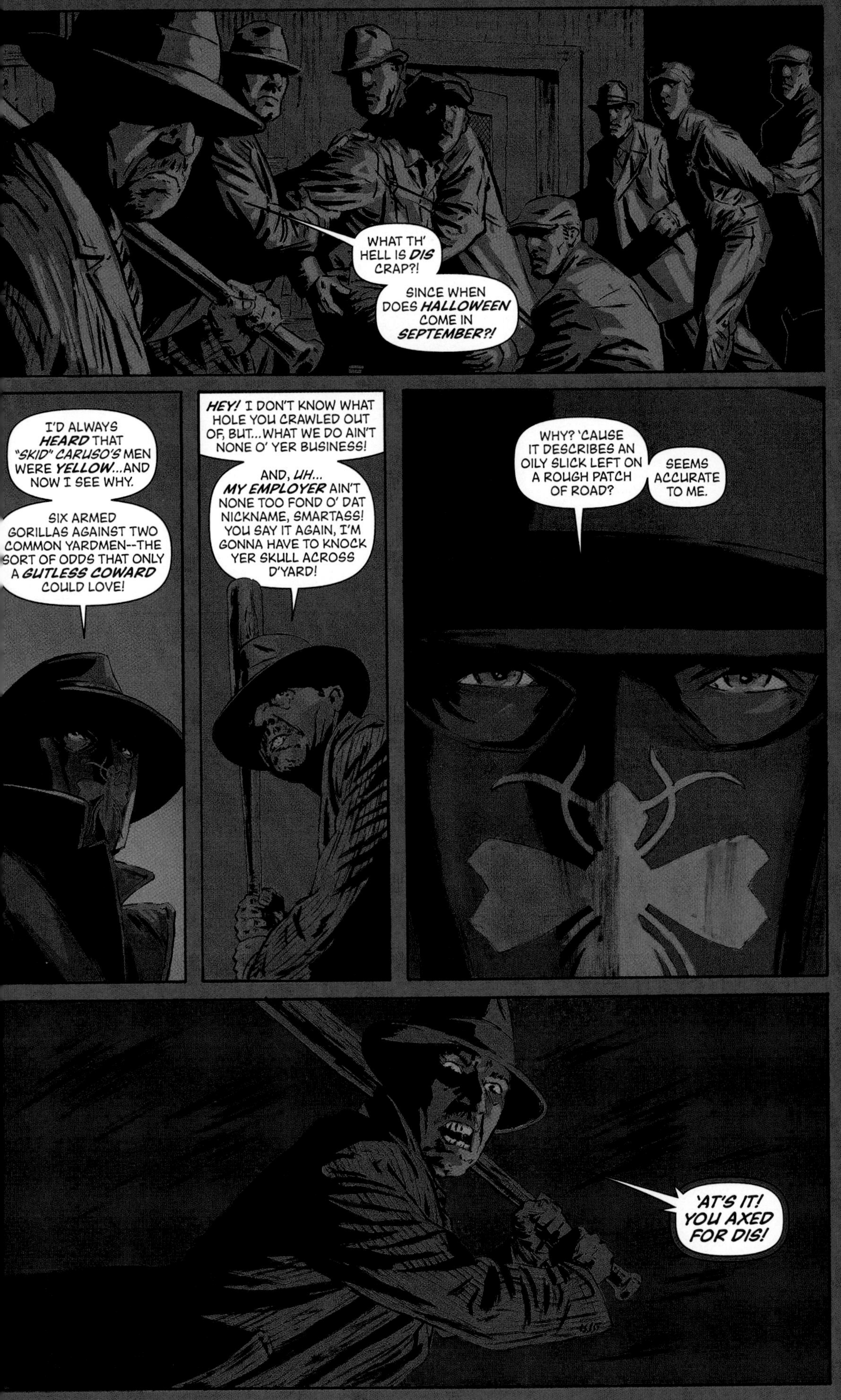

WHAT TH' HELL IS DIS CRAP?!
SINCE WHEN DOES HALLOWEEN COME IN SEPTEMBER?!
I'D ALWAYS HEARD THAT "SKID" CARUSO'S MEN WERE YELLOW...AND NOW I SEE WHY.
SIX ARMED GORILLAS AGAINST TWO COMMON YARDMEN--THE SORT OF ODDS THAT ONLY A GUTLESS COWARD COULD LOVE!
HEY! I DON'T KNOW WHAT HOLE YOU CRAWLED OUT OF, BUT...WHAT WE DO AIN'T NONE O' YER BUSINESS!
AND, UH... MY EMPLOYER AIN'T NONE TOO FOND O' DAT NICKNAME, SMARTASS! YOU SAY IT AGAIN, I'M GONNA HAVE TO KNOCK YER SKULL ACROSS D'YARD!
WHY? 'CAUSE IT DESCRIBES AN OILY SLICK LEFT ON A ROUGH PATCH OF ROAD?
SEEMS ACCURATE TO ME.
'AT'S IT! YOU AXED FOR DIS!

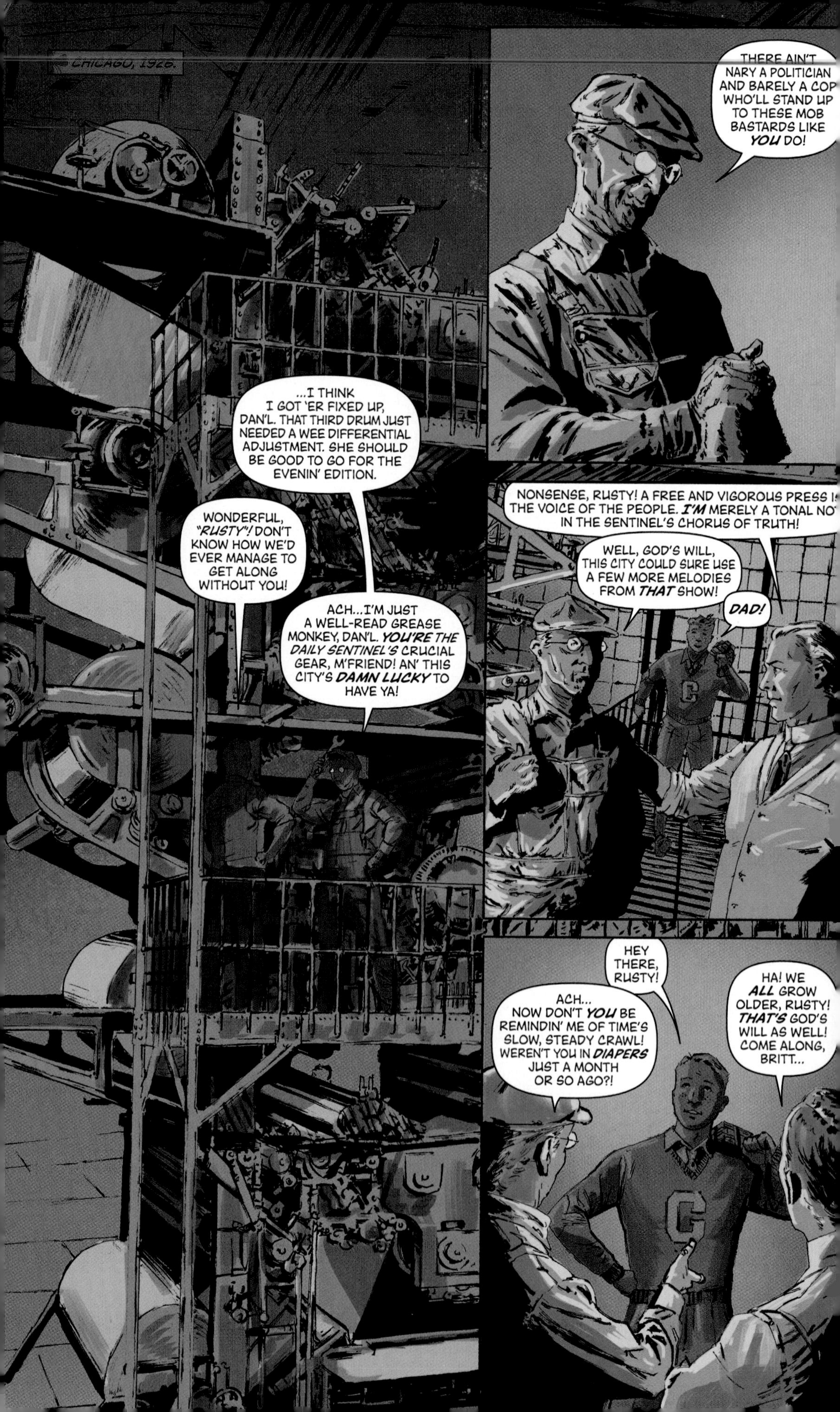
CHICAGO, 1926.
...I THINK I GOT 'ER FIXED UP, DAN'L. THAT THIRD DRUM JUST NEEDED A WEE DIFFERENTIAL ADJUSTMENT. SHE SHOULD BE GOOD TO GO FOR THE EVENIN' EDITION.
WONDERFUL, "RUSTY"! DON'T KNOW HOW WE'D EVER MANAGE TO GET ALONG WITHOUT YOU!
ACH...I'M JUST A WELL-READ GREASE MONKEY, DAN'L. YOU'RE THE DAILY SENTINEL'S CRUCIAL GEAR, M'FRIEND! AN' THIS CITY'S DAMN LUCKY TO HAVE YA!
THERE AIN'T NARY A POLITICIAN AND BARELY A COP WHO'LL STAND UP TO THESE MOB BASTARDS LIKE YOU DO!
NONSENSE, RUSTY! A FREE AND VIGOROUS PRESS IS THE VOICE OF THE PEOPLE. I'M MERELY A TONAL NOTE IN THE SENTINEL'S CHORUS OF TRUTH!
WELL, GOD'S WILL, THIS CITY COULD SURE USE A FEW MORE MELODIES FROM THAT SHOW!
DAD!
HEY THERE, RUSTY!
ACH... NOW DON'T YOU BE REMINDIN' ME OF TIME'S SLOW, STEADY CRAWL! WEREN'T YOU IN DIAPERS JUST A MONTH OR SO AGO?!
HA! WE ALL GROW OLDER, RUSTY! THAT'S GOD'S WILL AS WELL! COME ALONG, BRITT...

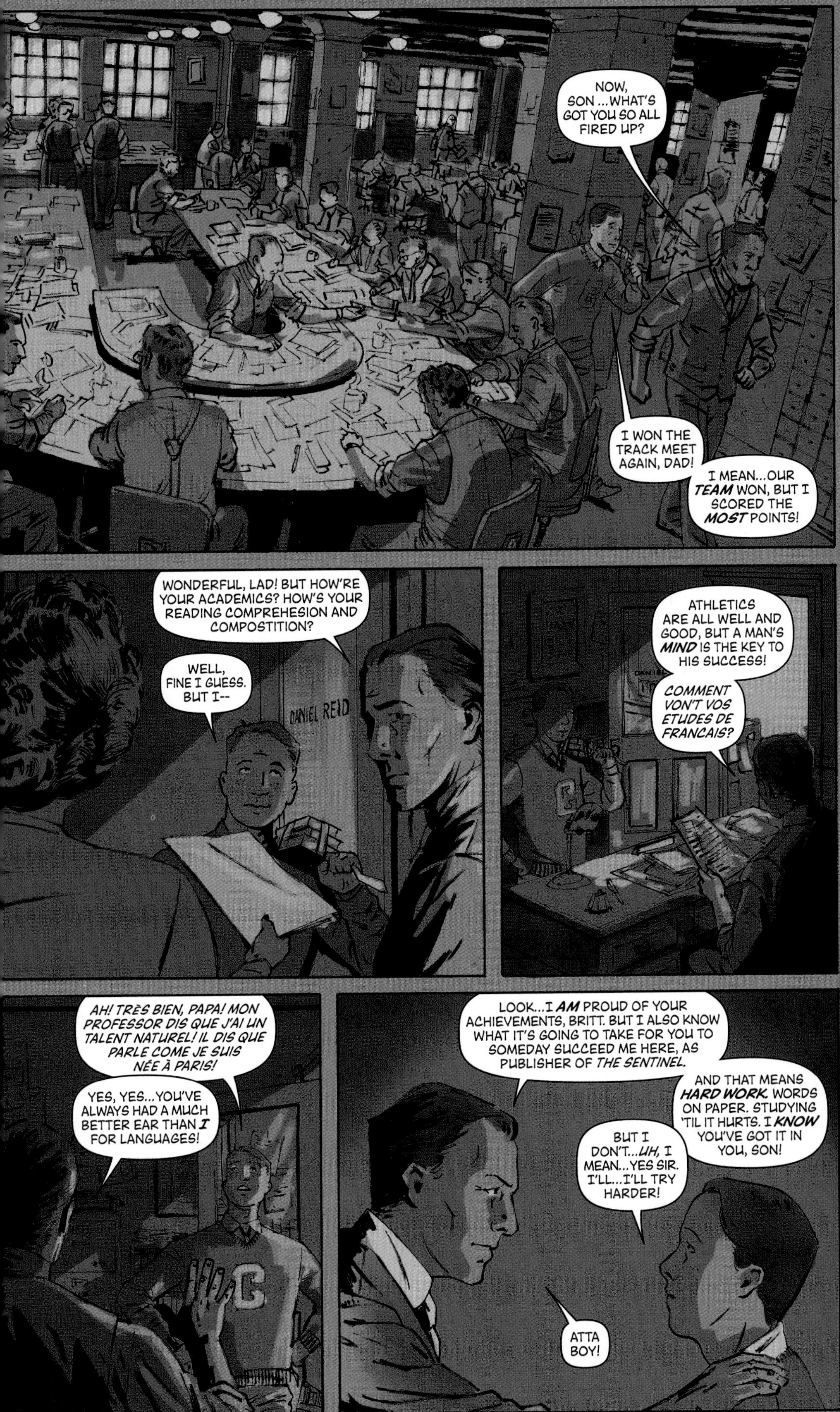
NOW, SON ...WHAT'S GOT YOU SO ALL FIRED UP?
I WON THE TRACK MEET AGAIN, DAD!
I MEAN...OUR TEAM WON, BUT I SCORED THE MOST POINTS!
WONDERFUL, LAD! BUT HOW'RE YOUR ACADEMICS? HOW'S YOUR READING COMPREHENSION AND COMPOSTITION?
WELL, FINE I GUESS. BUT I--
DANIEL REID
ATHLETICS ARE ALL WELL AND GOOD, BUT A MAN'S MIND IS THE KEY TO HIS SUCCESS!
COMMENT VON'T VOS ETUDES DE FRANCAIS?
AH! TRÈS BIEN, PAPA! MON PROFESSOR DIS QUE J'AI UN TALENT NATUREL! IL DIS QUE PARLE COME JE SUIS NÉE À PARIS!
YES, YES...YOU'VE ALWAYS HAD A MUCH BETTER EAR THAN I FOR LANGUAGES!
LOOK...I AM PROUD OF YOUR ACHIEVEMENTS, BRITT. BUT I ALSO KNOW WHAT IT'S GOING TO TAKE FOR YOU TO SOMEDAY SUCCEED ME HERE, AS PUBLISHER OF THE SENTINEL.
AND THAT MEANS HARD WORK. WORDS ON PAPER. STUDYING 'TIL IT HURTS. I KNOW YOU'VE GOT IT IN YOU, SON!
BUT I DON'T...UH, I MEAN...YES SIR. I'LL...I'LL TRY HARDER!
ATTA BOY!

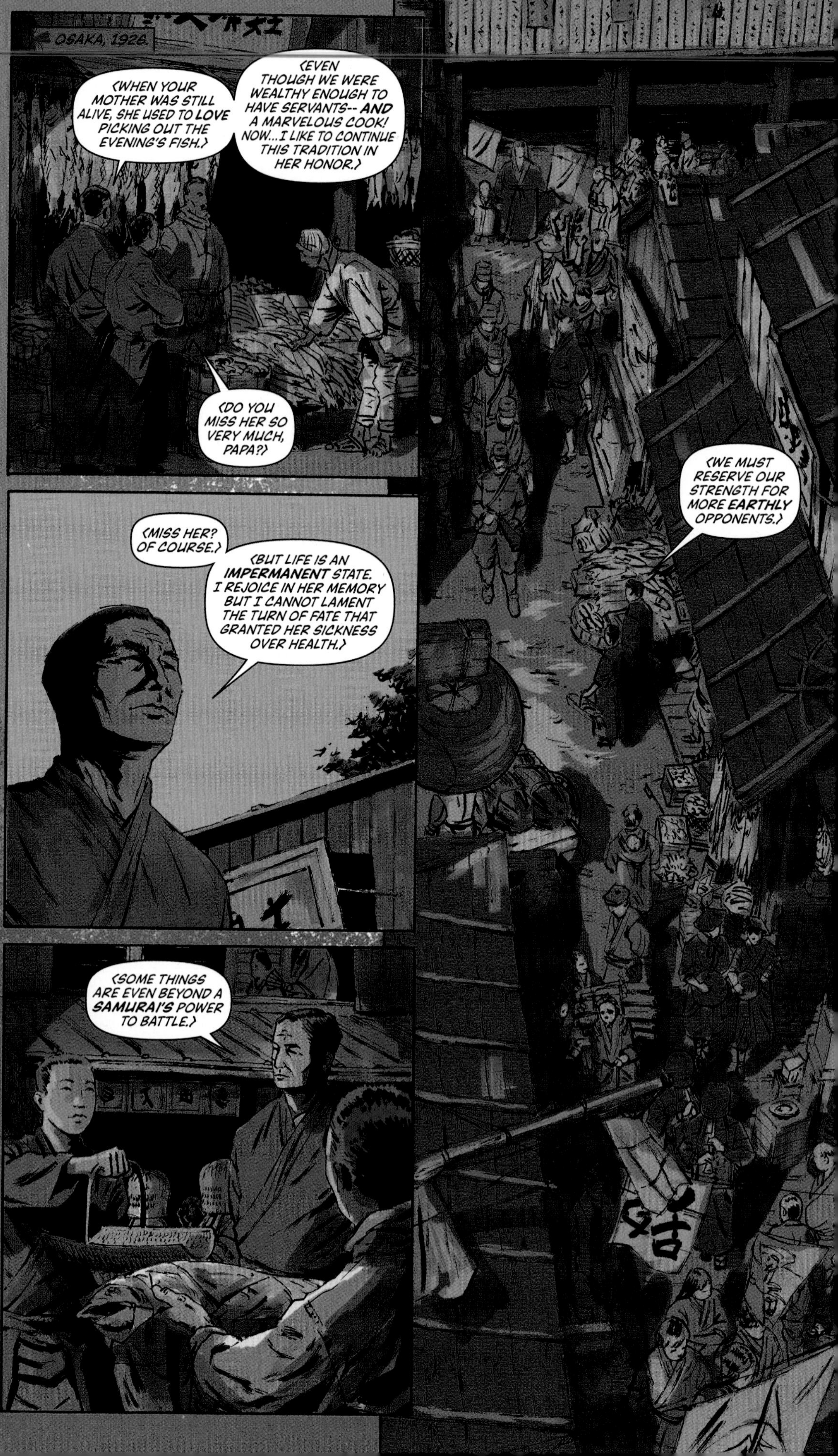
OSAKA, 1926.
<WHEN YOUR MOTHER WAS STILL ALIVE, SHE USED TO LOVE PICKING OUT THE EVENING'S FISH.>
<EVEN THOUGH WE WERE WEALTHY ENOUGH TO HAVE SERVANTS-- AND A MARVELOUS COOK! NOW...I LIKE TO CONTINUE THIS TRADITION IN HER HONOR.>
<DO YOU MISS HER SO VERY MUCH, PAPA?>
<MISS HER? OF COURSE.>
<BUT LIFE IS AN IMPERMANENT STATE. I REJOICE IN HER MEMORY BUT I CANNOT LAMENT THE TURN OF FATE THAT GRANTED HER SICKNESS OVER HEALTH.>
<SOME THINGS ARE EVEN BEYOND A SAMURAI'S POWER TO BATTLE.>
<WE MUST RESERVE OUR STRENGTH FOR MORE EARTHLY OPPONENTS.>

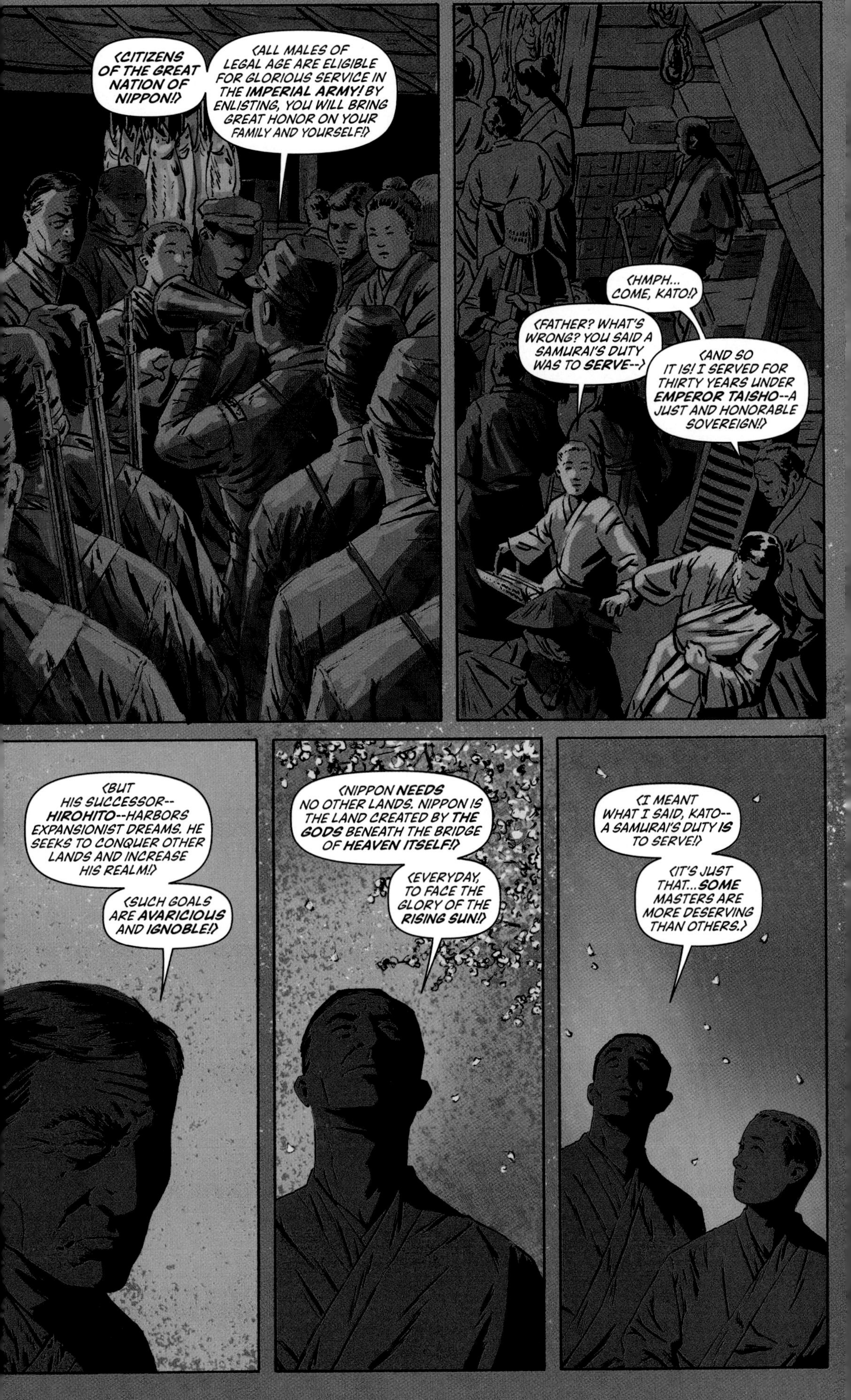

<CITIZENS OF THE GREAT NATION OF NIPPON!>
<ALL MALES OF LEGAL AGE ARE ELIGIBLE FOR GLORIOUS SERVICE IN THE IMPERIAL ARMY! BY ENLISTING, YOU WILL BRING GREAT HONOR ON YOUR FAMILY AND YOURSELF!>
<HMPH... COME, KATO!>
<FATHER? WHAT'S WRONG? YOU SAID A SAMURAI'S DUTY WAS TO SERVE-->
<AND SO IT IS! I SERVED FOR THIRTY YEARS UNDER EMPEROR TAISHO--A JUST AND HONORABLE SOVEREIGN!>
<BUT HIS SUCCESSOR--HIROHITO--HARBORS EXPANSIONIST DREAMS. HE SEEKS TO CONQUER OTHER LANDS AND INCREASE HIS REALM!>
<SUCH GOALS ARE AVARICIOUS AND IGNOBLE!>
<NIPPON NEEDS NO OTHER LANDS. NIPPON IS THE LAND CREATED BY THE GODS BENEATH THE BRIDGE OF HEAVEN ITSELF!>
<EVERYDAY, TO FACE THE GLORY OF THE RISING SUN!>
<I MEANT WHAT I SAID, KATO--A SAMURAI'S DUTY IS TO SERVE!>
<IT'S JUST THAT...SOME MASTERS ARE MORE DESERVING THAN OTHERS.>

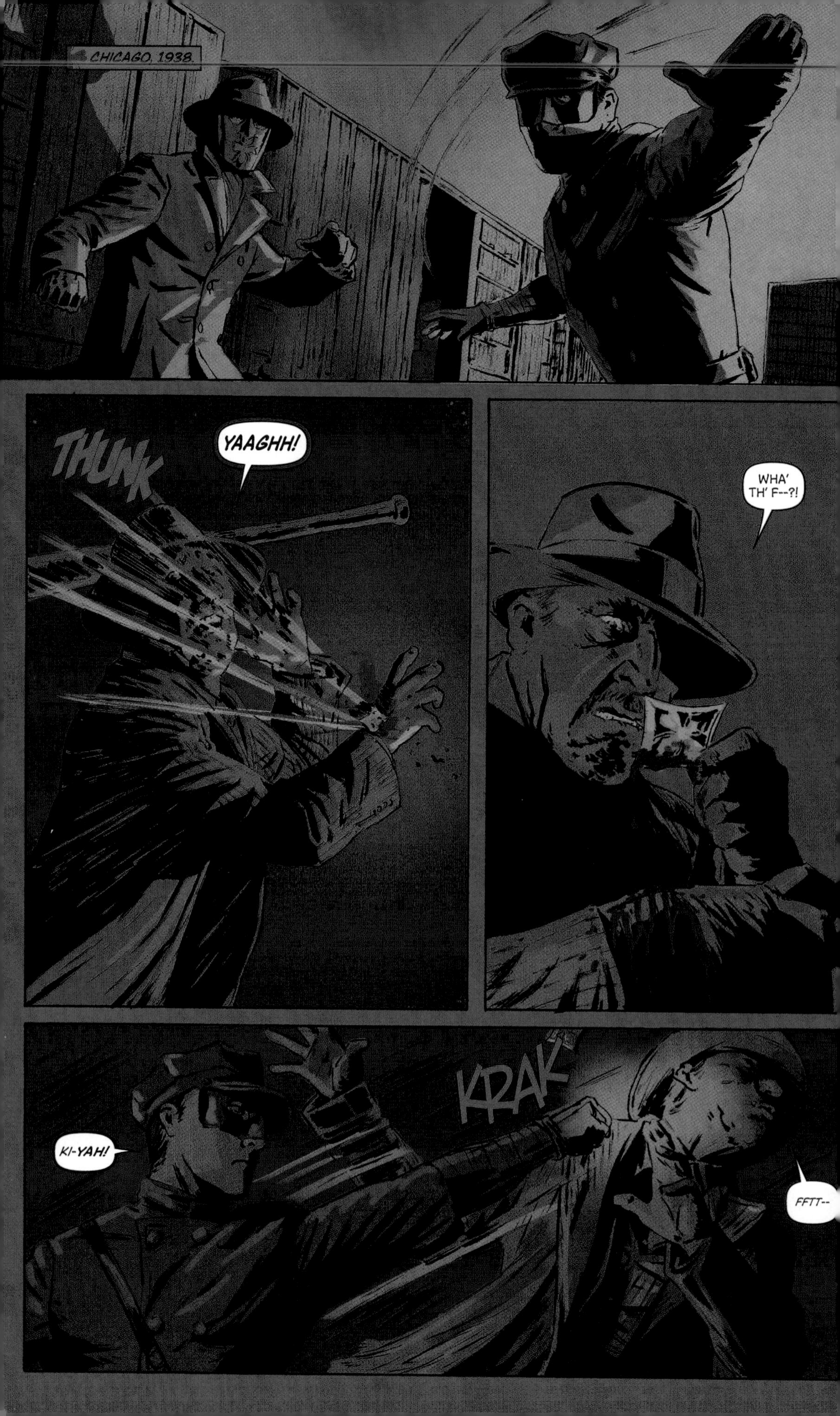

CHICAGO, 1938.
THUNK
YAAGHH!
WHA' TH' F--?!
KRAK
KI-YAH!
FFTT--

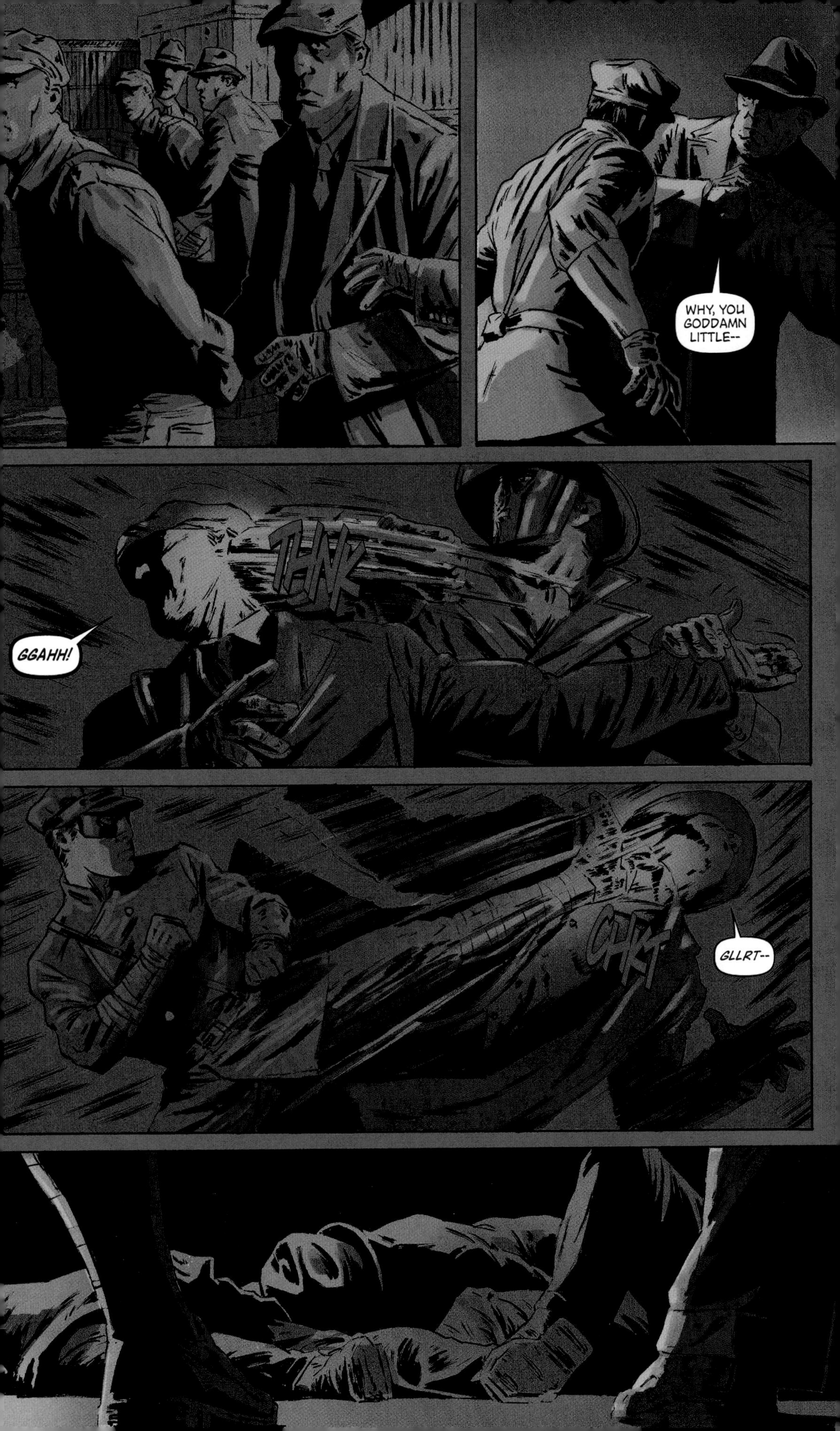
WHY, YOU GODDAMN LITTLE--
THNK
GGAHH!
CHKT
GLLRT--

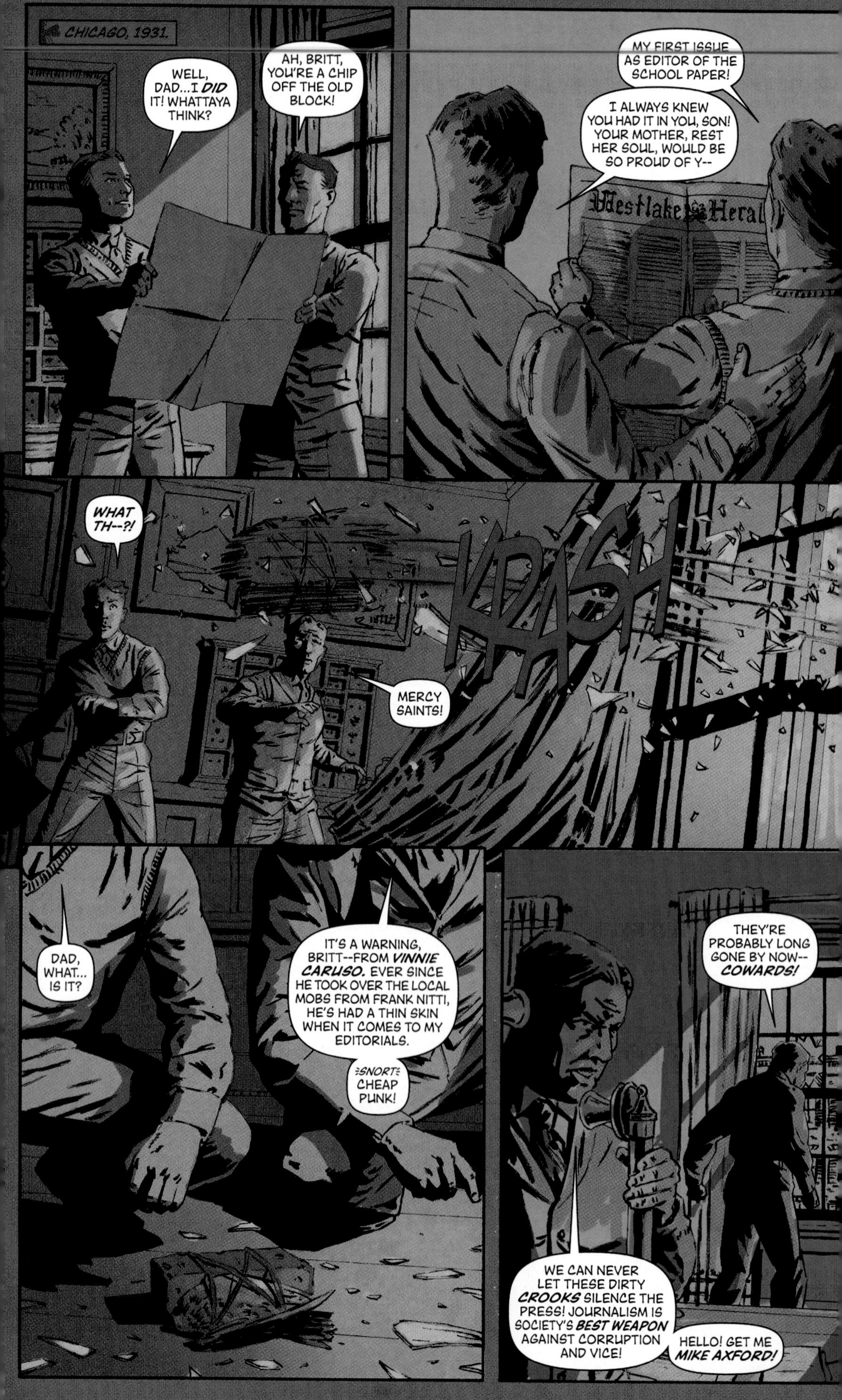
CHICAGO, 1931.
WELL, DAD...I DID IT! WHATTAYA THINK?
AH, BRITT, YOU'RE A CHIP OFF THE OLD BLOCK!
MY FIRST ISSUE AS EDITOR OF THE SCHOOL PAPER!
I ALWAYS KNEW YOU HAD IT IN YOU, SON! YOUR MOTHER, REST HER SOUL, WOULD BE SO PROUD OF Y--
Westlake Heral
WHAT TH--?!
KRASH
MERCY SAINTS!
DAD, WHAT... IS IT?
IT'S A WARNING, BRITT--FROM VINNIE CARUSO. EVER SINCE HE TOOK OVER THE LOCAL MOBS FROM FRANK NITTI, HE'S HAD A THIN SKIN WHEN IT COMES TO MY EDITORIALS.
SNORT CHEAP PUNK!
THEY'RE PROBABLY LONG GONE BY NOW-- COWARDS!
WE CAN NEVER LET THESE DIRTY CROOKS SILENCE THE PRESS! JOURNALISM IS SOCIETY'S BEST WEAPON AGAINST CORRUPTION AND VICE!
HELLO! GET ME MIKE AXFORD!

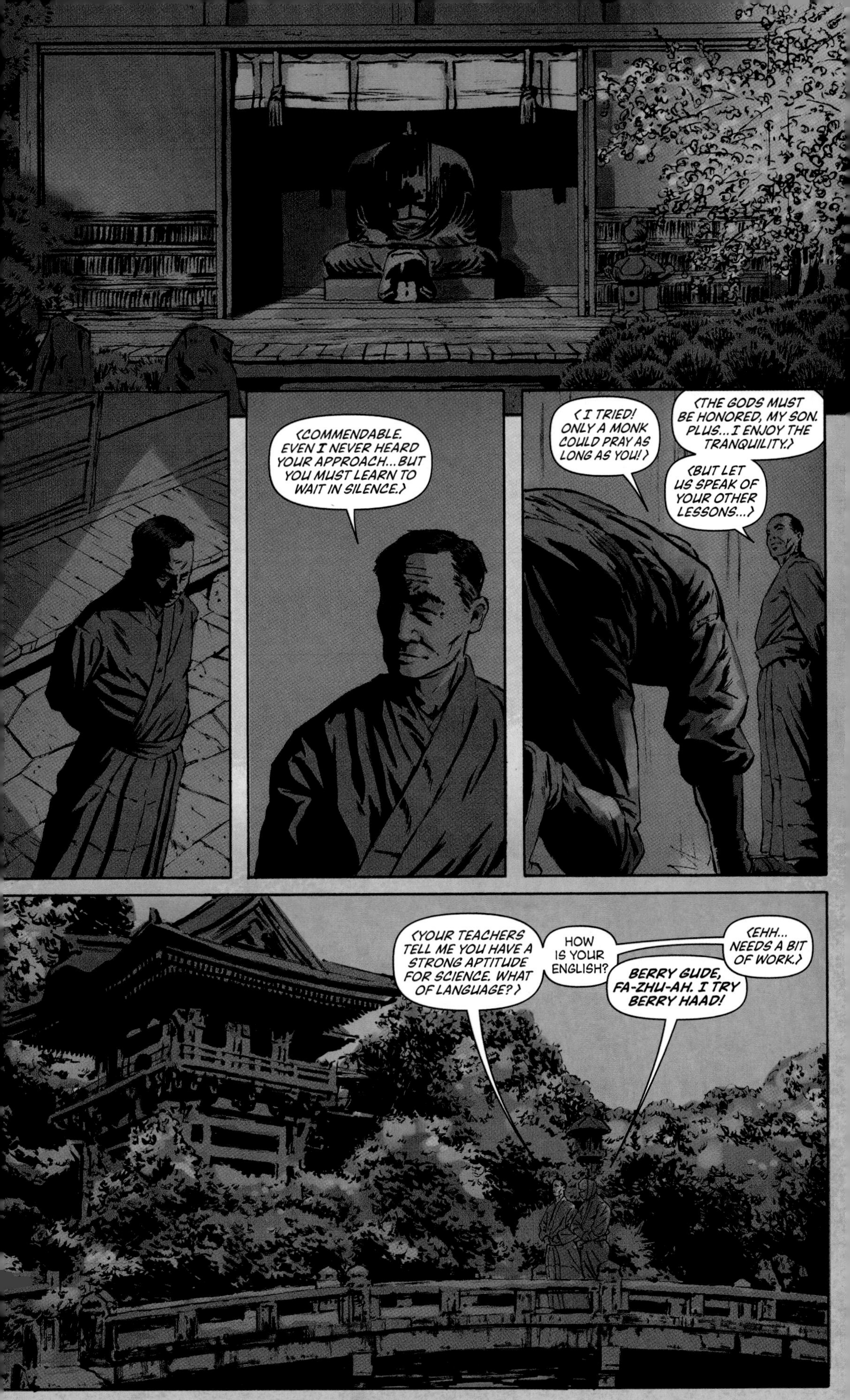

‹COMMENDABLE. EVEN I NEVER HEARD YOUR APPROACH...BUT YOU MUST LEARN TO WAIT IN SILENCE.›
‹I TRIED! ONLY A MONK COULD PRAY AS LONG AS YOU!›
‹THE GODS MUST BE HONORED, MY SON. PLUS...I ENJOY THE TRANQUILITY.›
‹BUT LET US SPEAK OF YOUR OTHER LESSONS...›
‹YOUR TEACHERS TELL ME YOU HAVE A STRONG APTITUDE FOR SCIENCE. WHAT OF LANGUAGE?›
HOW IS YOUR ENGLISH?
BERRY GUDE, FA-ZHU-AH. I TRY BERRY HAAD!
‹EHH... NEEDS A BIT OF WORK.›

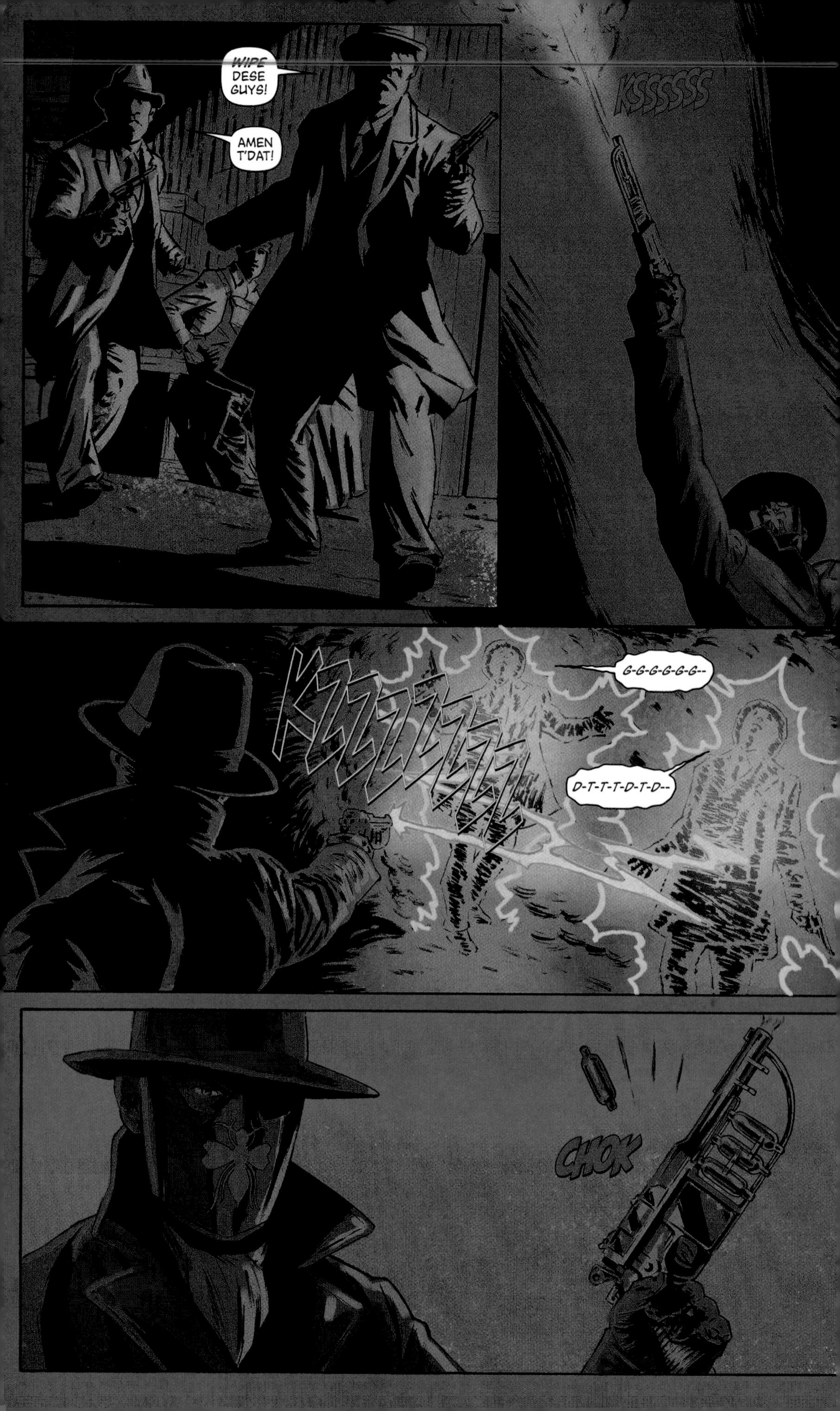
WIPE DESE GUYS!
AMEN T'DAT!
KSSSSSS
KZZZZZZZZT
G-G-G-G-G-G--
D-T-T-T-D-T-D--
CHOK

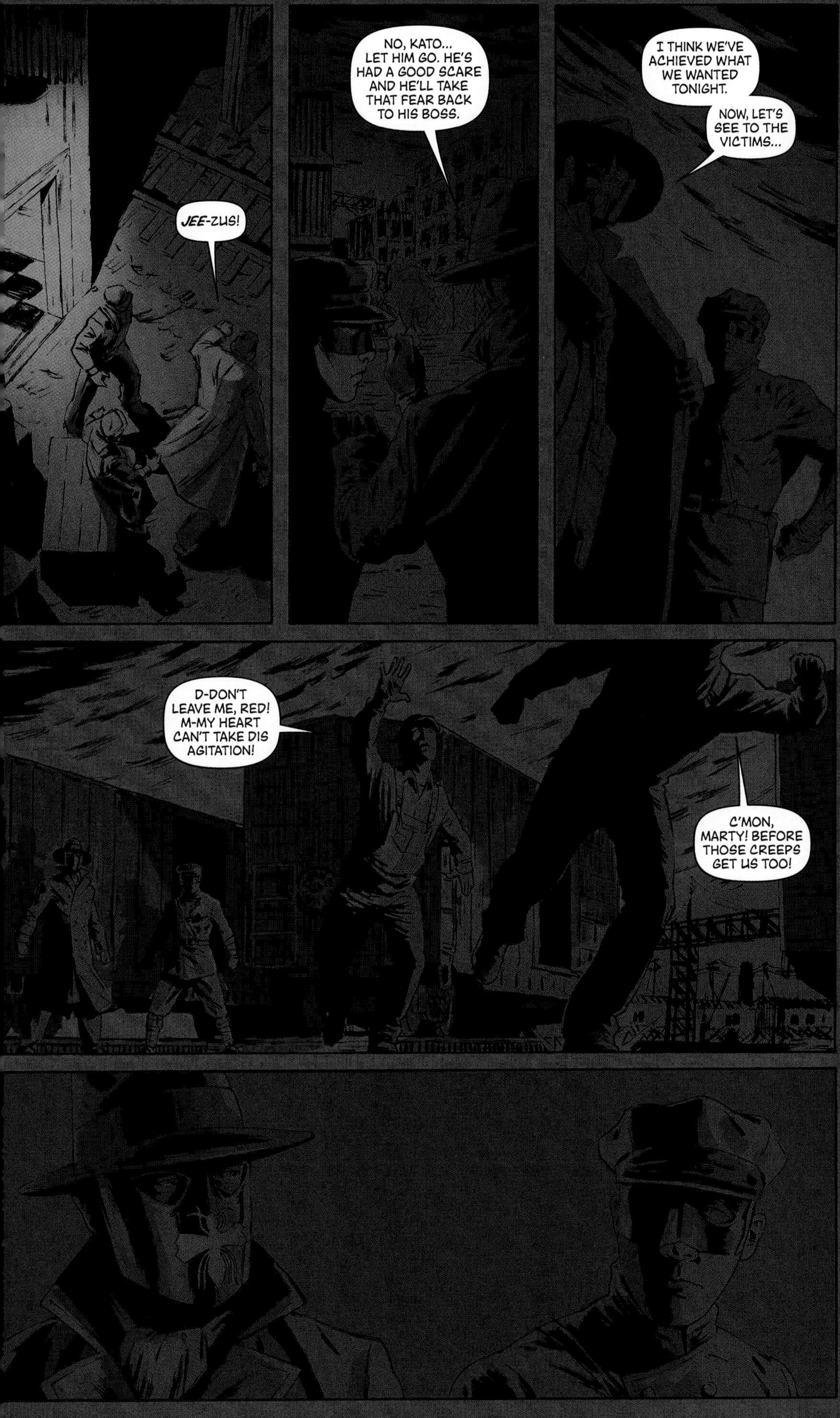
JEE-ZUS!
NO, KATO... LET HIM GO. HE'S HAD A GOOD SCARE AND HE'LL TAKE THAT FEAR BACK TO HIS BOSS.
I THINK WE'VE ACHIEVED WHAT WE WANTED TONIGHT.
NOW, LET'S SEE TO THE VICTIMS...
D-DON'T LEAVE ME, RED! M-MY HEART CAN'T TAKE DIS AGITATION!
C'MON, MARTY! BEFORE THOSE CREEPS GET US TOO!

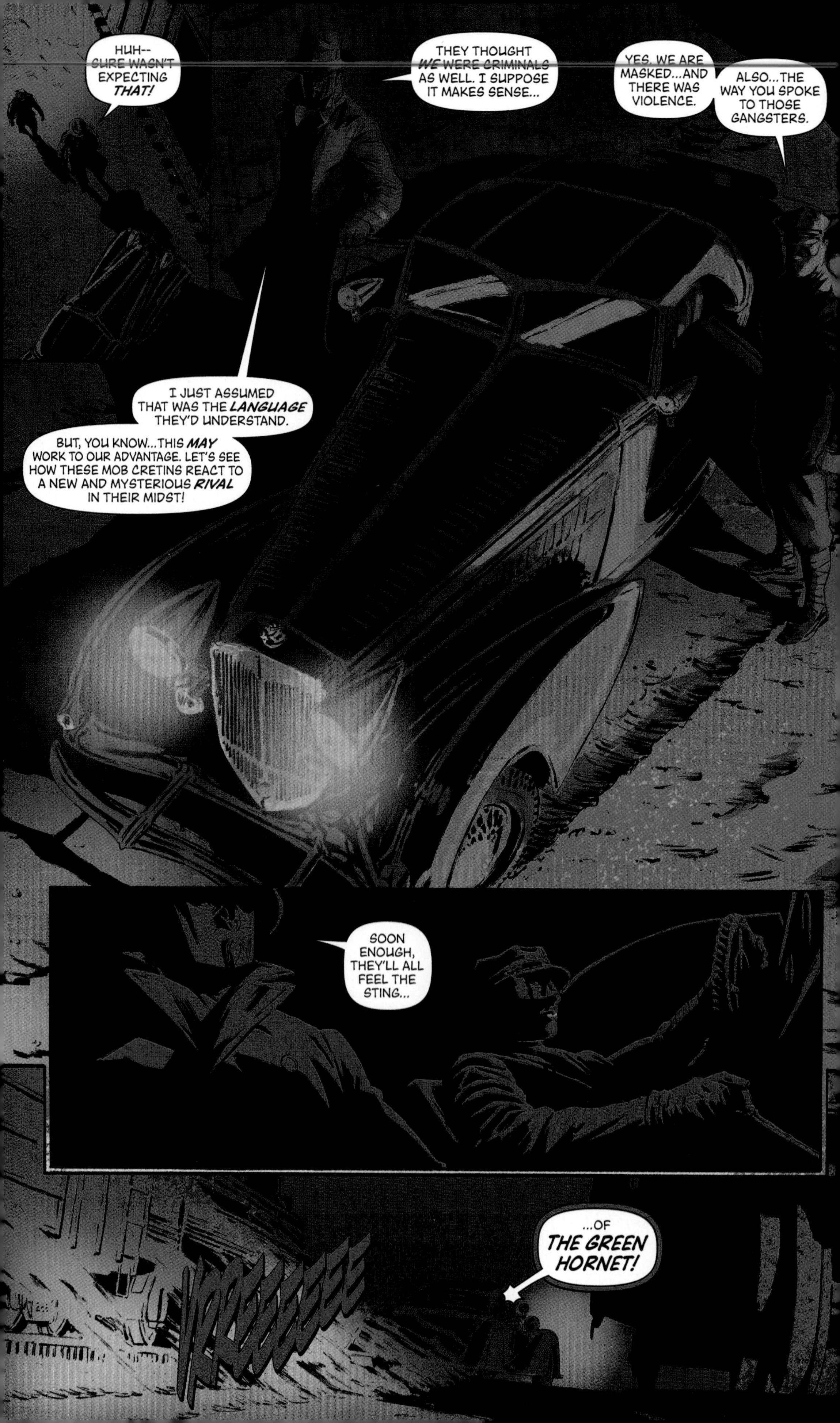
HUH-- SURE WASN'T EXPECTING *THAT!*
THEY THOUGHT *WE* WERE CRIMINALS AS WELL. I SUPPOSE IT MAKES SENSE...
YES. WE ARE MASKED...AND THERE WAS VIOLENCE.
ALSO...THE WAY YOU SPOKE TO THOSE GANGSTERS.
I JUST ASSUMED THAT WAS THE *LANGUAGE* THEY'D UNDERSTAND.
BUT, YOU KNOW...THIS *MAY* WORK TO OUR ADVANTAGE. LET'S SEE HOW THESE MOB CRETINS REACT TO A NEW AND MYSTERIOUS *RIVAL* IN THEIR MIDST!
SOON ENOUGH, THEY'LL ALL FEEL THE STING...
...OF *THE GREEN HORNET!*

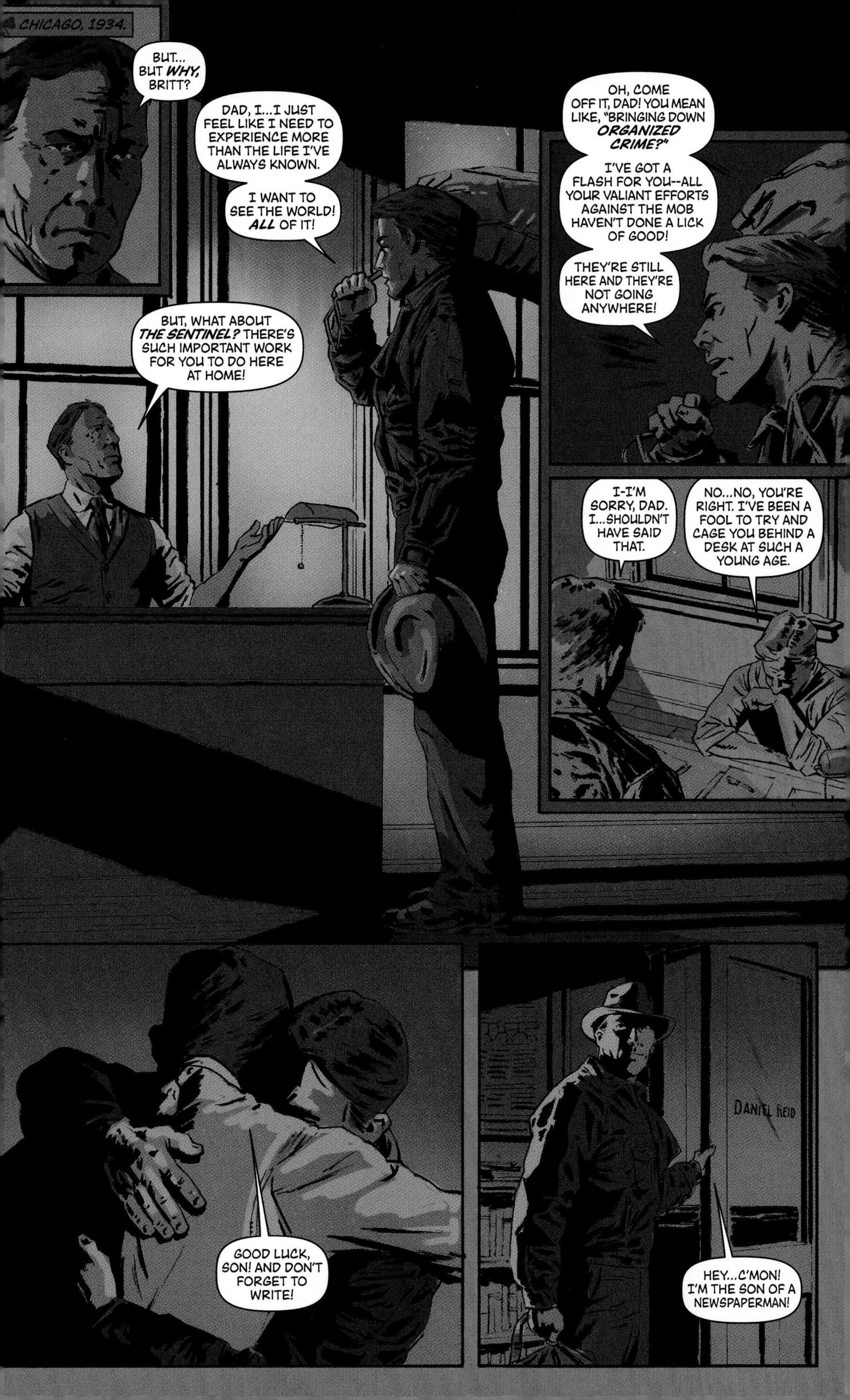
CHICAGO, 1934.
BUT... BUT WHY, BRITT?
DAD, I...I JUST FEEL LIKE I NEED TO EXPERIENCE MORE THAN THE LIFE I'VE ALWAYS KNOWN.
I WANT TO SEE THE WORLD! ALL OF IT!
BUT, WHAT ABOUT THE SENTINEL? THERE'S SUCH IMPORTANT WORK FOR YOU TO DO HERE AT HOME!
OH, COME OFF IT, DAD! YOU MEAN LIKE, "BRINGING DOWN ORGANIZED CRIME?"
I'VE GOT A FLASH FOR YOU--ALL YOUR VALIANT EFFORTS AGAINST THE MOB HAVEN'T DONE A LICK OF GOOD!
THEY'RE STILL HERE AND THEY'RE NOT GOING ANYWHERE!
I-I'M SORRY, DAD. I...SHOULDN'T HAVE SAID THAT.
NO...NO, YOU'RE RIGHT. I'VE BEEN A FOOL TO TRY AND CAGE YOU BEHIND A DESK AT SUCH A YOUNG AGE.
GOOD LUCK, SON! AND DON'T FORGET TO WRITE!
DANIEL REID
HEY...C'MON! I'M THE SON OF A NEWSPAPERMAN!

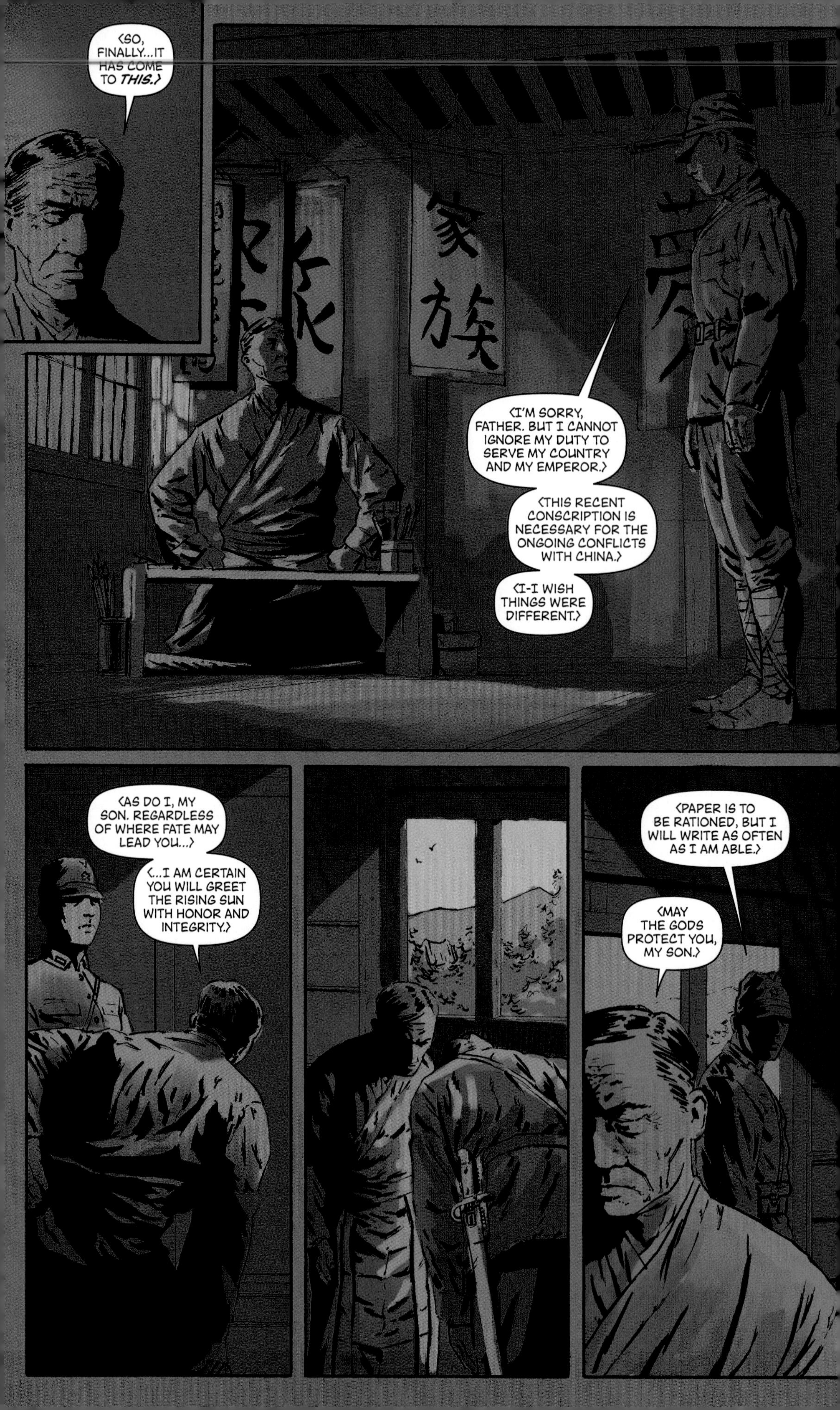

<SO, FINALLY...IT HAS COME TO *THIS.*>
家族
<I'M SORRY, FATHER. BUT I CANNOT IGNORE MY DUTY TO SERVE MY COUNTRY AND MY EMPEROR.>
<THIS RECENT CONSCRIPTION IS NECESSARY FOR THE ONGOING CONFLICTS WITH CHINA.>
<I-I WISH THINGS WERE DIFFERENT.>
<AS DO I, MY SON. REGARDLESS OF WHERE FATE MAY LEAD YOU...>
<...I AM CERTAIN YOU WILL GREET THE RISING SUN WITH HONOR AND INTEGRITY.>
<PAPER IS TO BE RATIONED, BUT I WILL WRITE AS OFTEN AS I AM ABLE.>
<MAY THE GODS PROTECT YOU, MY SON.>

ISSUE TWO

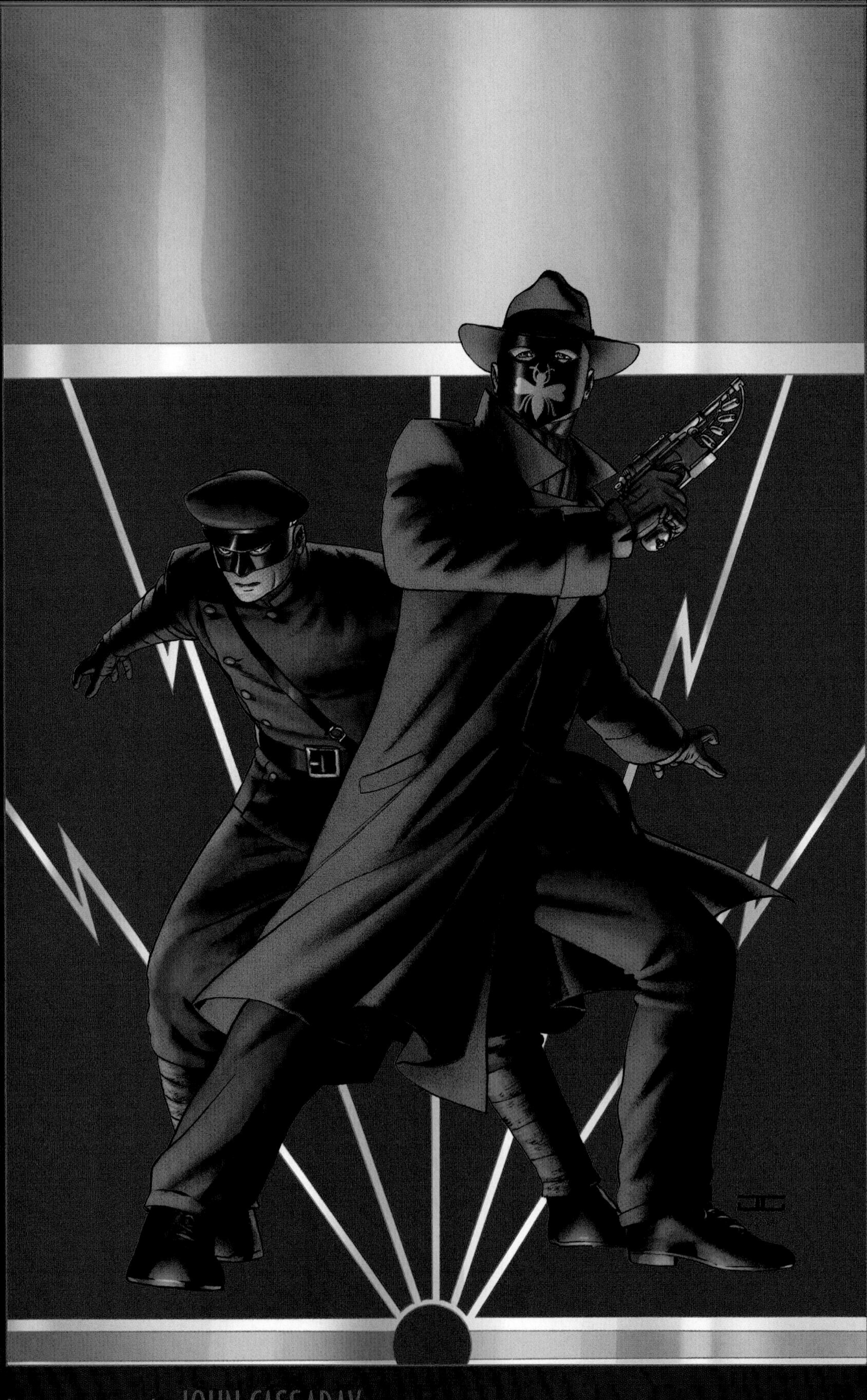

Issue two cover by JOHN CASSADAY

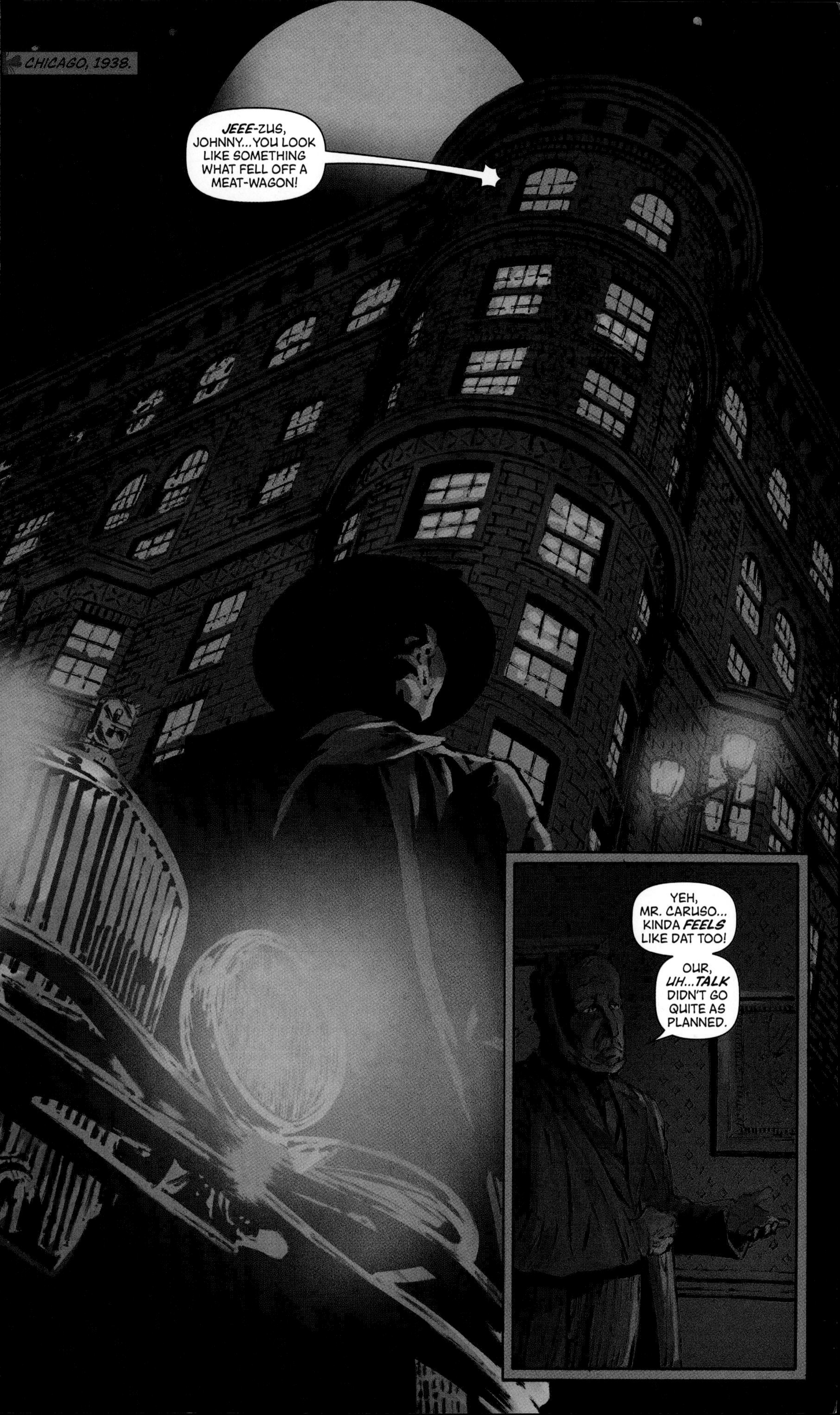
CHICAGO, 1938.
JEEE-ZUS, JOHNNY...YOU LOOK LIKE SOMETHING WHAT FELL OFF A MEAT-WAGON!
YEH, MR. CARUSO... KINDA FEELS LIKE DAT TOO!
OUR, UH...TALK DIDN'T GO QUITE AS PLANNED.

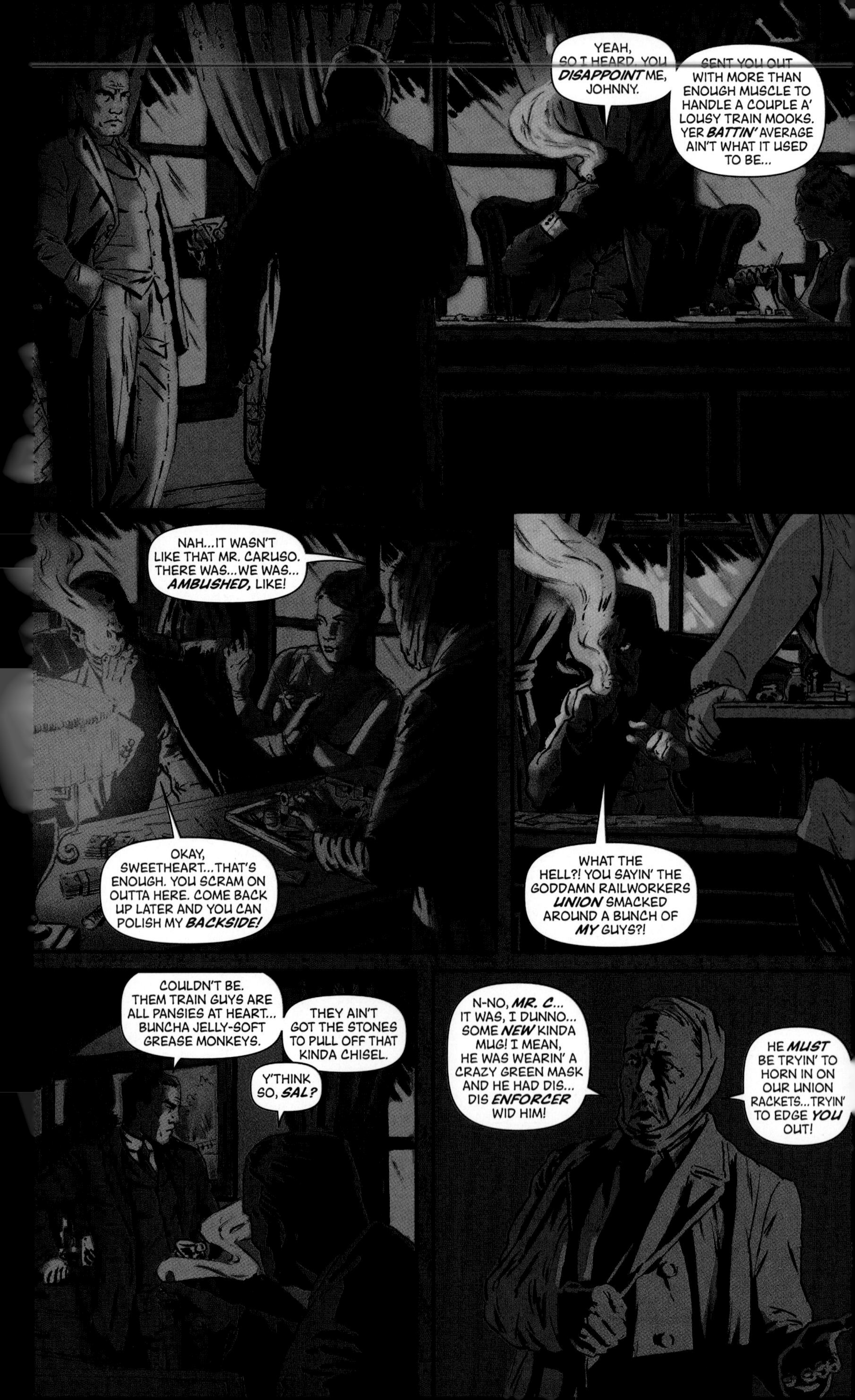
YEAH, SO I HEARD. YOU DISAPPOINT ME, JOHNNY.
SENT YOU OUT WITH MORE THAN ENOUGH MUSCLE TO HANDLE A COUPLE A' LOUSY TRAIN MOOKS. YER BATTIN' AVERAGE AIN'T WHAT IT USED TO BE...
NAH...IT WASN'T LIKE THAT MR. CARUSO. THERE WAS...WE WAS... AMBUSHED, LIKE!
OKAY, SWEETHEART...THAT'S ENOUGH. YOU SCRAM ON OUTTA HERE. COME BACK UP LATER AND YOU CAN POLISH MY BACKSIDE!
WHAT THE HELL?! YOU SAYIN' THE GODDAMN RAILWORKERS UNION SMACKED AROUND A BUNCH OF MY GUYS?!
COULDN'T BE. THEM TRAIN GUYS ARE ALL PANSIES AT HEART... BUNCHA JELLY-SOFT GREASE MONKEYS.
THEY AIN'T GOT THE STONES TO PULL OFF THAT KINDA CHISEL.
Y'THINK SO, SAL?
N-NO, MR. C... IT WAS, I DUNNO... SOME NEW KINDA MUG! I MEAN, HE WAS WEARIN' A CRAZY GREEN MASK AND HE HAD DIS... DIS ENFORCER WID HIM!
HE MUST BE TRYIN' TO HORN IN ON OUR UNION RACKETS...TRYIN' TO EDGE YOU OUT!

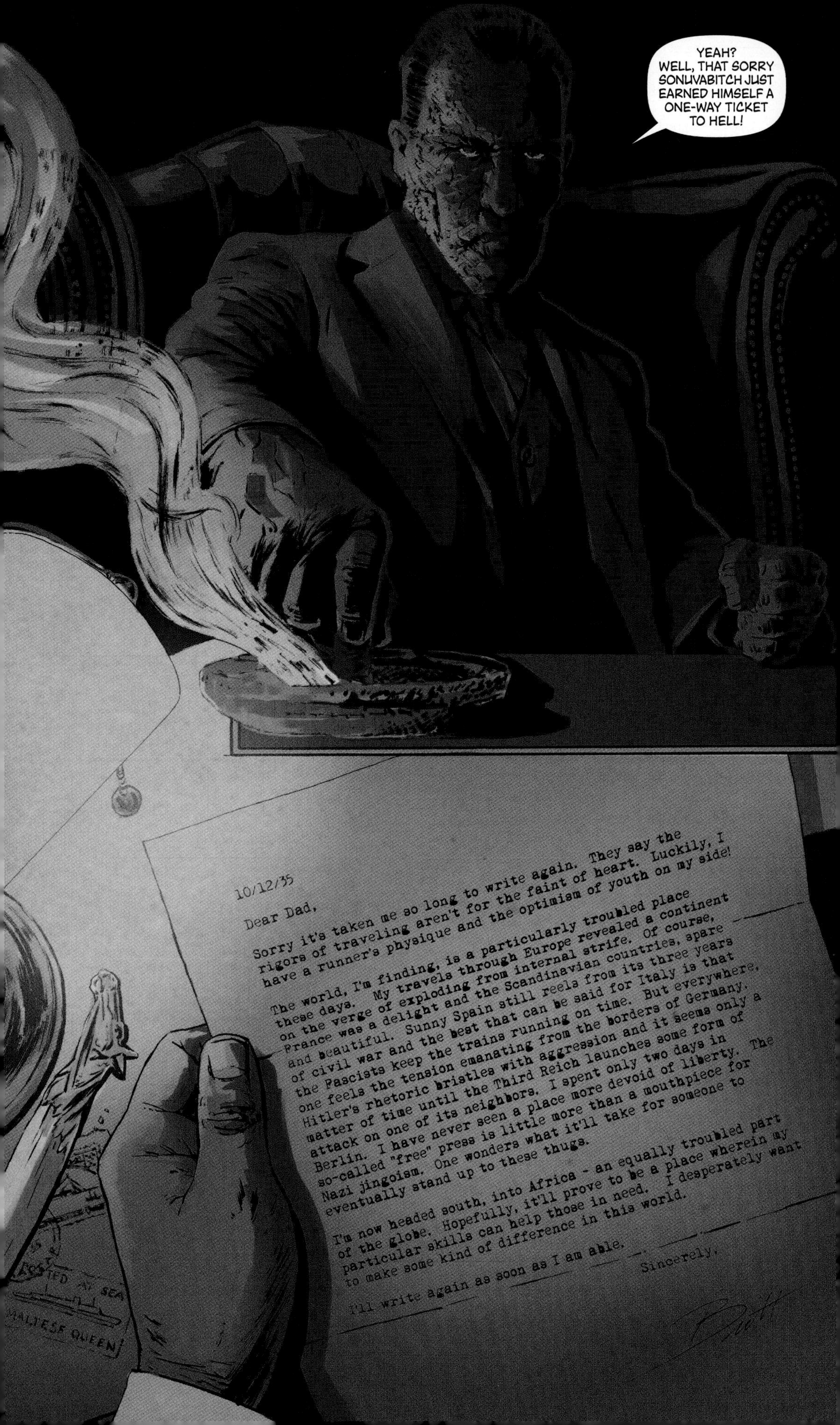
YEAH? WELL, THAT SORRY SONUVABITCH JUST EARNED HIMSELF A ONE-WAY TICKET TO HELL!
10/12/35
Dear Dad,
Sorry it's taken me so long to write again. They say the rigors of traveling aren't for the faint of heart. Luckily, I have a runner's physique and the optimism of youth on my side!
The world, I'm finding, is a particularly troubled place these days. My travels through Europe revealed a continent on the verge of exploding from internal strife. Of course, Prance was a delight and the Scandinavian countries, spare and beautiful. Sunny Spain still reels from its three years of civil war and the best that can be said for Italy is that the Pascists keep the trains running on time. But everywhere, one feels the tension emanating from the borders of Germany. Hitler's rhetoric bristles with aggression and it seems only a matter of time until the Third Reich launches some form of attack on one of its neighbors. I spent only two days in Berlin. I have never seen a place more devoid of liberty. The so-called "free" press is little more than a mouthpiece for Nazi jingoism. One wonders what it'll take for someone to eventually stand up to these thugs.
I'm now headed south, into Africa - an equally troubled part of the globe. Hopefully, it'll prove to be a place wherein my particular skills can help those in need. I desperately want to make some kind of difference in this world.
I'll write again as soon as I am able.
Sincerely,

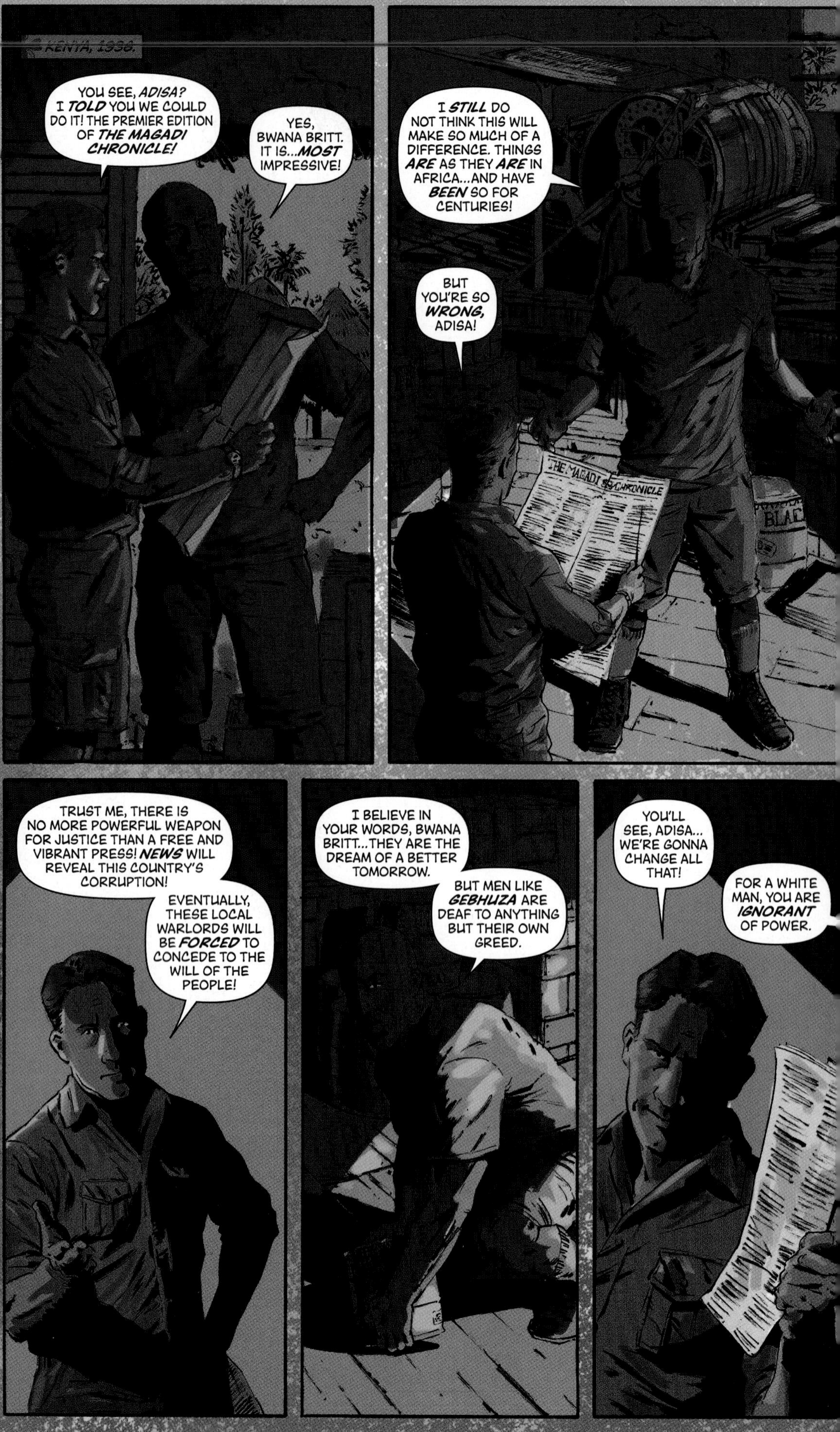
KENYA, 1938.
YOU SEE, ADISA? I TOLD YOU WE COULD DO IT! THE PREMIER EDITION OF THE MAGADI CHRONICLE!
YES, BWANA BRITT. IT IS...MOST IMPRESSIVE!
I STILL DO NOT THINK THIS WILL MAKE SO MUCH OF A DIFFERENCE. THINGS ARE AS THEY ARE IN AFRICA...AND HAVE BEEN SO FOR CENTURIES!
BUT YOU'RE SO WRONG, ADISA!
THE MAGADI CHRONICLE
TRUST ME, THERE IS NO MORE POWERFUL WEAPON FOR JUSTICE THAN A FREE AND VIBRANT PRESS! NEWS WILL REVEAL THIS COUNTRY'S CORRUPTION!
EVENTUALLY, THESE LOCAL WARLORDS WILL BE FORCED TO CONCEDE TO THE WILL OF THE PEOPLE!
I BELIEVE IN YOUR WORDS, BWANA BRITT...THEY ARE THE DREAM OF A BETTER TOMORROW.
BUT MEN LIKE GEBHUZA ARE DEAF TO ANYTHING BUT THEIR OWN GREED.
YOU'LL SEE, ADISA... WE'RE GONNA CHANGE ALL THAT!
FOR A WHITE MAN, YOU ARE IGNORANT OF POWER.

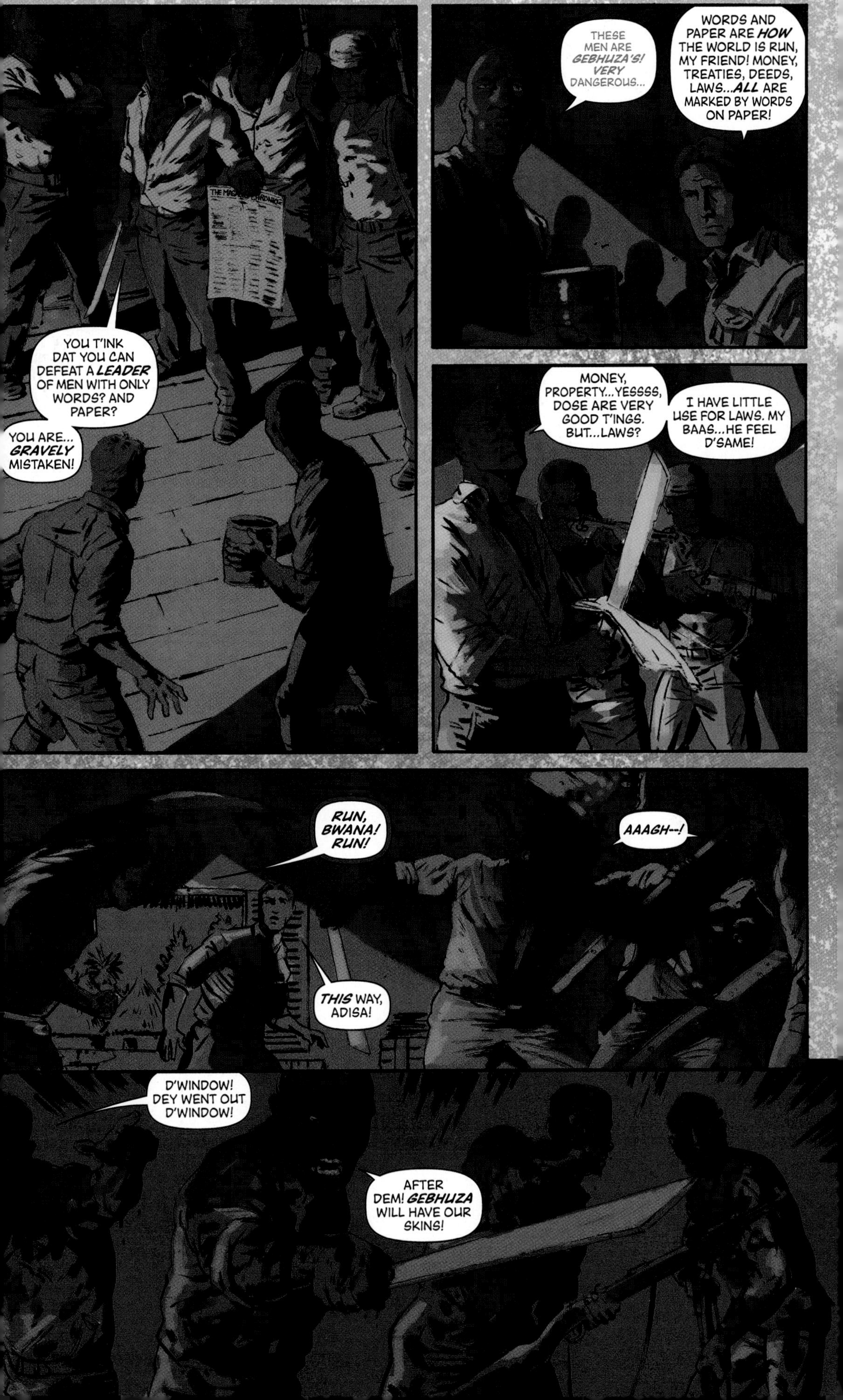
YOU T'INK DAT YOU CAN DEFEAT A LEADER OF MEN WITH ONLY WORDS? AND PAPER?
YOU ARE... GRAVELY MISTAKEN!
THESE MEN ARE GEBHUZA'S! VERY DANGEROUS...
WORDS AND PAPER ARE HOW THE WORLD IS RUN, MY FRIEND! MONEY, TREATIES, DEEDS, LAWS...ALL ARE MARKED BY WORDS ON PAPER!
MONEY, PROPERTY...YESSSS, DOSE ARE VERY GOOD T'INGS. BUT...LAWS?
I HAVE LITTLE USE FOR LAWS. MY BAAS...HE FEEL D'SAME!
RUN, BWANA! RUN!
AAAGH--!
THIS WAY, ADISA!
D'WINDOW! DEY WENT OUT D'WINDOW!
AFTER DEM! GEBHUZA WILL HAVE OUR SKINS!

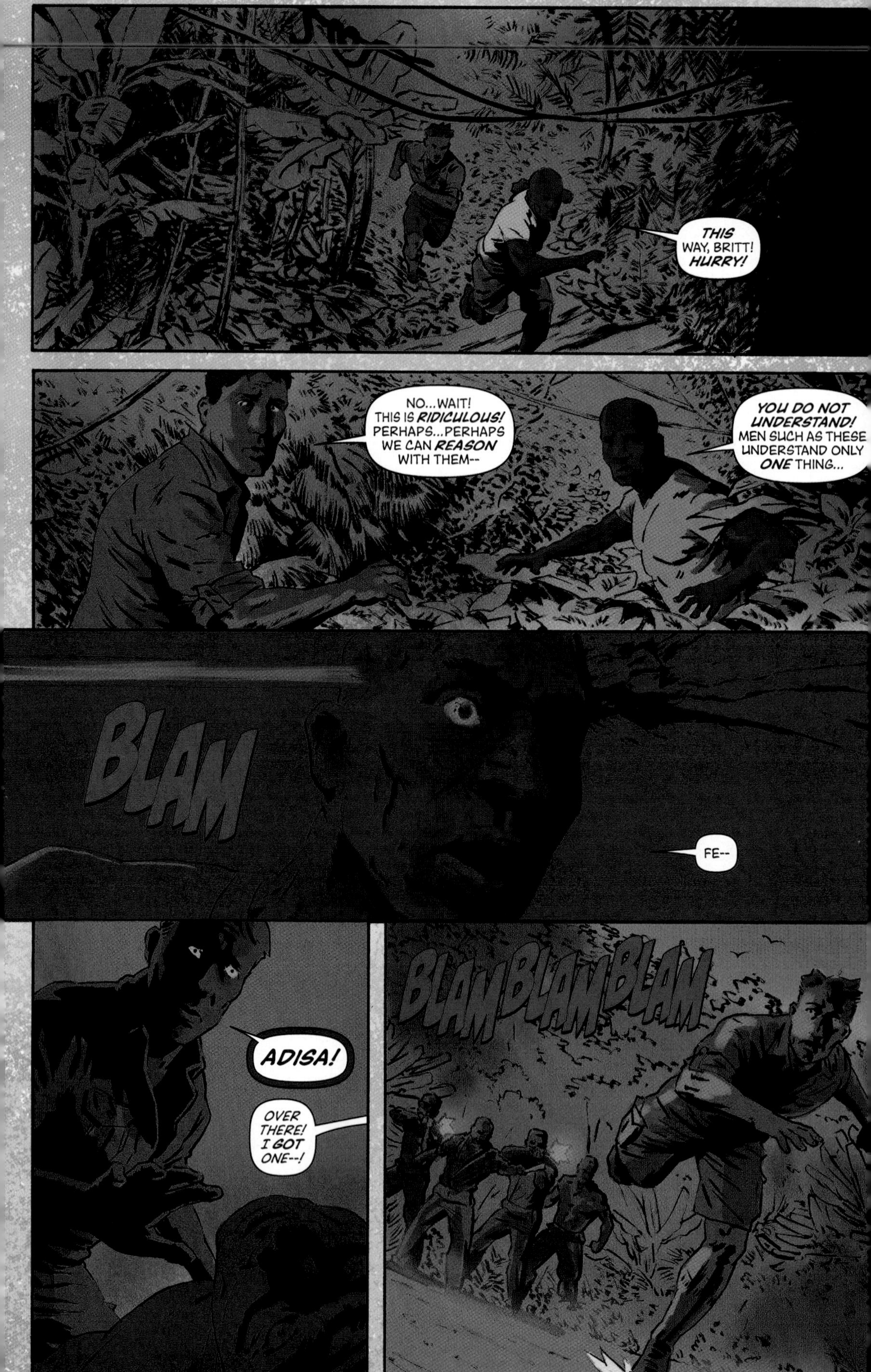
THIS WAY, BRITT! HURRY!
NO...WAIT! THIS IS RIDICULOUS! PERHAPS...PERHAPS WE CAN REASON WITH THEM--
YOU DO NOT UNDERSTAND! MEN SUCH AS THESE UNDERSTAND ONLY ONE THING...
BLAM
FE--
ADISA!
OVER THERE! I GOT ONE--!
BLAM BLAM BLAM

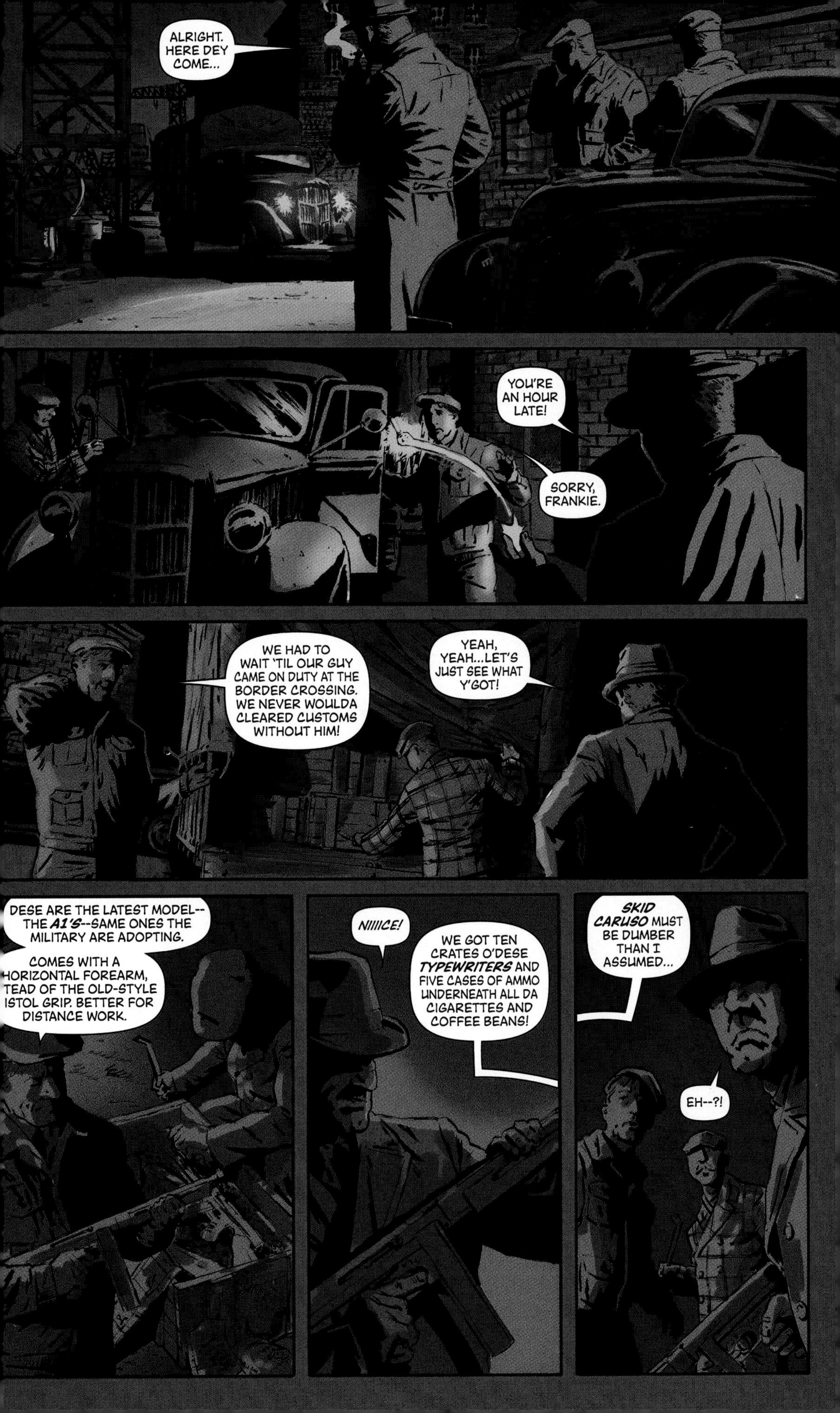
ALRIGHT. HERE DEY COME...
YOU'RE AN HOUR LATE!
SORRY, FRANKIE.
WE HAD TO WAIT 'TIL OUR GUY CAME ON DUTY AT THE BORDER CROSSING. WE NEVER WOULDA CLEARED CUSTOMS WITHOUT HIM!
YEAH, YEAH...LET'S JUST SEE WHAT Y'GOT!
DESE ARE THE LATEST MODEL-- THE *A1'S*--SAME ONES THE MILITARY ARE ADOPTING.
COMES WITH A HORIZONTAL FOREARM, TEAD OF THE OLD-STYLE ISTOL GRIP. BETTER FOR DISTANCE WORK.
NIIIICE!
WE GOT TEN CRATES O'DESE *TYPEWRITERS* AND FIVE CASES OF AMMO UNDERNEATH ALL DA CIGARETTES AND COFFEE BEANS!
SKID CARUSO MUST BE DUMBER THAN I ASSUMED...
EH--?!

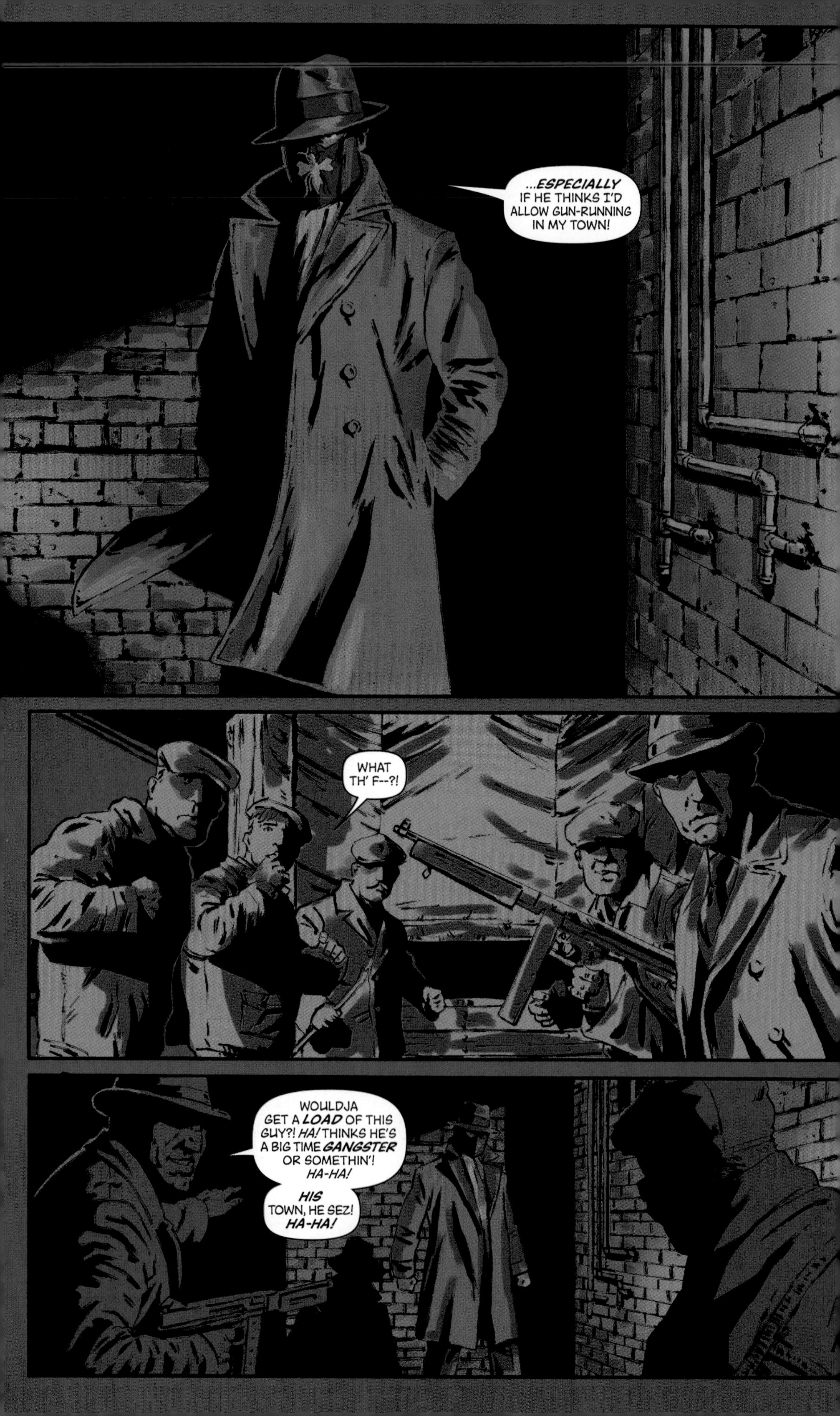
...ESPECIALLY IF HE THINKS I'D ALLOW GUN-RUNNING IN MY TOWN!
WHAT TH' F--?!
WOULDJA GET A LOAD OF THIS GUY?! HA! THINKS HE'S A BIG TIME GANGSTER OR SOMETHIN'! HA-HA!
HIS TOWN, HE SEZ! HA-HA!

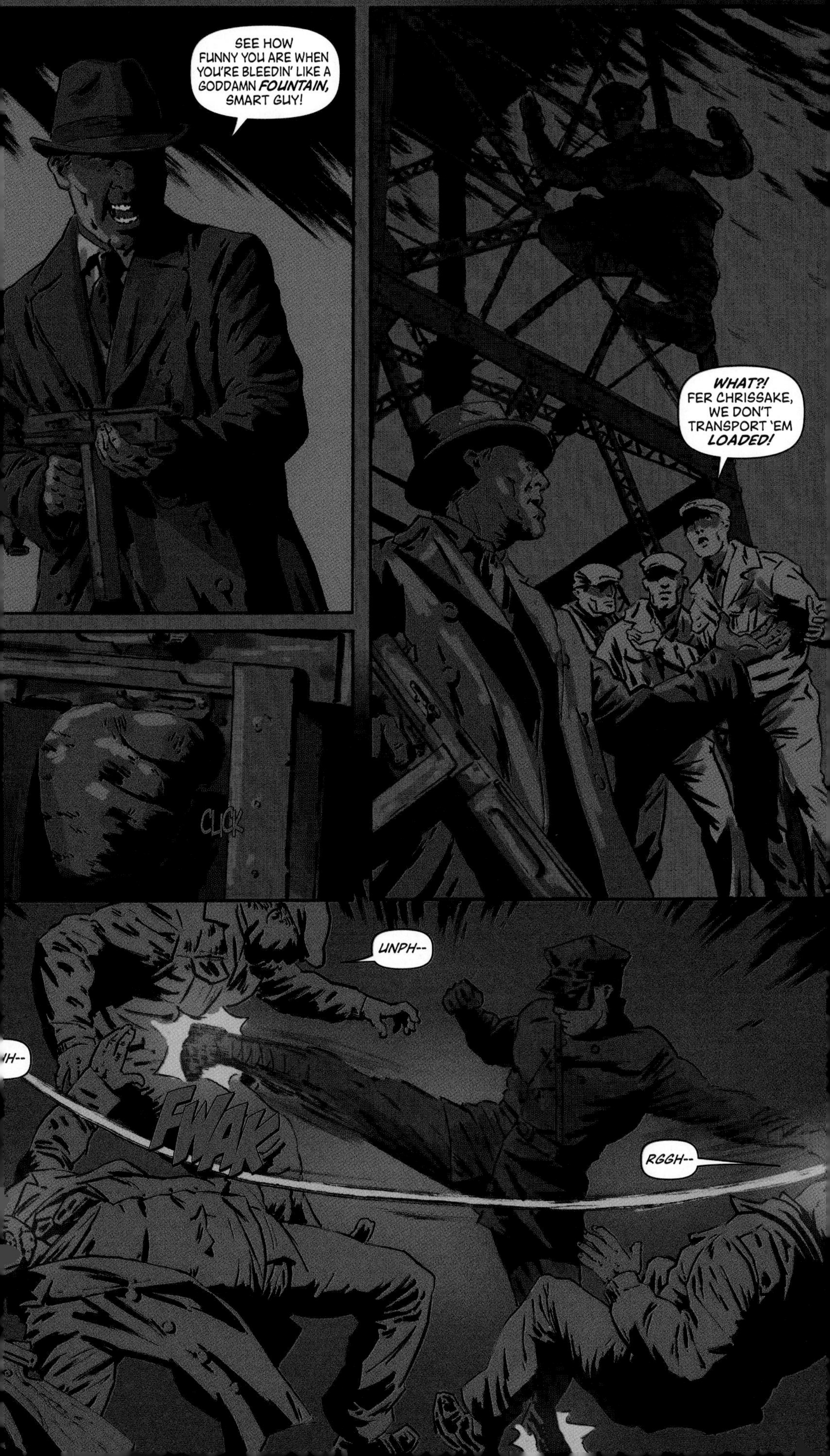
SEE HOW FUNNY YOU ARE WHEN YOU'RE BLEEDIN' LIKE A GODDAMN FOUNTAIN, SMART GUY!
CLICK
WHAT?! FER CHRISSAKE, WE DON'T TRANSPORT 'EM LOADED!
UNPH--
FWAK
RGGH--

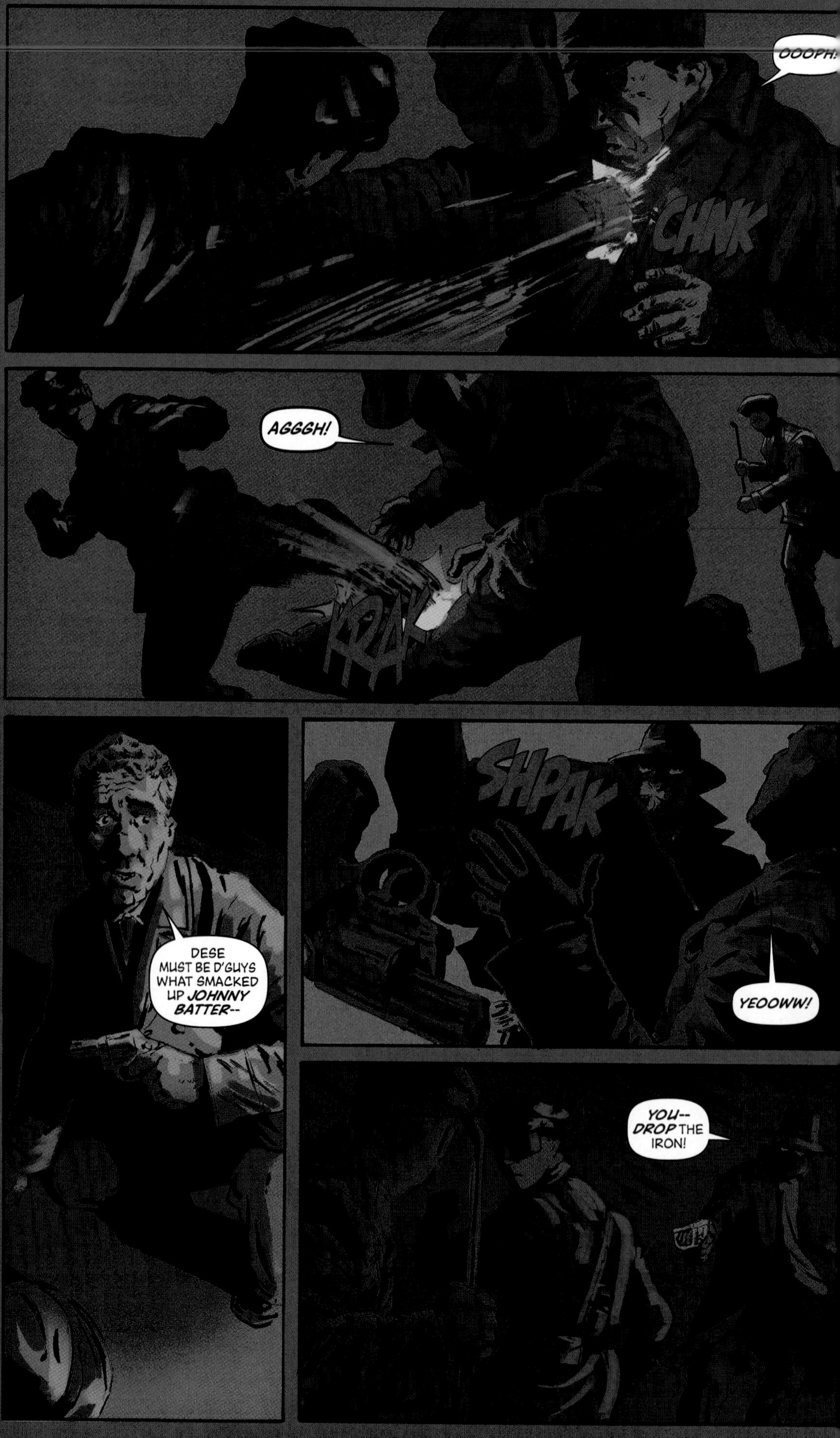
OOOPH!
CHNK
AGGGH!
KRAK
DESE MUST BE D'GUYS WHAT SMACKED UP JOHNNY BATTER--
SHPAK
YEOOWW!
YOU-- DROP THE IRON!

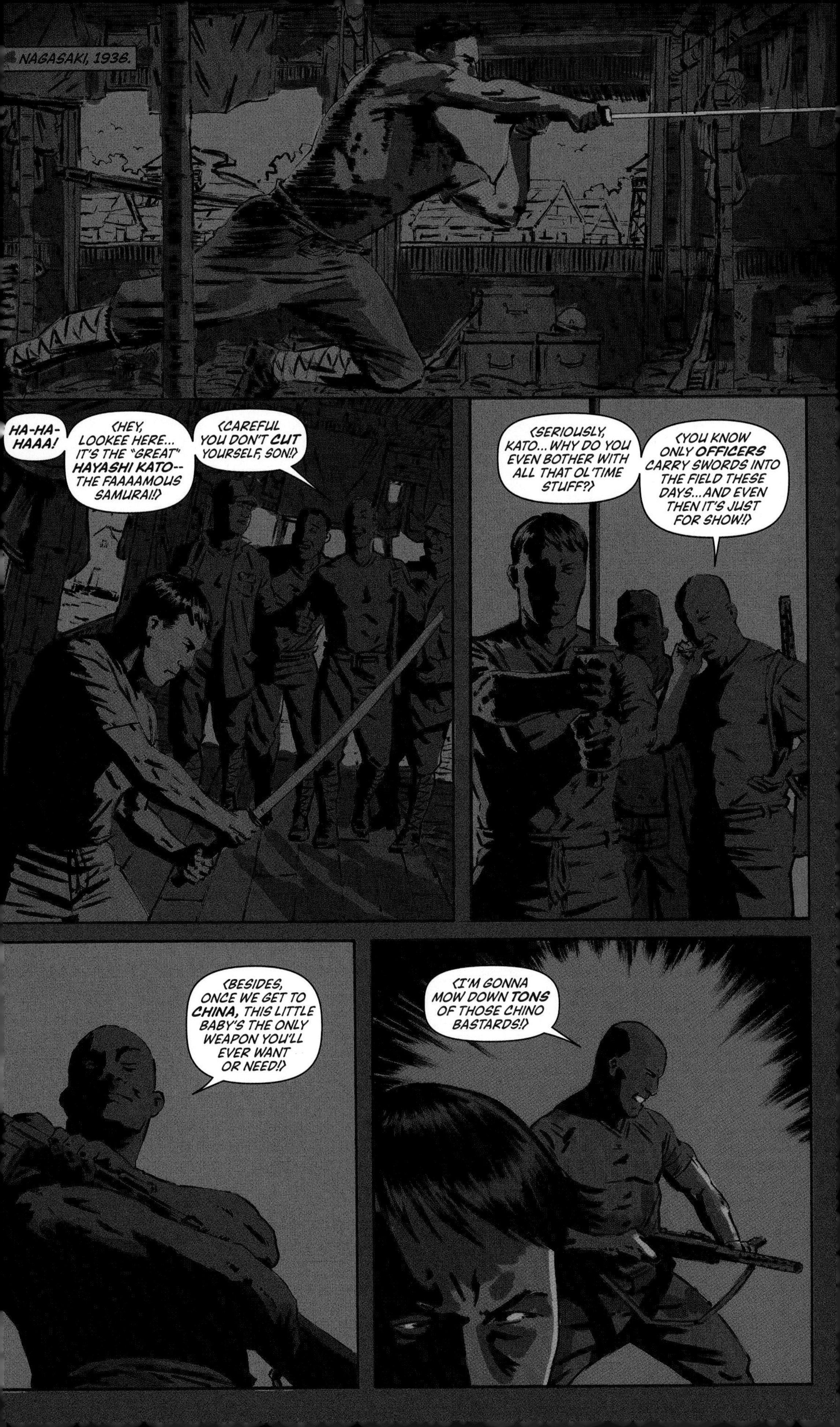
NAGASAKI, 1936.
HA-HA-HAAA!
<HEY, LOOKEE HERE... IT'S THE "GREAT" HAYASHI KATO-- THE FAAAAMOUS SAMURAI!>
<CAREFUL YOU DON'T CUT YOURSELF, SON!>
<SERIOUSLY, KATO... WHY DO YOU EVEN BOTHER WITH ALL THAT OL' TIME STUFF?>
<YOU KNOW ONLY OFFICERS CARRY SWORDS INTO THE FIELD THESE DAYS... AND EVEN THEN IT'S JUST FOR SHOW!>
<BESIDES, ONCE WE GET TO CHINA, THIS LITTLE BABY'S THE ONLY WEAPON YOU'LL EVER WANT OR NEED!>
<I'M GONNA MOW DOWN TONS OF THOSE CHINO BASTARDS!>

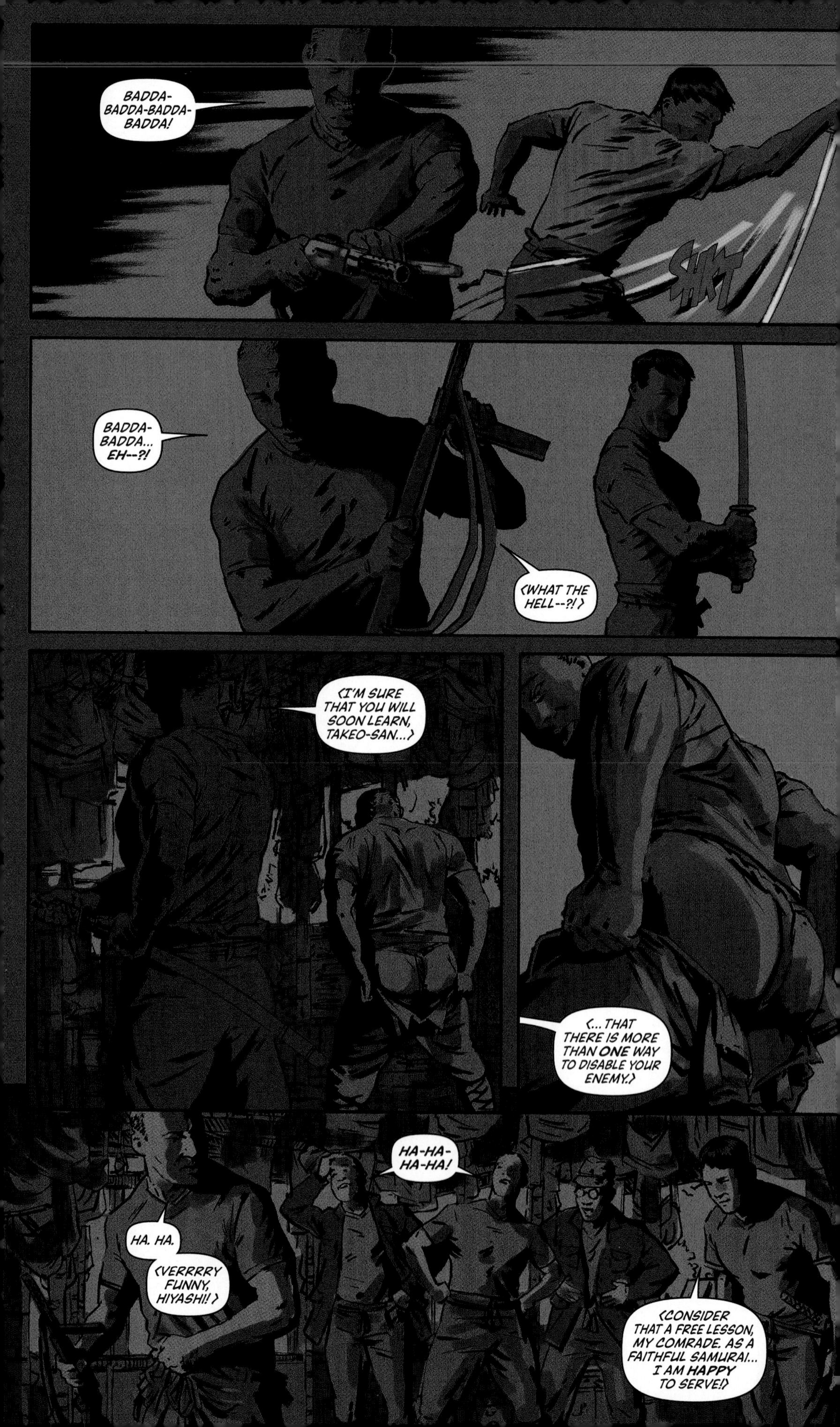
BADDA-BADDA-BADDA-BADDA!
SHKT
BADDA-BADDA... EH--?!
‹WHAT THE HELL--?!›
‹I'M SURE THAT YOU WILL SOON LEARN, TAKEO-SAN...›
‹... THAT THERE IS MORE THAN ONE WAY TO DISABLE YOUR ENEMY.›
HA-HA-HA-HA!
HA. HA.
‹VERRRRY FUNNY, HIYASHI!›
‹CONSIDER THAT A FREE LESSON, MY COMRADE. AS A FAITHFUL SAMURAI... I AM HAPPY TO SERVE!›

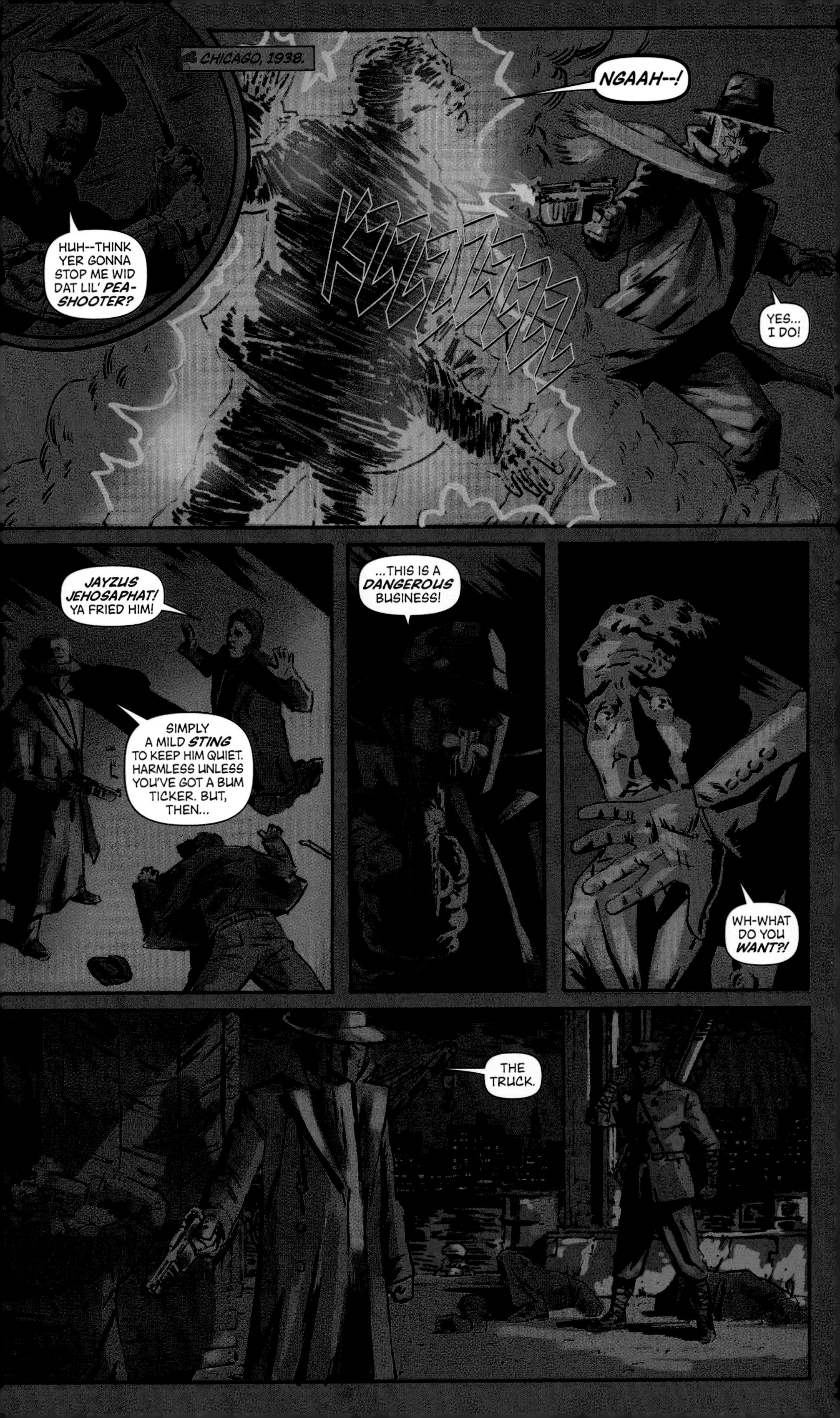
CHICAGO, 1938.
HUH--THINK YER GONNA STOP ME WID DAT LIL' PEA-SHOOTER?
NGAAH--!
KZZZZZZZZ
YES... I DO!
JAYZUS JEHOSAPHAT! YA FRIED HIM!
SIMPLY A MILD STING TO KEEP HIM QUIET. HARMLESS UNLESS YOU'VE GOT A BUM TICKER. BUT, THEN...
...THIS IS A DANGEROUS BUSINESS!
WH-WHAT DO YOU WANT?!
THE TRUCK.

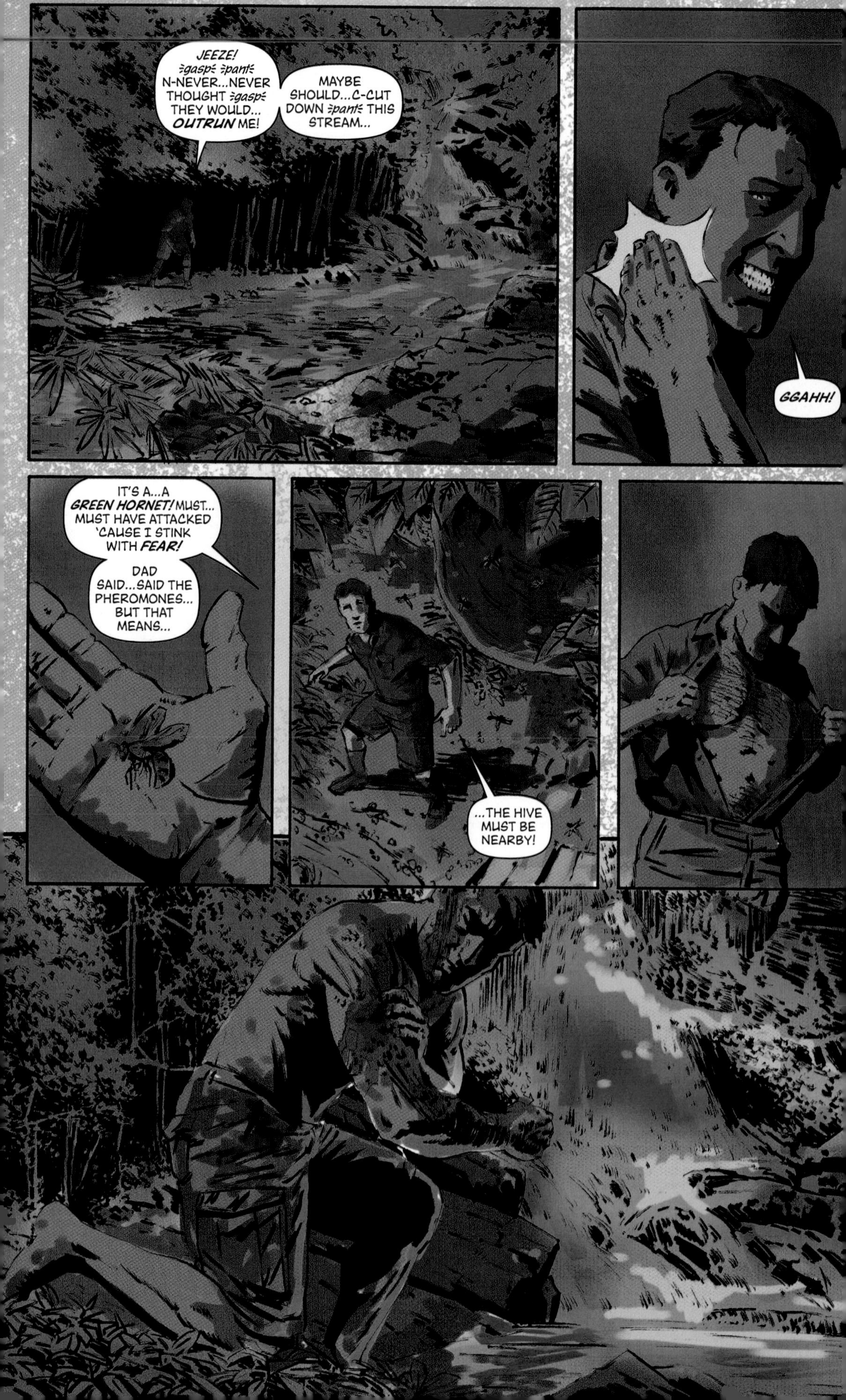
JEEZE! ≷gasp≶ ≷pant≶ N-NEVER...NEVER THOUGHT ≷gasp≶ THEY WOULD... OUTRUN ME!
MAYBE SHOULD...C-CUT DOWN ≷pant≶ THIS STREAM...
GGAHH!
IT'S A...A GREEN HORNET! MUST... MUST HAVE ATTACKED 'CAUSE I STINK WITH FEAR!
DAD SAID...SAID THE PHEROMONES... BUT THAT MEANS...
...THE HIVE MUST BE NEARBY!

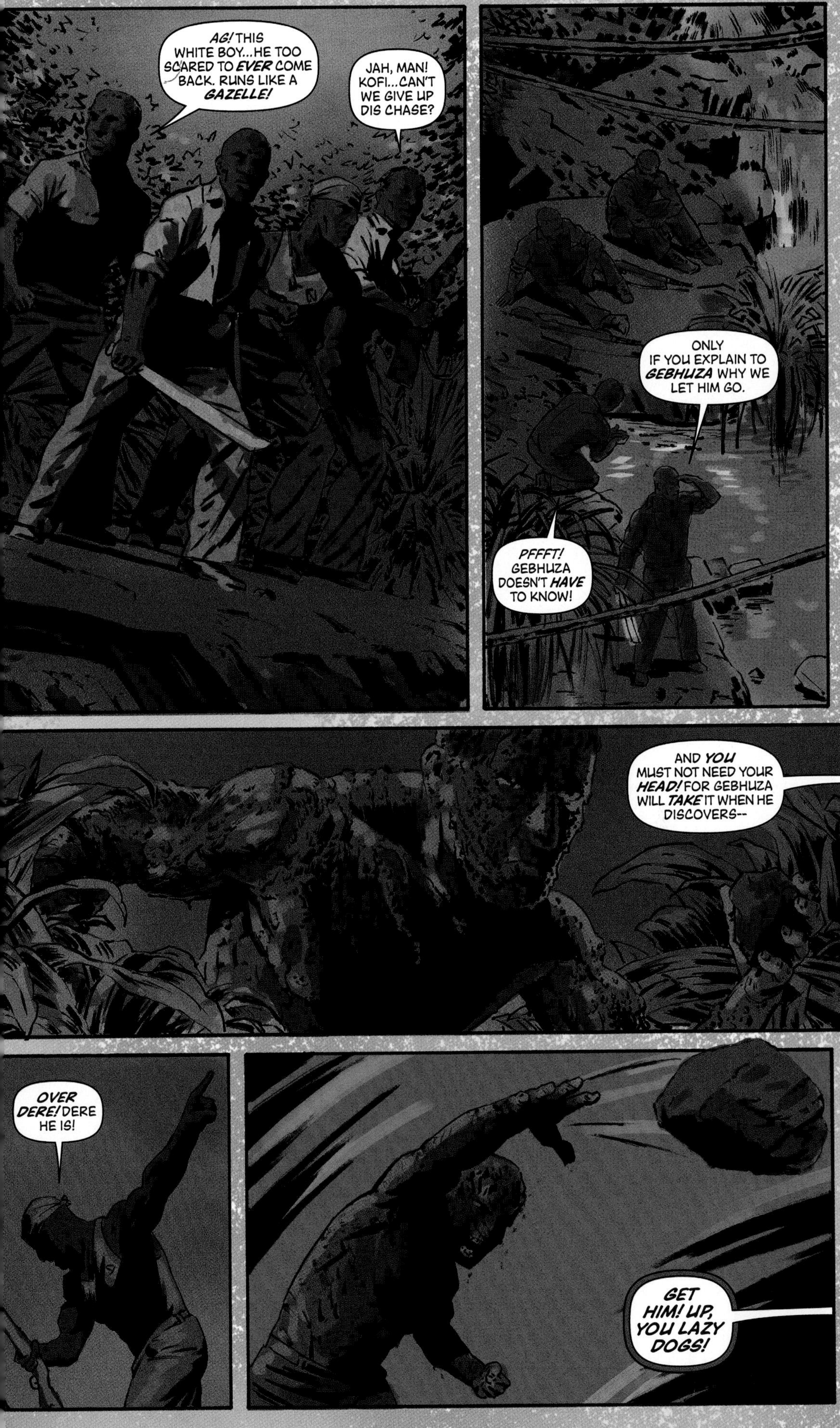
AG! THIS WHITE BOY...HE TOO SCARED TO EVER COME BACK. RUNS LIKE A GAZELLE!
JAH, MAN! KOFI...CAN'T WE GIVE UP DIS CHASE?
ONLY IF YOU EXPLAIN TO GEBHUZA WHY WE LET HIM GO.
PFFFT! GEBHUZA DOESN'T HAVE TO KNOW!
AND YOU MUST NOT NEED YOUR HEAD! FOR GEBHUZA WILL TAKE IT WHEN HE DISCOVERS--
OVER DERE! DERE HE IS!
GET HIM! UP, YOU LAZY DOGS!

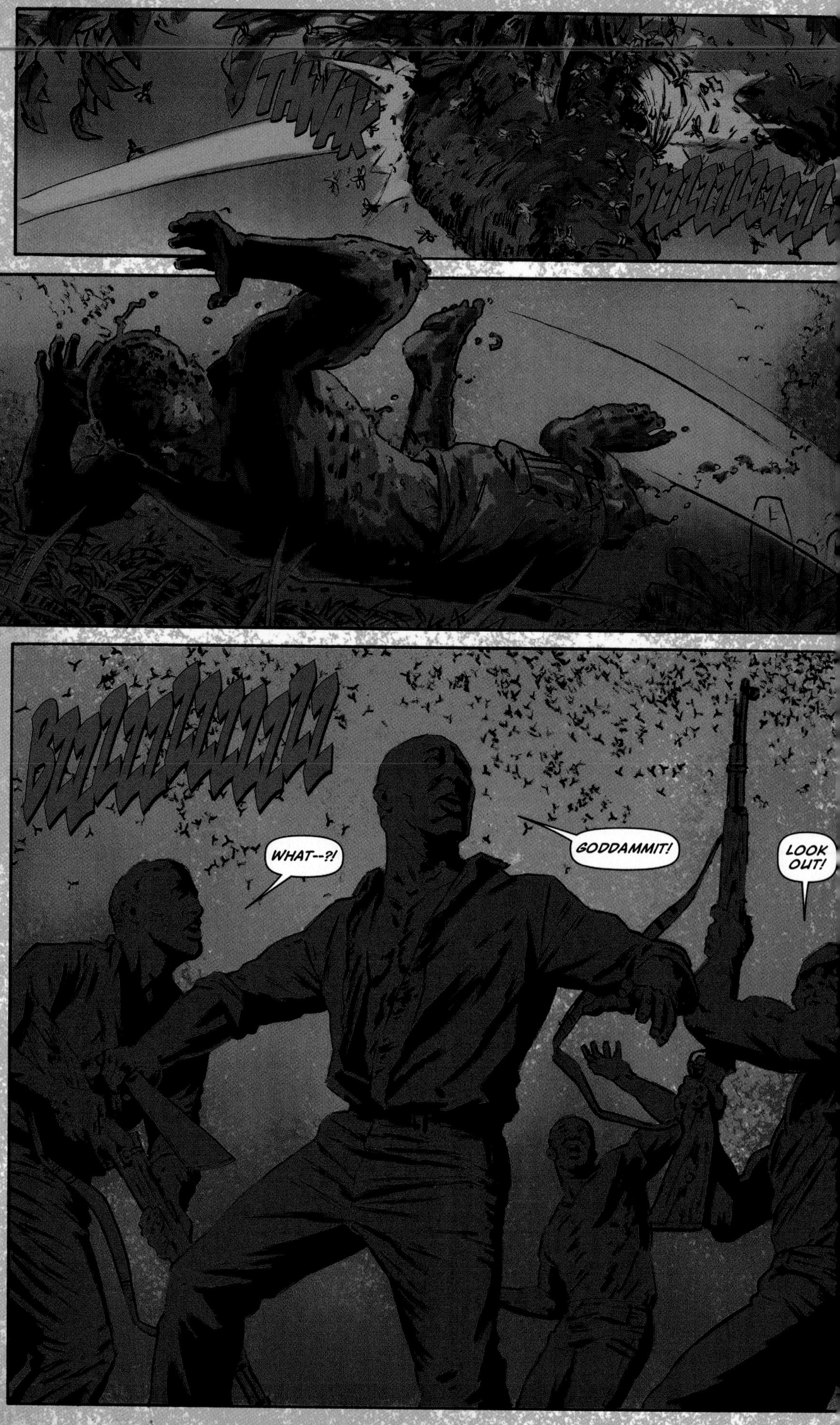
THWAK
BZZZZZZZZZ
WHAT--?!
GODDAMMIT!
LOOK OUT!

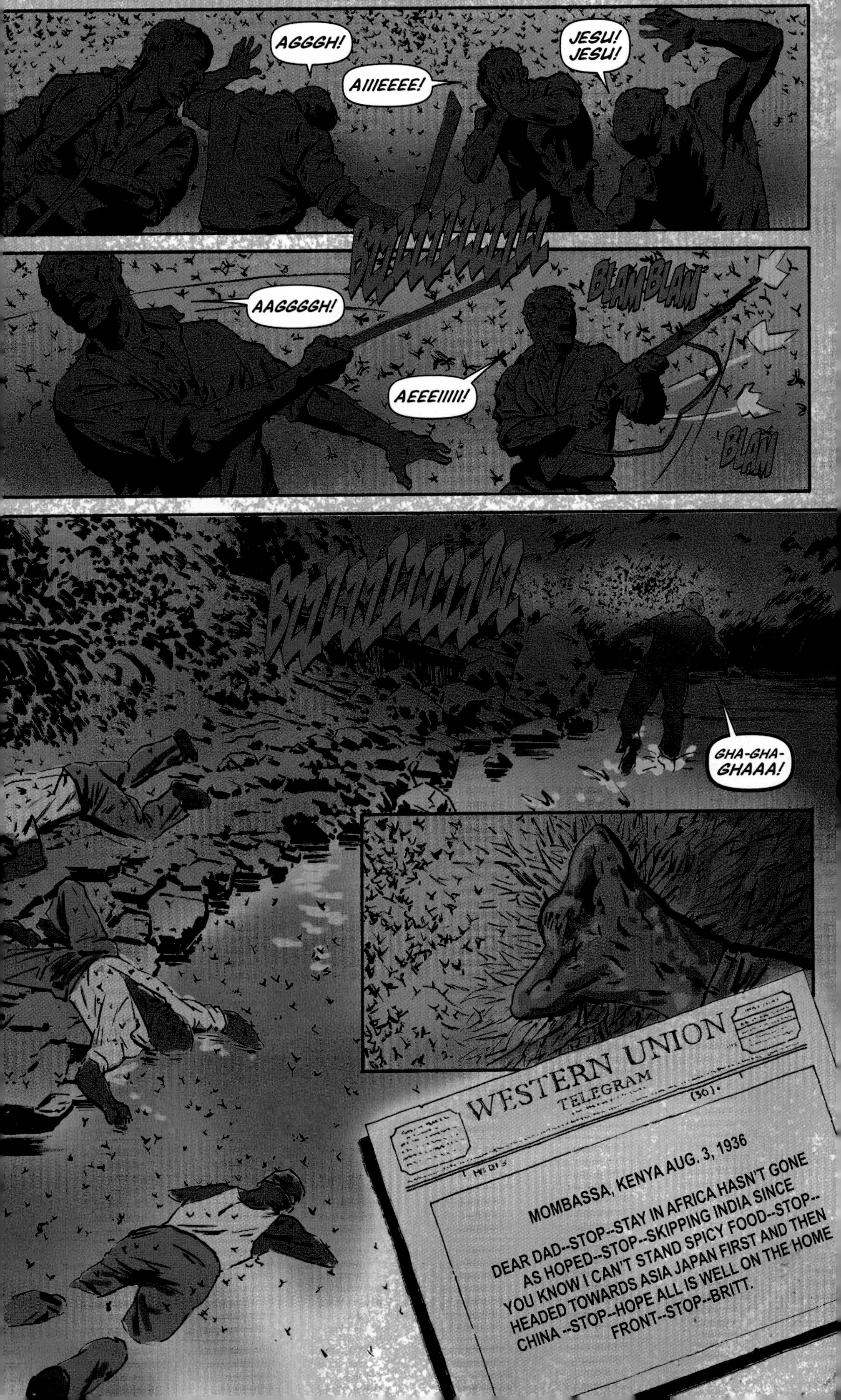
AGGGH!
AIIIEEEE!
JESU! JESU!
BZZZZZZZZZZZZ
AAGGGGH!
BLAM BLAM
AEEEIIIII!
BLAM
BZZZZZZZZZZZZ
GHA-GHA-GHAAA!
WESTERN UNION
TELEGRAM
MOMBASSA, KENYA AUG. 3, 1936
DEAR DAD--STOP--STAY IN AFRICA HASN'T GONE AS HOPED--STOP--SKIPPING INDIA SINCE YOU KNOW I CAN'T STAND SPICY FOOD--STOP--HEADED TOWARDS ASIA JAPAN FIRST AND THEN CHINA --STOP--HOPE ALL IS WELL ON THE HOME FRONT--STOP--BRITT.

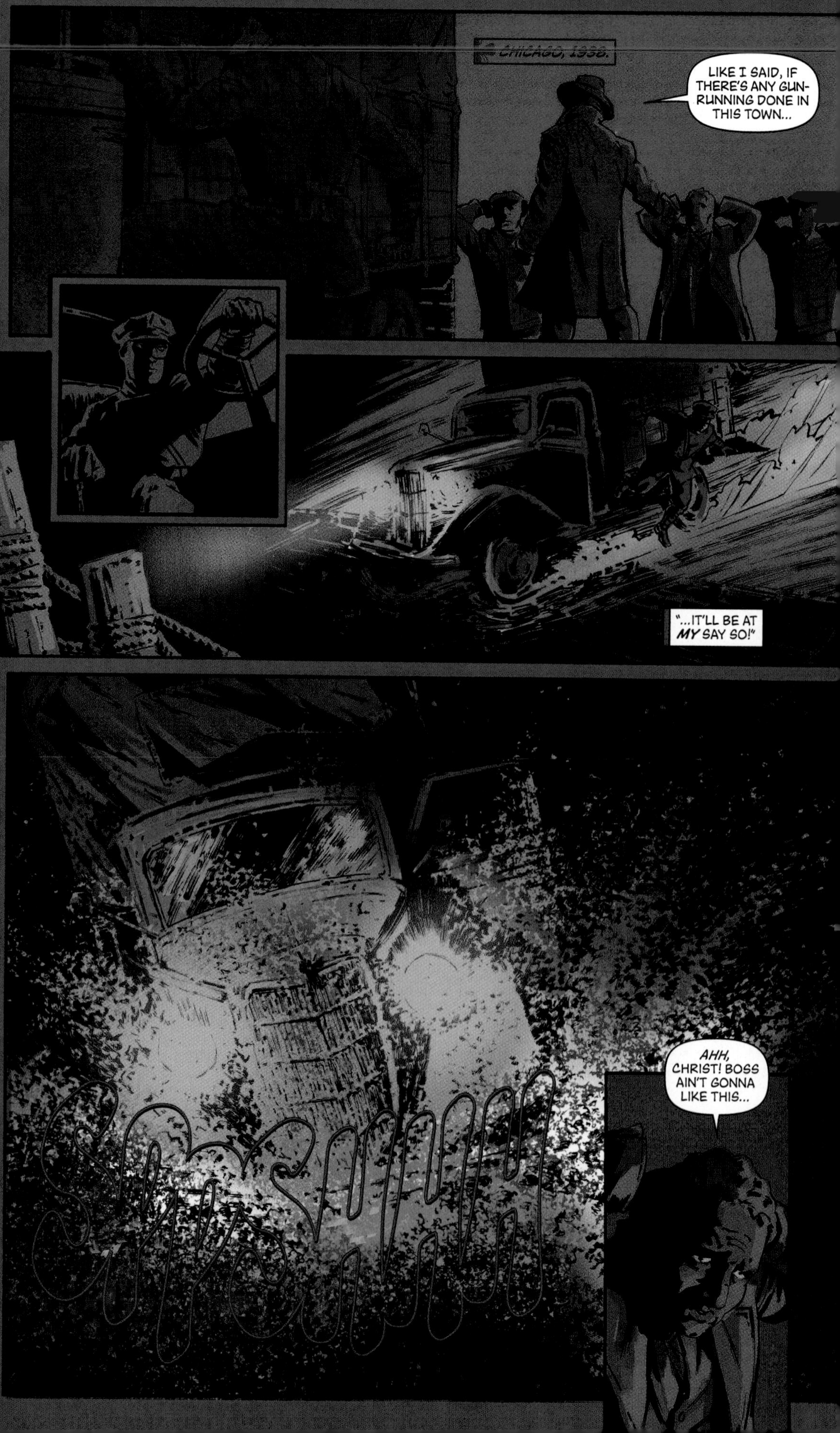
CHICAGO, 1938.
LIKE I SAID, IF THERE'S ANY GUN-RUNNING DONE IN THIS TOWN...
"...IT'LL BE AT *MY* SAY SO!"
AHH, CHRIST! BOSS AIN'T GONNA LIKE THIS...

REPUBLIC OF CHINA, 1937.

Honorable Father,
I hope this letter manages to find you well if, indeed, it finds you at all. As you predicted, our emperor's expansionist dreams have at last led us to invade the Chinese mainland.

The mood among my fellow soldiers is tense. Most are young and undisciplined, eager to play at war, eager to deal out death.

The locals offer little resistance as we make our way towards the capital city. I am different than when last we met, father, for I have now killed other men — an experience that changes one forever. I am even more grateful for your instruction and your wisdom.

Still, nothing could have prepared me for the carnage and horrors that now greet me daily. We have occupied the capital for three weeks, an event I feel certain will someday be known as...

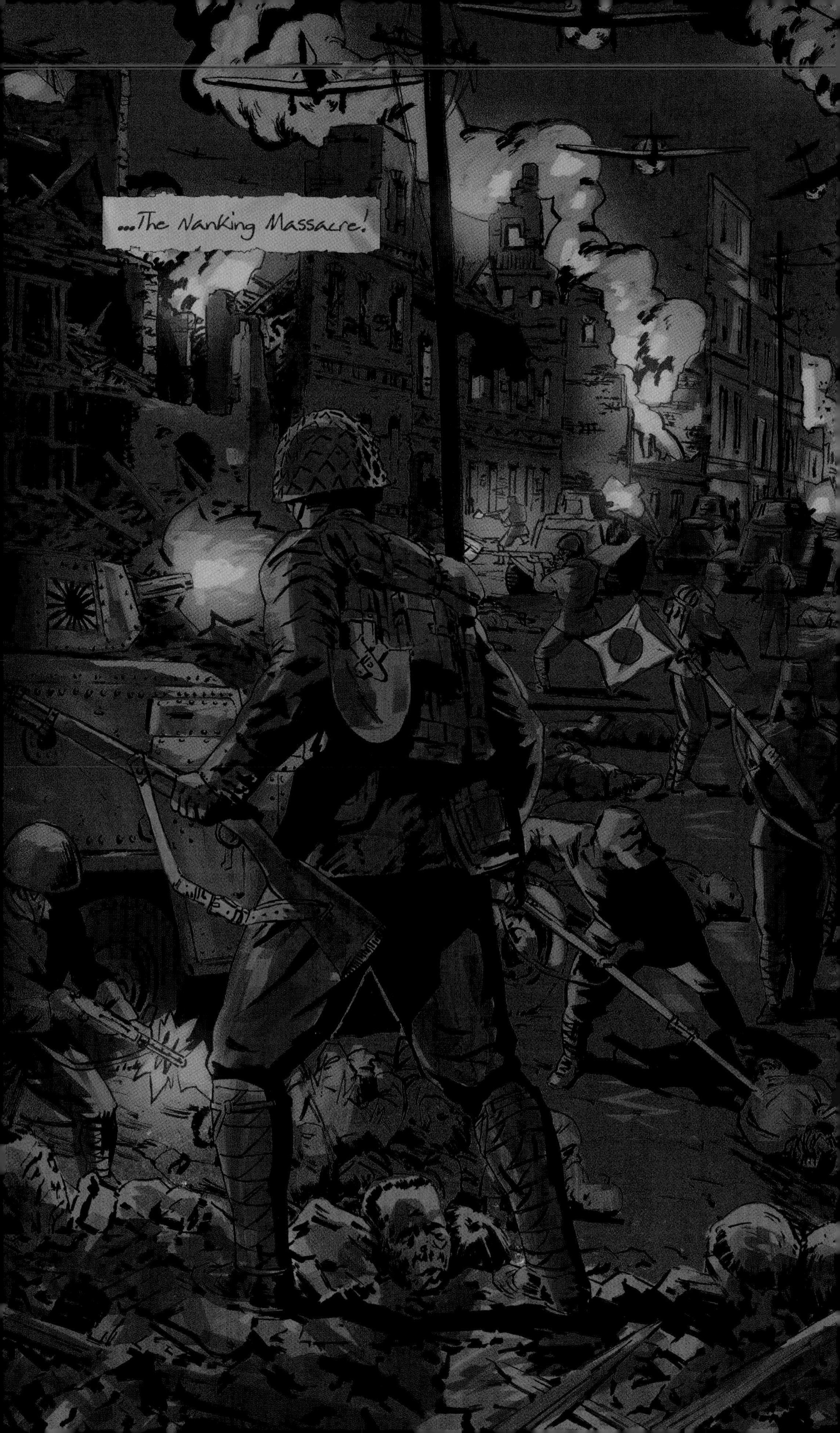
...The Nanking Massacre!

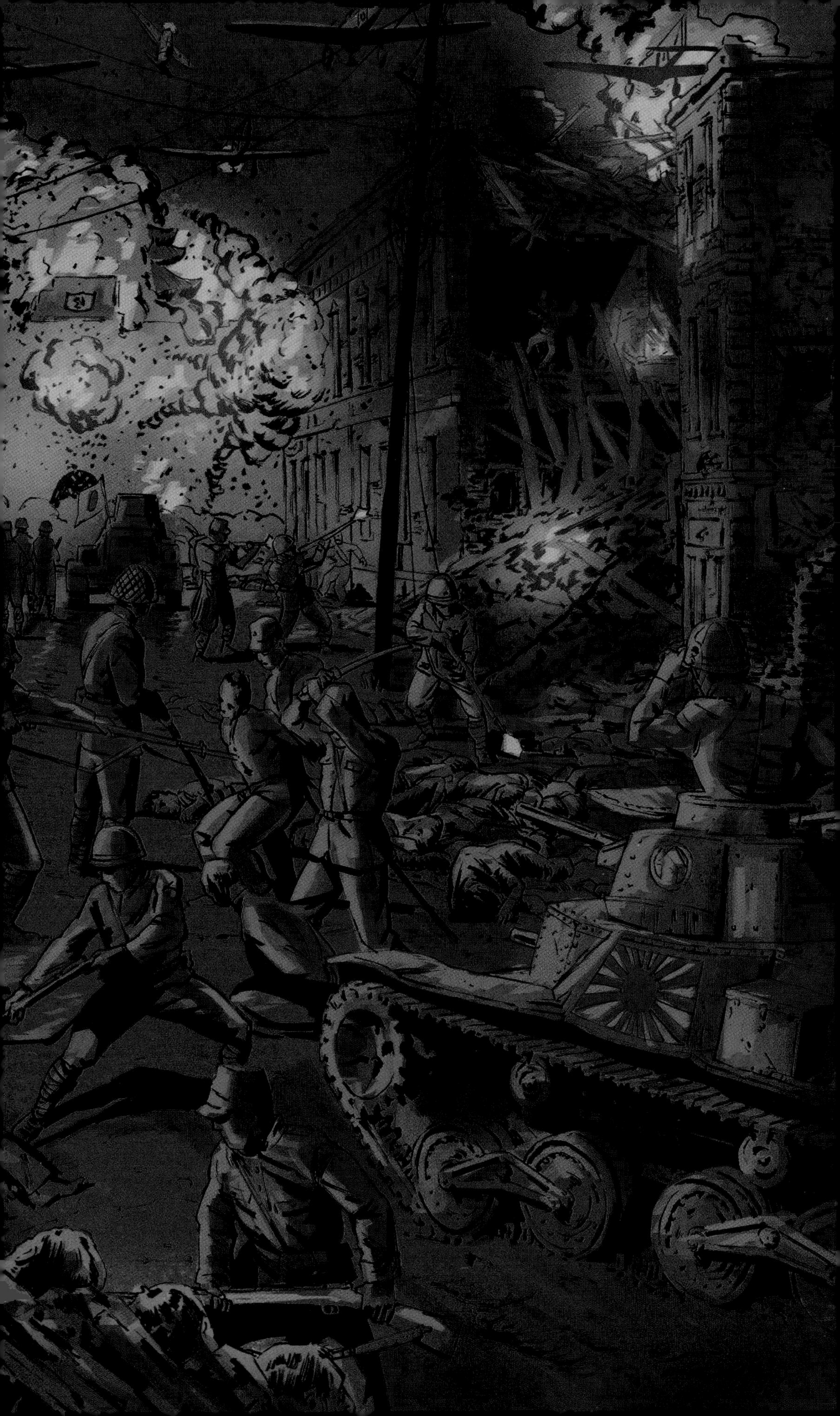

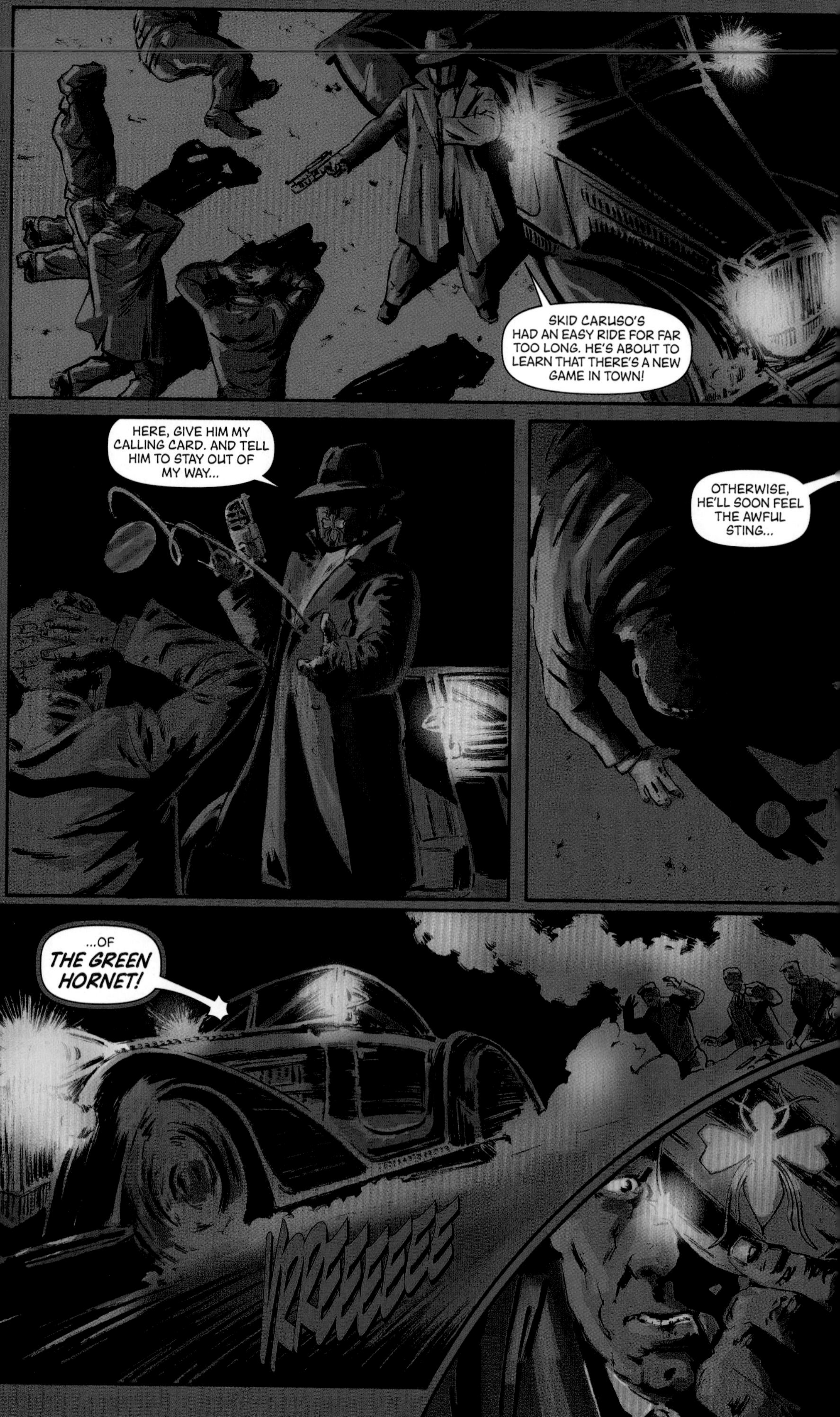
SKID CARUSO'S HAD AN EASY RIDE FOR FAR TOO LONG. HE'S ABOUT TO LEARN THAT THERE'S A NEW GAME IN TOWN!
HERE, GIVE HIM MY CALLING CARD. AND TELL HIM TO STAY OUT OF MY WAY...
OTHERWISE, HE'LL SOON FEEL THE AWFUL STING...
...OF THE GREEN HORNET!
VRREEEEEE

ISSUE THREE

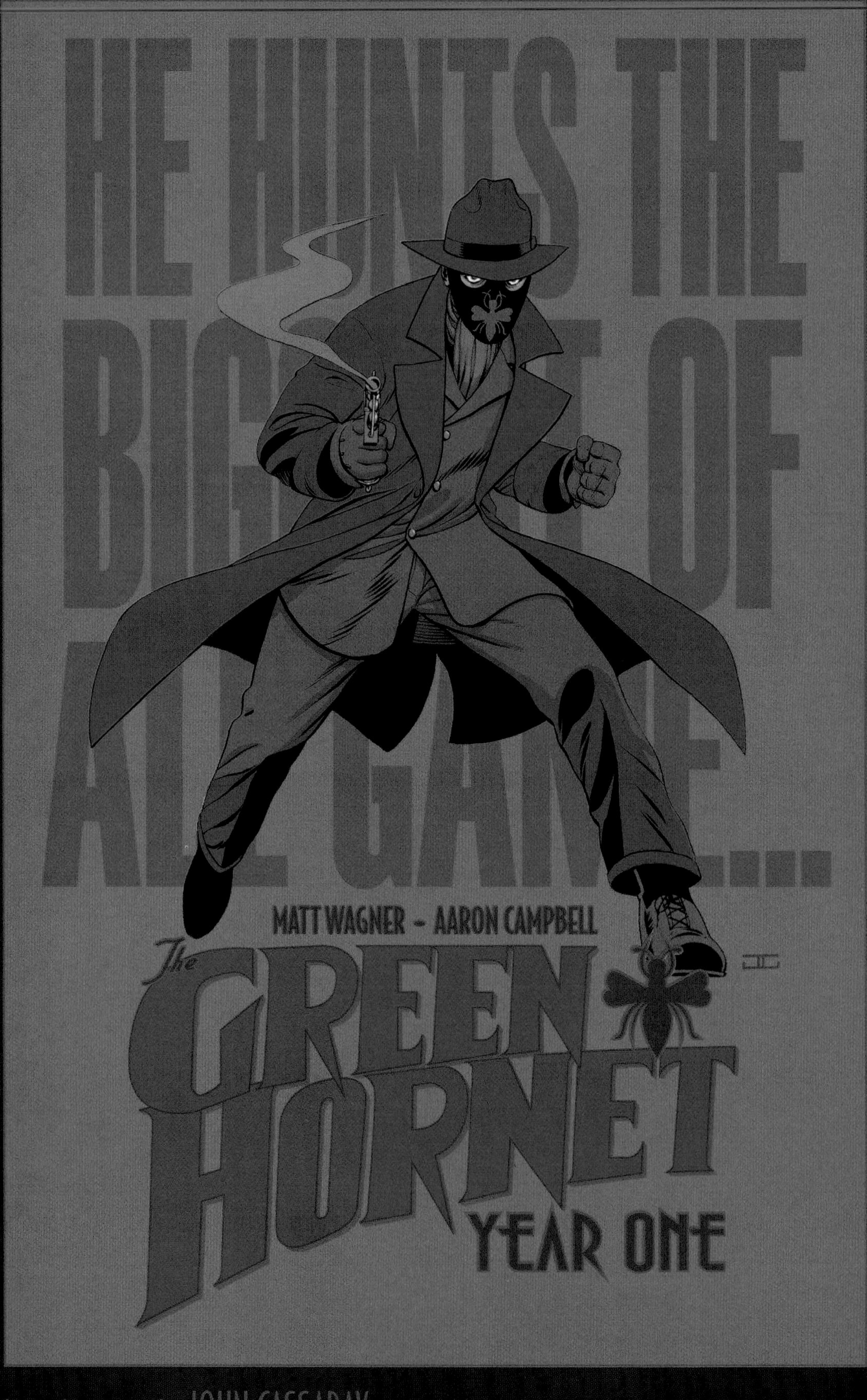
HE HUNTS THE
MATT WAGNER - AARON CAMPBELL
The GREEN HORNET
YEAR ONE

Issue three cover by JOHN CASSADAY

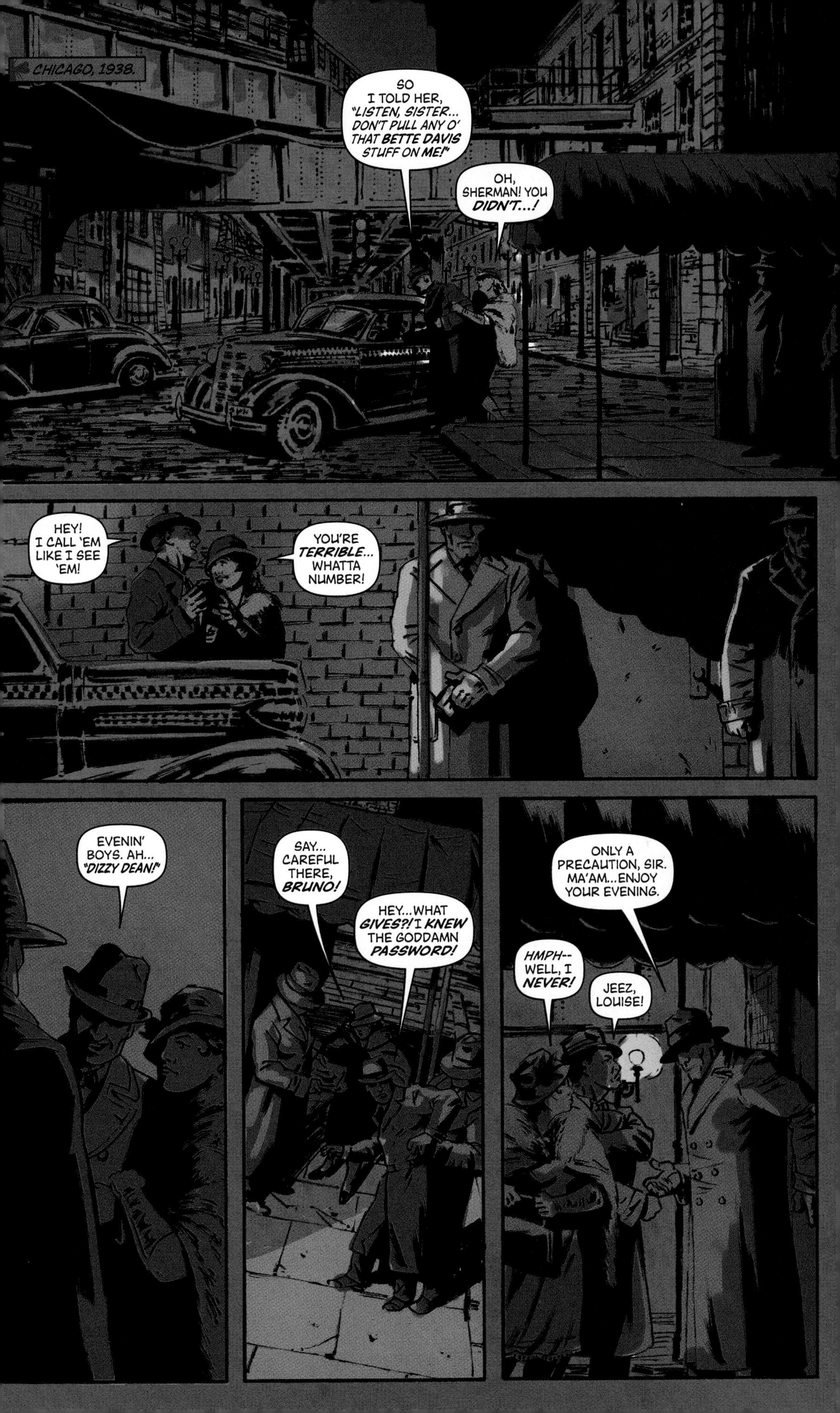
CHICAGO, 1938.
SO I TOLD HER, "LISTEN, SISTER... DON'T PULL ANY O' THAT BETTE DAVIS STUFF ON ME!"
OH, SHERMAN! YOU DIDN'T...!
HEY! I CALL 'EM LIKE I SEE 'EM!
YOU'RE TERRIBLE... WHATTA NUMBER!
EVENIN' BOYS. AH... "DIZZY DEAN!"
SAY... CAREFUL THERE, BRUNO!
HEY...WHAT GIVES?! I KNEW THE GODDAMN PASSWORD!
ONLY A PRECAUTION, SIR. MA'AM...ENJOY YOUR EVENING.
HMPH-- WELL, I NEVER!
JEEZ, LOUISE!

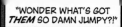

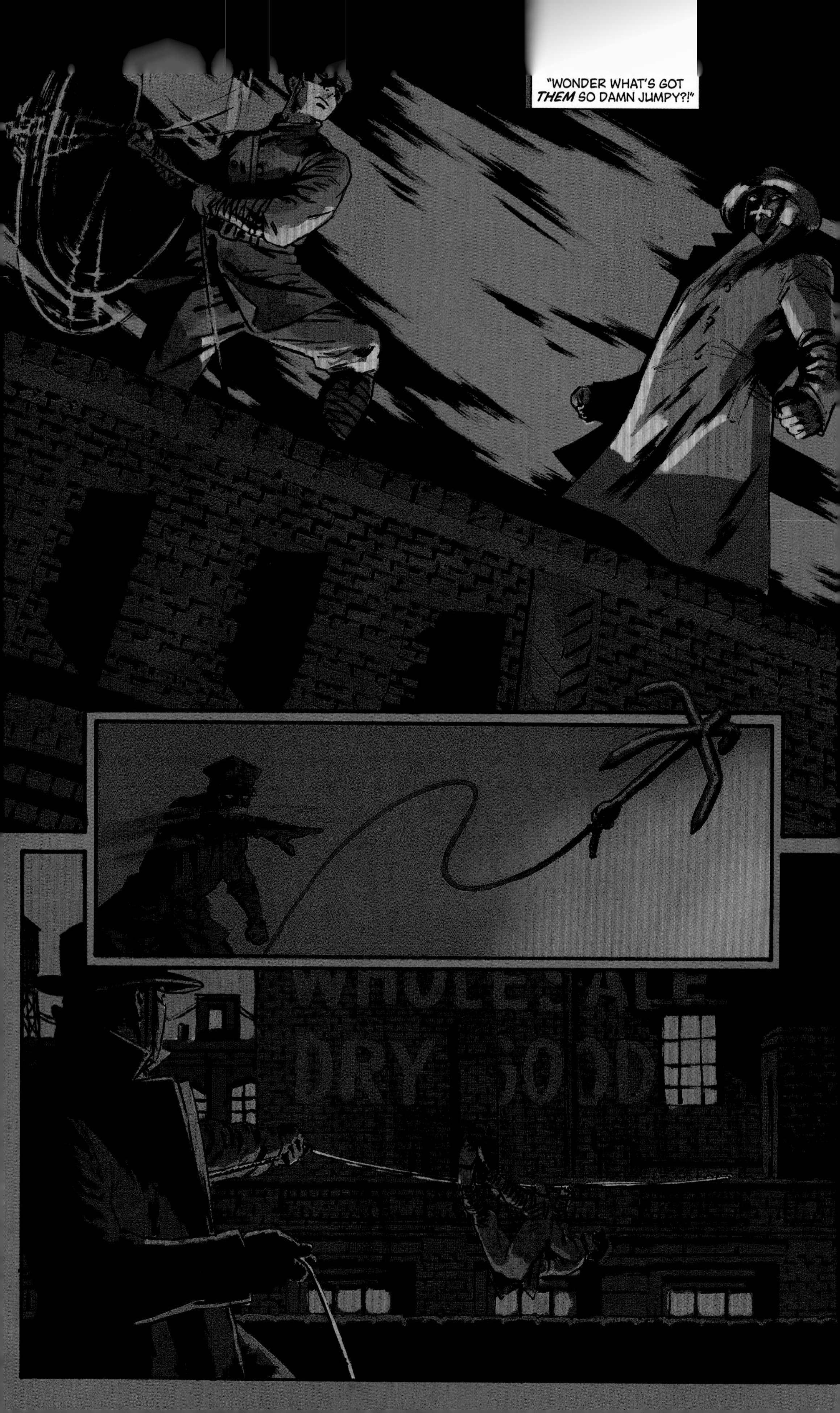

"WONDER WHAT'S GOT *THEM* SO DAMN JUMPY?!"

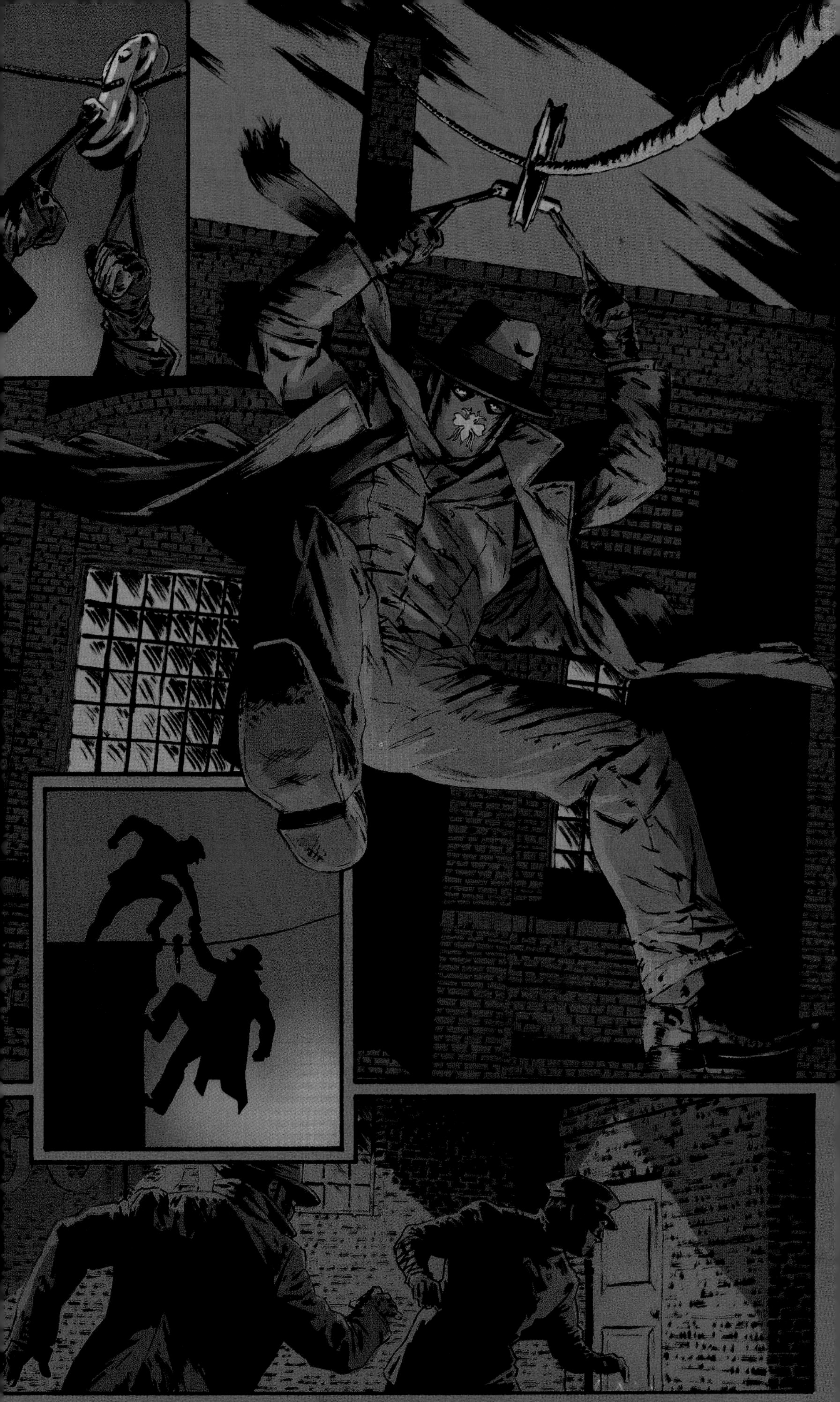

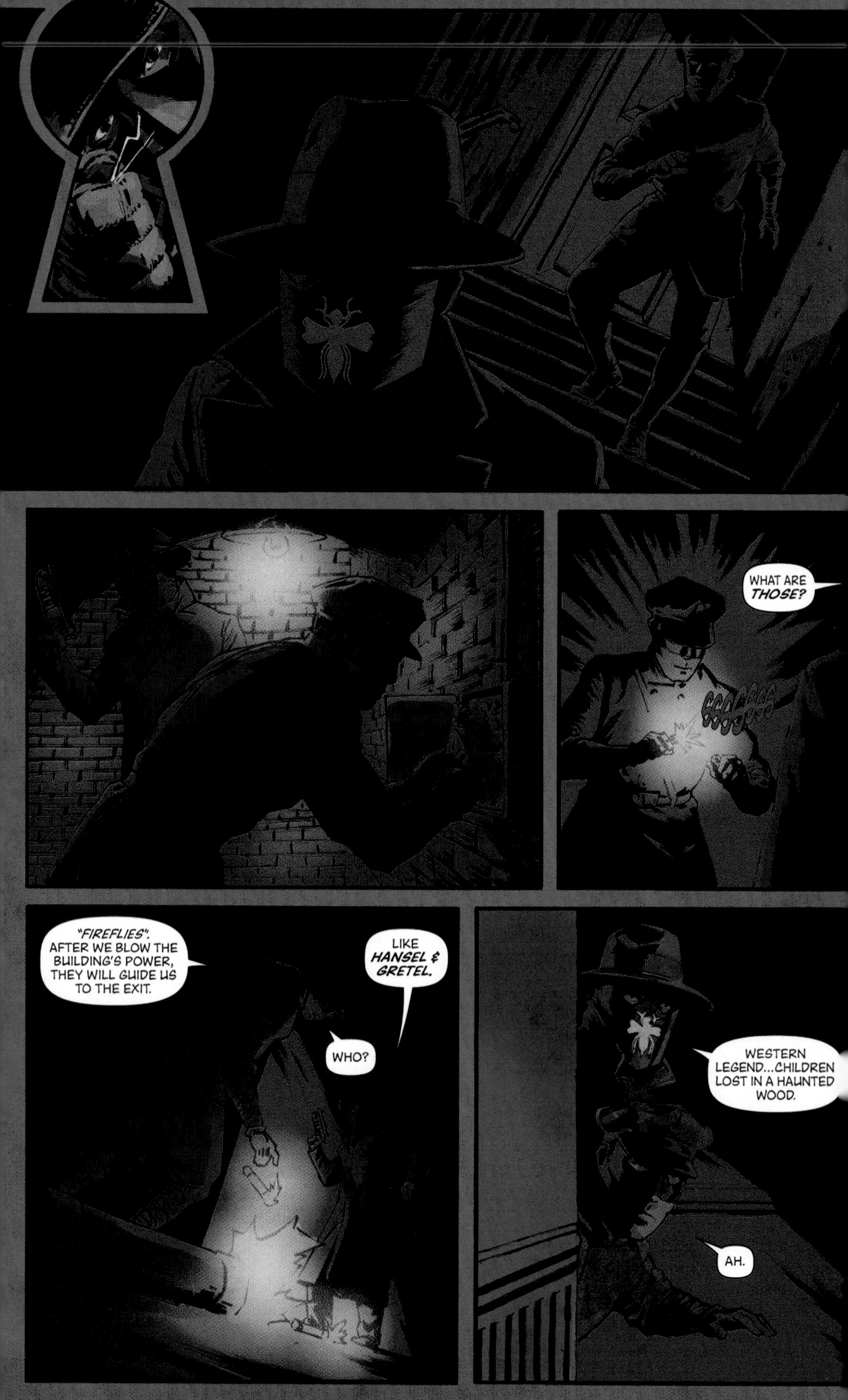
WHAT ARE THOSE?
"FIREFLIES". AFTER WE BLOW THE BUILDING'S POWER, THEY WILL GUIDE US TO THE EXIT.
LIKE HANSEL & GRETEL.
WHO?
WESTERN LEGEND...CHILDREN LOST IN A HAUNTED WOOD.
AH.

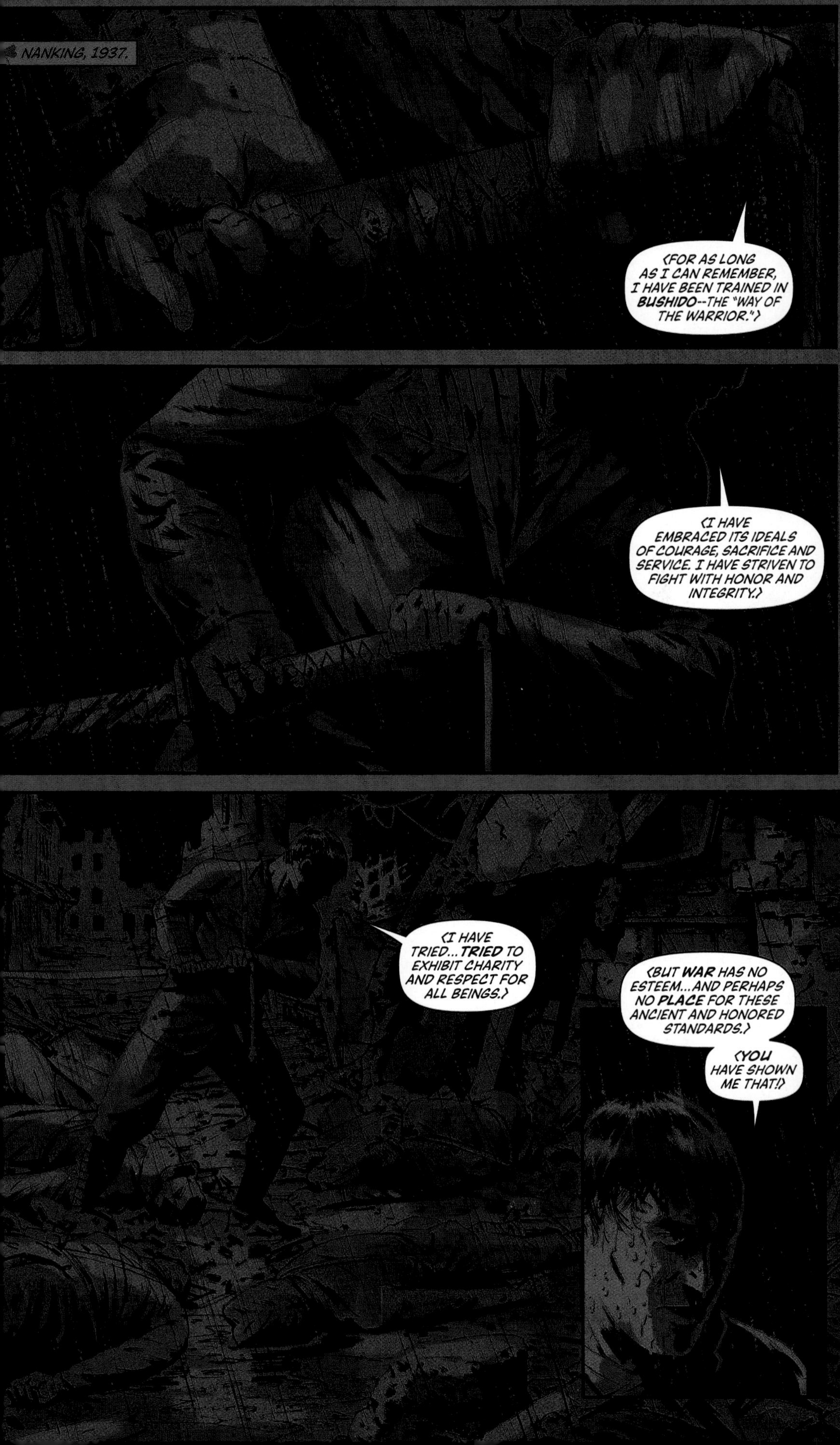
NANKING, 1937.
<FOR AS LONG AS I CAN REMEMBER, I HAVE BEEN TRAINED IN BUSHIDO--THE "WAY OF THE WARRIOR.">
<I HAVE EMBRACED ITS IDEALS OF COURAGE, SACRIFICE AND SERVICE. I HAVE STRIVEN TO FIGHT WITH HONOR AND INTEGRITY.>
<I HAVE TRIED... TRIED TO EXHIBIT CHARITY AND RESPECT FOR ALL BEINGS.>
<BUT WAR HAS NO ESTEEM... AND PERHAPS NO PLACE FOR THESE ANCIENT AND HONORED STANDARDS.>
<YOU HAVE SHOWN ME THAT!>

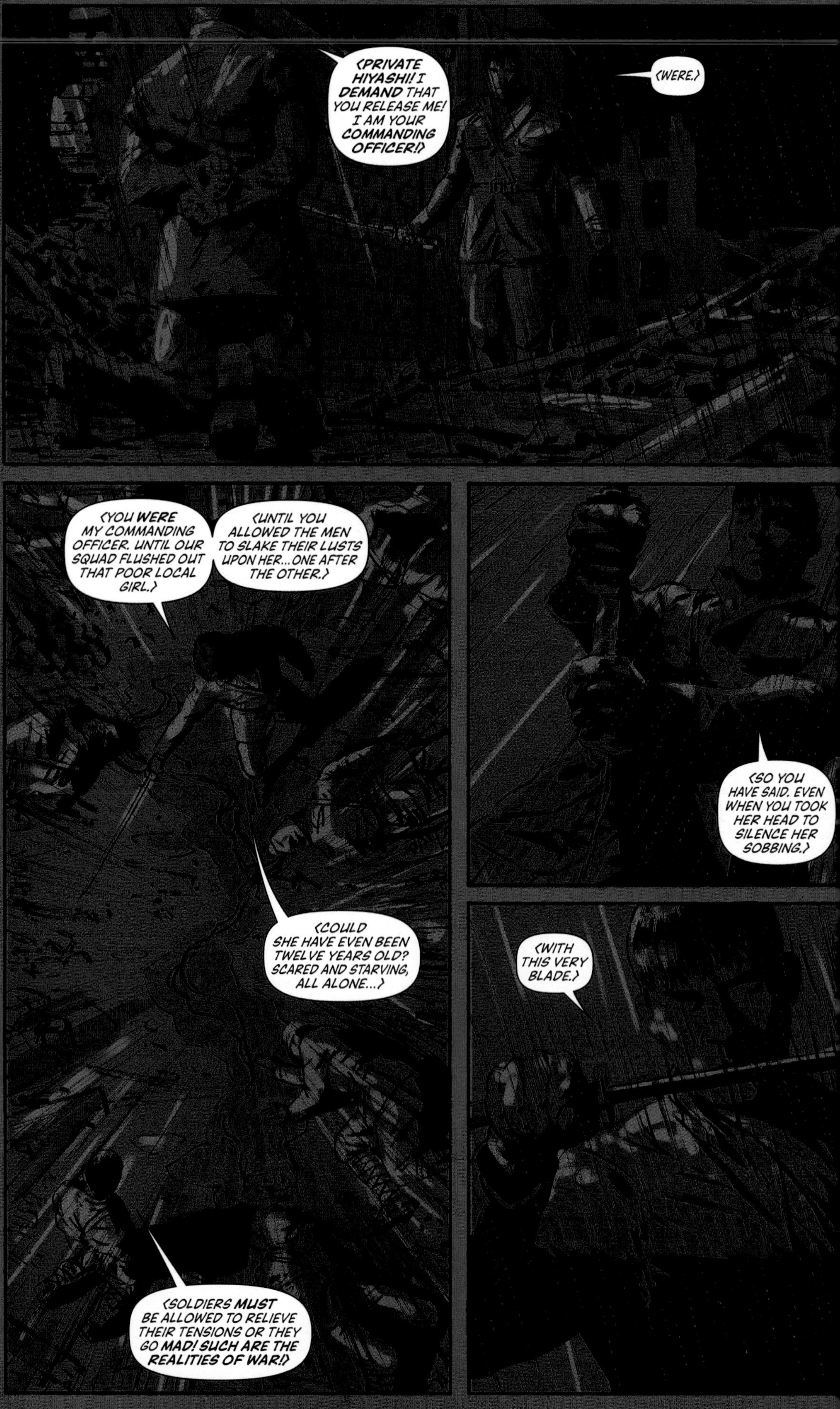

<PRIVATE HIYASHI! I DEMAND THAT YOU RELEASE ME! I AM YOUR COMMANDING OFFICER!>
<WERE.>
<YOU WERE MY COMMANDING OFFICER. UNTIL OUR SQUAD FLUSHED OUT THAT POOR LOCAL GIRL.>
<UNTIL YOU ALLOWED THE MEN TO SLAKE THEIR LUSTS UPON HER...ONE AFTER THE OTHER.>
<COULD SHE HAVE EVEN BEEN TWELVE YEARS OLD? SCARED AND STARVING, ALL ALONE...>
<SOLDIERS MUST BE ALLOWED TO RELIEVE THEIR TENSIONS OR THEY GO MAD! SUCH ARE THE REALITIES OF WAR!>
<SO YOU HAVE SAID. EVEN WHEN YOU TOOK HER HEAD TO SILENCE HER SOBBING.>
<WITH THIS VERY BLADE.>

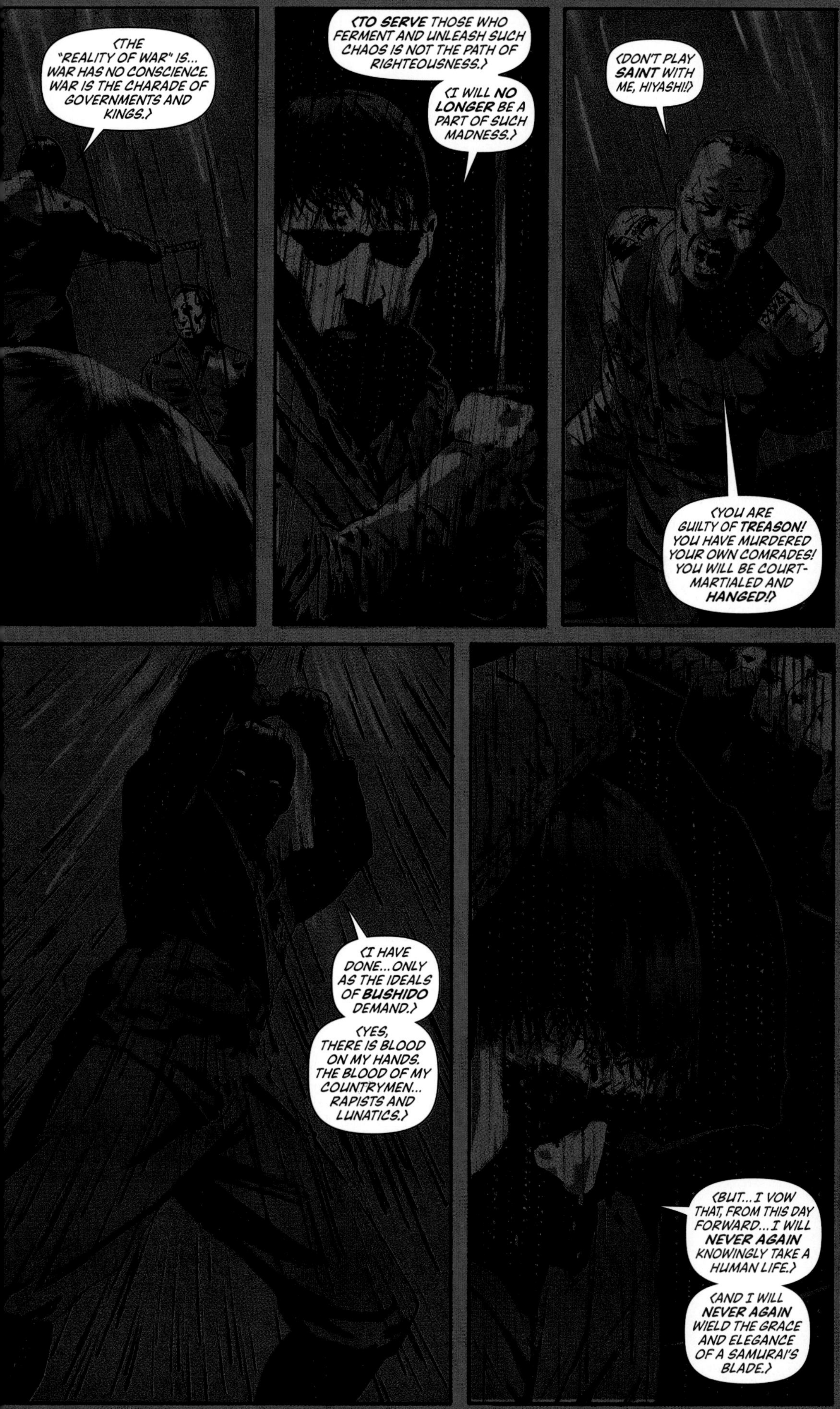

<THE "REALITY OF WAR" IS... WAR HAS NO CONSCIENCE. WAR IS THE CHARADE OF GOVERNMENTS AND KINGS.>
<TO SERVE THOSE WHO FERMENT AND UNLEASH SUCH CHAOS IS NOT THE PATH OF RIGHTEOUSNESS.>
<I WILL NO LONGER BE A PART OF SUCH MADNESS.>
<DON'T PLAY SAINT WITH ME, HIYASHI!>
<YOU ARE GUILTY OF TREASON! YOU HAVE MURDERED YOUR OWN COMRADES! YOU WILL BE COURT-MARTIALED AND HANGED!>
<I HAVE DONE...ONLY AS THE IDEALS OF BUSHIDO DEMAND.>
<YES, THERE IS BLOOD ON MY HANDS. THE BLOOD OF MY COUNTRYMEN... RAPISTS AND LUNATICS.>
<BUT...I VOW THAT, FROM THIS DAY FORWARD...I WILL NEVER AGAIN KNOWINGLY TAKE A HUMAN LIFE.>
<AND I WILL NEVER AGAIN WIELD THE GRACE AND ELEGANCE OF A SAMURAI'S BLADE.>

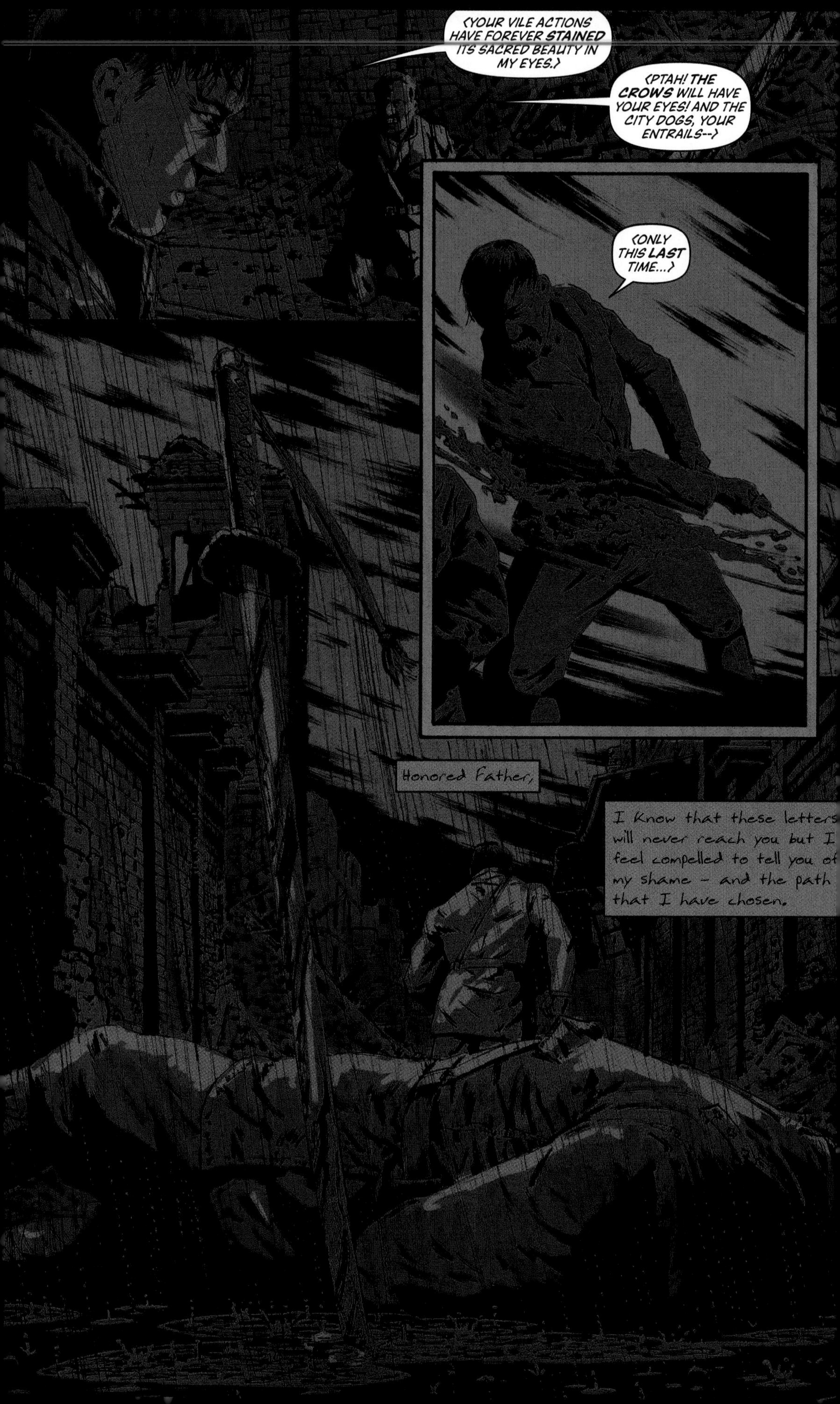

<YOUR VILE ACTIONS HAVE FOREVER STAINED ITS SACRED BEAUTY IN MY EYES.>
<PTAH! THE CROWS WILL HAVE YOUR EYES! AND THE CITY DOGS, YOUR ENTRAILS-->
<ONLY THIS LAST TIME...>
Honored Father,
I know that these letters will never reach you but I feel compelled to tell you of my shame - and the path that I have chosen.

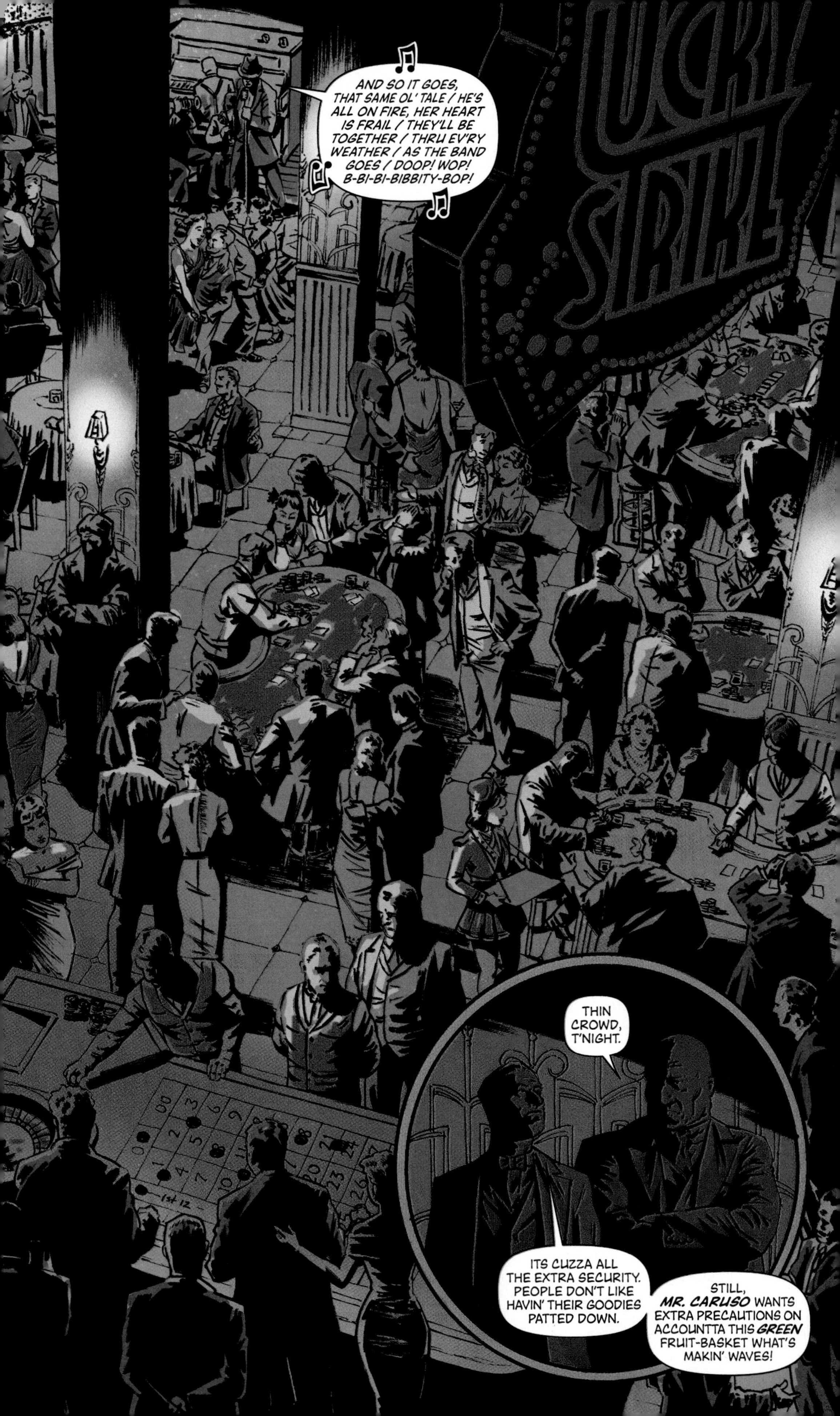
AND SO IT GOES, THAT SAME OL' TALE / HE'S ALL ON FIRE, HER HEART IS FRAIL / THEY'LL BE TOGETHER / THRU EV'RY WEATHER / AS THE BAND GOES / DOOP! WOP! B-BI-BI-BIBBITY-BOP!
LUCKY STRIKE
THIN CROWD, T'NIGHT.
ITS CUZZA ALL THE EXTRA SECURITY. PEOPLE DON'T LIKE HAVIN' THEIR GOODIES PATTED DOWN.
STILL, MR. CARUSO WANTS EXTRA PRECAUTIONS ON ACCOUNTTA THIS GREEN FRUIT-BASKET WHAT'S MAKIN' WAVES!

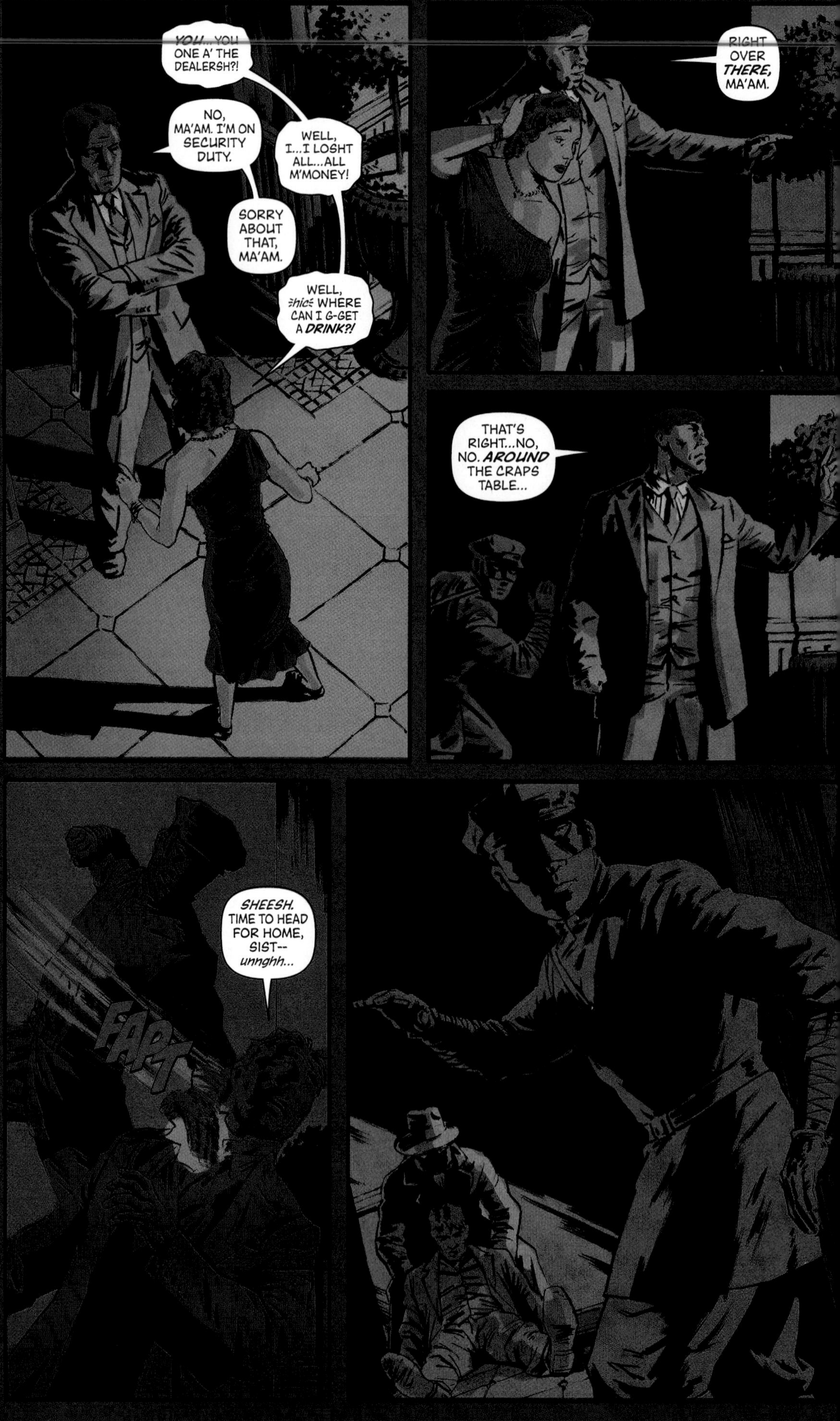
YOU...YOU ONE A' THE DEALERSH?!
NO, MA'AM. I'M ON SECURITY DUTY.
WELL, I...I LOSHT ALL...ALL M'MONEY!
SORRY ABOUT THAT, MA'AM.
WELL, *hic* WHERE CAN I G-GET A DRINK?!
RIGHT OVER THERE, MA'AM.
THAT'S RIGHT...NO, NO. AROUND THE CRAPS TABLE...
SHEESH. TIME TO HEAD FOR HOME, SIST-- unnghh...
FAPP

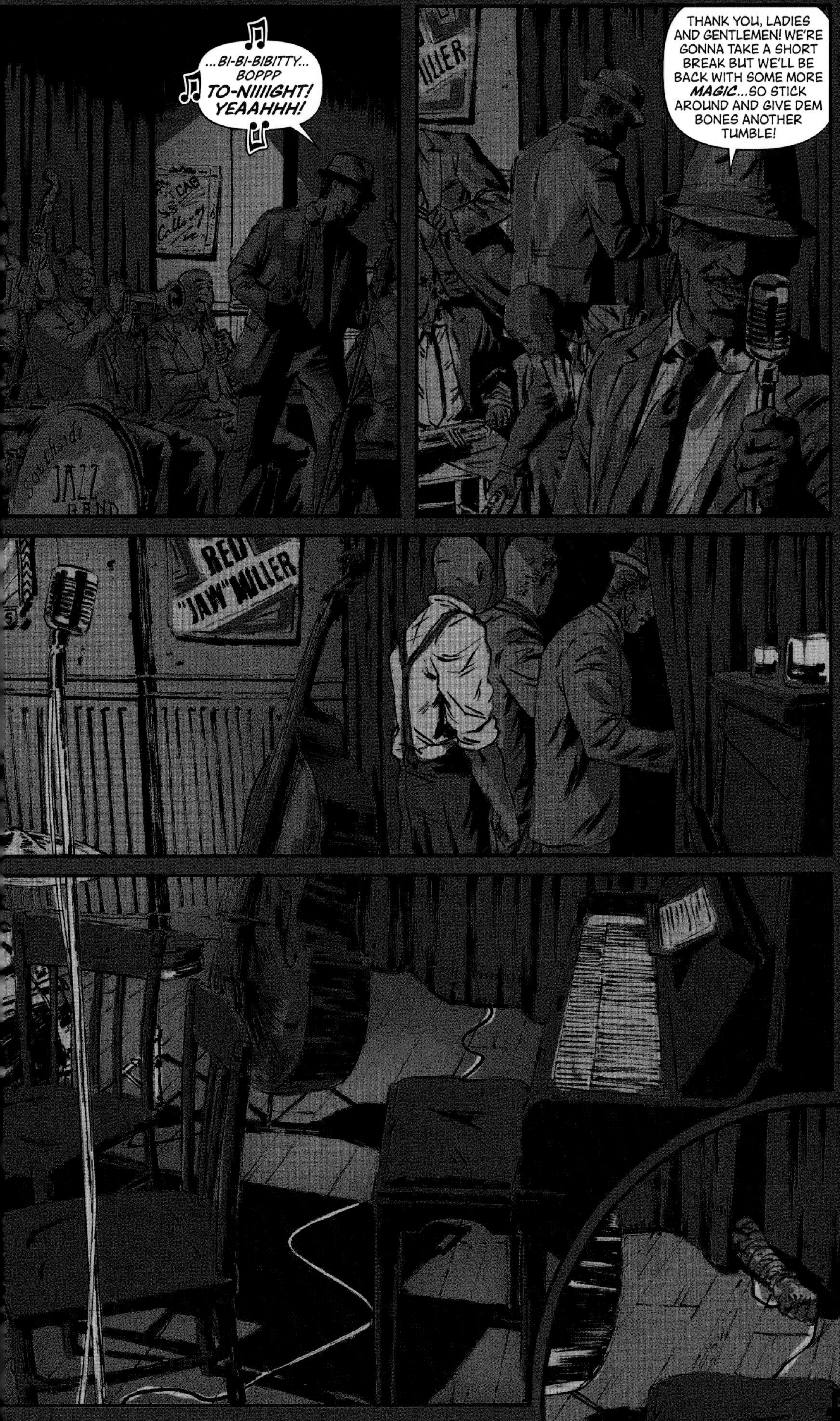
...BI-BI-BIBITTY... BOPPP TO-NIIIIGHT! YEAAHHH!
CAB Calloway
Southside JAZZ BAND
THANK YOU, LADIES AND GENTLEMEN! WE'RE GONNA TAKE A SHORT BREAK BUT WE'LL BE BACK WITH SOME MORE MAGIC...SO STICK AROUND AND GIVE DEM BONES ANOTHER TUMBLE!
RED "JAW" MILLER

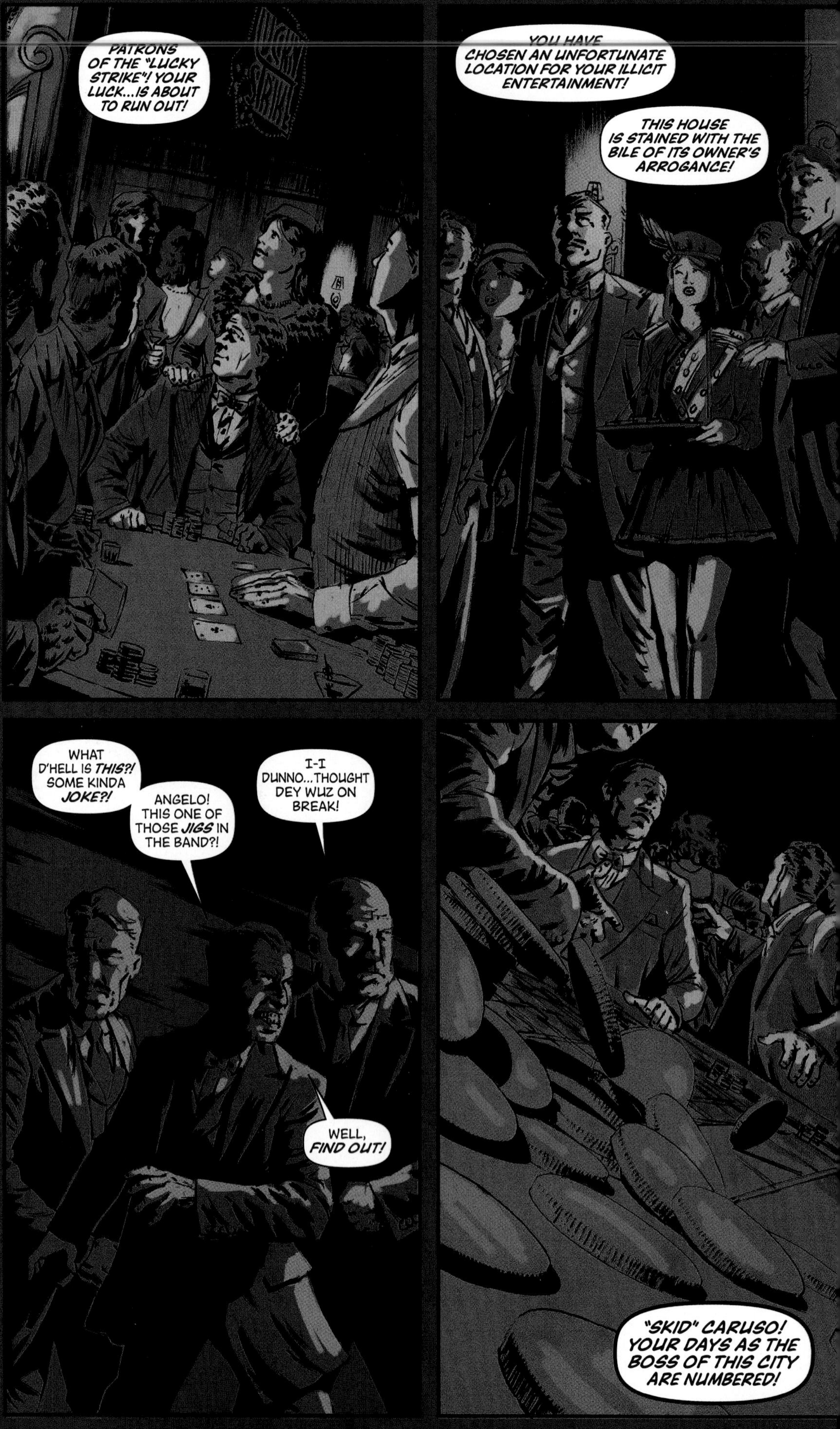
PATRONS OF THE "LUCKY STRIKE"! YOUR LUCK...IS ABOUT TO RUN OUT!
YOU HAVE CHOSEN AN UNFORTUNATE LOCATION FOR YOUR ILLICIT ENTERTAINMENT!
THIS HOUSE IS STAINED WITH THE BILE OF ITS OWNER'S ARROGANCE!
WHAT D'HELL IS *THIS?!* SOME KINDA *JOKE?!*
ANGELO! THIS ONE OF THOSE *JIGS* IN THE BAND?!
I-I DUNNO...THOUGHT DEY WUZ ON BREAK!
WELL, *FIND OUT!*
"SKID" CARUSO! YOUR DAYS AS THE BOSS OF THIS CITY ARE NUMBERED!

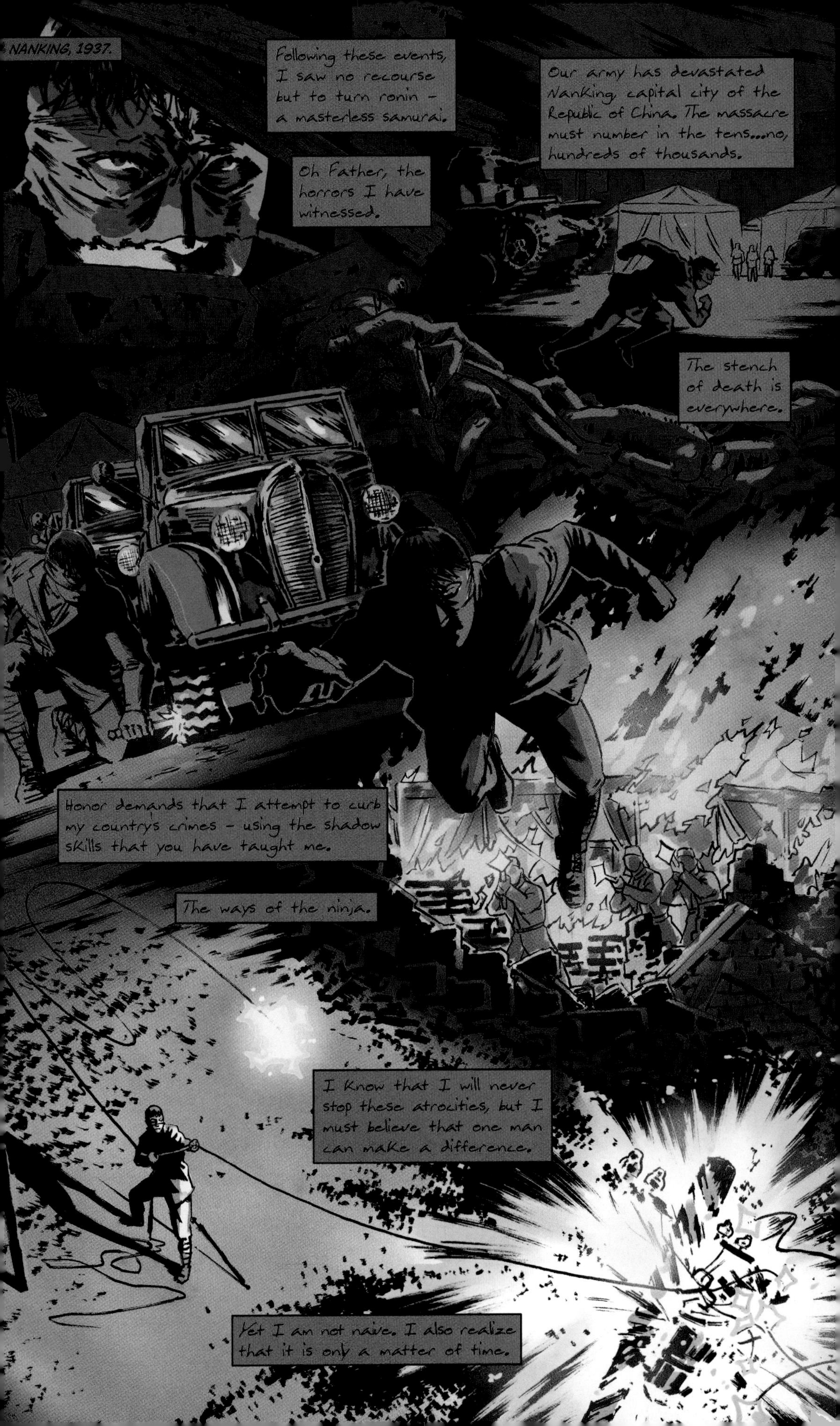
NANKING, 1937.
Following these events, I saw no recourse but to turn ronin - a masterless samurai.
Oh Father, the horrors I have witnessed.
Our army has devastated Nanking, capital city of the Republic of China. The massacre must number in the tens...no, hundreds of thousands.
The stench of death is everywhere.
Honor demands that I attempt to curb my country's crimes - using the shadow skills that you have taught me.
The ways of the ninja.
I know that I will never stop these atrocities, but I must believe that one man can make a difference.
Yet I am not naive. I also realize that it is only a matter of time.

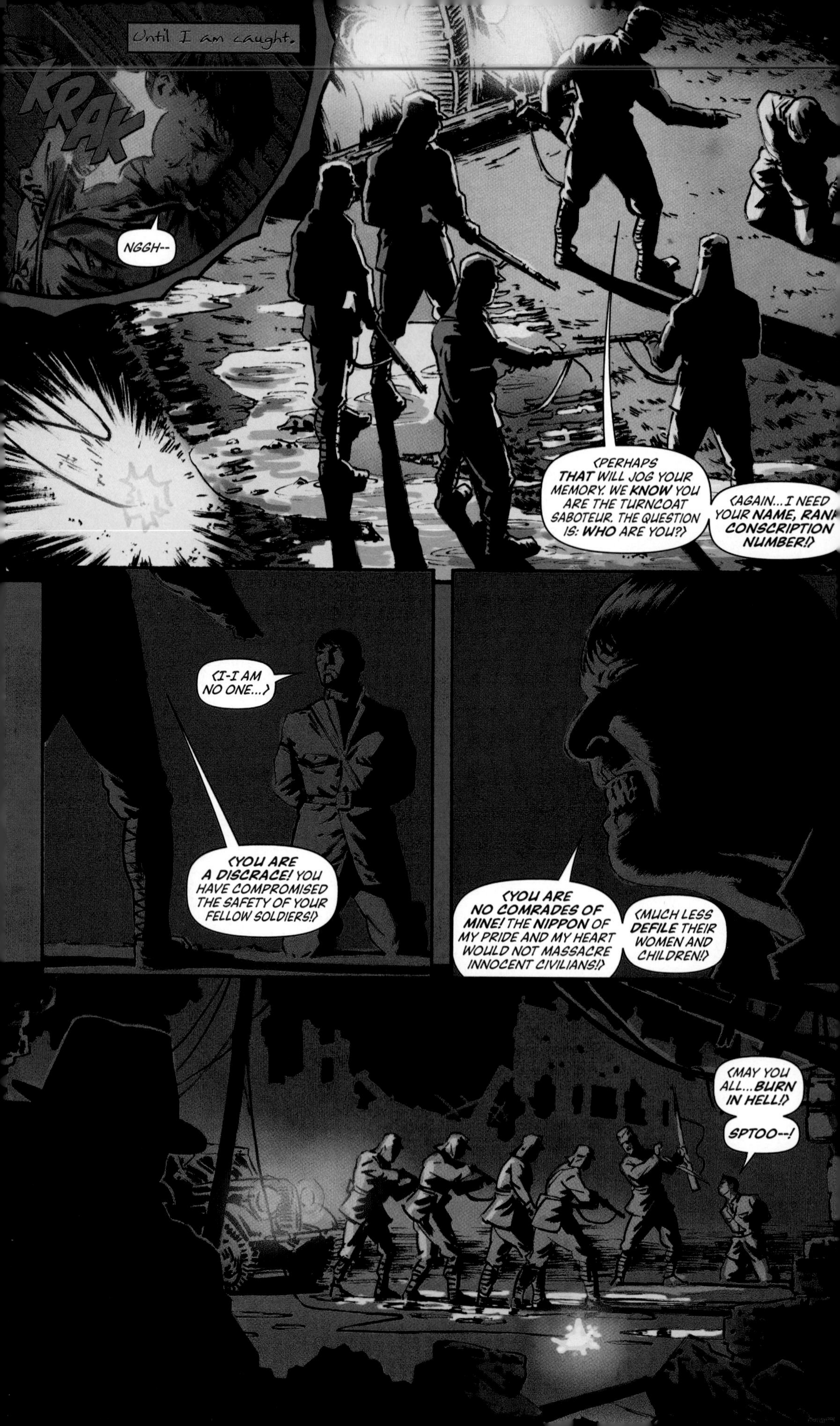
Until I am caught.
KRAK
NGGH--
<PERHAPS THAT WILL JOG YOUR MEMORY. WE KNOW YOU ARE THE TURNCOAT SABOTEUR. THE QUESTION IS: WHO ARE YOU?>
<AGAIN... I NEED YOUR NAME, RAN CONSCRIPTION NUMBER!>
<I-I AM NO ONE...>
<YOU ARE A DISGRACE! YOU HAVE COMPROMISED THE SAFETY OF YOUR FELLOW SOLDIERS!>
<YOU ARE NO COMRADES OF MINE! THE NIPPON OF MY PRIDE AND MY HEART WOULD NOT MASSACRE INNOCENT CIVILIANS!>
<MUCH LESS DEFILE THEIR WOMEN AND CHILDREN!>
<MAY YOU ALL... BURN IN HELL!>
SPTOO--!

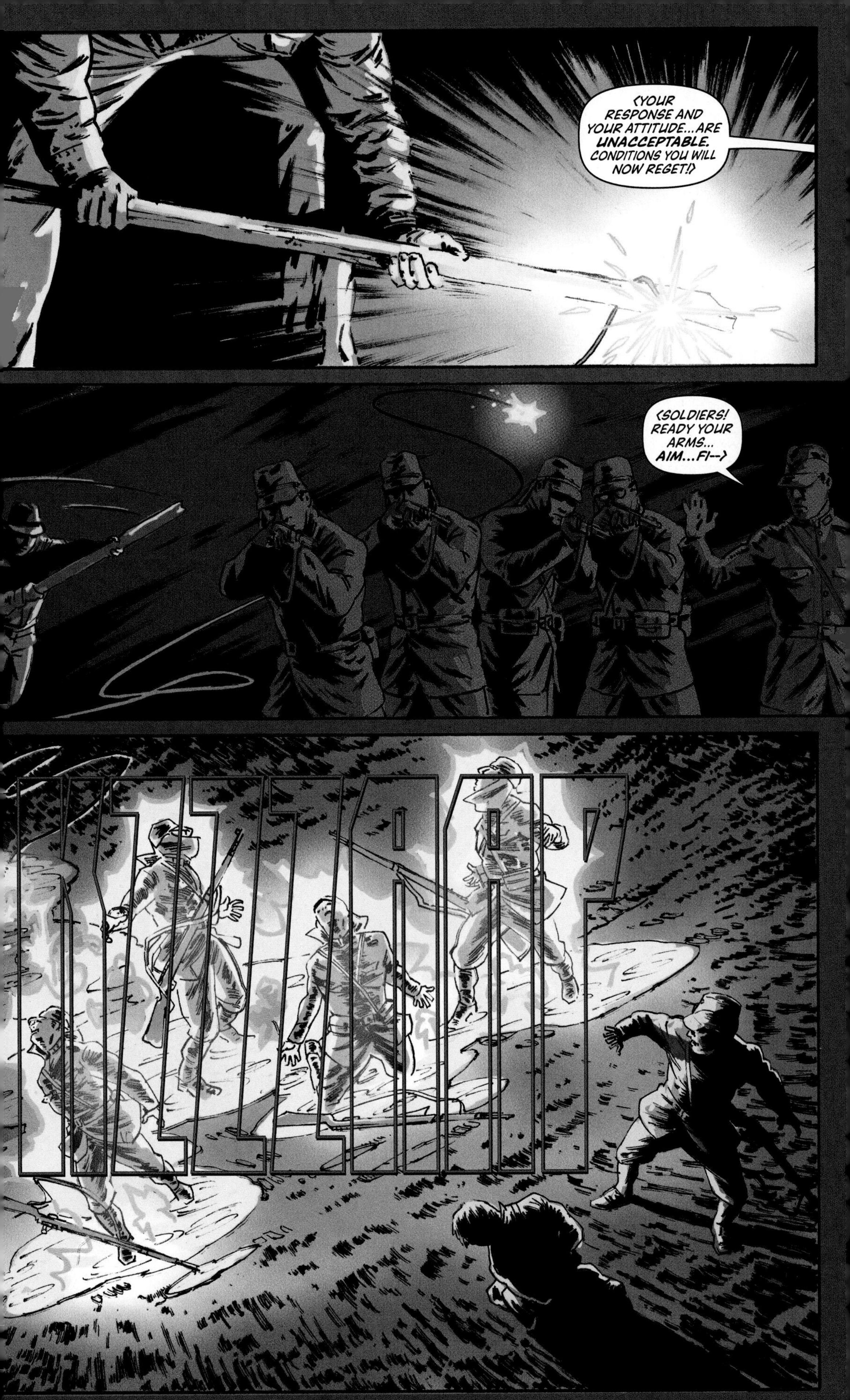

<YOUR RESPONSE AND YOUR ATTITUDE...ARE **UNACCEPTABLE.** CONDITIONS YOU WILL NOW REGET!>
<SOLDIERS! READY YOUR ARMS... **AIM...FI-->**

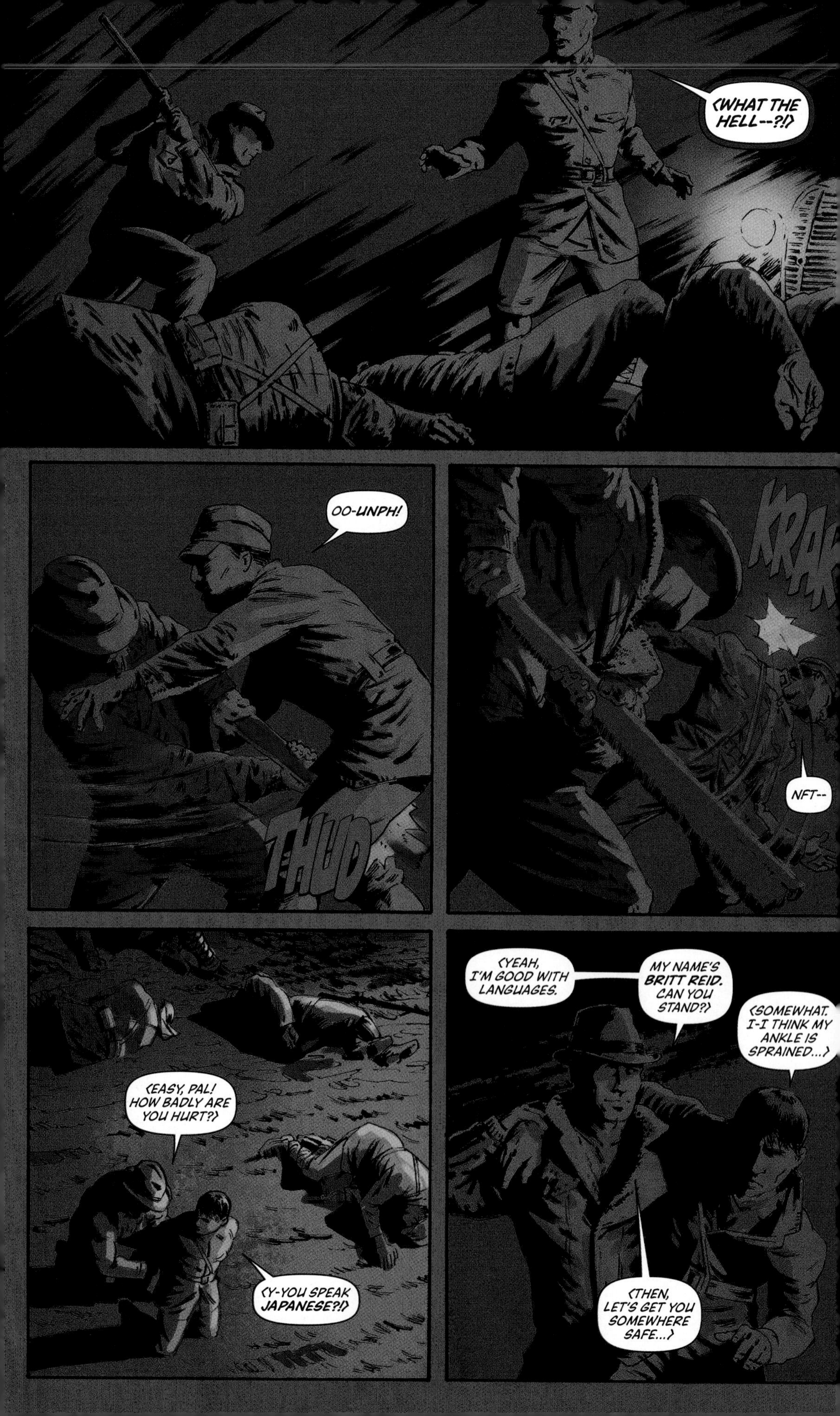
‹WHAT THE HELL--?!›
OO-UNPH!
THUD
KRAK
NFT--
‹EASY, PAL! HOW BADLY ARE YOU HURT?›
‹Y-YOU SPEAK JAPANESE?!›
‹YEAH, I'M GOOD WITH LANGUAGES.
MY NAME'S BRITT REID. CAN YOU STAND?›
‹SOMEWHAT. I-I THINK MY ANKLE IS SPRAINED...›
‹THEN, LET'S GET YOU SOMEWHERE SAFE...›

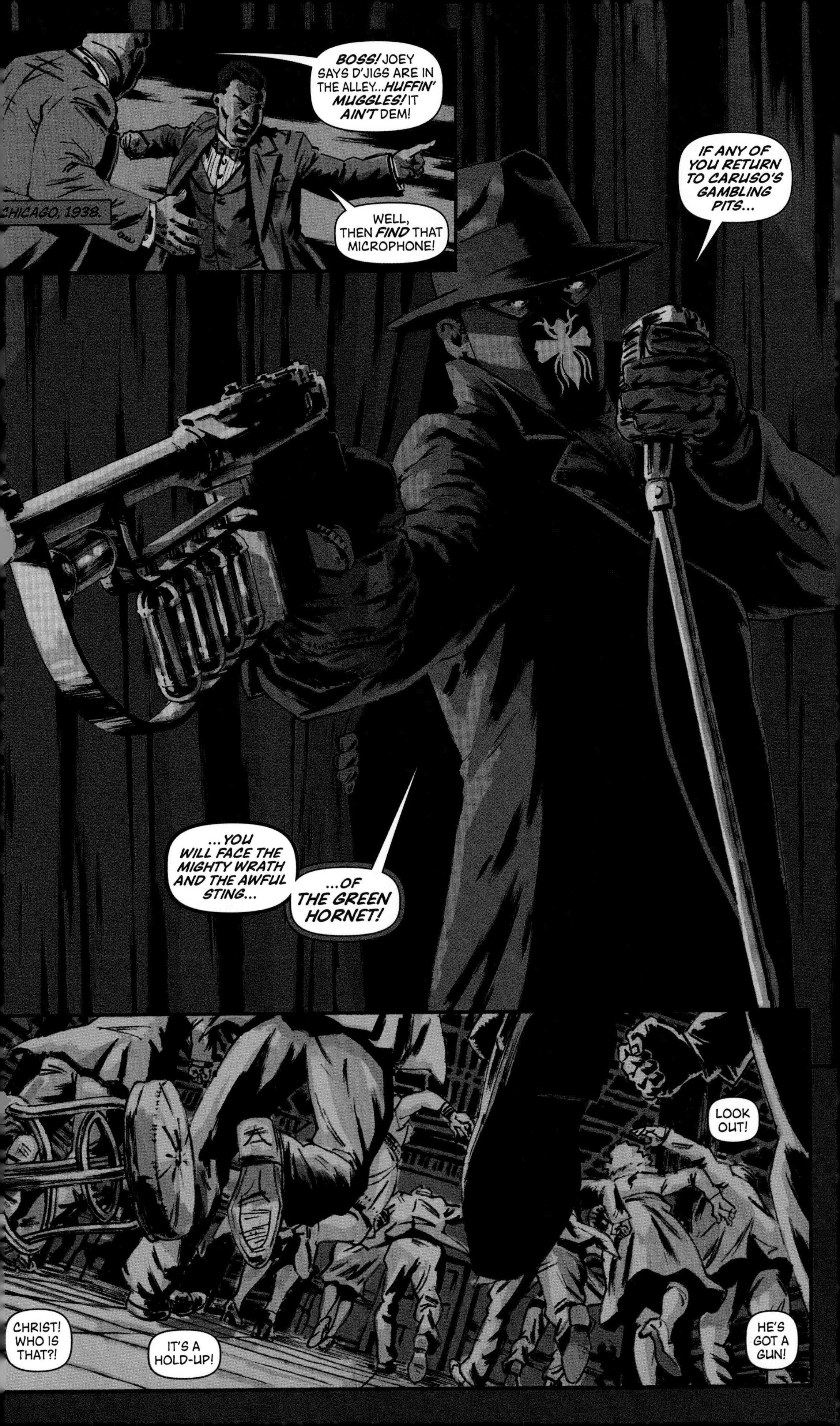
CHICAGO, 1938.
BOSS! JOEY SAYS D'JIGS ARE IN THE ALLEY...HUFFIN' MUGGLES! IT AIN'T DEM!
WELL, THEN FIND THAT MICROPHONE!
IF ANY OF YOU RETURN TO CARUSO'S GAMBLING PITS...
...YOU WILL FACE THE MIGHTY WRATH AND THE AWFUL STING...
...OF THE GREEN HORNET!
LOOK OUT!
CHRIST! WHO IS THAT?!
IT'S A HOLD-UP!
HE'S GOT A GUN!

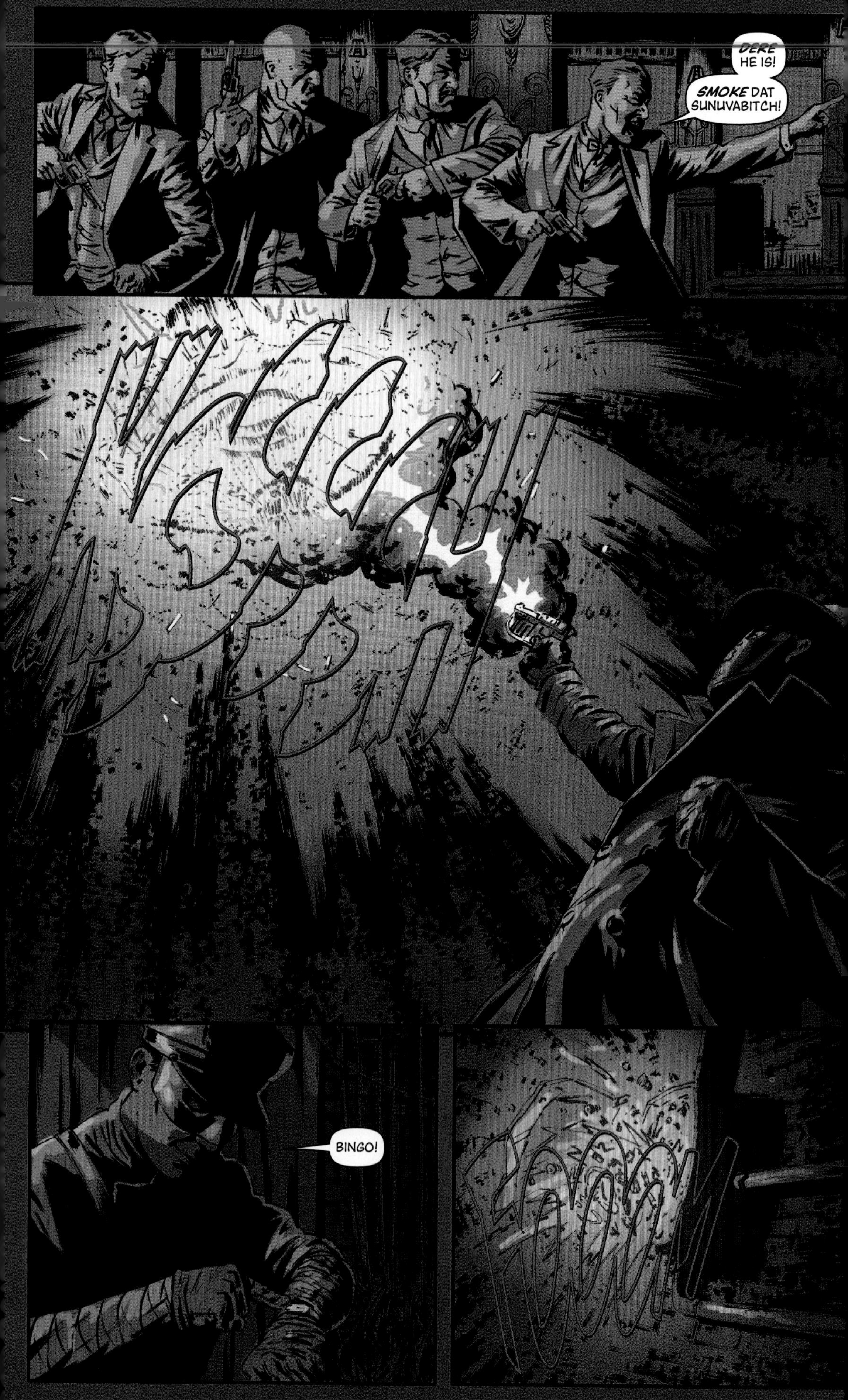
DERE HE IS!
SMOKE DAT SUNUVABITCH!
BINGO!

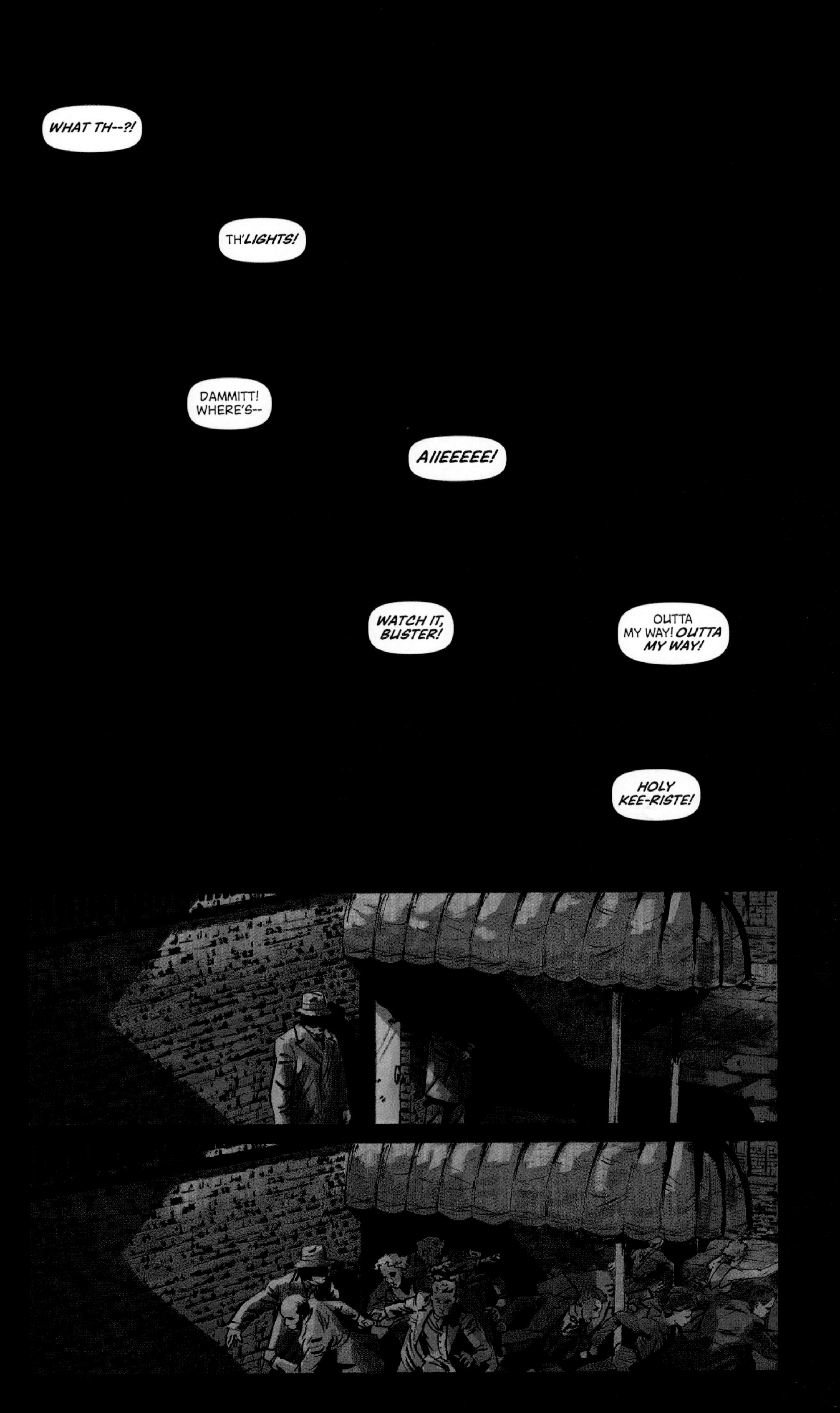
WHAT TH--?!
TH'LIGHTS!
DAMMITT! WHERE'S--
AIIEEEEE!
WATCH IT, BUSTER!
OUTTA MY WAY! OUTTA MY WAY!
HOLY KEE-RISTE!

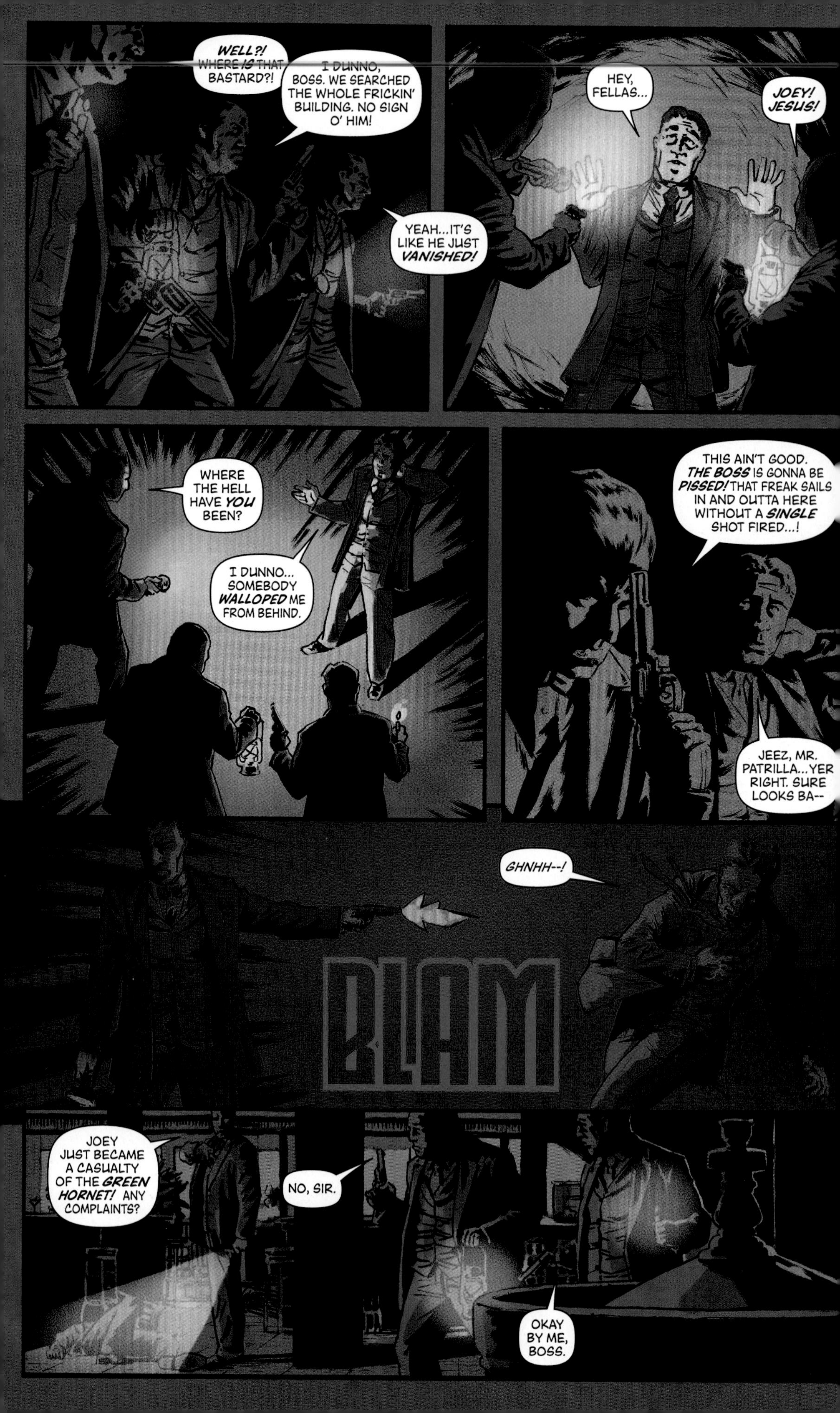
WELL?! WHERE IS THAT BASTARD?!
I DUNNO, BOSS. WE SEARCHED THE WHOLE FRICKIN' BUILDING. NO SIGN O' HIM!
YEAH...IT'S LIKE HE JUST VANISHED!
HEY, FELLAS...
JOEY! JESUS!
WHERE THE HELL HAVE YOU BEEN?
I DUNNO... SOMEBODY WALLOPED ME FROM BEHIND.
THIS AIN'T GOOD. THE BOSS IS GONNA BE PISSED! THAT FREAK SAILS IN AND OUTTA HERE WITHOUT A SINGLE SHOT FIRED...!
JEEZ, MR. PATRILLA...YER RIGHT. SURE LOOKS BA--
GHNHH--!
BLAM
JOEY JUST BECAME A CASUALTY OF THE GREEN HORNET! ANY COMPLAINTS?
NO, SIR.
OKAY BY ME, BOSS.

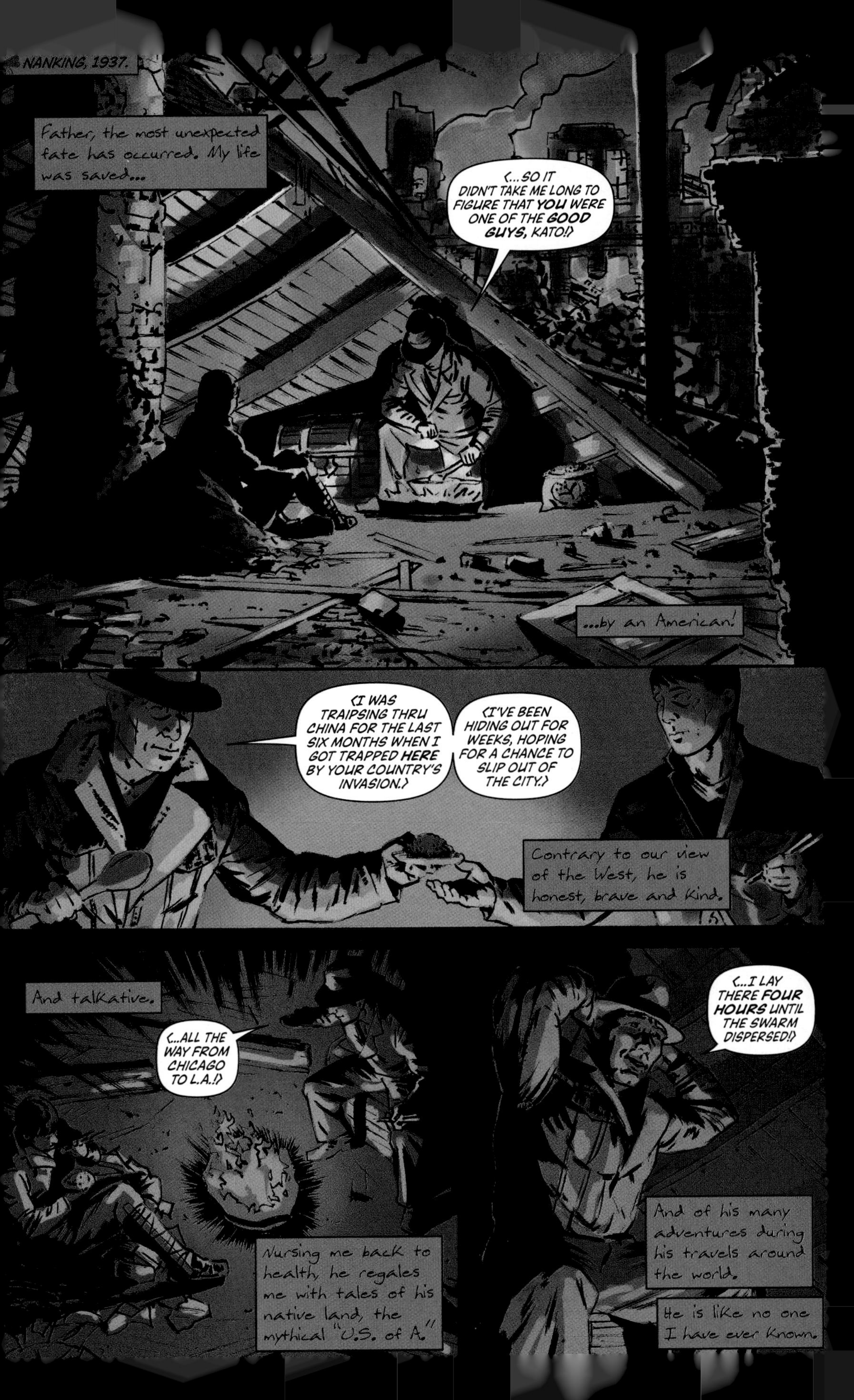
NANKING, 1937.
Father, the most unexpected fate has occurred. My life was saved...
<...SO IT DIDN'T TAKE ME LONG TO FIGURE THAT YOU WERE ONE OF THE GOOD GUYS, KATO!>
...by an American!
<I WAS TRAIPSING THRU CHINA FOR THE LAST SIX MONTHS WHEN I GOT TRAPPED HERE BY YOUR COUNTRY'S INVASION.>
<I'VE BEEN HIDING OUT FOR WEEKS, HOPING FOR A CHANCE TO SLIP OUT OF THE CITY.>
Contrary to our view of the West, he is honest, brave and kind.
And talkative.
<...ALL THE WAY FROM CHICAGO TO L.A.!>
Nursing me back to health, he regales me with tales of his native land, the mythical "U.S. of A."
<...I LAY THERE FOUR HOURS UNTIL THE SWARM DISPERSED!>
And of his many adventures during his travels around the world.
He is like no one I have ever known.

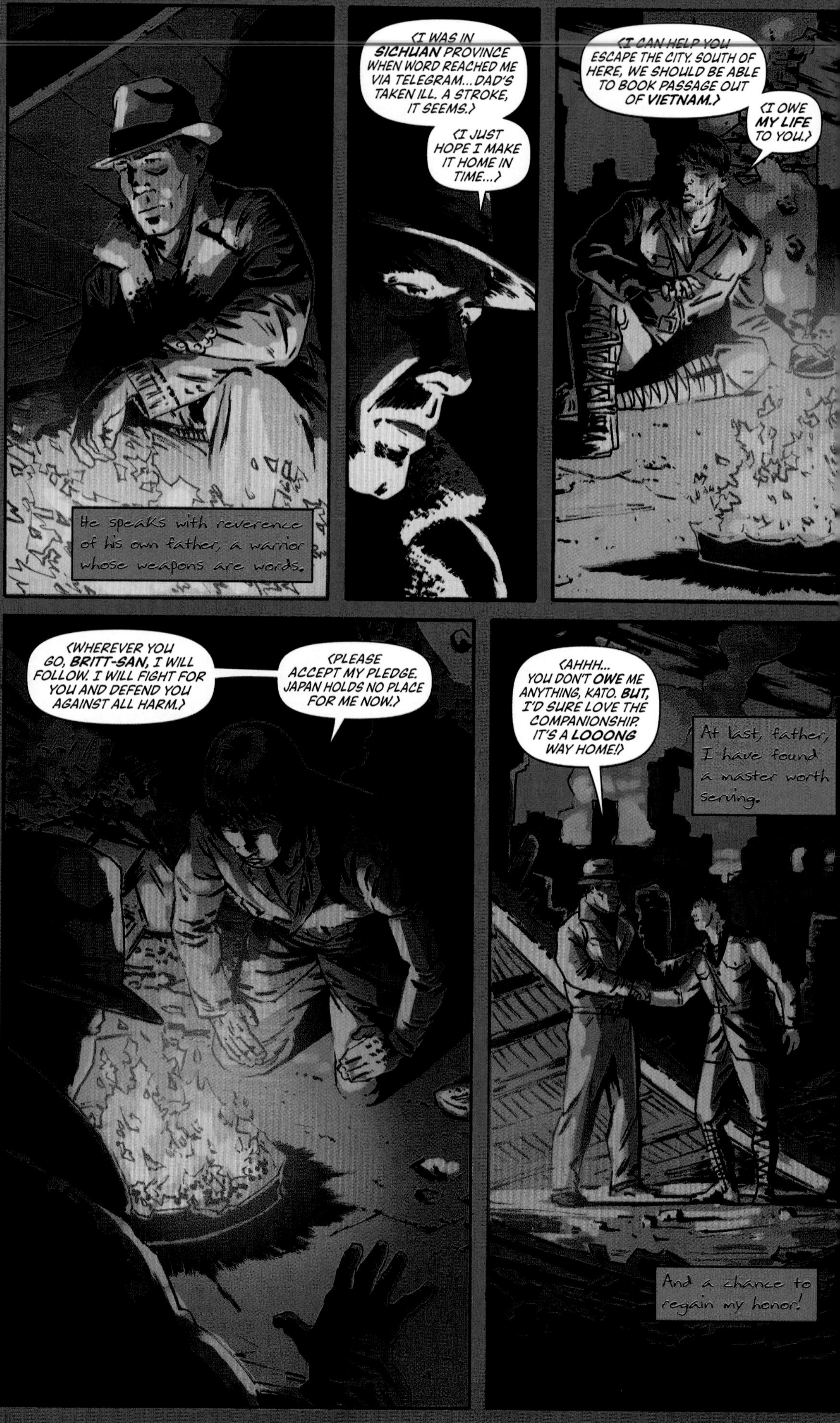
He speaks with reverence of his own father, a warrior whose weapons are words.
<I WAS IN SICHUAN PROVINCE WHEN WORD REACHED ME VIA TELEGRAM... DAD'S TAKEN ILL. A STROKE, IT SEEMS.>
<I JUST HOPE I MAKE IT HOME IN TIME...>
<I CAN HELP YOU ESCAPE THE CITY. SOUTH OF HERE, WE SHOULD BE ABLE TO BOOK PASSAGE OUT OF VIETNAM.>
<I OWE MY LIFE TO YOU.>
<WHEREVER YOU GO, BRITT-SAN, I WILL FOLLOW. I WILL FIGHT FOR YOU AND DEFEND YOU AGAINST ALL HARM.>
<PLEASE ACCEPT MY PLEDGE. JAPAN HOLDS NO PLACE FOR ME NOW.>
<AHHH... YOU DON'T OWE ME ANYTHING, KATO. BUT, I'D SURE LOVE THE COMPANIONSHIP. IT'S A LOOONG WAY HOME!>
At last, father, I have found a master worth serving.
And a chance to regain my honor!

ISSUE FOUR

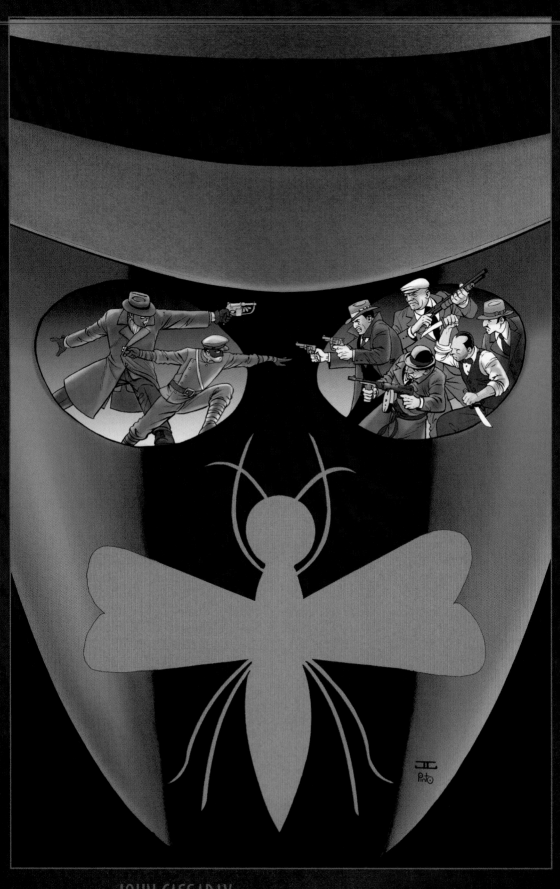

Issue four cover by JOHN CASSADAY

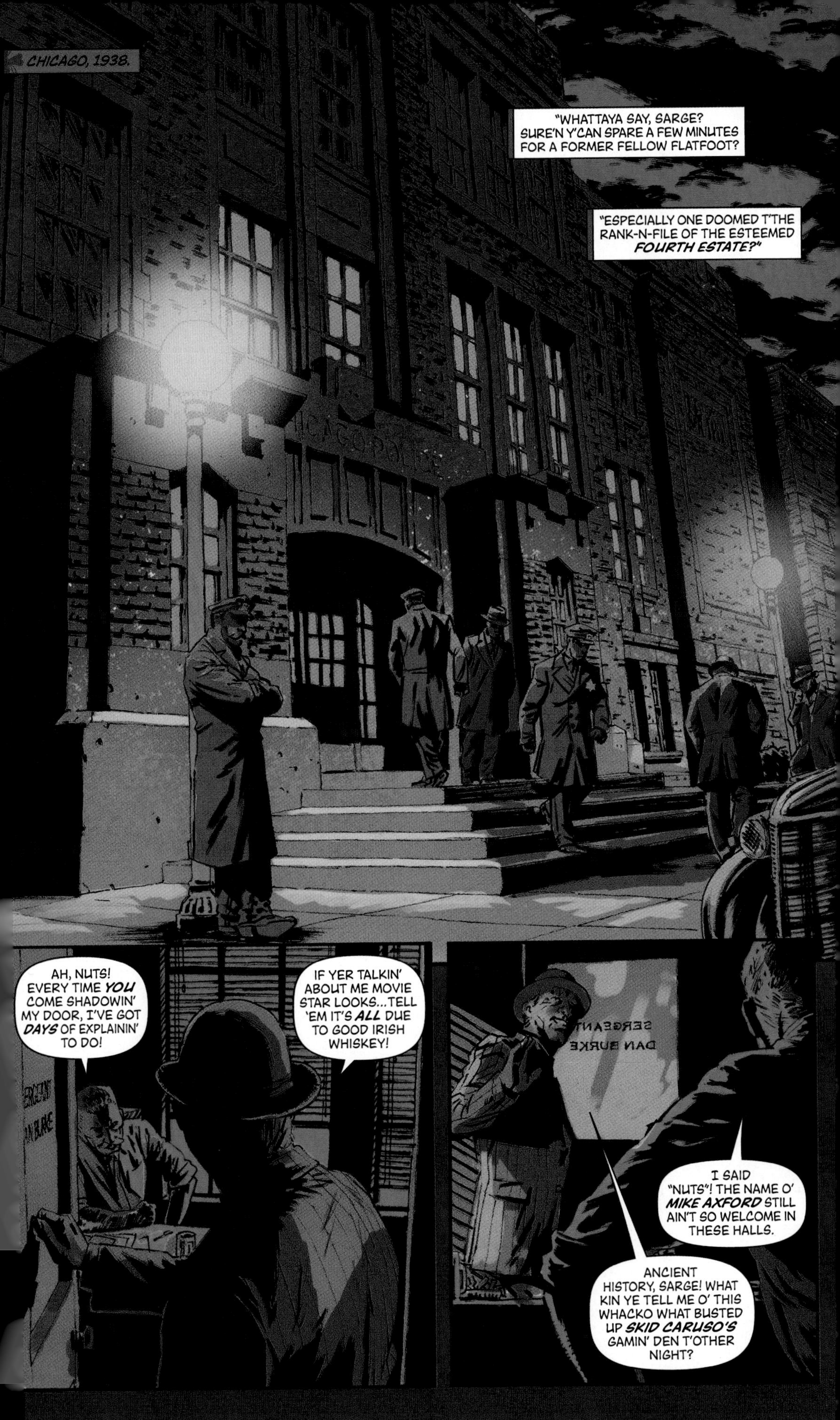
CHICAGO, 1938.
"WHATTAYA SAY, SARGE? SURE'N Y'CAN SPARE A FEW MINUTES FOR A FORMER FELLOW FLATFOOT?
"ESPECIALLY ONE DOOMED T'THE RANK-N-FILE OF THE ESTEEMED FOURTH ESTATE?"
AH, NUTS! EVERY TIME YOU COME SHADOWIN' MY DOOR, I'VE GOT DAYS OF EXPLAININ' TO DO!
IF YER TALKIN' ABOUT ME MOVIE STAR LOOKS...TELL 'EM IT'S ALL DUE TO GOOD IRISH WHISKEY!
I SAID "NUTS"! THE NAME O' MIKE AXFORD STILL AIN'T SO WELCOME IN THESE HALLS.
ANCIENT HISTORY, SARGE! WHAT KIN YE TELL ME O' THIS WHACKO WHAT BUSTED UP SKID CARUSO'S GAMIN' DEN T'OTHER NIGHT?

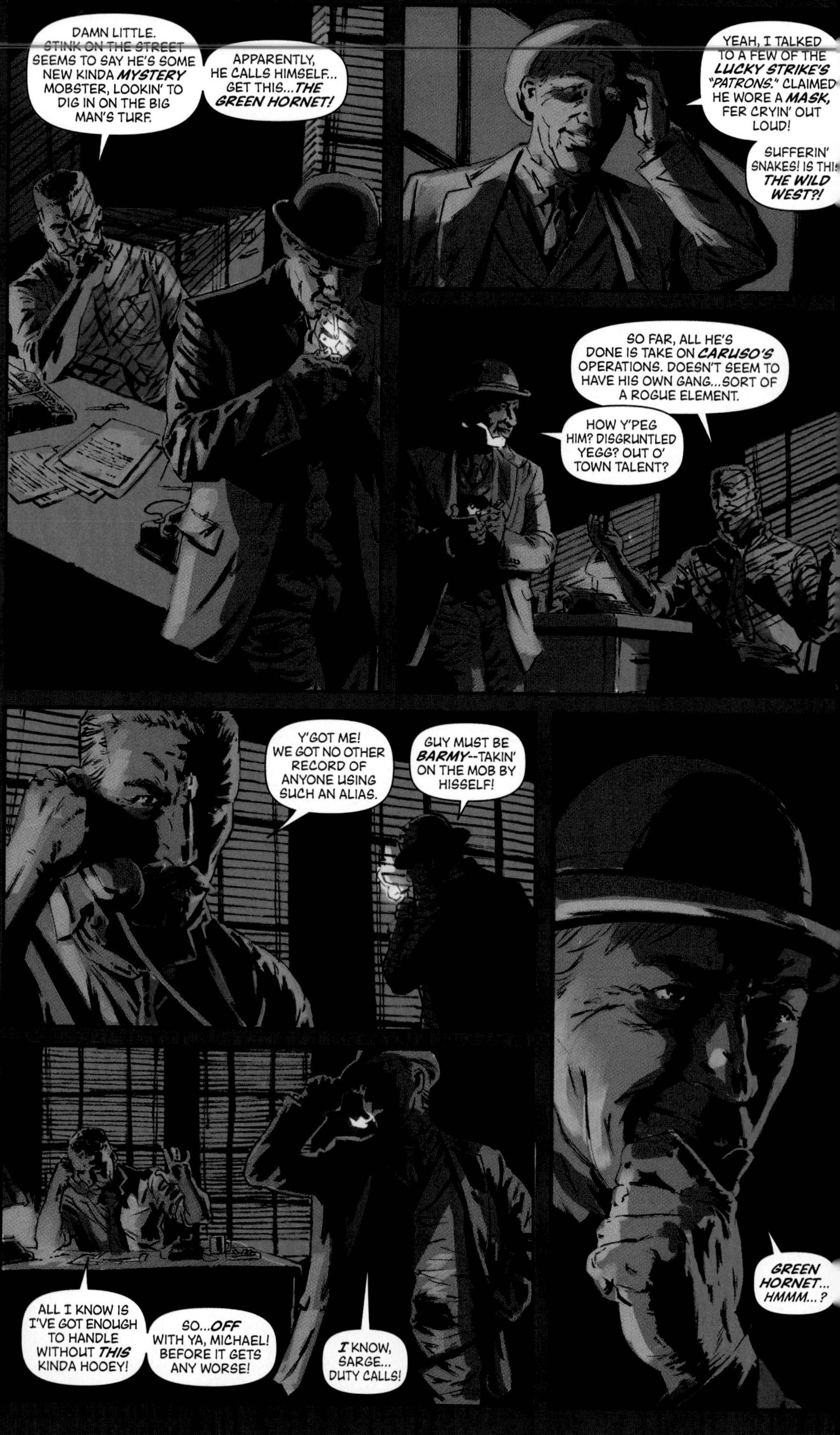
DAMN LITTLE. STINK ON THE STREET SEEMS TO SAY HE'S SOME NEW KINDA *MYSTERY* MOBSTER, LOOKIN' TO DIG IN ON THE BIG MAN'S TURF.
APPARENTLY, HE CALLS HIMSELF... GET THIS... *THE GREEN HORNET!*
YEAH, I TALKED TO A FEW OF THE *LUCKY STRIKE'S* "*PATRONS.*" CLAIMED HE WORE A *MASK*, FER CRYIN' OUT LOUD!
SUFFERIN' SNAKES! IS THIS *THE WILD WEST?!*
SO FAR, ALL HE'S DONE IS TAKE ON *CARUSO'S* OPERATIONS. DOESN'T SEEM TO HAVE HIS OWN GANG... SORT OF A ROGUE ELEMENT.
HOW Y'PEG HIM? DISGRUNTLED YEGG? OUT O' TOWN TALENT?
Y'GOT ME! WE GOT NO OTHER RECORD OF ANYONE USING SUCH AN ALIAS.
GUY MUST BE *BARMY*--TAKIN' ON THE MOB BY HISSELF!
ALL I KNOW IS I'VE GOT ENOUGH TO HANDLE WITHOUT *THIS* KINDA HOOEY!
SO... *OFF* WITH YA, MICHAEL! BEFORE IT GETS ANY WORSE!
I KNOW, SARGE... DUTY CALLS!
GREEN HORNET... HMMM...?

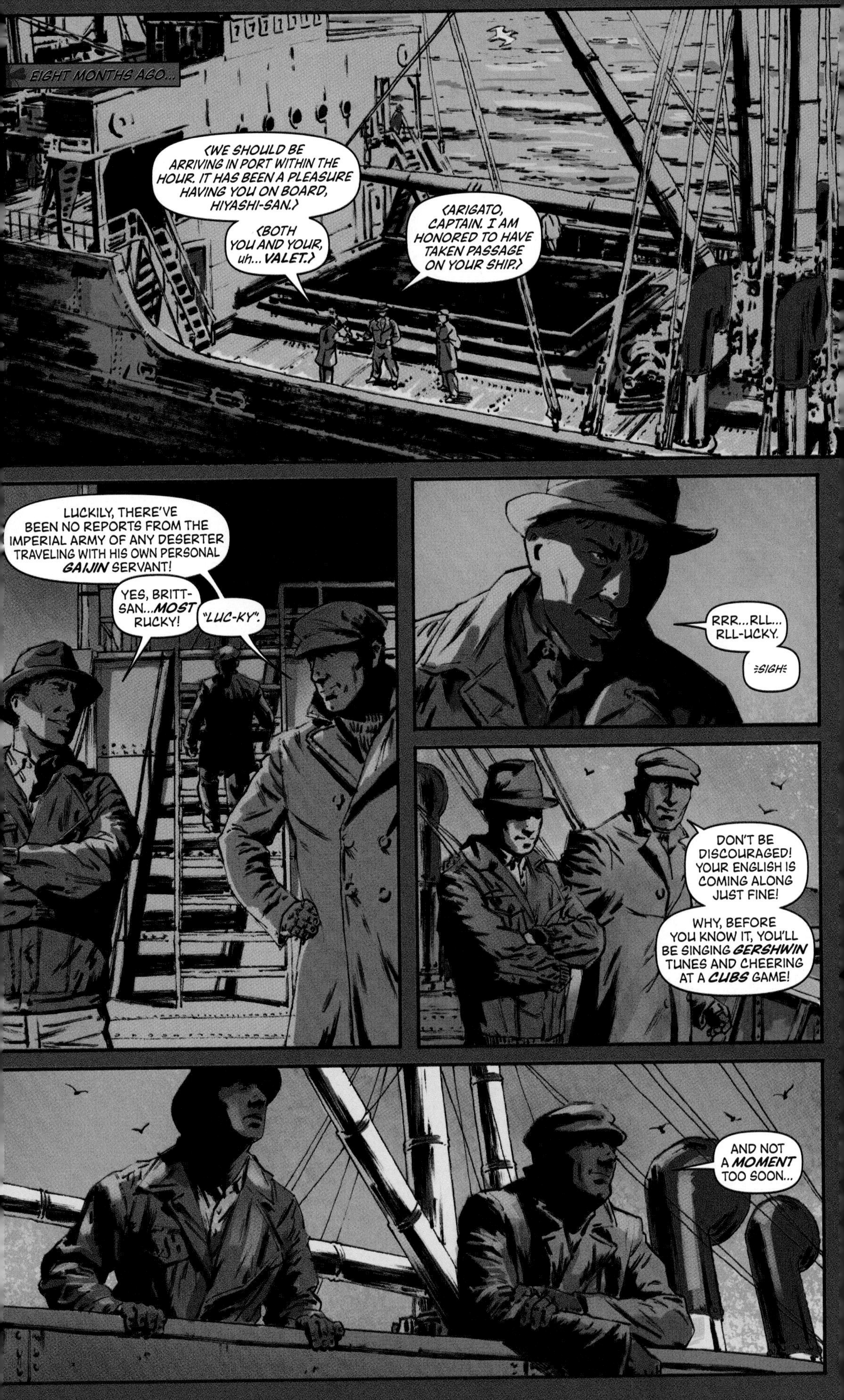
EIGHT MONTHS AGO...
<WE SHOULD BE ARRIVING IN PORT WITHIN THE HOUR. IT HAS BEEN A PLEASURE HAVING YOU ON BOARD, HIYASHI-SAN.>
<BOTH YOU AND YOUR, uh... VALET.>
<ARIGATO, CAPTAIN. I AM HONORED TO HAVE TAKEN PASSAGE ON YOUR SHIP.>
LUCKILY, THERE'VE BEEN NO REPORTS FROM THE IMPERIAL ARMY OF ANY DESERTER TRAVELING WITH HIS OWN PERSONAL GAIJIN SERVANT!
YES, BRITT-SAN...MOST RUCKY!
"LUC-KY".
RRR...RLL... RLL-UCKY.
SIGH
DON'T BE DISCOURAGED! YOUR ENGLISH IS COMING ALONG JUST FINE!
WHY, BEFORE YOU KNOW IT, YOU'LL BE SINGING GERSHWIN TUNES AND CHEERING AT A CUBS GAME!
AND NOT A MOMENT TOO SOON...

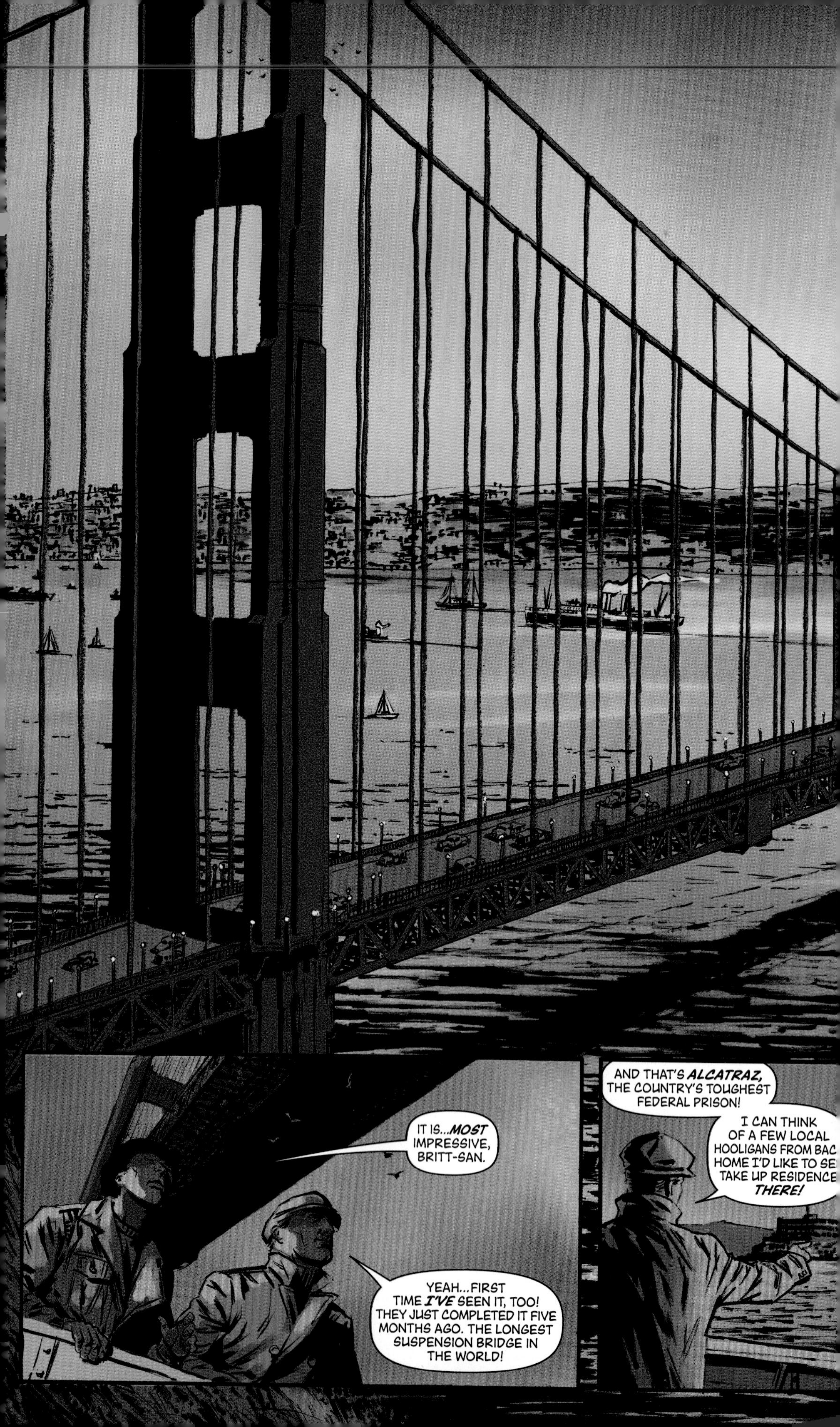
IT IS...MOST IMPRESSIVE, BRITT-SAN.
YEAH...FIRST TIME I'VE SEEN IT, TOO! THEY JUST COMPLETED IT FIVE MONTHS AGO. THE LONGEST SUSPENSION BRIDGE IN THE WORLD!
AND THAT'S ALCATRAZ, THE COUNTRY'S TOUGHEST FEDERAL PRISON!
I CAN THINK OF A FEW LOCAL HOOLIGANS FROM BAC HOME I'D LIKE TO SE TAKE UP RESIDENCE THERE!

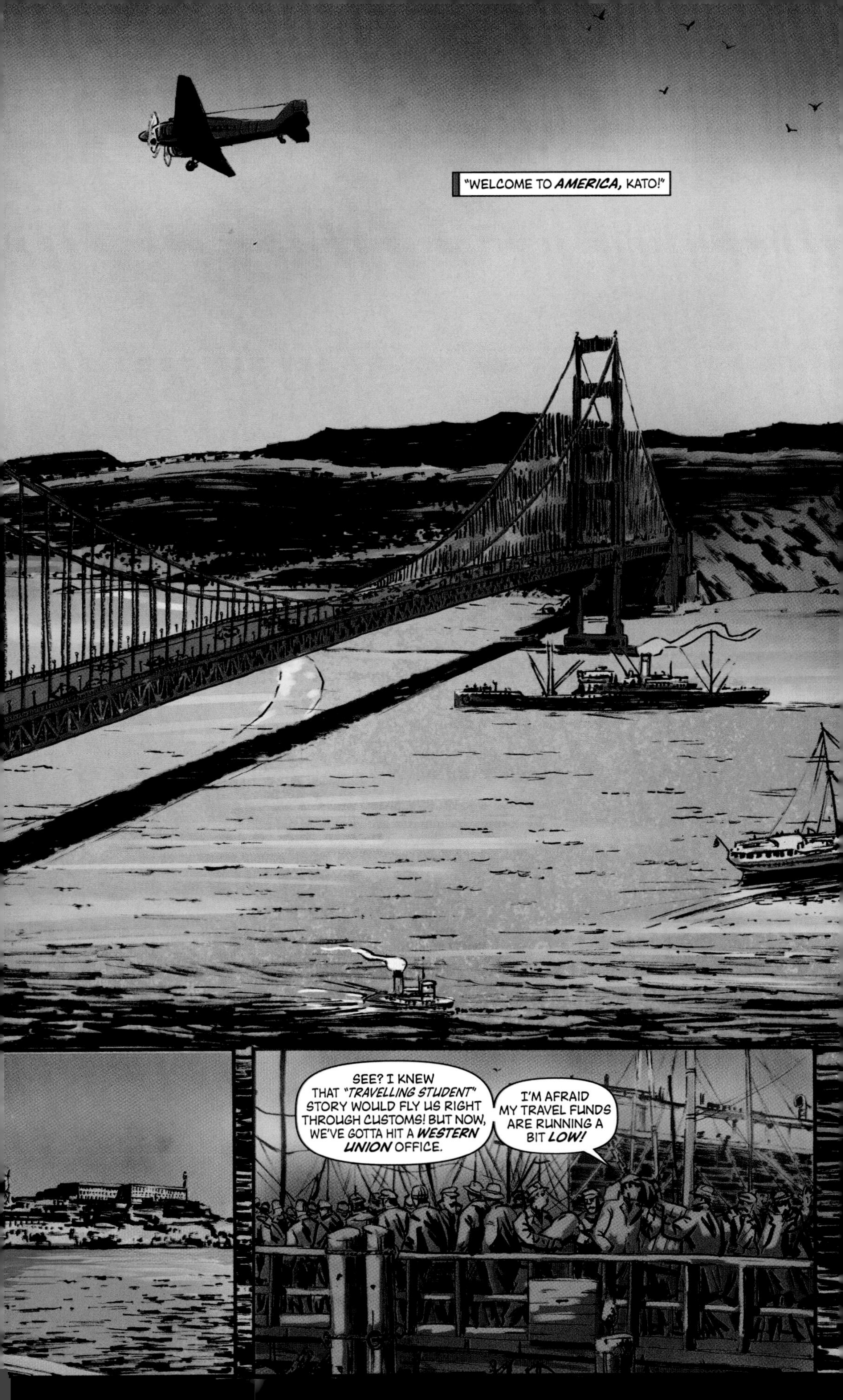
"WELCOME TO AMERICA, KATO!"
SEE? I KNEW THAT "TRAVELLING STUDENT" STORY WOULD FLY US RIGHT THROUGH CUSTOMS! BUT NOW, WE'VE GOTTA HIT A WESTERN UNION OFFICE.
I'M AFRAID MY TRAVEL FUNDS ARE RUNNING A BIT LOW!

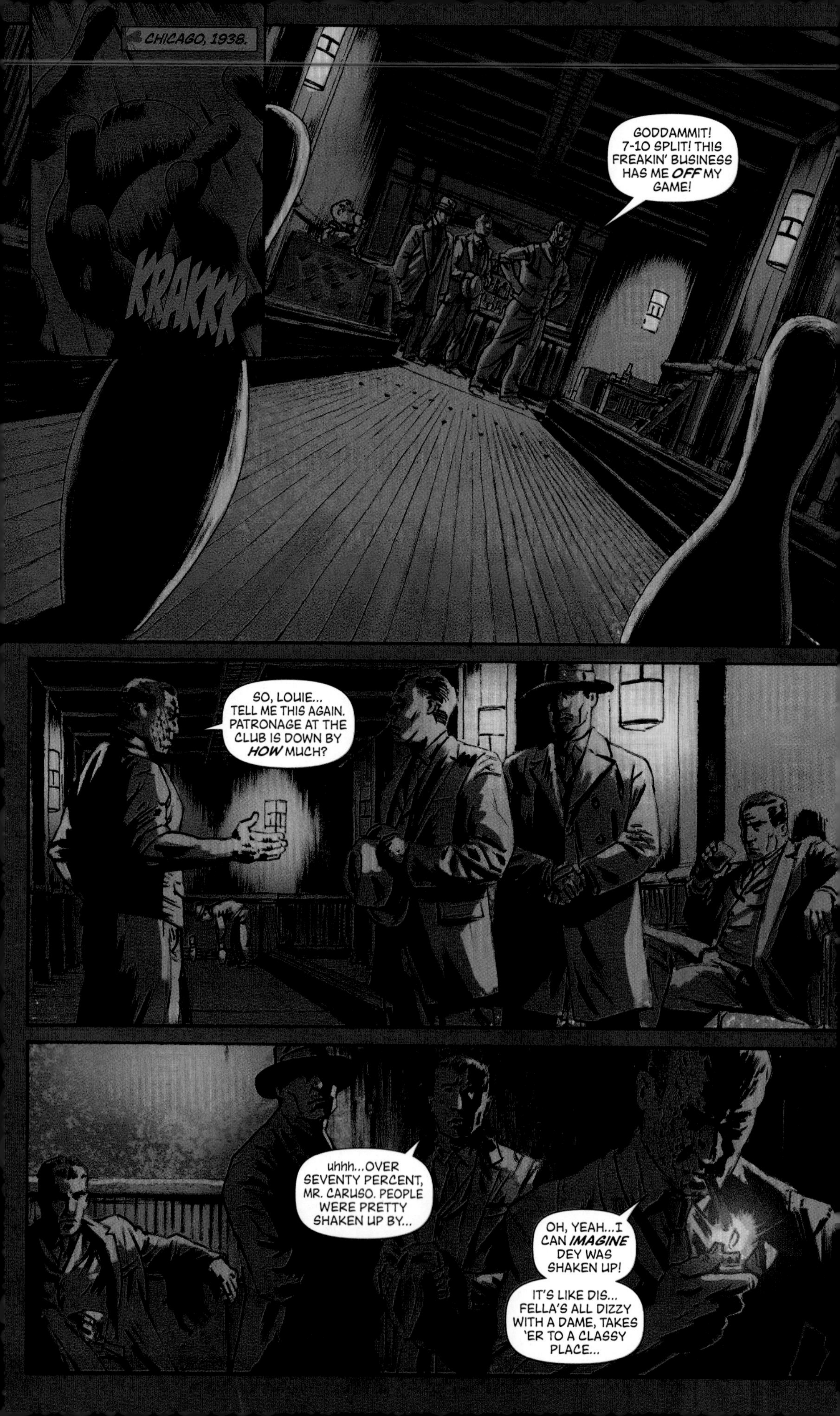
CHICAGO, 1938.
KRAKKK
GODDAMMIT! 7-10 SPLIT! THIS FREAKIN' BUSINESS HAS ME OFF MY GAME!
SO, LOUIE... TELL ME THIS AGAIN. PATRONAGE AT THE CLUB IS DOWN BY HOW MUCH?
uhhh...OVER SEVENTY PERCENT, MR. CARUSO. PEOPLE WERE PRETTY SHAKEN UP BY...
OH, YEAH...I CAN IMAGINE DEY WAS SHAKEN UP!
IT'S LIKE DIS... FELLA'S ALL DIZZY WITH A DAME, TAKES 'ER TO A CLASSY PLACE...

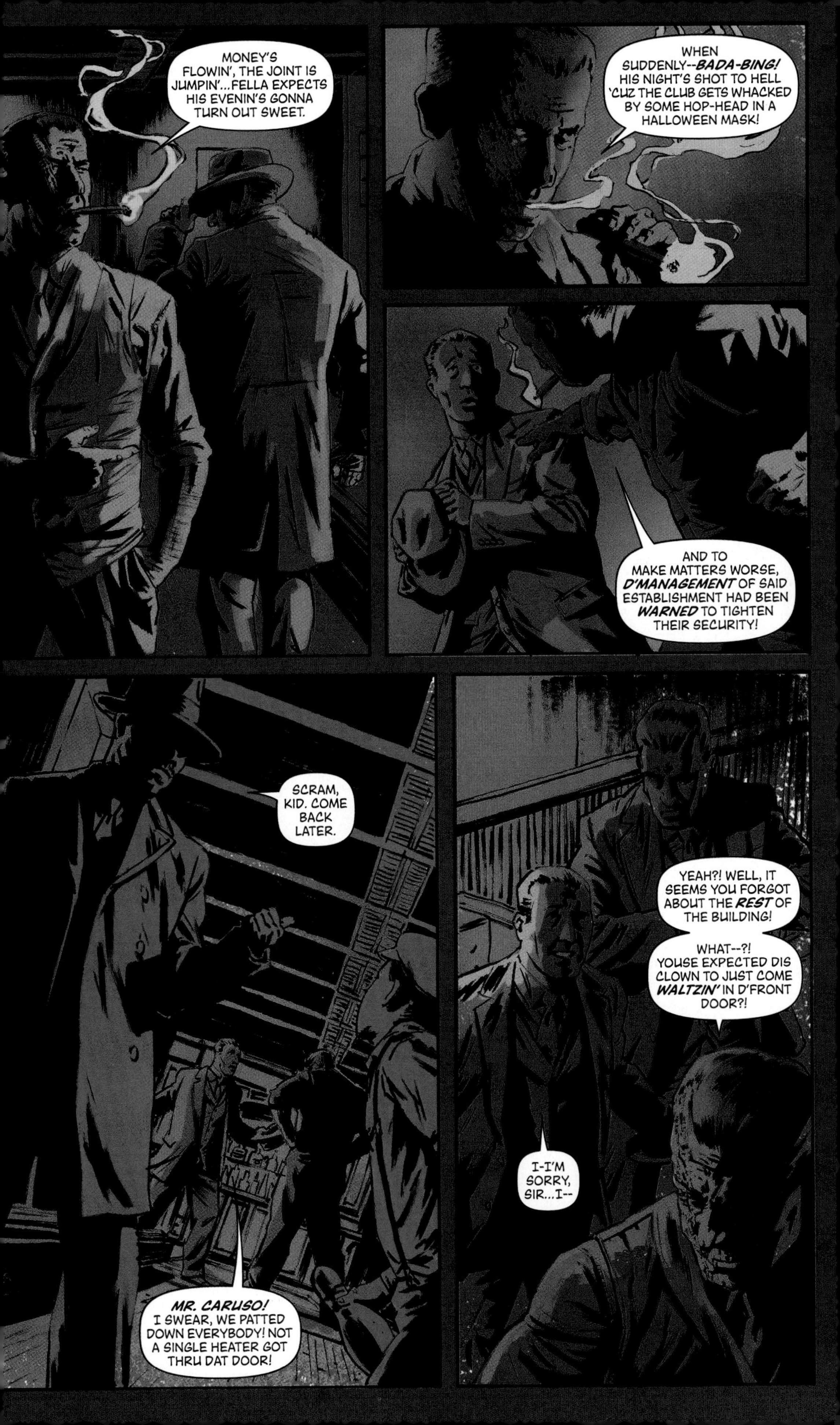
MONEY'S FLOWIN', THE JOINT IS JUMPIN'...FELLA EXPECTS HIS EVENIN'S GONNA TURN OUT SWEET.
WHEN SUDDENLY--BADA-BING! HIS NIGHT'S SHOT TO HELL 'CUZ THE CLUB GETS WHACKED BY SOME HOP-HEAD IN A HALLOWEEN MASK!
AND TO MAKE MATTERS WORSE, D'MANAGEMENT OF SAID ESTABLISHMENT HAD BEEN WARNED TO TIGHTEN THEIR SECURITY!
SCRAM, KID. COME BACK LATER.
MR. CARUSO! I SWEAR, WE PATTED DOWN EVERYBODY! NOT A SINGLE HEATER GOT THRU DAT DOOR!
YEAH?! WELL, IT SEEMS YOU FORGOT ABOUT THE REST OF THE BUILDING!
WHAT--?! YOUSE EXPECTED DIS CLOWN TO JUST COME WALTZIN' IN D'FRONT DOOR?!
I-I'M SORRY, SIR...I--

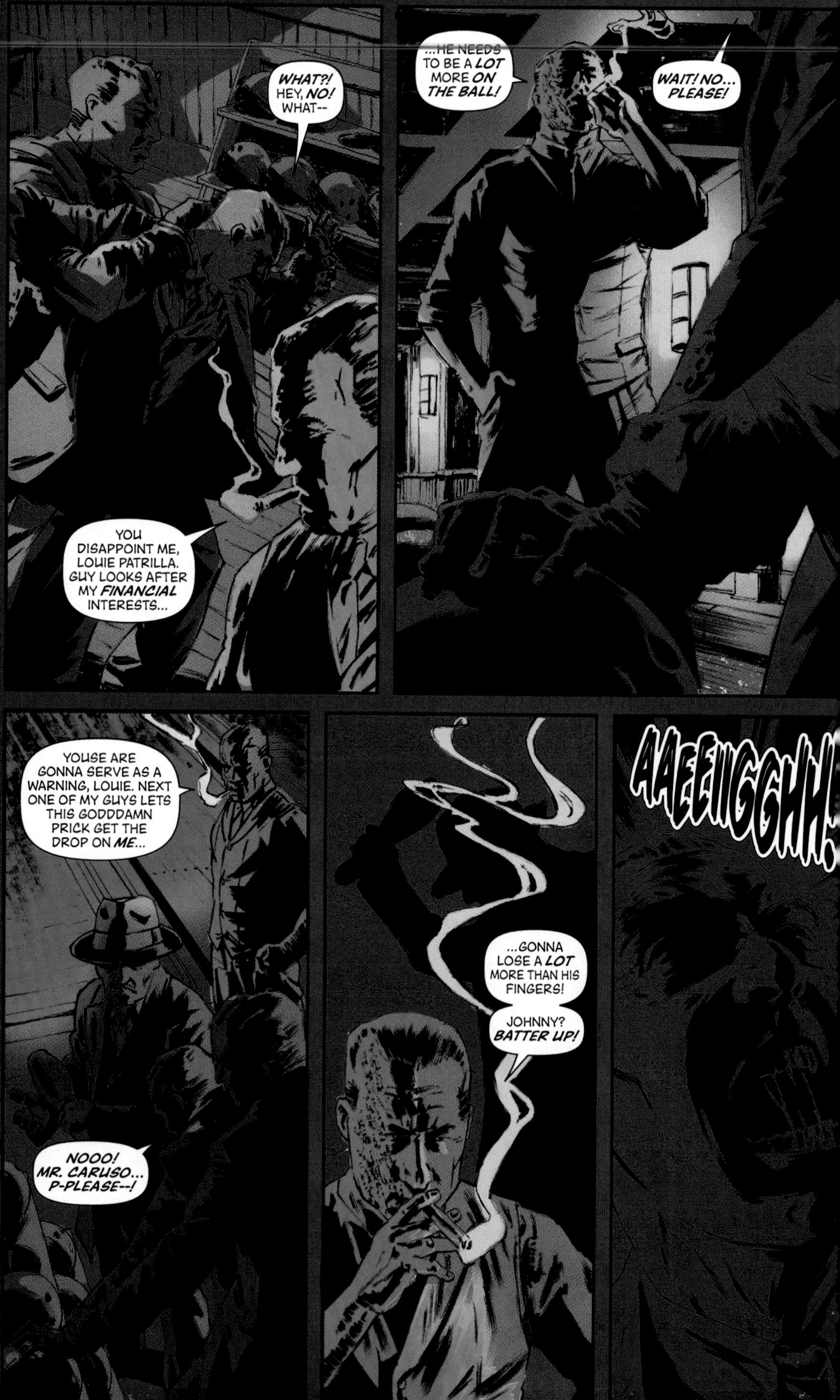
WHAT?! HEY, NO! WHAT--
YOU DISAPPOINT ME, LOUIE PATRILLA. GUY LOOKS AFTER MY FINANCIAL INTERESTS...
...HE NEEDS TO BE A LOT MORE ON THE BALL!
WAIT! NO... PLEASE!
YOUSE ARE GONNA SERVE AS A WARNING, LOUIE. NEXT ONE OF MY GUYS LETS THIS GODDDAMN PRICK GET THE DROP ON ME...
NOOO! MR. CARUSO... P-PLEASE--!
...GONNA LOSE A LOT MORE THAN HIS FINGERS!
JOHNNY? BATTER UP!
AAEEIIGGHH!

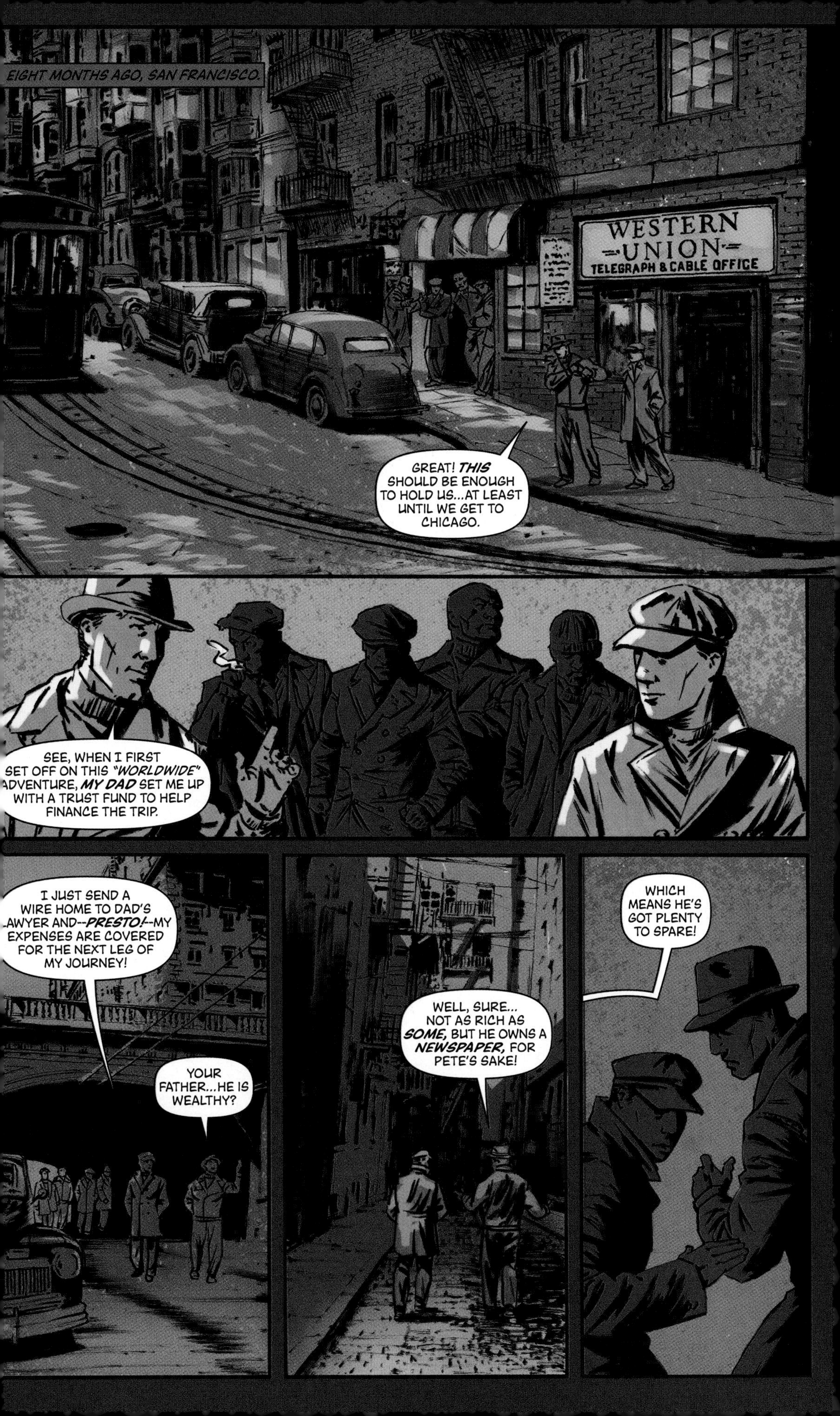
EIGHT MONTHS AGO, SAN FRANCISCO.
WESTERN UNION TELEGRAPH & CABLE OFFICE
GREAT! THIS SHOULD BE ENOUGH TO HOLD US...AT LEAST UNTIL WE GET TO CHICAGO.
SEE, WHEN I FIRST SET OFF ON THIS "WORLDWIDE" ADVENTURE, MY DAD SET ME UP WITH A TRUST FUND TO HELP FINANCE THE TRIP.
I JUST SEND A WIRE HOME TO DAD'S LAWYER AND--PRESTO!--MY EXPENSES ARE COVERED FOR THE NEXT LEG OF MY JOURNEY!
YOUR FATHER...HE IS WEALTHY?
WELL, SURE... NOT AS RICH AS SOME, BUT HE OWNS A NEWSPAPER, FOR PETE'S SAKE!
WHICH MEANS HE'S GOT PLENTY TO SPARE!

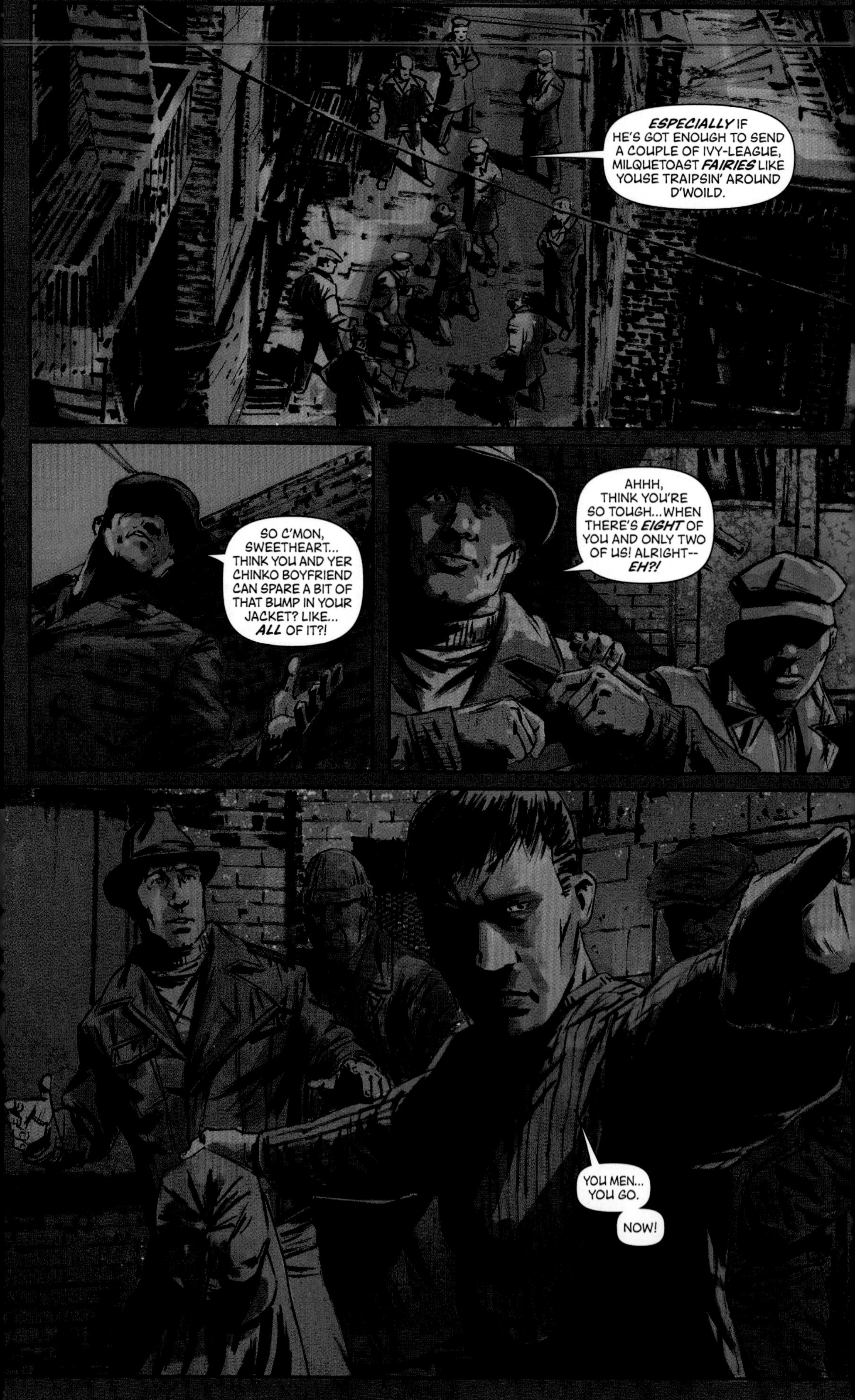
ESPECIALLY IF HE'S GOT ENOUGH TO SEND A COUPLE OF IVY-LEAGUE, MILQUETOAST FAIRIES LIKE YOUSE TRAIPSIN' AROUND D'WOILD.
SO C'MON, SWEETHEART... THINK YOU AND YER CHINKO BOYFRIEND CAN SPARE A BIT OF THAT BUMP IN YOUR JACKET? LIKE... ALL OF IT?!
AHHH, THINK YOU'RE SO TOUGH...WHEN THERE'S EIGHT OF YOU AND ONLY TWO OF US! ALRIGHT-- EH?!
YOU MEN... YOU GO.
NOW!

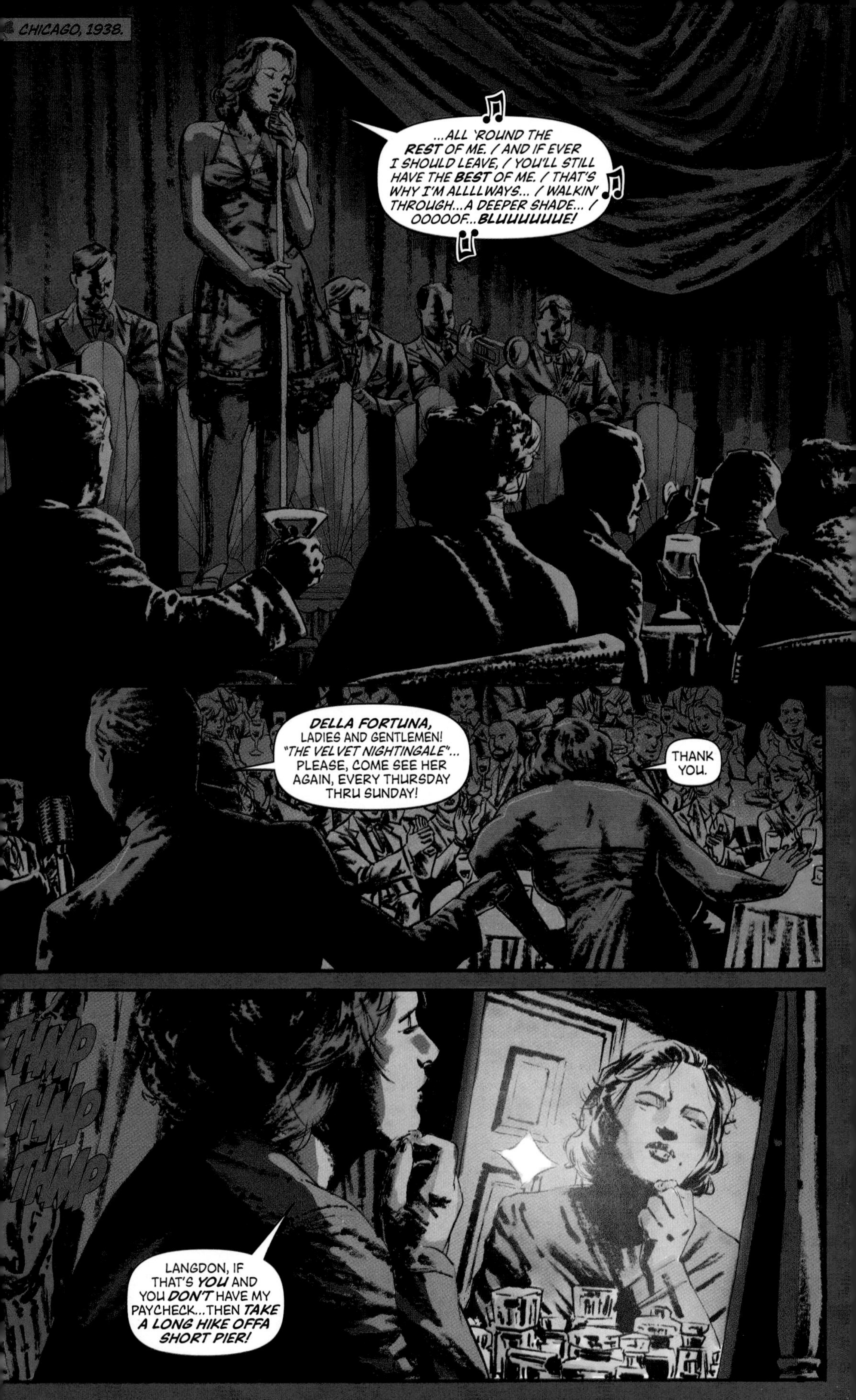
CHICAGO, 1938.
...ALL 'ROUND THE REST OF ME. / AND IF EVER I SHOULD LEAVE, / YOU'LL STILL HAVE THE BEST OF ME. / THAT'S WHY I'M ALLLLWAYS... / WALKIN' THROUGH...A DEEPER SHADE... / OOOOOF...BLUUUUUUE!
DELLA FORTUNA, LADIES AND GENTLEMEN! "THE VELVET NIGHTINGALE"... PLEASE, COME SEE HER AGAIN, EVERY THURSDAY THRU SUNDAY!
THANK YOU.
THMP THMP THMP
LANGDON, IF THAT'S YOU AND YOU DON'T HAVE MY PAYCHECK...THEN TAKE A LONG HIKE OFFA SHORT PIER!

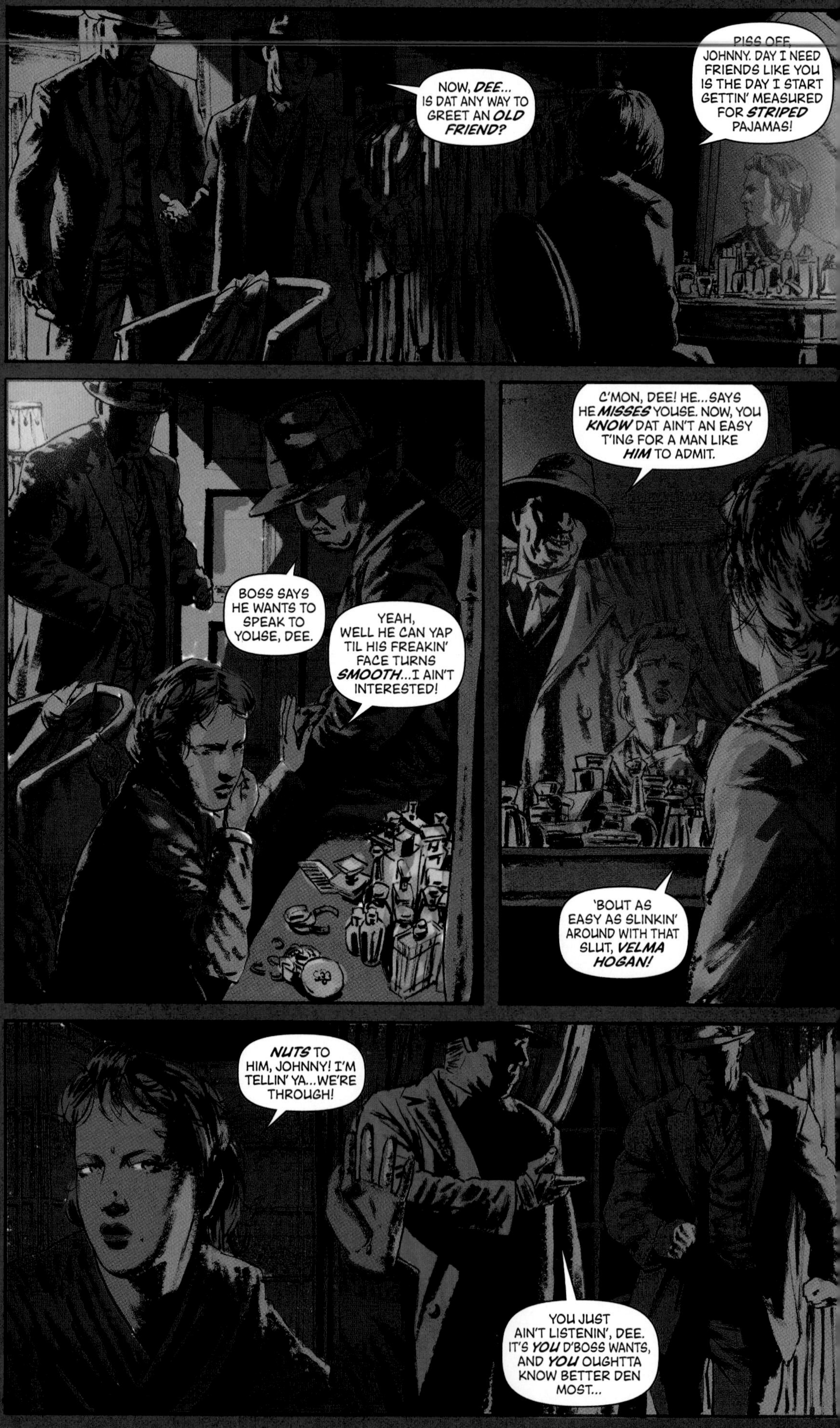
NOW, DEE... IS DAT ANY WAY TO GREET AN OLD FRIEND?
PISS OFF, JOHNNY. DAY I NEED FRIENDS LIKE YOU IS THE DAY I START GETTIN' MEASURED FOR STRIPED PAJAMAS!
BOSS SAYS HE WANTS TO SPEAK TO YOUSE, DEE.
YEAH, WELL HE CAN YAP TIL HIS FREAKIN' FACE TURNS SMOOTH...I AIN'T INTERESTED!
C'MON, DEE! HE...SAYS HE MISSES YOUSE. NOW, YOU KNOW DAT AIN'T AN EASY T'ING FOR A MAN LIKE HIM TO ADMIT.
'BOUT AS EASY AS SLINKIN' AROUND WITH THAT SLUT, VELMA HOGAN!
NUTS TO HIM, JOHNNY! I'M TELLIN' YA...WE'RE THROUGH!
YOU JUST AIN'T LISTENIN', DEE. IT'S YOU D'BOSS WANTS, AND YOU OUGHTTA KNOW BETTER DEN MOST...

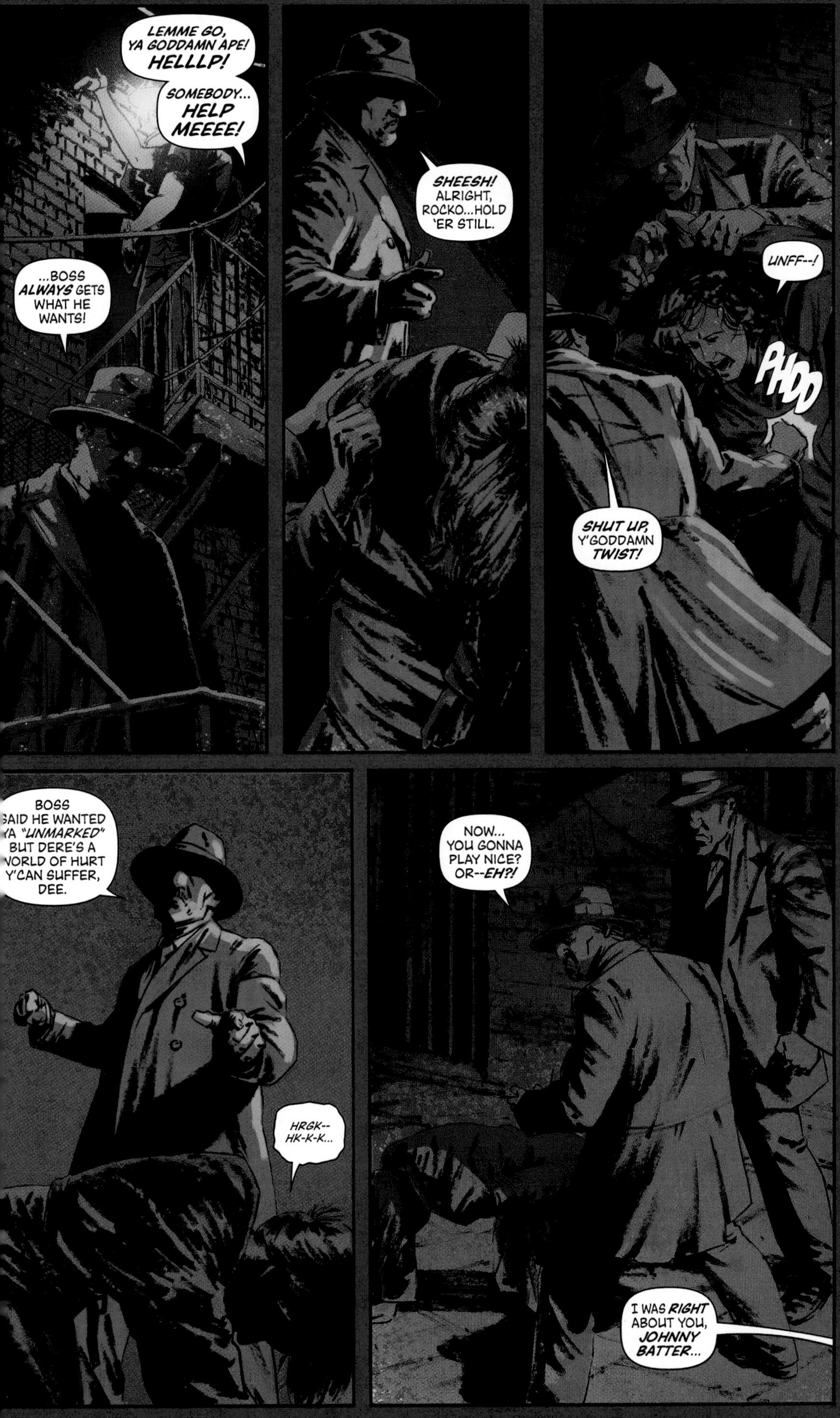
LEMME GO, YA GODDAMN APE! HELLLP!
SOMEBODY... HELP MEEEE!
...BOSS ALWAYS GETS WHAT HE WANTS!
SHEESH! ALRIGHT, ROCKO...HOLD 'ER STILL.
UNFF--!
PHDD
SHUT UP, Y'GODDAMN TWIST!
BOSS SAID HE WANTED YA "UNMARKED" BUT DERE'S A WORLD OF HURT Y'CAN SUFFER, DEE.
HRGK-- HK-K-K...
NOW... YOU GONNA PLAY NICE? OR--EH?!
I WAS RIGHT ABOUT YOU, JOHNNY BATTER...

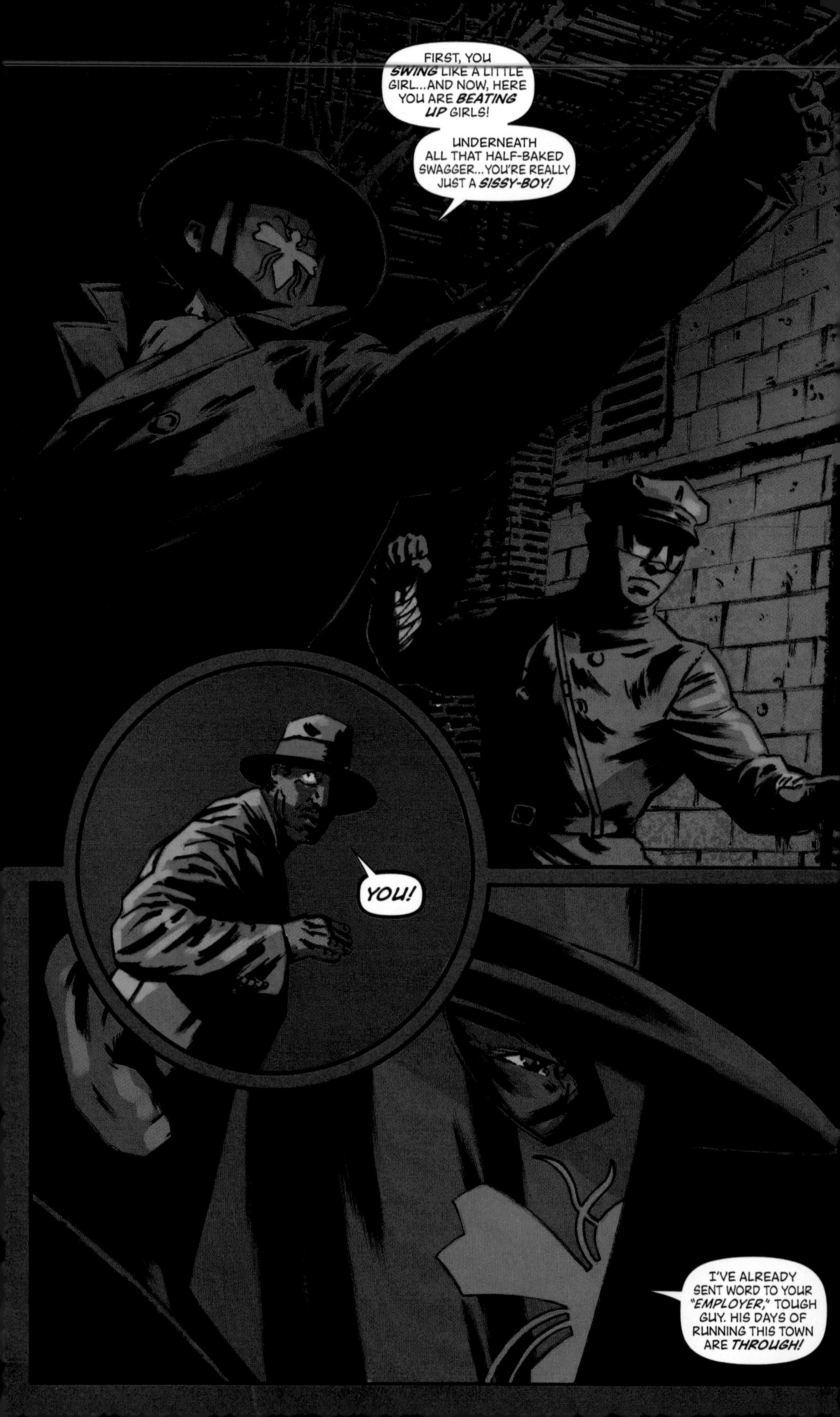
FIRST, YOU SWING LIKE A LITTLE GIRL...AND NOW, HERE YOU ARE BEATING UP GIRLS!
UNDERNEATH ALL THAT HALF-BAKED SWAGGER...YOU'RE REALLY JUST A SISSY-BOY!
YOU!
I'VE ALREADY SENT WORD TO YOUR "EMPLOYER," TOUGH GUY. HIS DAYS OF RUNNING THIS TOWN ARE THROUGH!

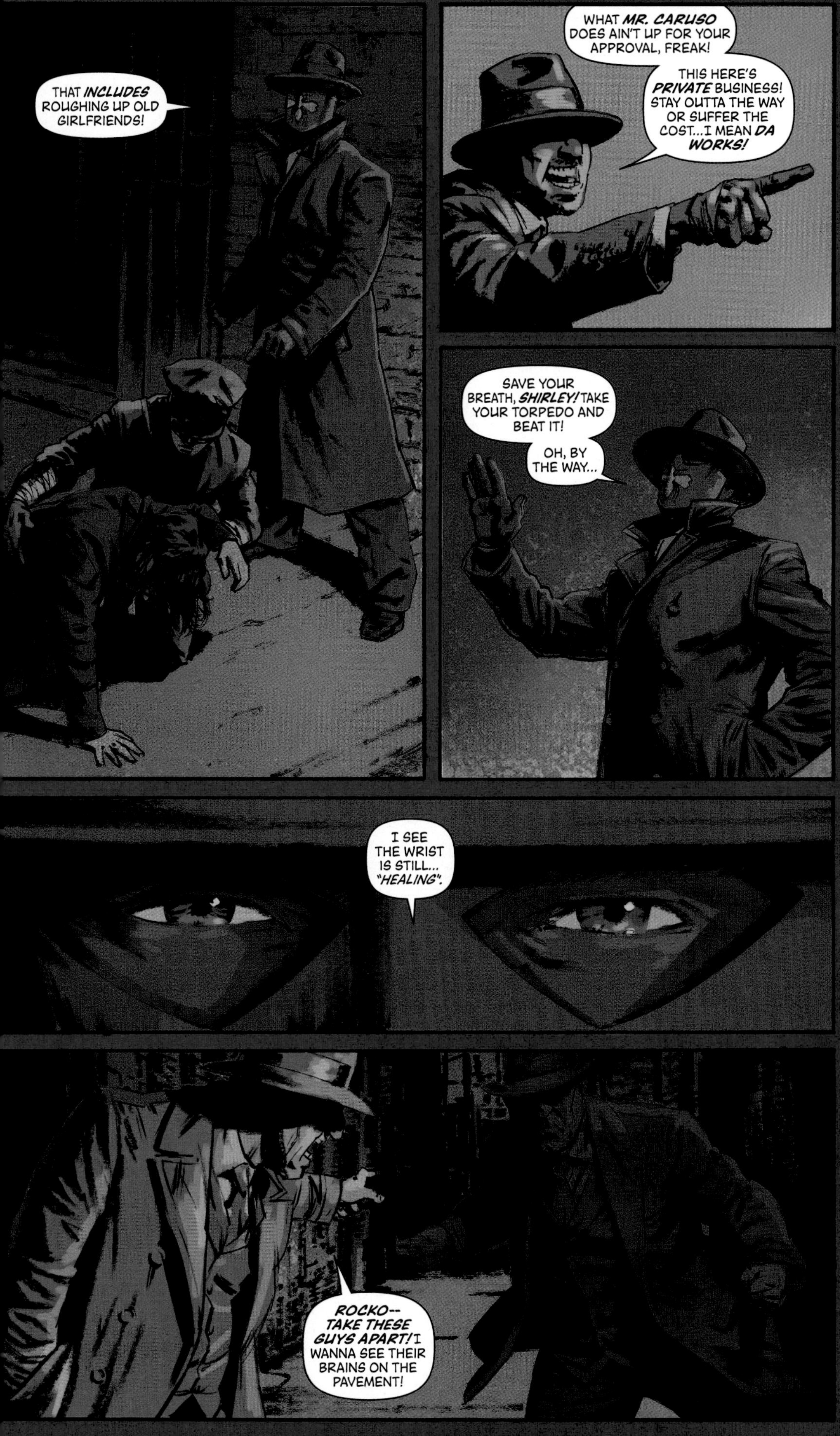
THAT INCLUDES ROUGHING UP OLD GIRLFRIENDS!
WHAT MR. CARUSO DOES AIN'T UP FOR YOUR APPROVAL, FREAK!
THIS HERE'S PRIVATE BUSINESS! STAY OUTTA THE WAY OR SUFFER THE COST...I MEAN DA WORKS!
SAVE YOUR BREATH, SHIRLEY! TAKE YOUR TORPEDO AND BEAT IT!
OH, BY THE WAY...
I SEE THE WRIST IS STILL... "HEALING".
ROCKO-- TAKE THESE GUYS APART! I WANNA SEE THEIR BRAINS ON THE PAVEMENT!

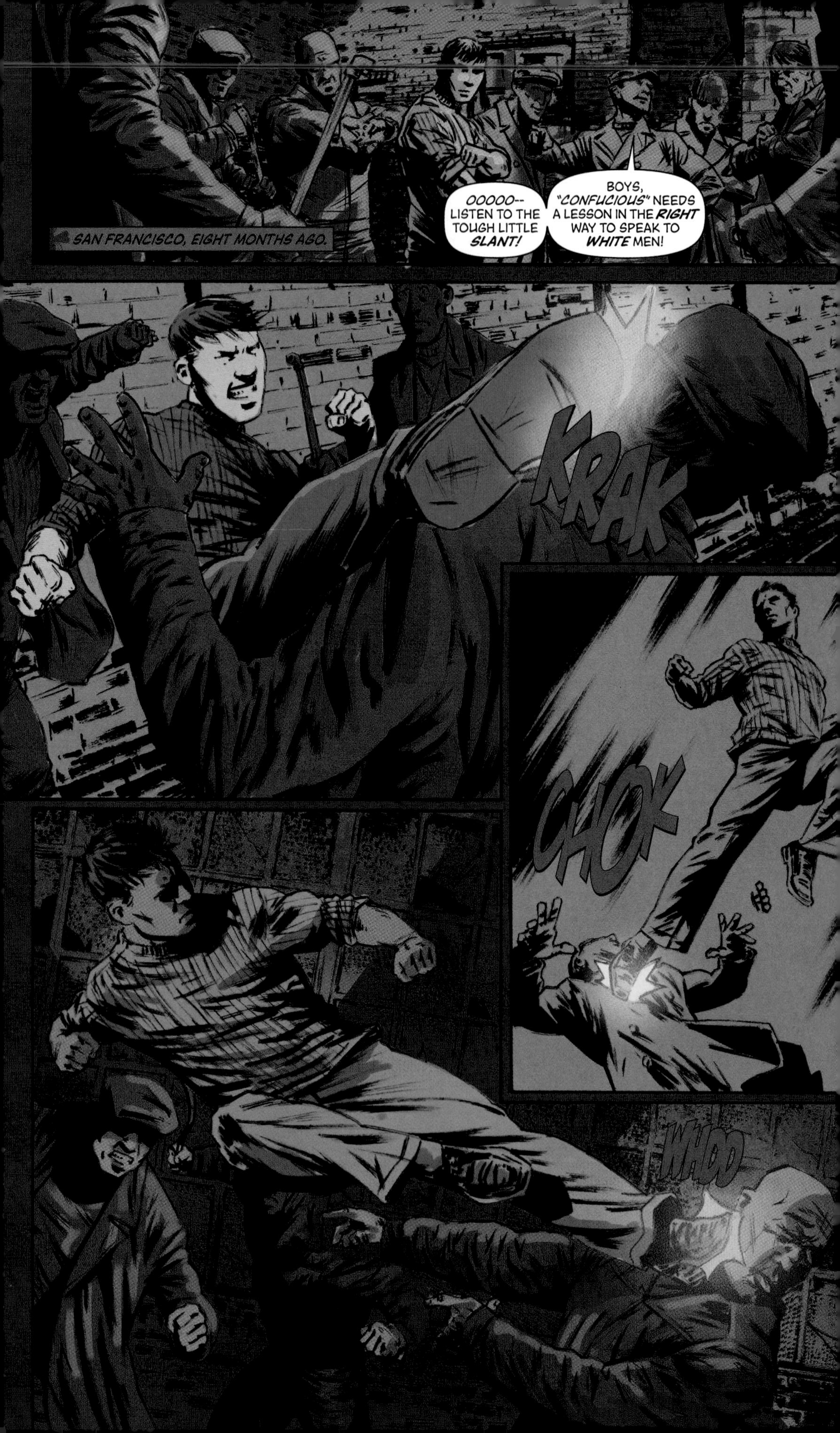
SAN FRANCISCO, EIGHT MONTHS AGO.
OOOOO-- LISTEN TO THE TOUGH LITTLE SLANT!
BOYS, "CONFUCIOUS" NEEDS A LESSON IN THE RIGHT WAY TO SPEAK TO WHITE MEN!
KRAK
CHOK
WHOO

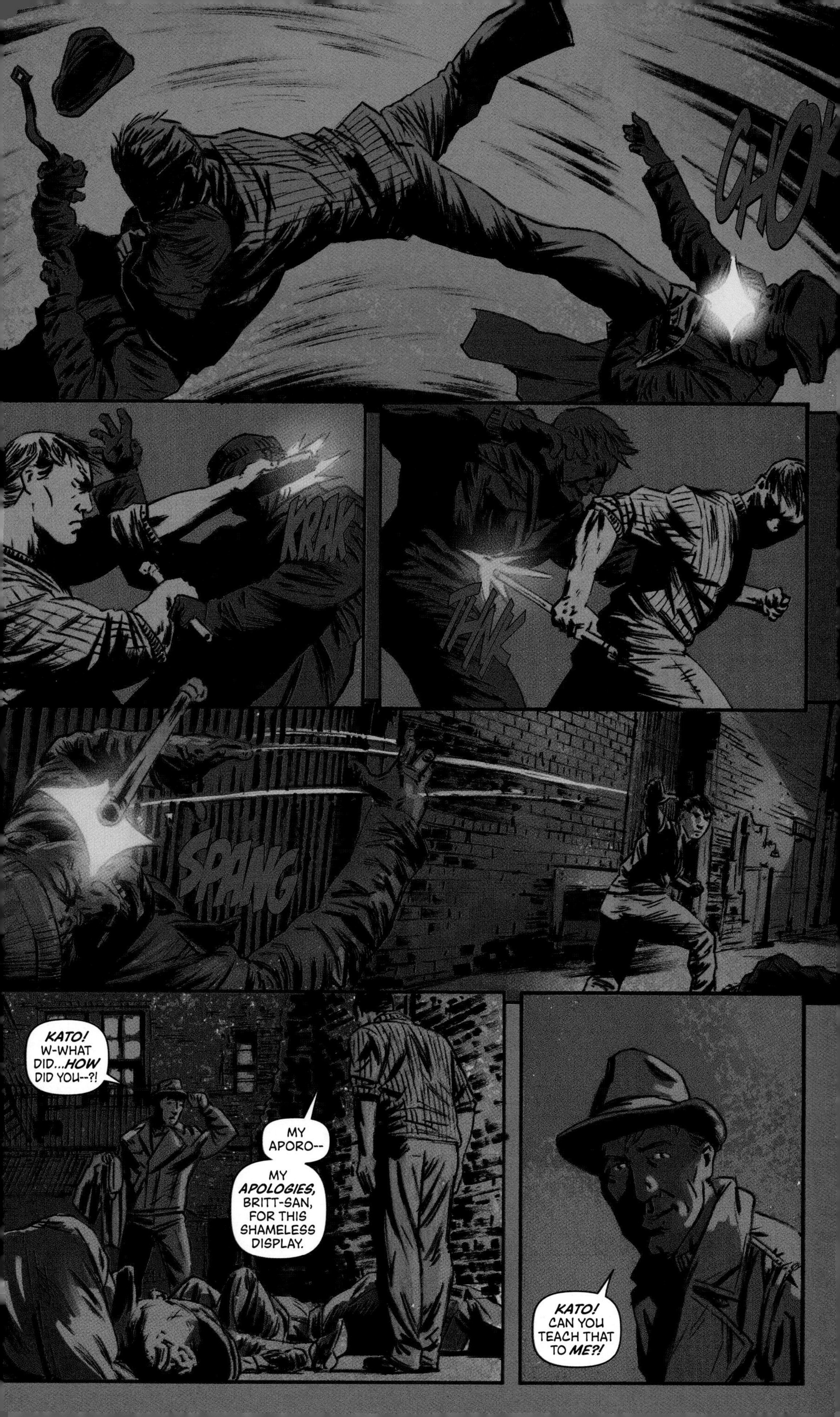
CHOK
KRAK
TANK
SPANG
KATO! W-WHAT DID...HOW DID YOU--?!
MY APORO--
MY APOLOGIES, BRITT-SAN, FOR THIS SHAMELESS DISPLAY.
KATO! CAN YOU TEACH THAT TO ME?!

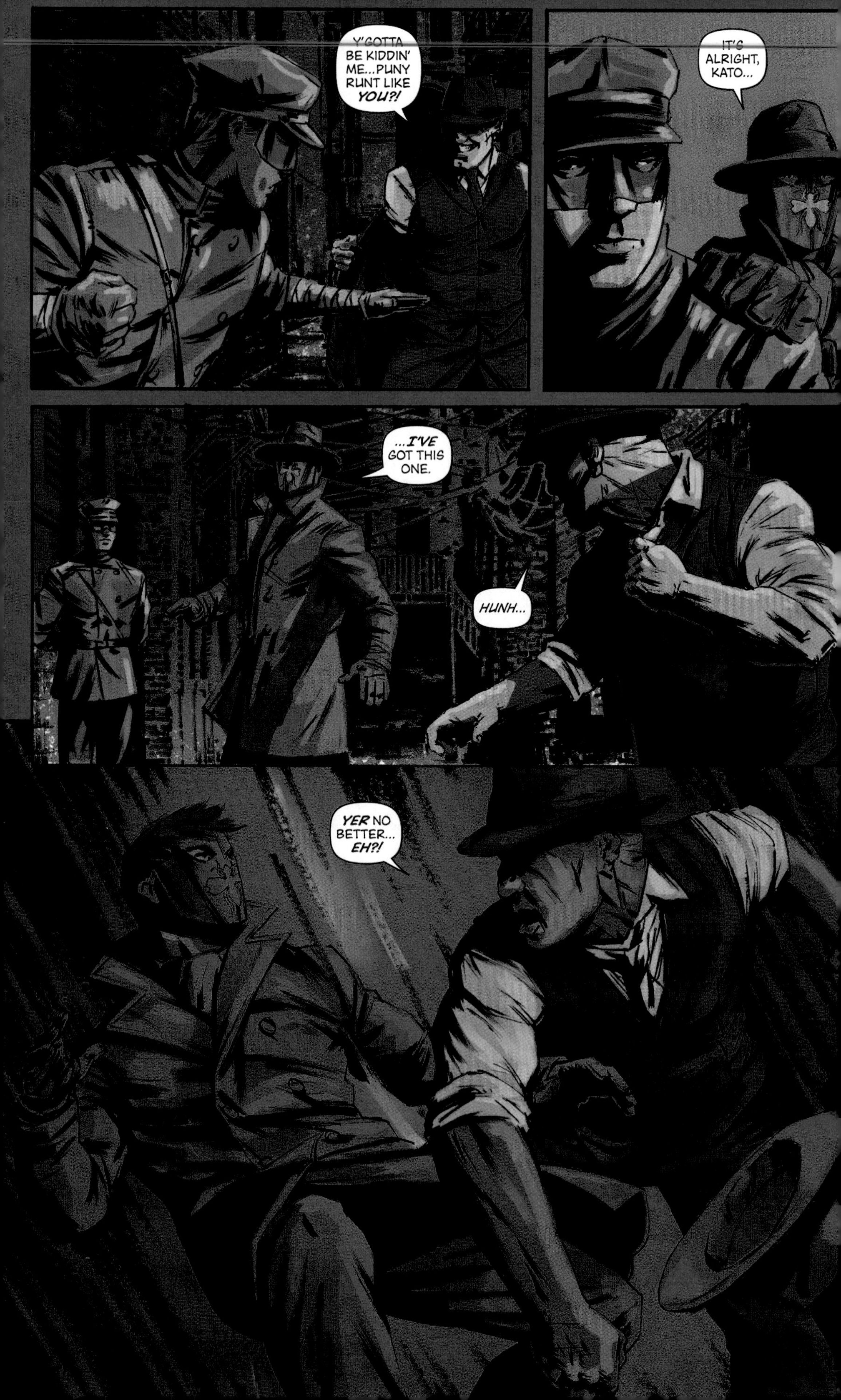
Y'GOTTA BE KIDDIN' ME...PUNY RUNT LIKE YOU?!
IT'S ALRIGHT, KATO...
...I'VE GOT THIS ONE.
HUNH...
YER NO BETTER... EH?!

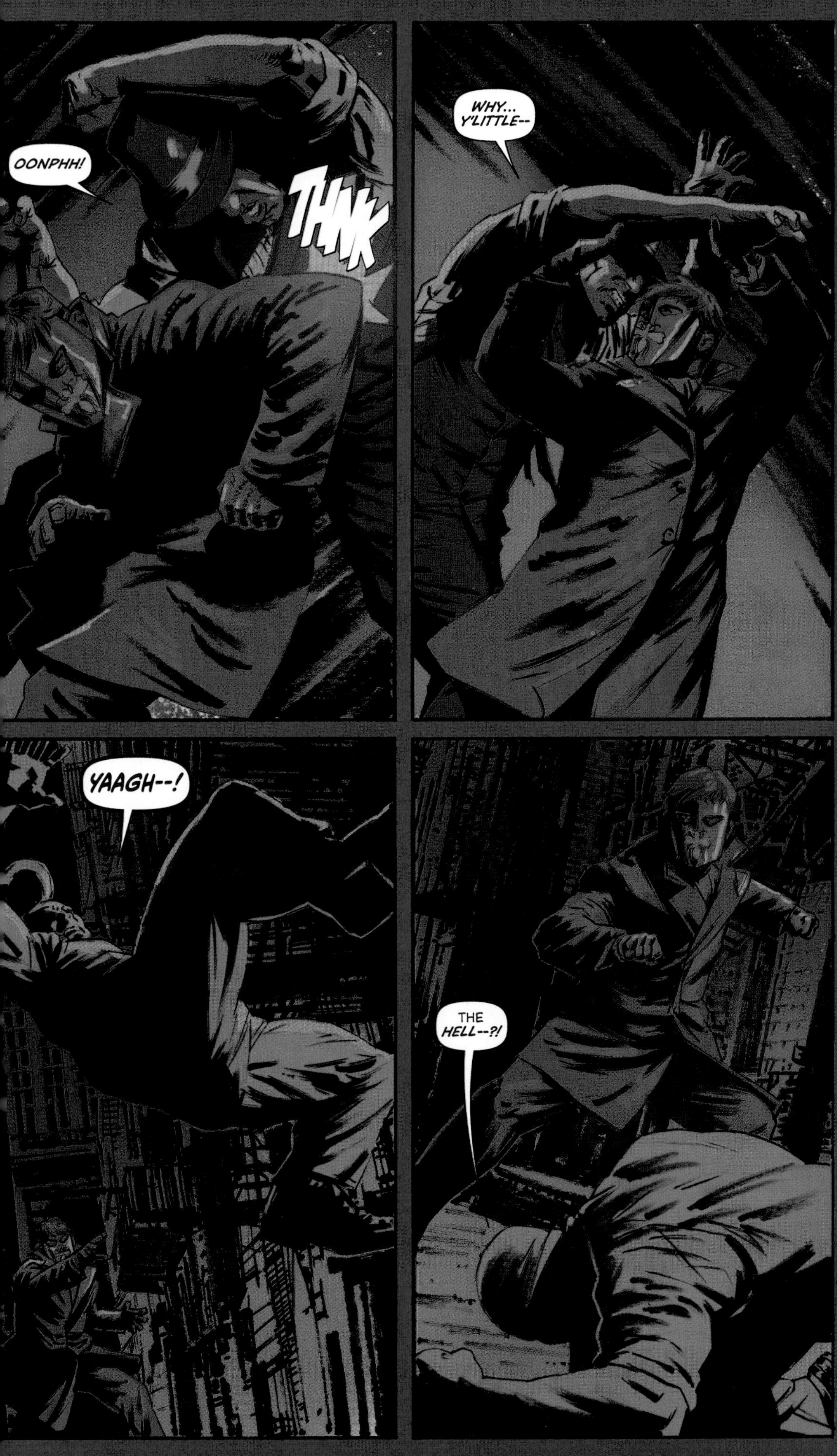
OONPHH!
THNK
WHY... Y'LITTLE--
YAAGH--!
THE HELL--?!

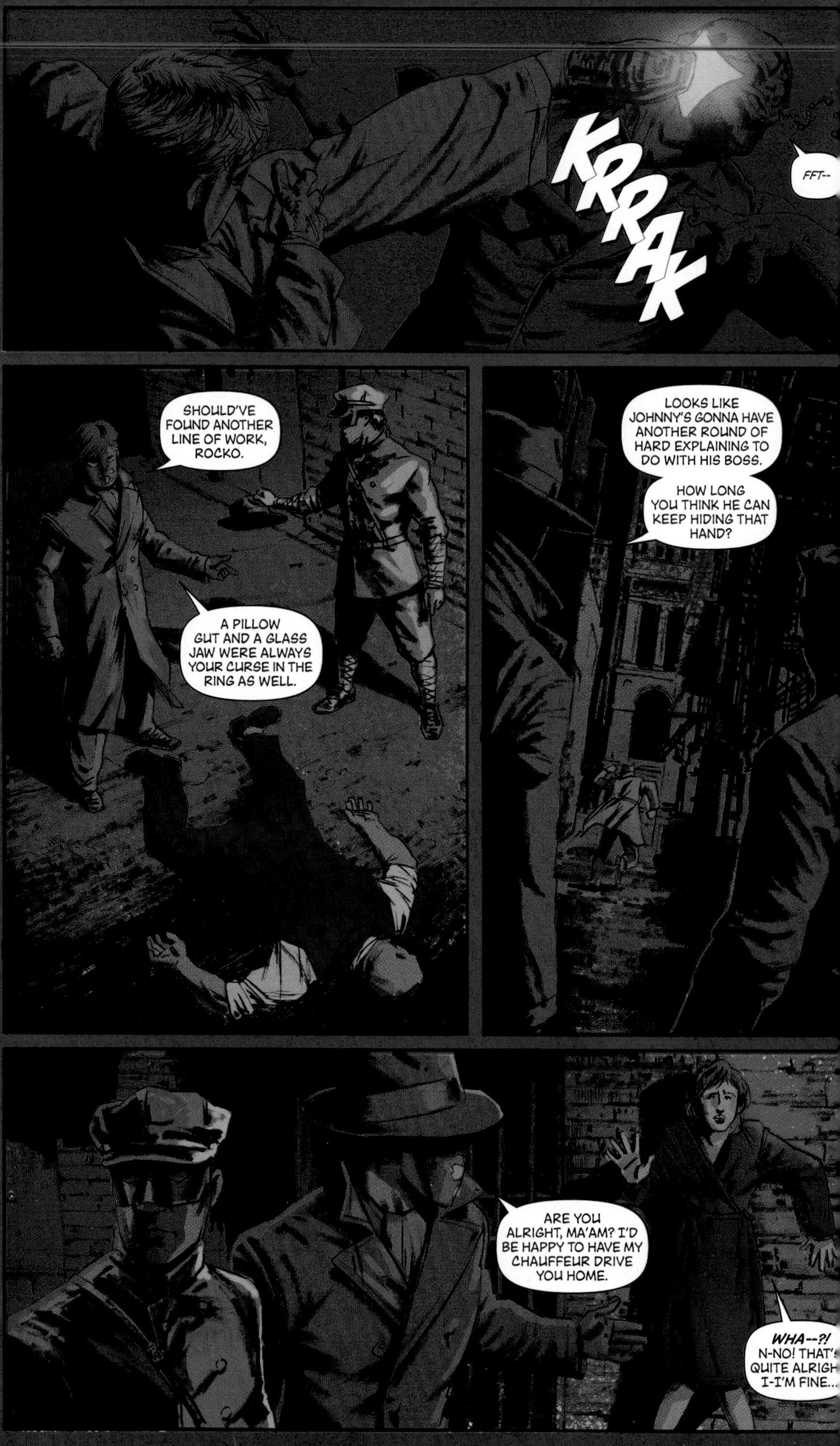
KRRAK
FFT--
SHOULD'VE FOUND ANOTHER LINE OF WORK, ROCKO.
A PILLOW GUT AND A GLASS JAW WERE ALWAYS YOUR CURSE IN THE RING AS WELL.
LOOKS LIKE JOHNNY'S GONNA HAVE ANOTHER ROUND OF HARD EXPLAINING TO DO WITH HIS BOSS.
HOW LONG YOU THINK HE CAN KEEP HIDING THAT HAND?
ARE YOU ALRIGHT, MA'AM? I'D BE HAPPY TO HAVE MY CHAUFFEUR DRIVE YOU HOME.
WHA--?! N-NO! THAT'S QUITE ALRIGH I-I'M FINE...

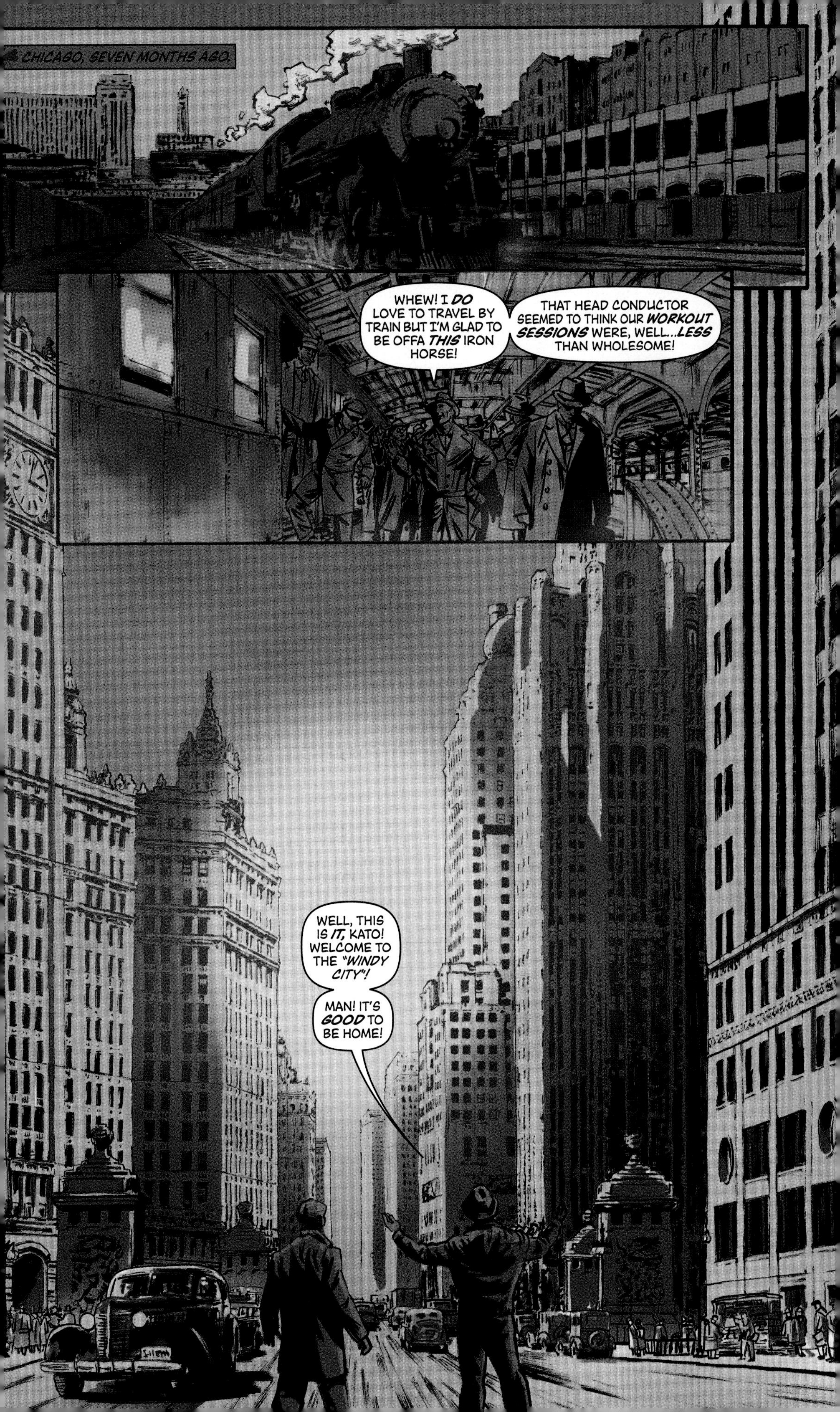
CHICAGO, SEVEN MONTHS AGO.
WHEW! I DO LOVE TO TRAVEL BY TRAIN BUT I'M GLAD TO BE OFFA THIS IRON HORSE!
THAT HEAD CONDUCTOR SEEMED TO THINK OUR WORKOUT SESSIONS WERE, WELL...LESS THAN WHOLESOME!
WELL, THIS IS IT, KATO! WELCOME TO THE "WINDY CITY"!
MAN! IT'S GOOD TO BE HOME!

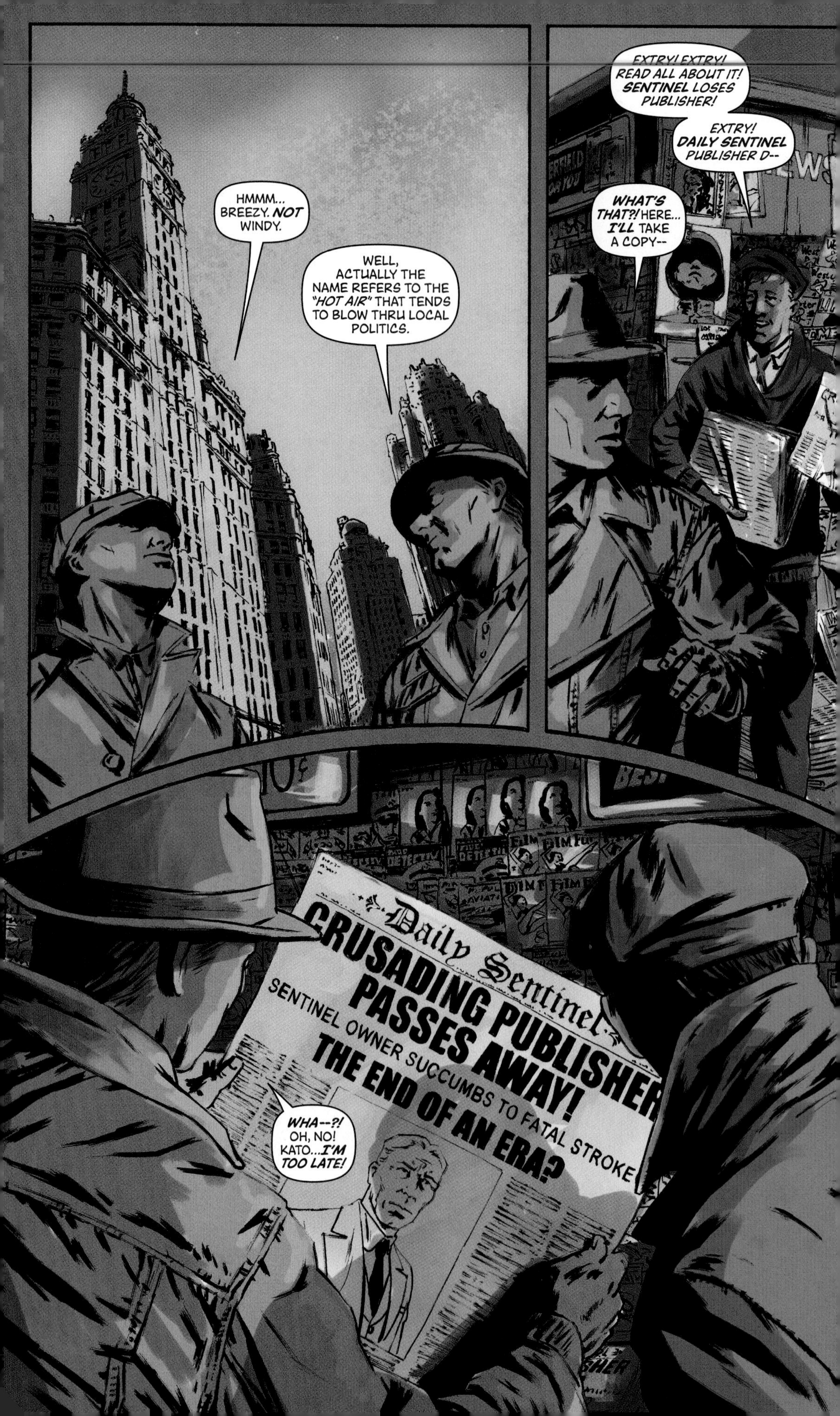
HMMM... BREEZY. NOT WINDY.
WELL, ACTUALLY THE NAME REFERS TO THE "HOT AIR" THAT TENDS TO BLOW THRU LOCAL POLITICS.
EXTRY! EXTRY! READ ALL ABOUT IT! SENTINEL LOSES PUBLISHER!
EXTRY! DAILY SENTINEL PUBLISHER D--
WHAT'S THAT?! HERE... I'LL TAKE A COPY--
Daily Sentinel
CRUSADING PUBLISHER PASSES AWAY!
SENTINEL OWNER SUCCUMBS TO FATAL STROKE
THE END OF AN ERA?
WHA--?! OH, NO! KATO...I'M TOO LATE!

ISSUE FIVE

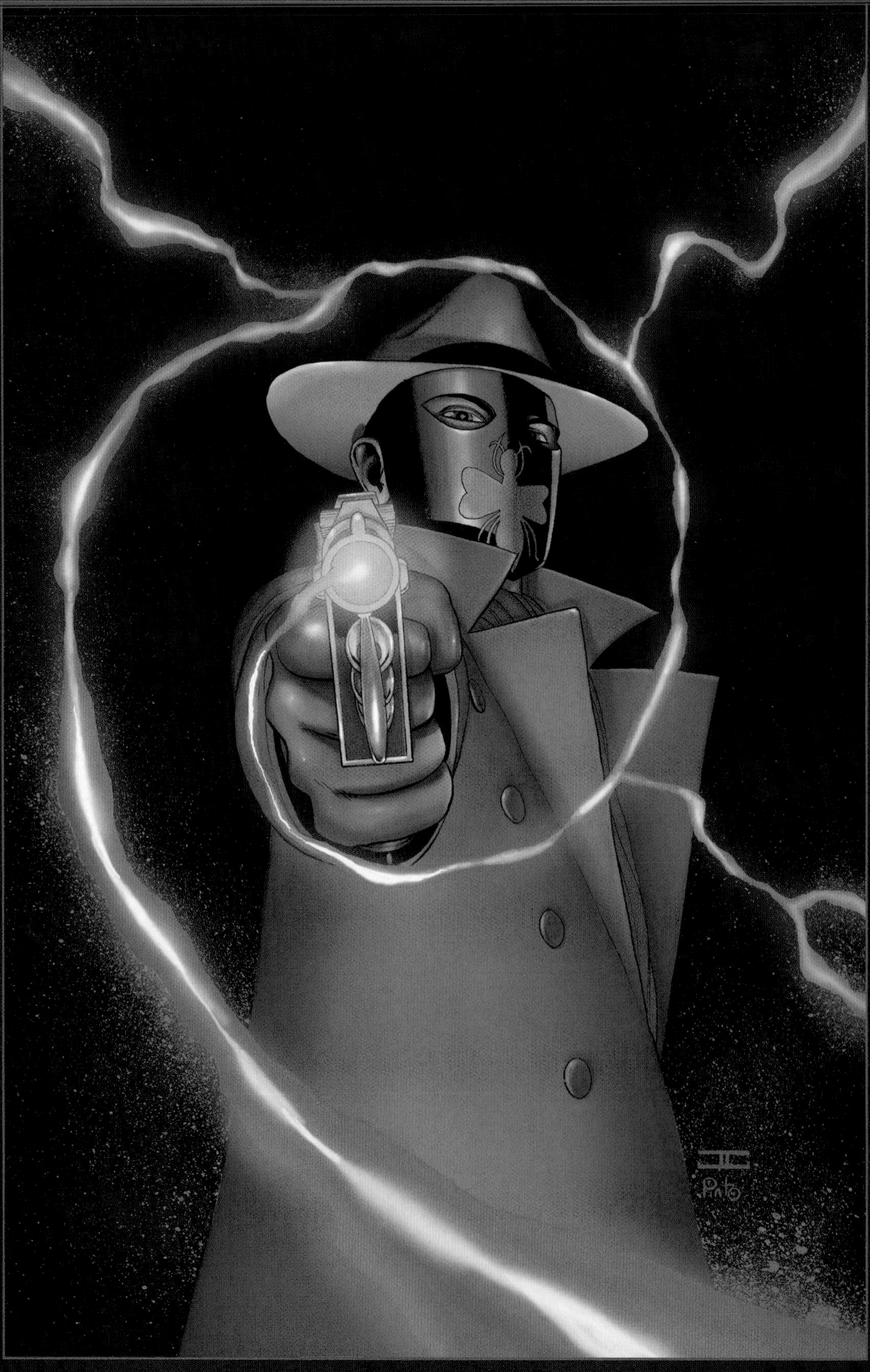

Issue five cover by JOHN CASSADAY

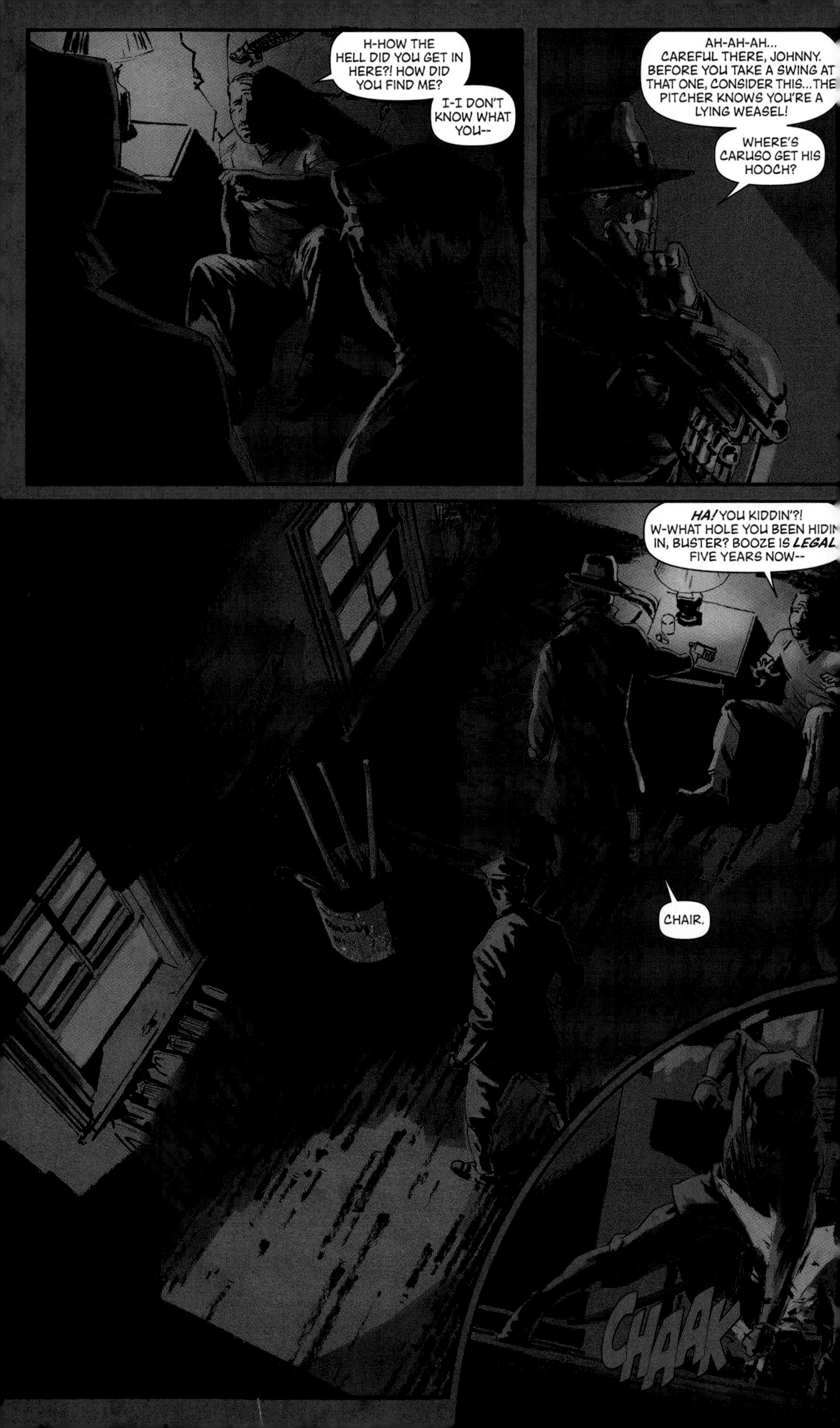
H-HOW THE HELL DID YOU GET IN HERE?! HOW DID YOU FIND ME?
I-I DON'T KNOW WHAT YOU--
AH-AH-AH... CAREFUL THERE, JOHNNY. BEFORE YOU TAKE A SWING AT THAT ONE, CONSIDER THIS...THE PITCHER KNOWS YOU'RE A LYING WEASEL!
WHERE'S CARUSO GET HIS HOOCH?
HA! YOU KIDDIN'?! W-WHAT HOLE YOU BEEN HIDIN IN, BUSTER? BOOZE IS *LEGAL* FIVE YEARS NOW--
CHAIR.
CHAAK

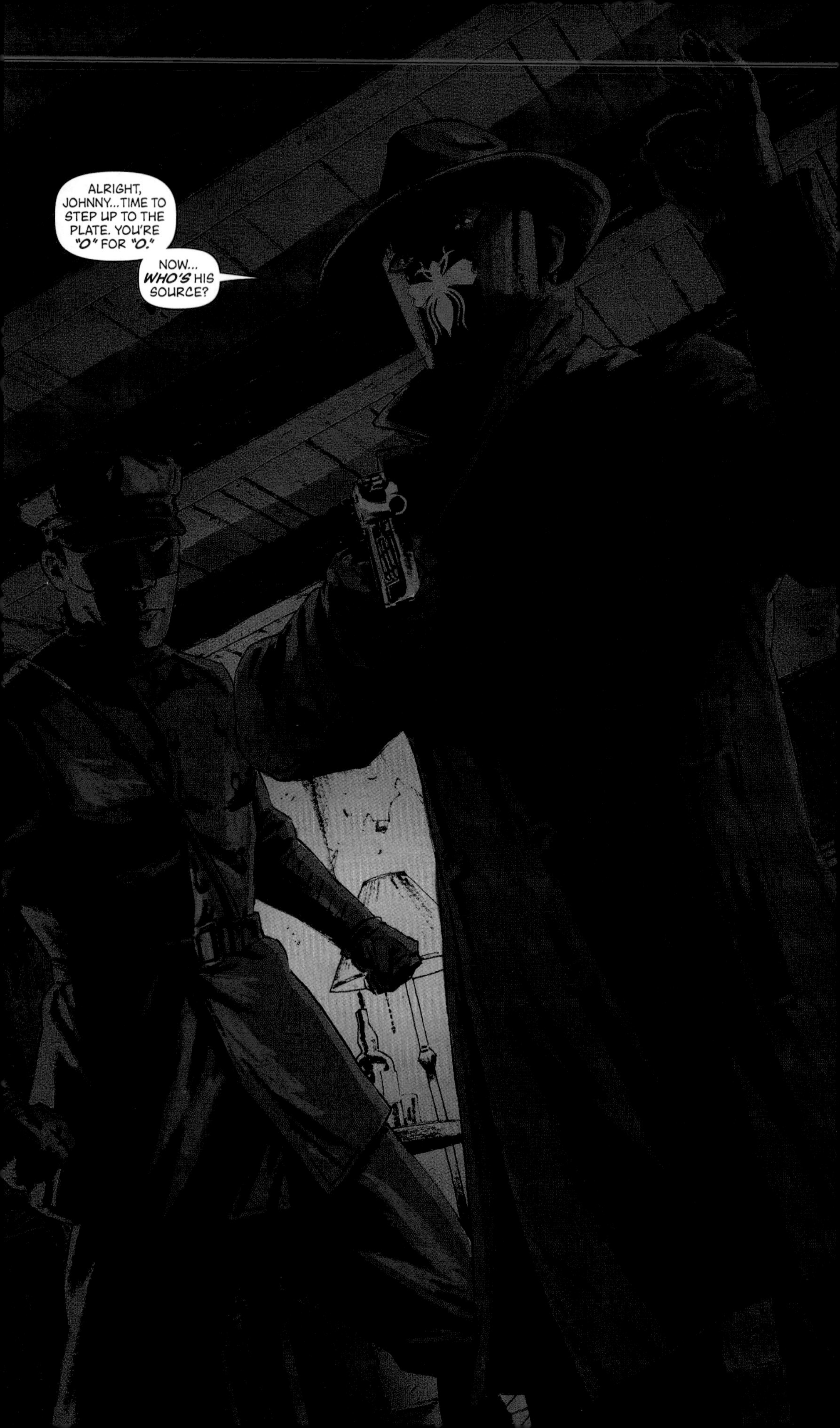
ALRIGHT, JOHNNY...TIME TO STEP UP TO THE PLATE. YOU'RE "O" FOR "O."
NOW... WHO'S HIS SOURCE?

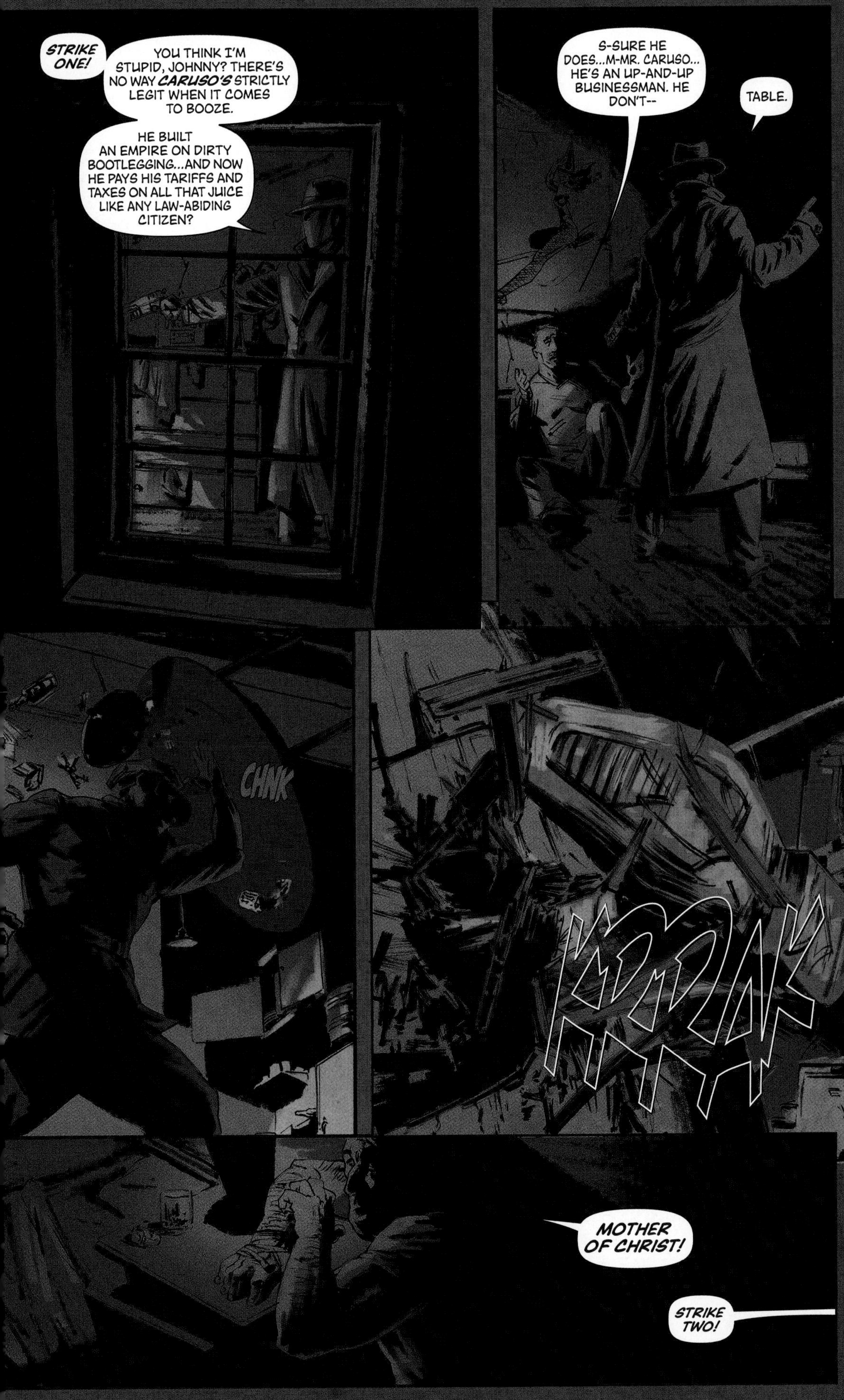
STRIKE ONE!
YOU THINK I'M STUPID, JOHNNY? THERE'S NO WAY CARUSO'S STRICTLY LEGIT WHEN IT COMES TO BOOZE.
HE BUILT AN EMPIRE ON DIRTY BOOTLEGGING...AND NOW HE PAYS HIS TARIFFS AND TAXES ON ALL THAT JUICE LIKE ANY LAW-ABIDING CITIZEN?
S-SURE HE DOES...M-MR. CARUSO... HE'S AN UP-AND-UP BUSINESSMAN. HE DON'T--
TABLE.
CHNK
KRRAK
MOTHER OF CHRIST!
STRIKE TWO!

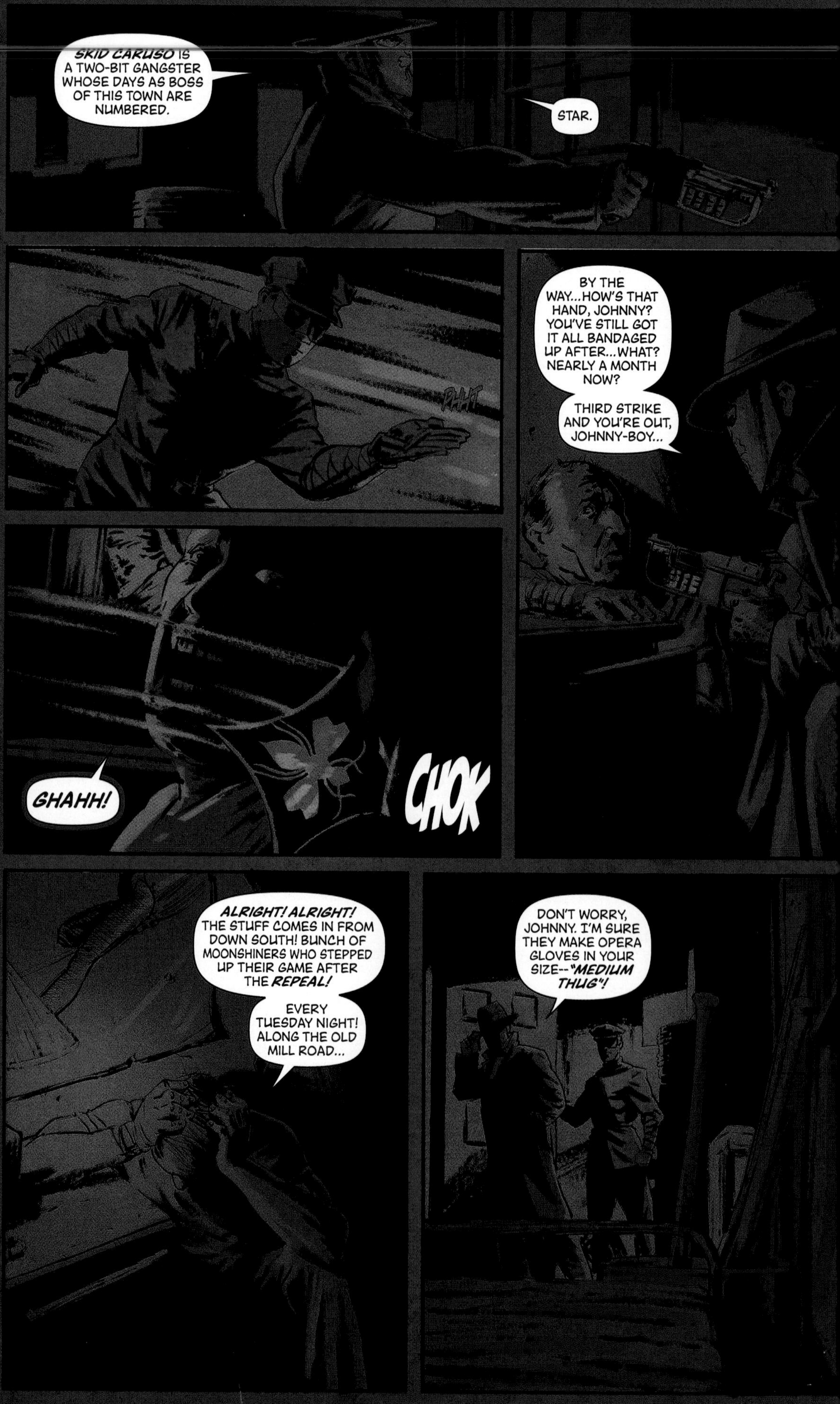
SKID CARUSO IS A TWO-BIT GANGSTER WHOSE DAYS AS BOSS OF THIS TOWN ARE NUMBERED.
STAR.
PHHT
BY THE WAY...HOW'S THAT HAND, JOHNNY? YOU'VE STILL GOT IT ALL BANDAGED UP AFTER...WHAT? NEARLY A MONTH NOW?
THIRD STRIKE AND YOU'RE OUT, JOHNNY-BOY...
GHAHH!
CHOK
ALRIGHT! ALRIGHT! THE STUFF COMES IN FROM DOWN SOUTH! BUNCH OF MOONSHINERS WHO STEPPED UP THEIR GAME AFTER THE REPEAL!
EVERY TUESDAY NIGHT! ALONG THE OLD MILL ROAD...
DON'T WORRY, JOHNNY. I'M SURE THEY MAKE OPERA GLOVES IN YOUR SIZE--"MEDIUM THUG"!

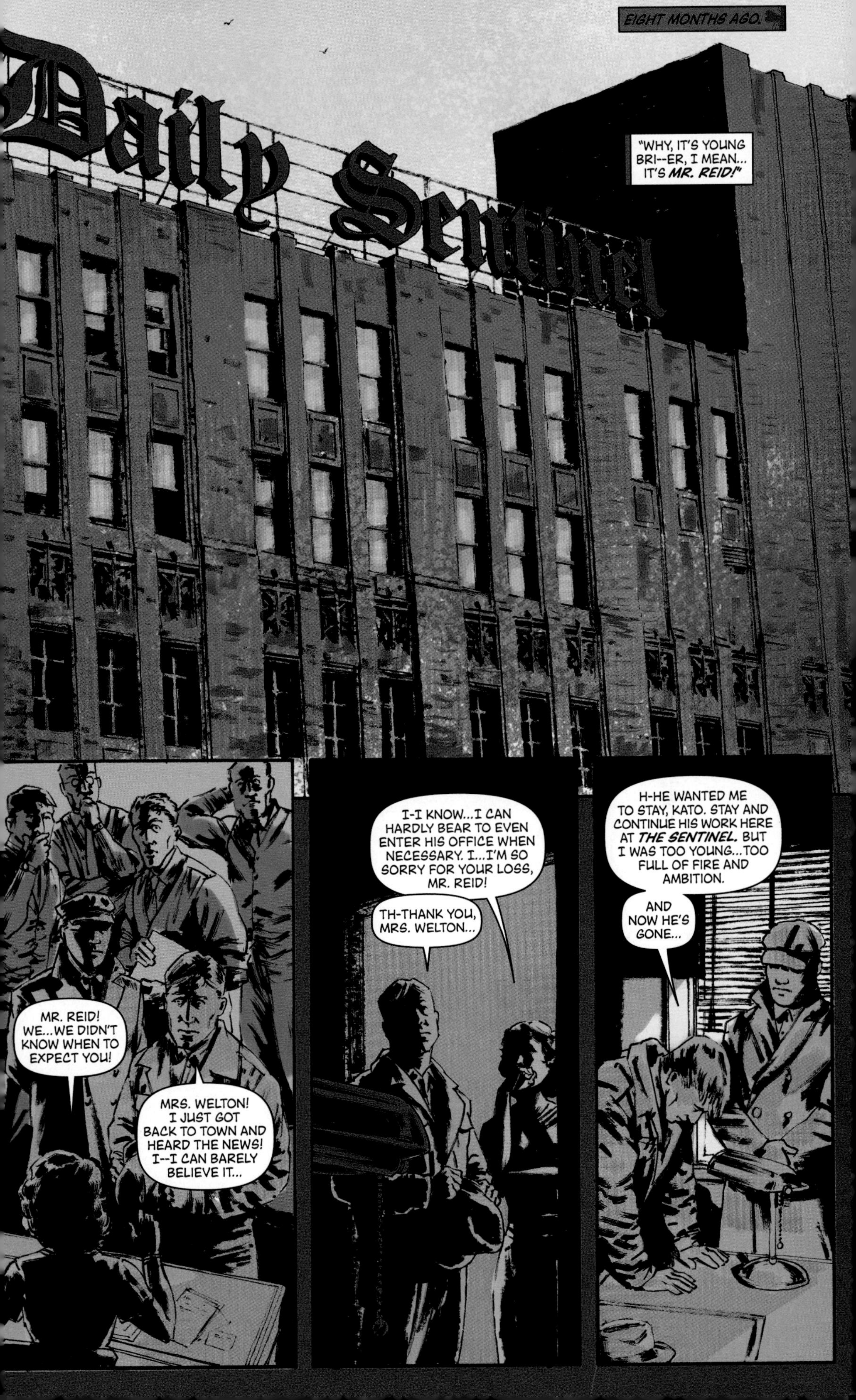
EIGHT MONTHS AGO.
Daily Sentinel
"WHY, IT'S YOUNG BRI--ER, I MEAN... IT'S MR. REID!"
MR. REID! WE...WE DIDN'T KNOW WHEN TO EXPECT YOU!
MRS. WELTON! I JUST GOT BACK TO TOWN AND HEARD THE NEWS! I--I CAN BARELY BELIEVE IT...
I-I KNOW...I CAN HARDLY BEAR TO EVEN ENTER HIS OFFICE WHEN NECESSARY. I...I'M SO SORRY FOR YOUR LOSS, MR. REID!
TH-THANK YOU, MRS. WELTON...
H-HE WANTED ME TO STAY, KATO. STAY AND CONTINUE HIS WORK HERE AT THE SENTINEL. BUT I WAS TOO YOUNG...TOO FULL OF FIRE AND AMBITION.
AND NOW HE'S GONE...

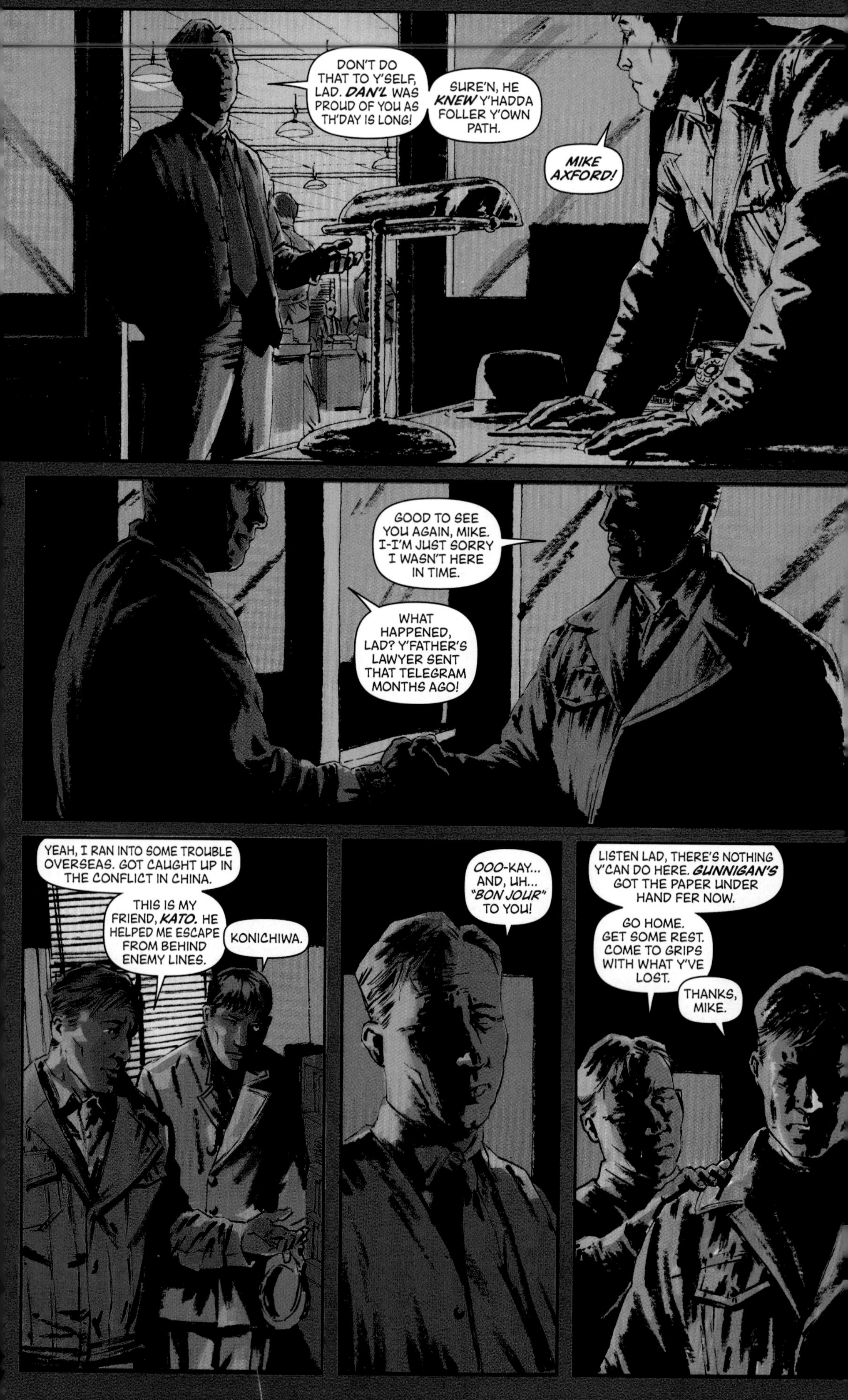
DON'T DO THAT TO Y'SELF, LAD. DAN'L WAS PROUD OF YOU AS TH'DAY IS LONG!
SURE'N, HE KNEW Y'HADDA FOLLER Y'OWN PATH.
MIKE AXFORD!
GOOD TO SEE YOU AGAIN, MIKE. I-I'M JUST SORRY I WASN'T HERE IN TIME.
WHAT HAPPENED, LAD? Y'FATHER'S LAWYER SENT THAT TELEGRAM MONTHS AGO!
YEAH, I RAN INTO SOME TROUBLE OVERSEAS. GOT CAUGHT UP IN THE CONFLICT IN CHINA.
THIS IS MY FRIEND, KATO. HE HELPED ME ESCAPE FROM BEHIND ENEMY LINES.
KONICHIWA.
OOO-KAY... AND, UH... "BON JOUR" TO YOU!
LISTEN LAD, THERE'S NOTHING Y'CAN DO HERE. GUNNIGAN'S GOT THE PAPER UNDER HAND FER NOW.
GO HOME. GET SOME REST. COME TO GRIPS WITH WHAT Y'VE LOST.
THANKS, MIKE.

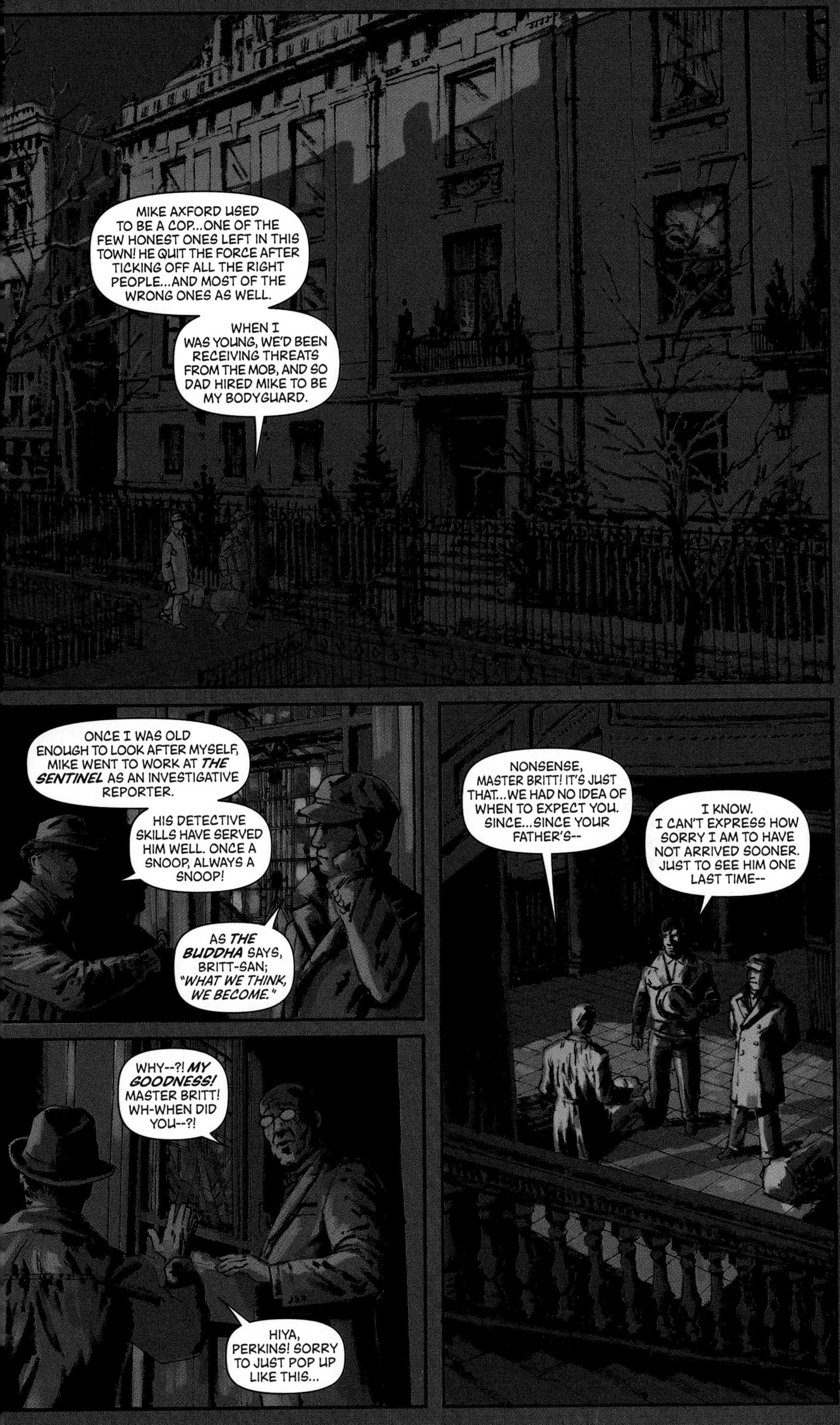
MIKE AXFORD USED TO BE A COP...ONE OF THE FEW HONEST ONES LEFT IN THIS TOWN! HE QUIT THE FORCE AFTER TICKING OFF ALL THE RIGHT PEOPLE...AND MOST OF THE WRONG ONES AS WELL.
WHEN I WAS YOUNG, WE'D BEEN RECEIVING THREATS FROM THE MOB, AND SO DAD HIRED MIKE TO BE MY BODYGUARD.
ONCE I WAS OLD ENOUGH TO LOOK AFTER MYSELF, MIKE WENT TO WORK AT *THE SENTINEL* AS AN INVESTIGATIVE REPORTER.
HIS DETECTIVE SKILLS HAVE SERVED HIM WELL. ONCE A SNOOP, ALWAYS A SNOOP!
AS *THE BUDDHA* SAYS, BRITT-SAN; *"WHAT WE THINK, WE BECOME."*
WHY--?! *MY GOODNESS!* MASTER BRITT! WH-WHEN DID YOU--?!
HIYA, PERKINS! SORRY TO JUST POP UP LIKE THIS...
NONSENSE, MASTER BRITT! IT'S JUST THAT...WE HAD NO IDEA OF WHEN TO EXPECT YOU. SINCE...SINCE YOUR FATHER'S--
I KNOW. I CAN'T EXPRESS HOW SORRY I AM TO HAVE NOT ARRIVED SOONER. JUST TO SEE HIM ONE LAST TIME--

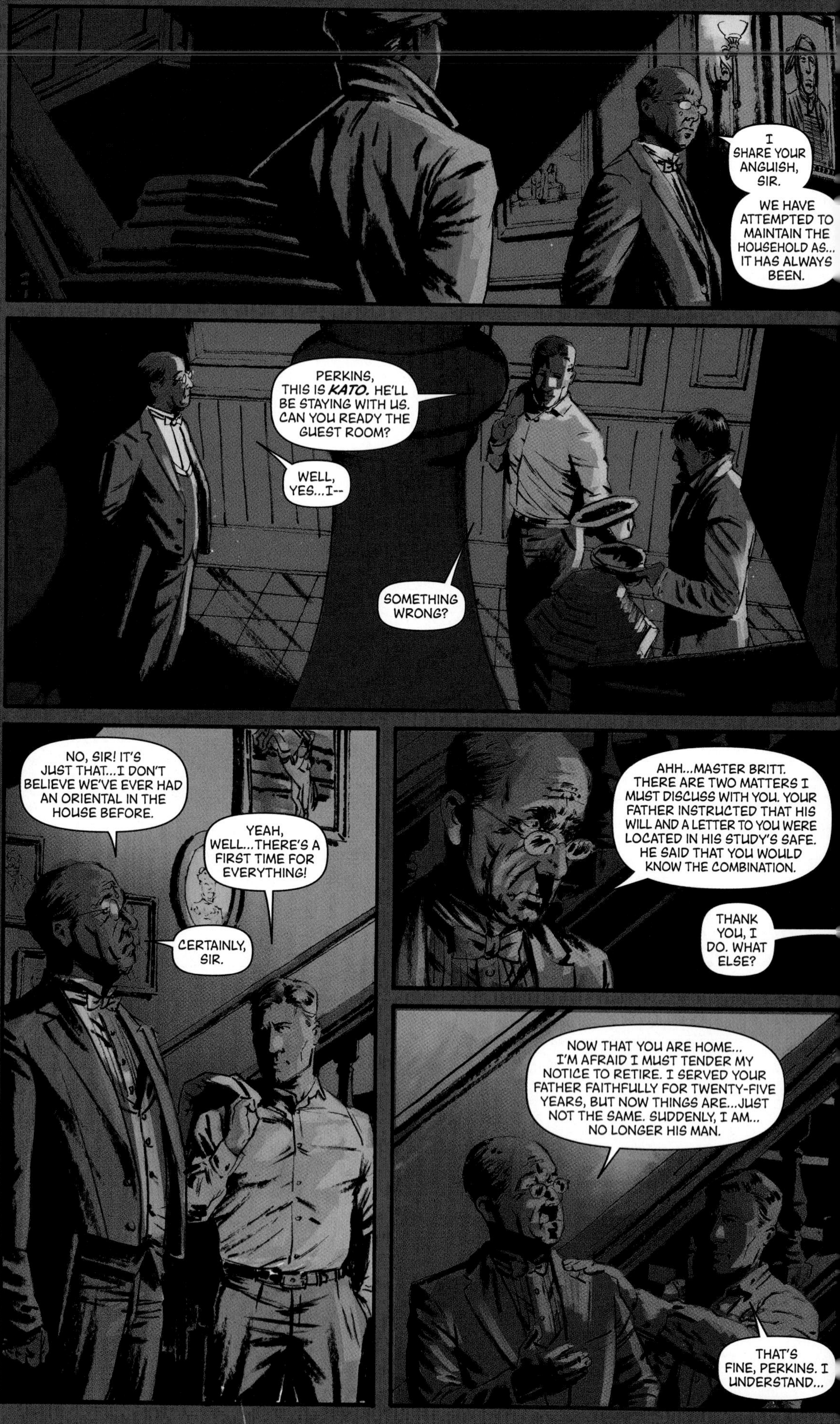
I SHARE YOUR ANGUISH, SIR.
WE HAVE ATTEMPTED TO MAINTAIN THE HOUSEHOLD AS... IT HAS ALWAYS BEEN.
PERKINS, THIS IS *KATO.* HE'LL BE STAYING WITH US. CAN YOU READY THE GUEST ROOM?
WELL, YES...I--
SOMETHING WRONG?
NO, SIR! IT'S JUST THAT...I DON'T BELIEVE WE'VE EVER HAD AN ORIENTAL IN THE HOUSE BEFORE.
YEAH, WELL...THERE'S A FIRST TIME FOR EVERYTHING!
CERTAINLY, SIR.
AHH...MASTER BRITT. THERE ARE TWO MATTERS I MUST DISCUSS WITH YOU. YOUR FATHER INSTRUCTED THAT HIS WILL AND A LETTER TO YOU WERE LOCATED IN HIS STUDY'S SAFE. HE SAID THAT YOU WOULD KNOW THE COMBINATION.
THANK YOU, I DO. WHAT ELSE?
NOW THAT YOU ARE HOME... I'M AFRAID I MUST TENDER MY NOTICE TO RETIRE. I SERVED YOUR FATHER FAITHFULLY FOR TWENTY-FIVE YEARS, BUT NOW THINGS ARE...JUST NOT THE SAME. SUDDENLY, I AM... NO LONGER HIS MAN.
THAT'S FINE, PERKINS. I UNDERSTAND...

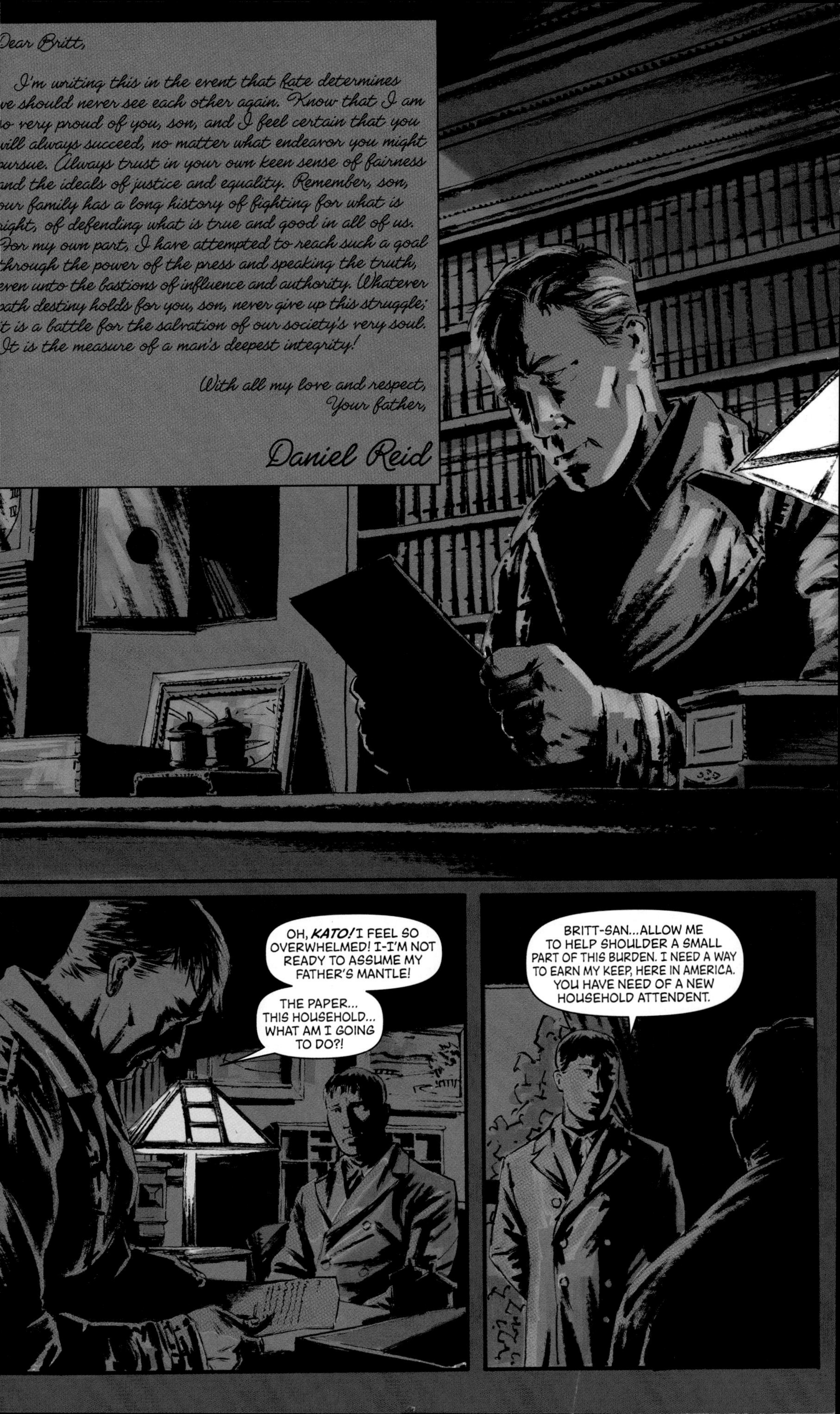
Dear Britt,
I'm writing this in the event that Kate determines we should never see each other again. Know that I am so very proud of you, son, and I feel certain that you will always succeed, no matter what endeavor you might pursue. Always trust in your own keen sense of fairness and the ideals of justice and equality. Remember, son, our family has a long history of fighting for what is right, of defending what is true and good in all of us. For my own part, I have attempted to reach such a goal through the power of the press and speaking the truth, even unto the bastions of influence and authority. Whatever path destiny holds for you, son, never give up this struggle; it is a battle for the salvation of our society's very soul. It is the measure of a man's deepest integrity!
With all my love and respect,
Your father,
Daniel Reid
OH, KATO! I FEEL SO OVERWHELMED! I-I'M NOT READY TO ASSUME MY FATHER'S MANTLE!
THE PAPER... THIS HOUSEHOLD... WHAT AM I GOING TO DO?!
BRITT-SAN...ALLOW ME TO HELP SHOULDER A SMALL PART OF THIS BURDEN. I NEED A WAY TO EARN MY KEEP, HERE IN AMERICA. YOU HAVE NEED OF A NEW HOUSEHOLD ATTENDENT.

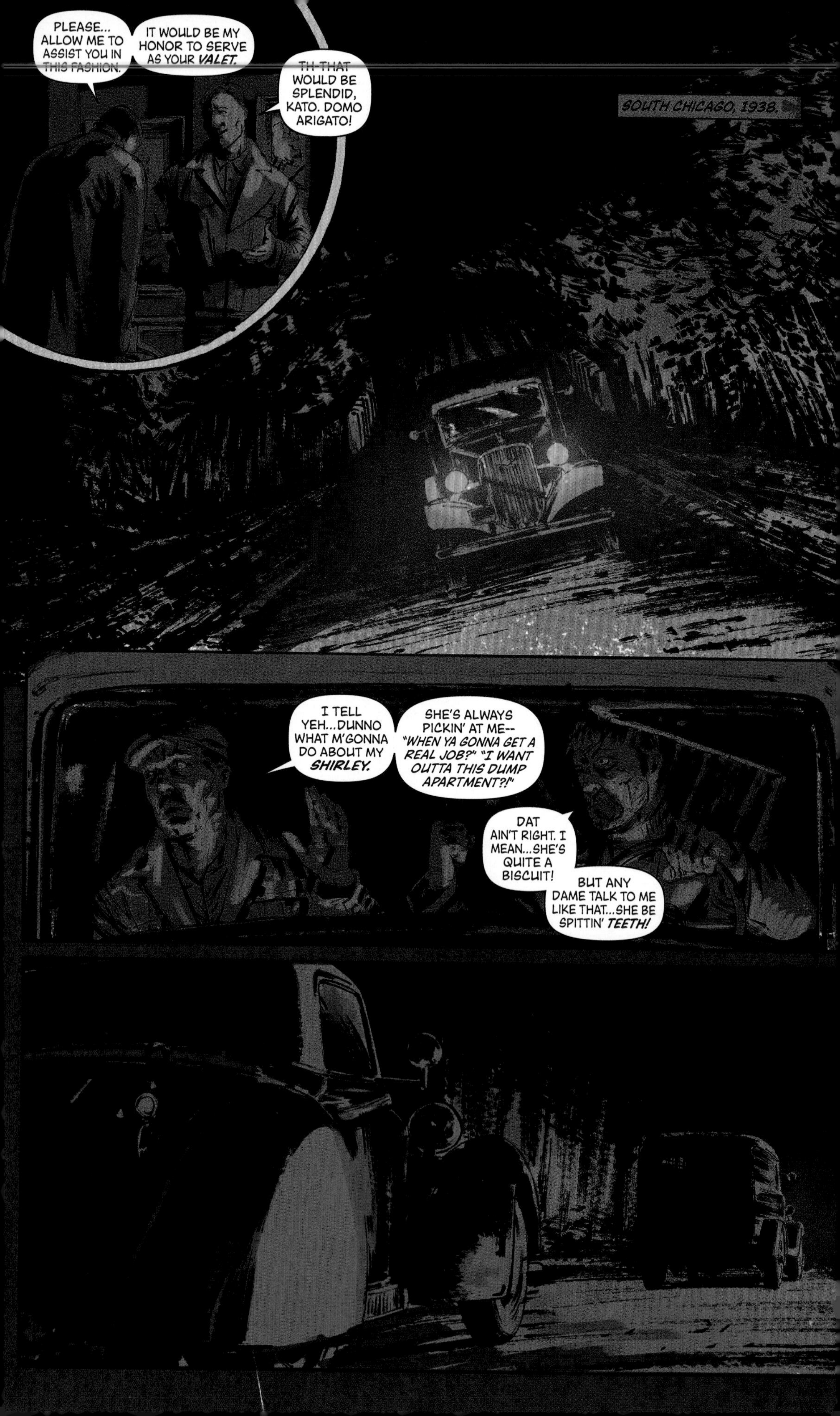
PLEASE... ALLOW ME TO ASSIST YOU IN THIS FASHION.
IT WOULD BE MY HONOR TO SERVE AS YOUR VALET.
TH-THAT WOULD BE SPLENDID, KATO. DOMO ARIGATO!
SOUTH CHICAGO, 1938.
I TELL YEH...DUNNO WHAT M'GONNA DO ABOUT MY SHIRLEY.
SHE'S ALWAYS PICKIN' AT ME-- "WHEN YA GONNA GET A REAL JOB?" "I WANT OUTTA THIS DUMP APARTMENT?!"
DAT AIN'T RIGHT. I MEAN...SHE'S QUITE A BISCUIT!
BUT ANY DAME TALK TO ME LIKE THAT...SHE BE SPITTIN' TEETH!

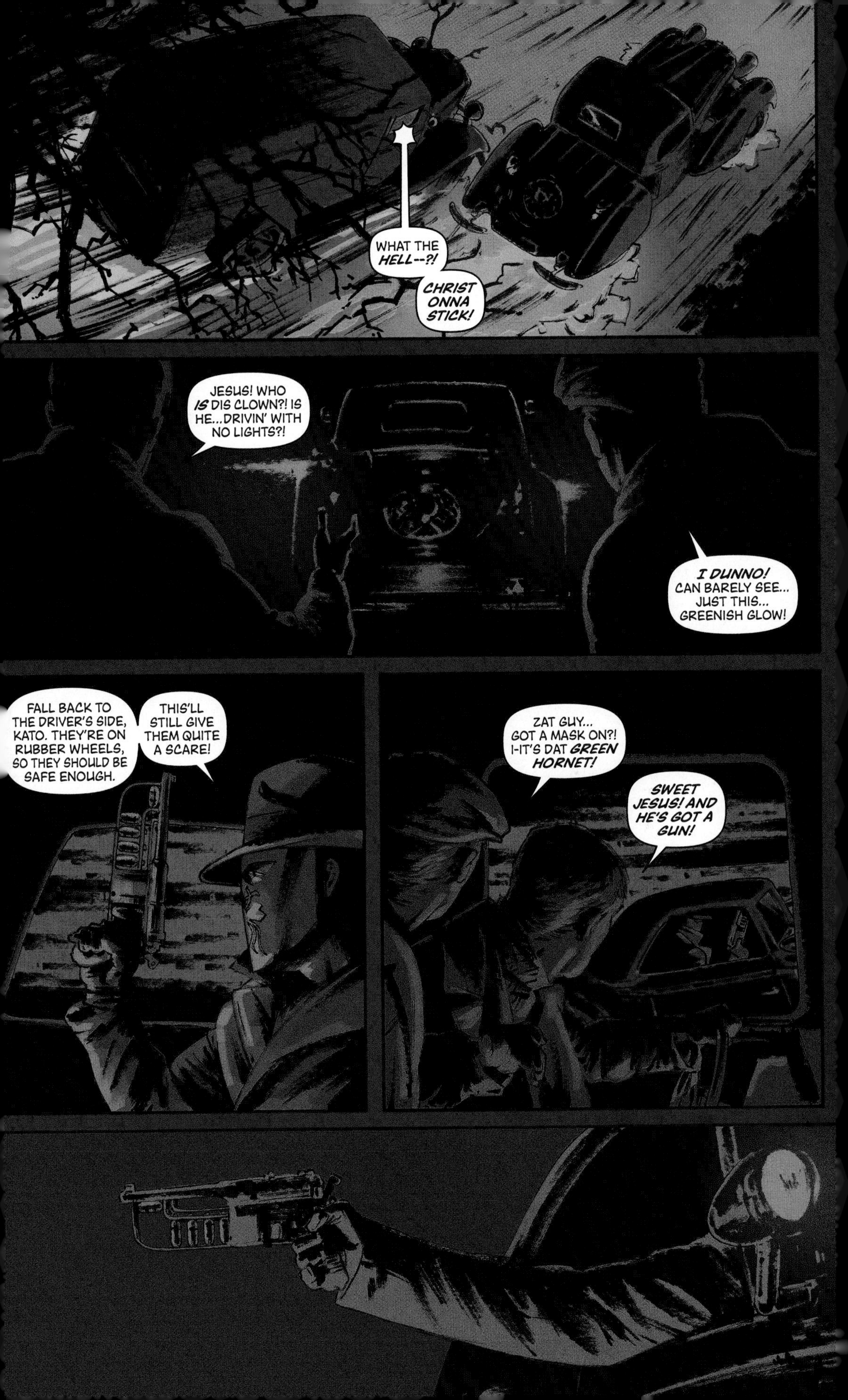
WHAT THE *HELL--?!*
CHRIST ONNA STICK!
JESUS! WHO *IS* DIS CLOWN?! IS HE...DRIVIN' WITH NO LIGHTS?!
I DUNNO! CAN BARELY SEE... JUST THIS... GREENISH GLOW!
FALL BACK TO THE DRIVER'S SIDE, KATO. THEY'RE ON RUBBER WHEELS, SO THEY SHOULD BE SAFE ENOUGH.
THIS'LL STILL GIVE THEM QUITE A SCARE!
ZAT GUY... GOT A MASK ON?! I-IT'S DAT *GREEN HORNET!*
SWEET JESUS! AND HE'S GOT A GUN!

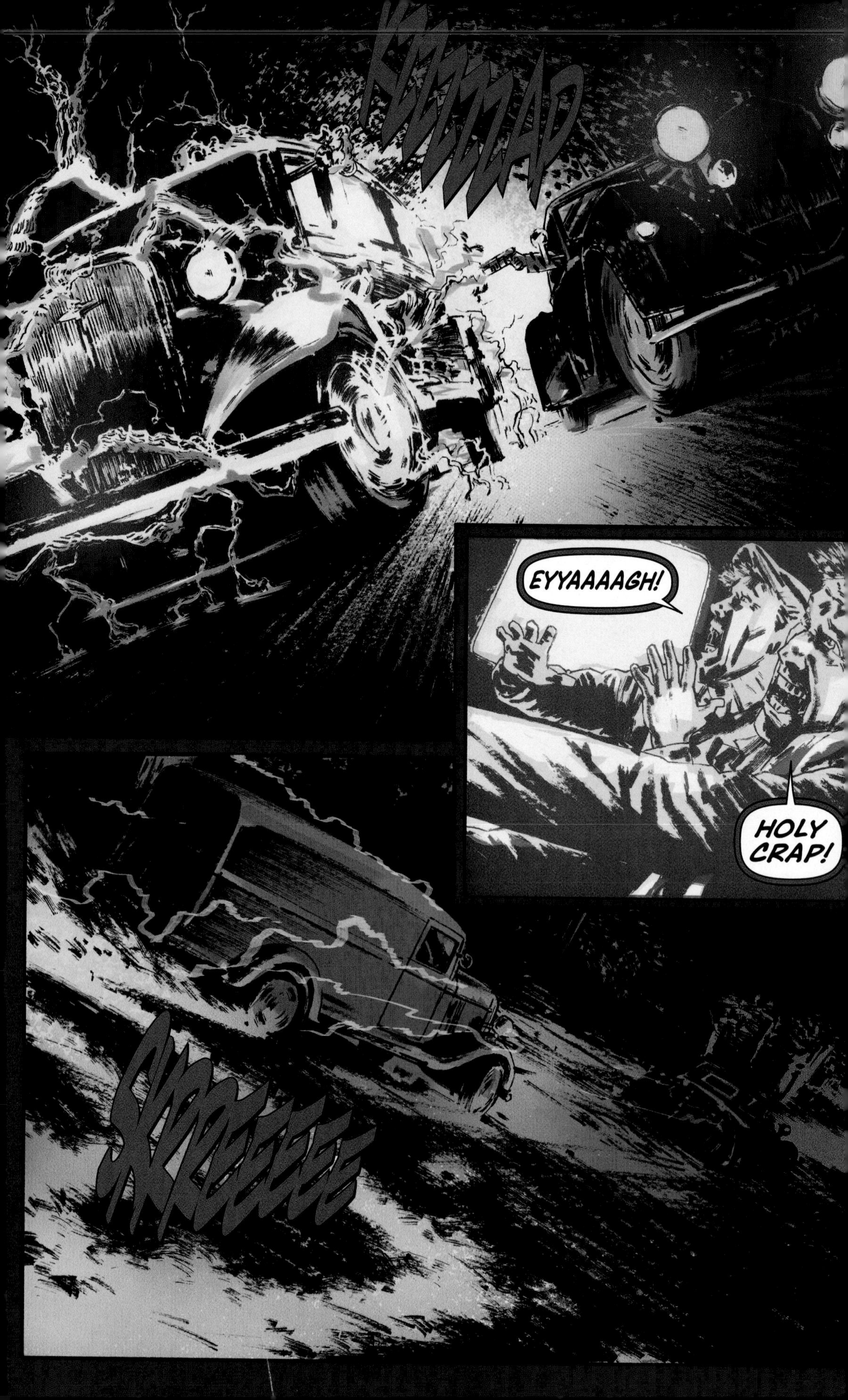
EYYAAAAGH!
HOLY CRAP!

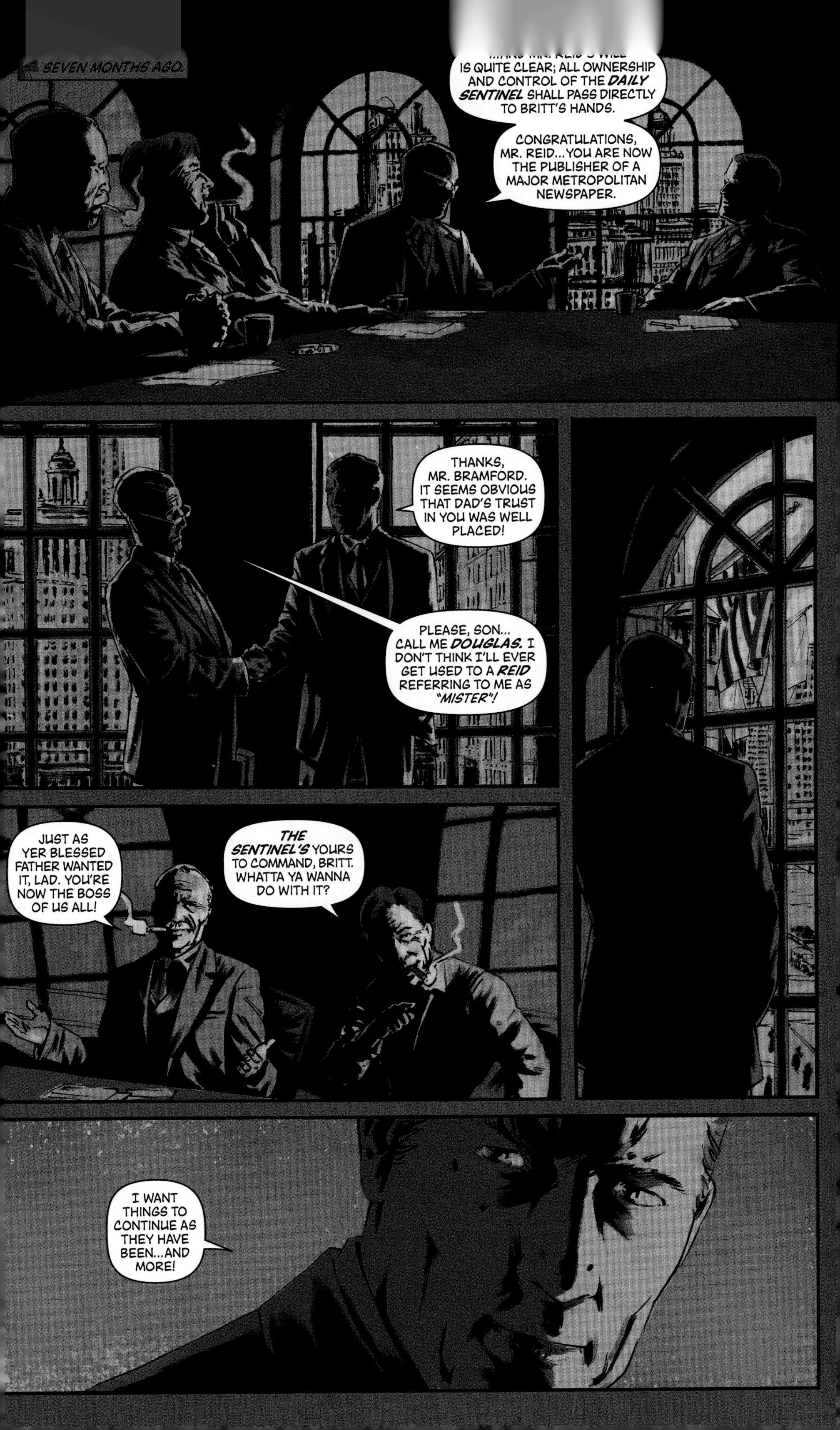
SEVEN MONTHS AGO.
IS QUITE CLEAR; ALL OWNERSHIP AND CONTROL OF THE *DAILY SENTINEL* SHALL PASS DIRECTLY TO BRITT'S HANDS.
CONGRATULATIONS, MR. REID... YOU ARE NOW THE PUBLISHER OF A MAJOR METROPOLITAN NEWSPAPER.
THANKS, MR. BRAMFORD. IT SEEMS OBVIOUS THAT DAD'S TRUST IN YOU WAS WELL PLACED!
PLEASE, SON... CALL ME *DOUGLAS.* I DON'T THINK I'LL EVER GET USED TO A *REID* REFERRING TO ME AS *"MISTER"*!
JUST AS YER BLESSED FATHER WANTED IT, LAD. YOU'RE NOW THE BOSS OF US ALL!
THE SENTINEL'S YOURS TO COMMAND, BRITT. WHATTA YA WANNA DO WITH IT?
I WANT THINGS TO CONTINUE AS THEY HAVE BEEN... AND MORE!

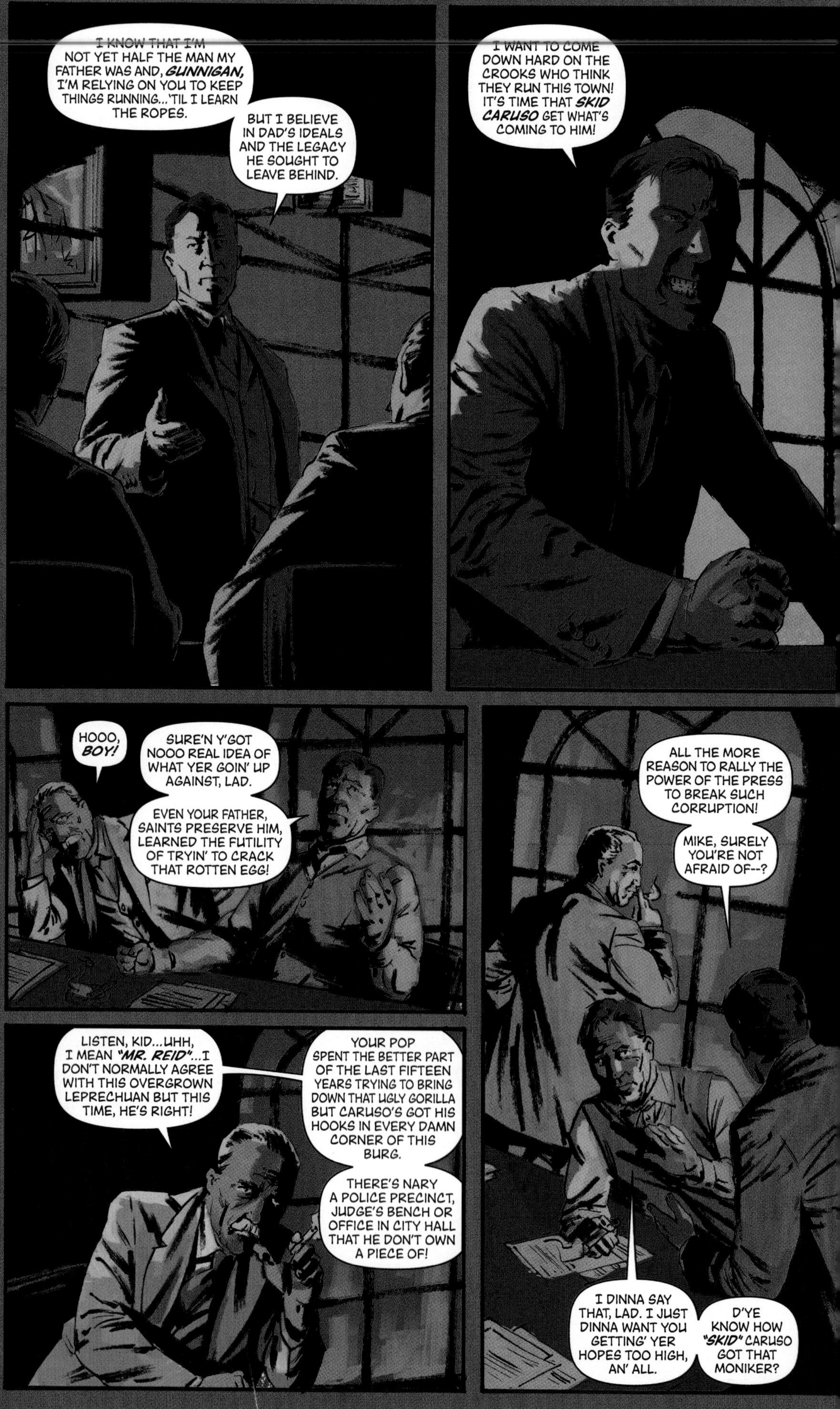

I KNOW THAT I'M NOT YET HALF THE MAN MY FATHER WAS AND, GUNNIGAN, I'M RELYING ON YOU TO KEEP THINGS RUNNING...'TIL I LEARN THE ROPES.
BUT I BELIEVE IN DAD'S IDEALS AND THE LEGACY HE SOUGHT TO LEAVE BEHIND.
I WANT TO COME DOWN HARD ON THE CROOKS WHO THINK THEY RUN THIS TOWN! IT'S TIME THAT SKID CARUSO GET WHAT'S COMING TO HIM!
HOOO, BOY!
SURE'N Y'GOT NOOO REAL IDEA OF WHAT YER GOIN' UP AGAINST, LAD.
EVEN YOUR FATHER, SAINTS PRESERVE HIM, LEARNED THE FUTILITY OF TRYIN' TO CRACK THAT ROTTEN EGG!
ALL THE MORE REASON TO RALLY THE POWER OF THE PRESS TO BREAK SUCH CORRUPTION!
MIKE, SURELY YOU'RE NOT AFRAID OF--?
LISTEN, KID...UHH, I MEAN "MR. REID"...I DON'T NORMALLY AGREE WITH THIS OVERGROWN LEPRECHUAN BUT THIS TIME, HE'S RIGHT!
YOUR POP SPENT THE BETTER PART OF THE LAST FIFTEEN YEARS TRYING TO BRING DOWN THAT UGLY GORILLA BUT CARUSO'S GOT HIS HOOKS IN EVERY DAMN CORNER OF THIS BURG.
THERE'S NARY A POLICE PRECINCT, JUDGE'S BENCH OR OFFICE IN CITY HALL THAT HE DON'T OWN A PIECE OF!
I DINNA SAY THAT, LAD. I JUST DINNA WANT YOU GETTING' YER HOPES TOO HIGH, AN' ALL.
D'YE KNOW HOW "SKID" CARUSO GOT THAT MONIKER?

...WAS BACK IN 19 AN' 19...CARUSO WAS AN UP-AN-COMIN' HOOLIGAN IN TH' SOUTHSIDE MOB. KNOWN FER IS BRUTAL WAYS AND DANDY DUDS.

RIVAL GANG TRIED TAKIN' 'IM FER *ONE-WAY RIDE* BUT, WHEN THEY THREW HIM OUT OF THE CAR...FAIR *VINCENT* HUNG ON--THO' HE CAUGHT FINE FACEFUL O' PAVEMENT.

"HE PLUGGED THOSE WESTSIDE TOUGHS USIN' ONE O' THEIR OWN GUNS!"

HE'S TENACIOUS AS A SNAPPIN' TURTLE, LAD.

IN THE END, EVEN YOUR FATHER--GOD REST HIS SOUL--WAS OVERCOME BY THE BATTLE GONE SOUR. FOR ALL DAN'L'S BRILLIANT, HEARTFELT EDITORIALS... CARUSO STILL RULES CHI-TOWN FROM HIS PRIVATE CASTLE IN THE *IMPERIAL HOTEL!*

AGAIN...ALL THE MORE REASON TO TRY AND TAKE THIS BASTARD DOWN!

EXTRY! EXTRY!

NEW PUBLISHER SETS SIGHTS ON MOB INFLUENCE! EXTRY!

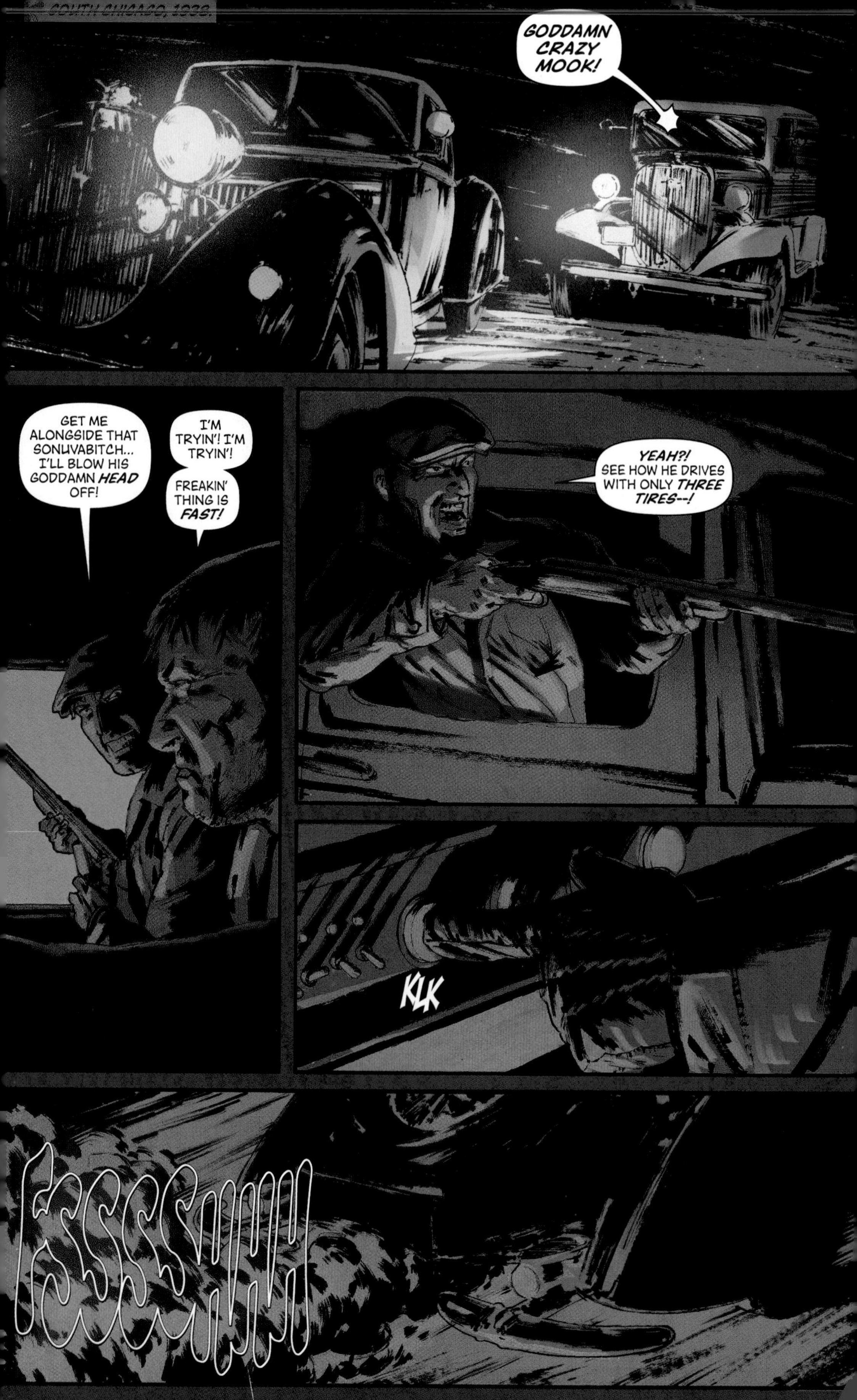
SOUTH CHICAGO,
GODDAMN CRAZY MOOK!
GET ME ALONGSIDE THAT SONUVABITCH... I'LL BLOW HIS GODDAMN *HEAD* OFF!
I'M TRYIN'! I'M TRYIN'!
FREAKIN' THING IS *FAST!*
YEAH?! SEE HOW HE DRIVES WITH ONLY *THREE TIRES--!*
KLK
FSSSSHHH

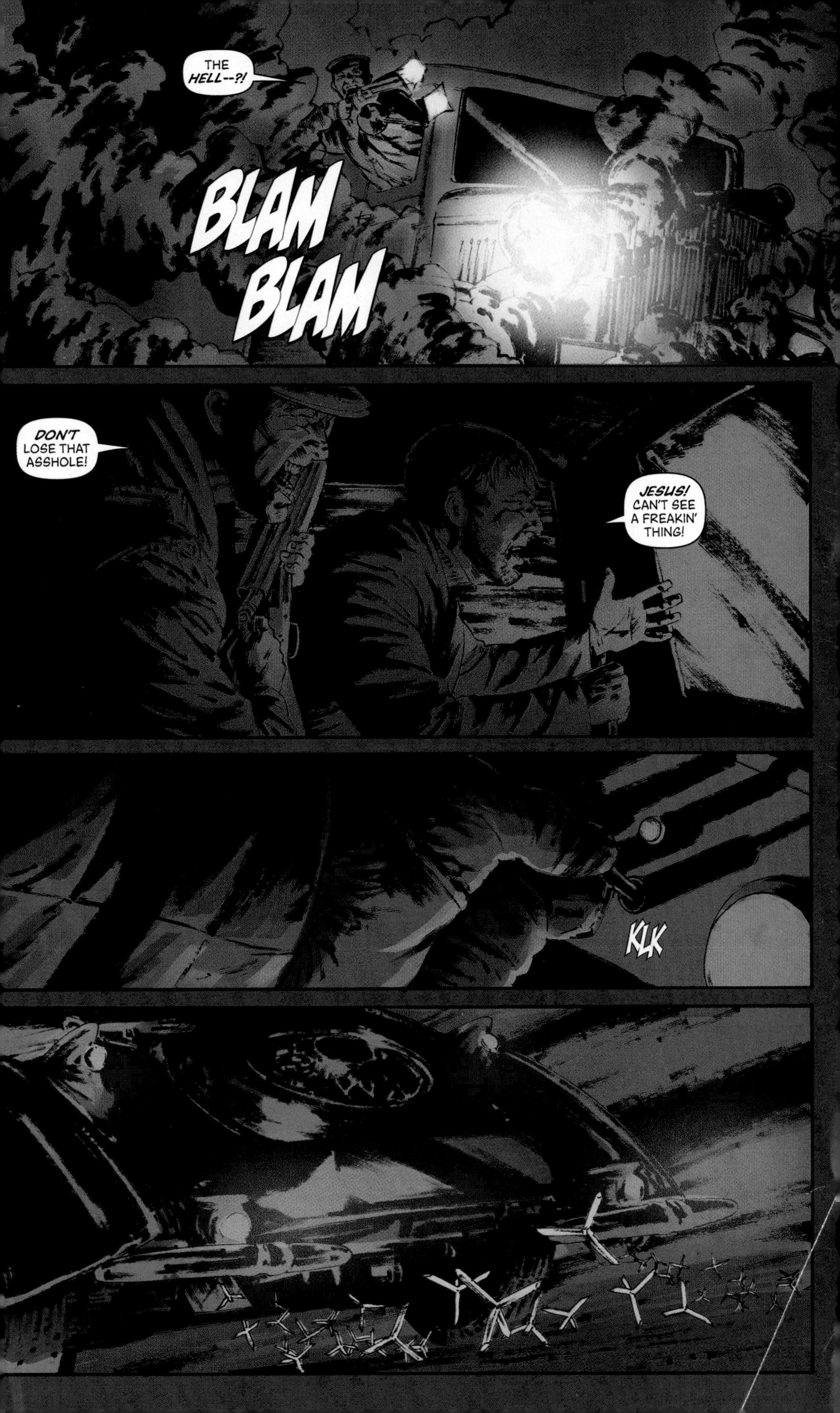
THE *HELL*--?!
BLAM BLAM
DON'T LOSE THAT ASSHOLE!
JESUS! CAN'T SEE A FREAKIN' THING!
KLK

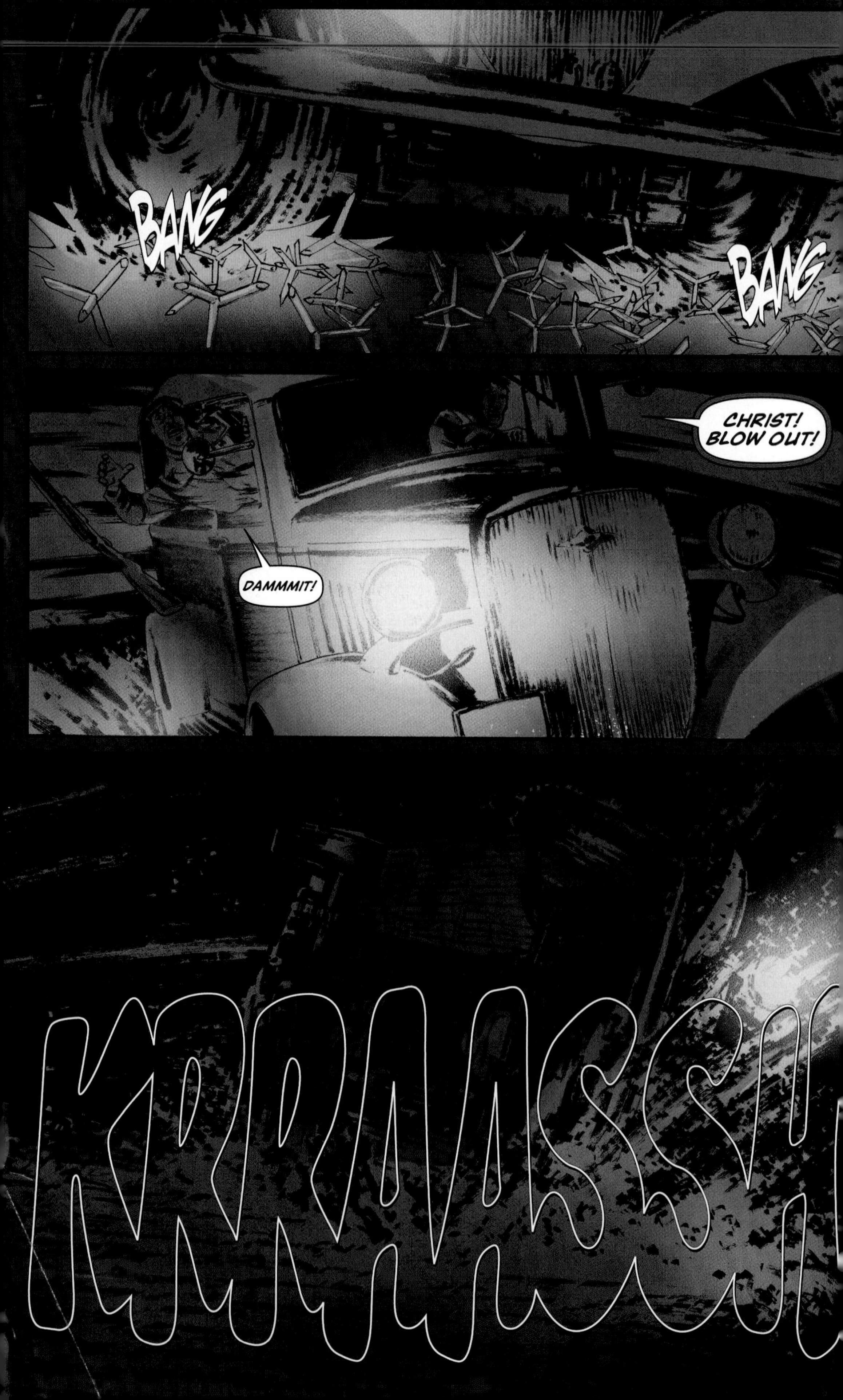
BANG
BANG
CHRIST! BLOW OUT!
DAMMMIT!
KRRAASCH

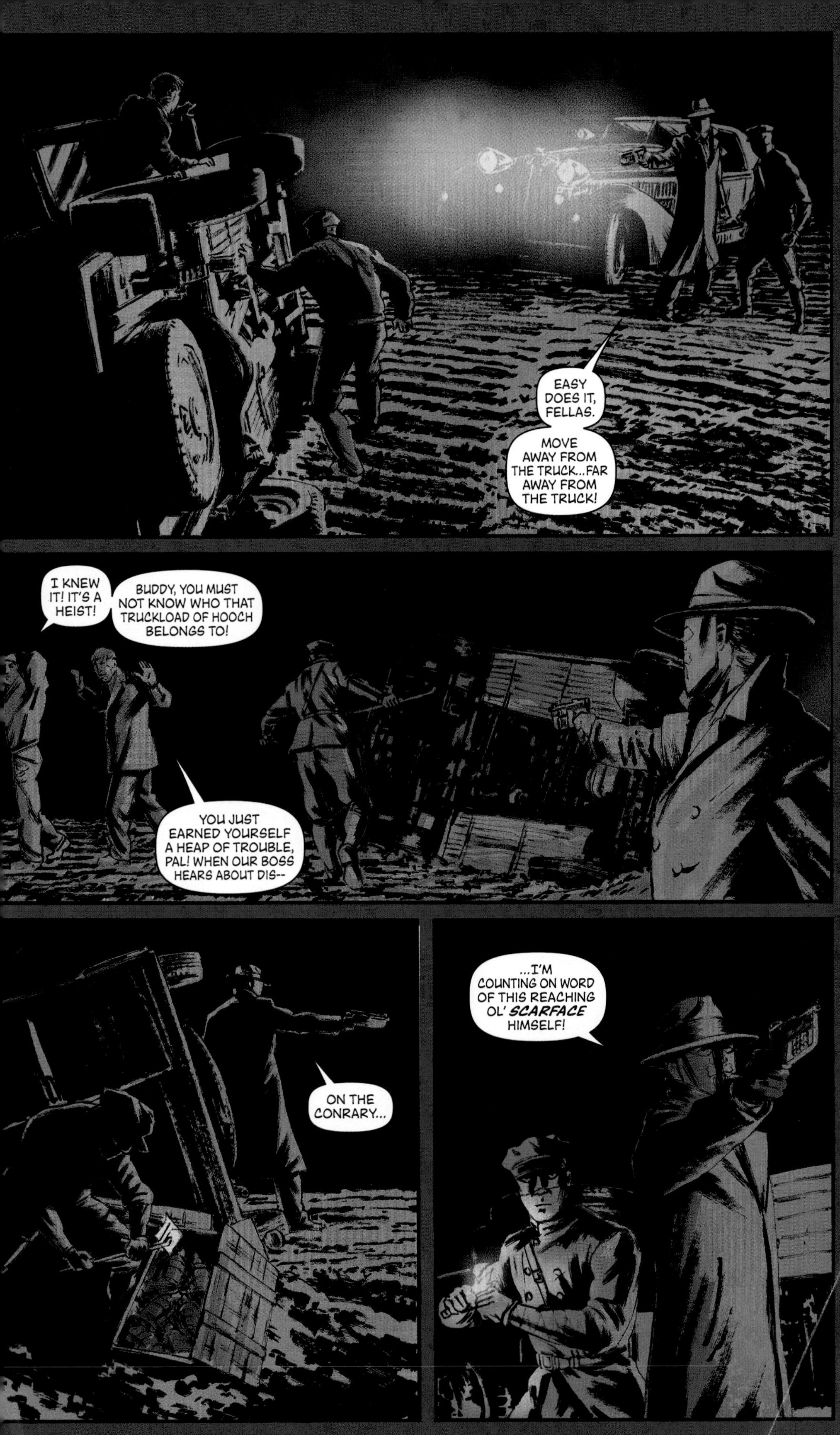
EASY DOES IT, FELLAS.
MOVE AWAY FROM THE TRUCK...FAR AWAY FROM THE TRUCK!
I KNEW IT! IT'S A HEIST!
BUDDY, YOU MUST NOT KNOW WHO THAT TRUCKLOAD OF HOOCH BELONGS TO!
YOU JUST EARNED YOURSELF A HEAP OF TROUBLE, PAL! WHEN OUR BOSS HEARS ABOUT DIS--
ON THE CONRARY...
...I'M COUNTING ON WORD OF THIS REACHING OL' *SCARFACE* HIMSELF!

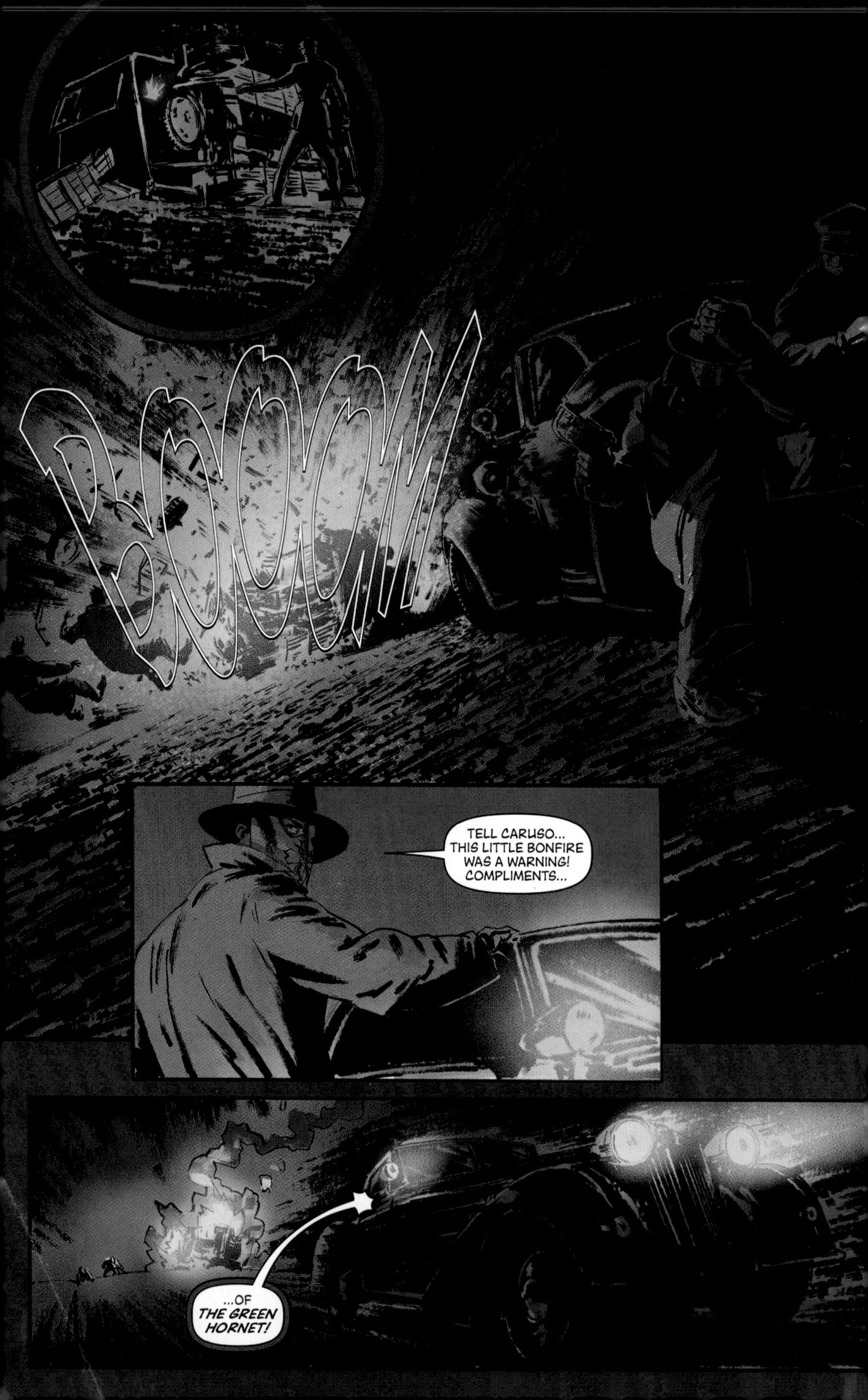
BOOOM
TELL CARUSO... THIS LITTLE BONFIRE WAS A WARNING! COMPLIMENTS...
...OF *THE GREEN HORNET!*

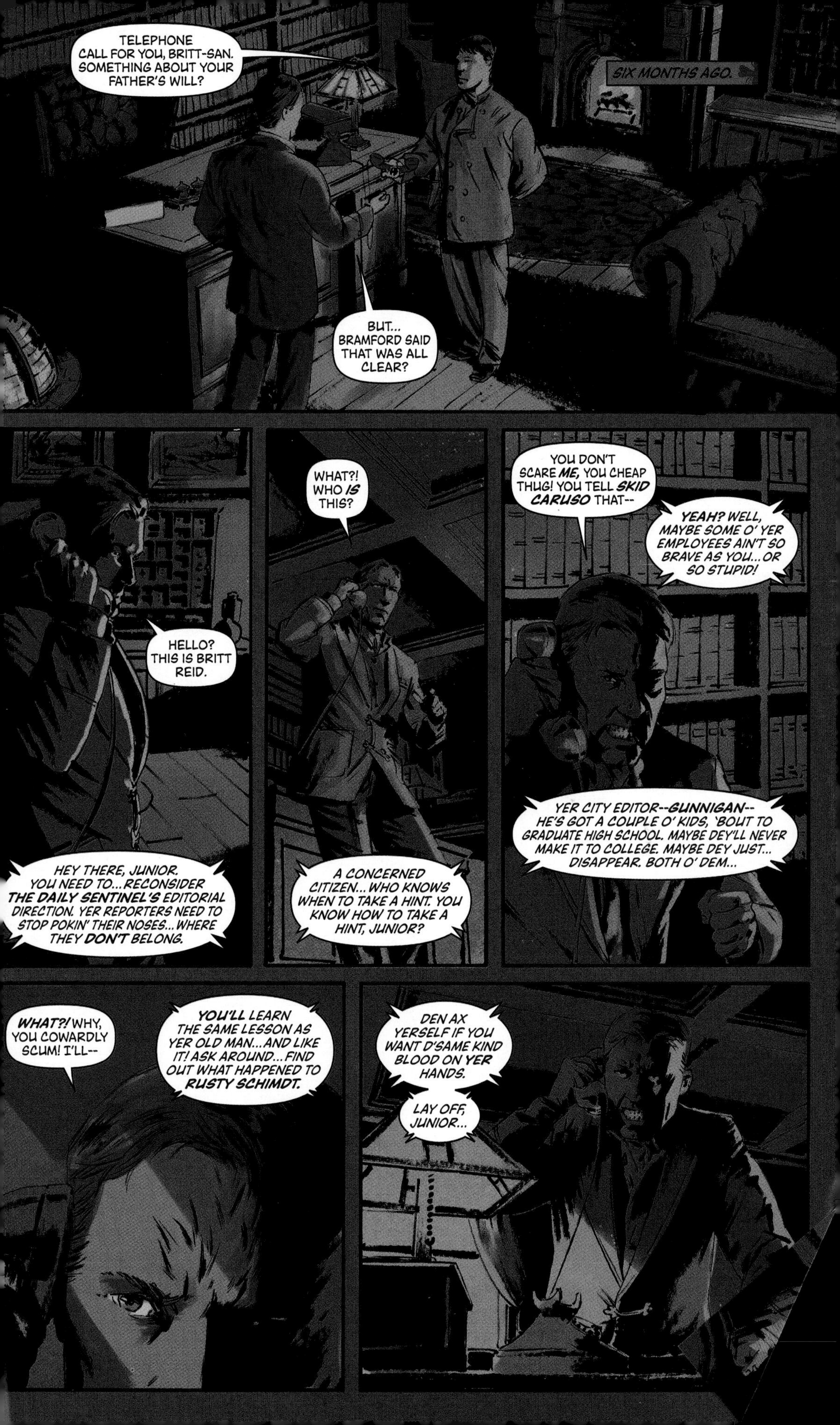
TELEPHONE CALL FOR YOU, BRITT-SAN. SOMETHING ABOUT YOUR FATHER'S WILL?
SIX MONTHS AGO.
BUT... BRAMFORD SAID THAT WAS ALL CLEAR?
HELLO? THIS IS BRITT REID.
HEY THERE, JUNIOR. YOU NEED TO... RECONSIDER THE DAILY SENTINEL'S EDITORIAL DIRECTION. YER REPORTERS NEED TO STOP POKIN' THEIR NOSES... WHERE THEY DON'T BELONG.
WHAT?! WHO IS THIS?
A CONCERNED CITIZEN... WHO KNOWS WHEN TO TAKE A HINT. YOU KNOW HOW TO TAKE A HINT, JUNIOR?
YOU DON'T SCARE ME, YOU CHEAP THUG! YOU TELL SKID CARUSO THAT--
YEAH? WELL, MAYBE SOME O' YER EMPLOYEES AIN'T SO BRAVE AS YOU... OR SO STUPID!
YER CITY EDITOR--GUNNIGAN-- HE'S GOT A COUPLE O' KIDS, 'BOUT TO GRADUATE HIGH SCHOOL. MAYBE DEY'LL NEVER MAKE IT TO COLLEGE. MAYBE DEY JUST... DISAPPEAR. BOTH O' DEM...
WHAT?! WHY, YOU COWARDLY SCUM! I'LL--
YOU'LL LEARN THE SAME LESSON AS YER OLD MAN... AND LIKE IT! ASK AROUND... FIND OUT WHAT HAPPENED TO RUSTY SCHIMDT.
DEN AX YERSELF IF YOU WANT D'SAME KIND BLOOD ON YER HANDS.
LAY OFF, JUNIOR...

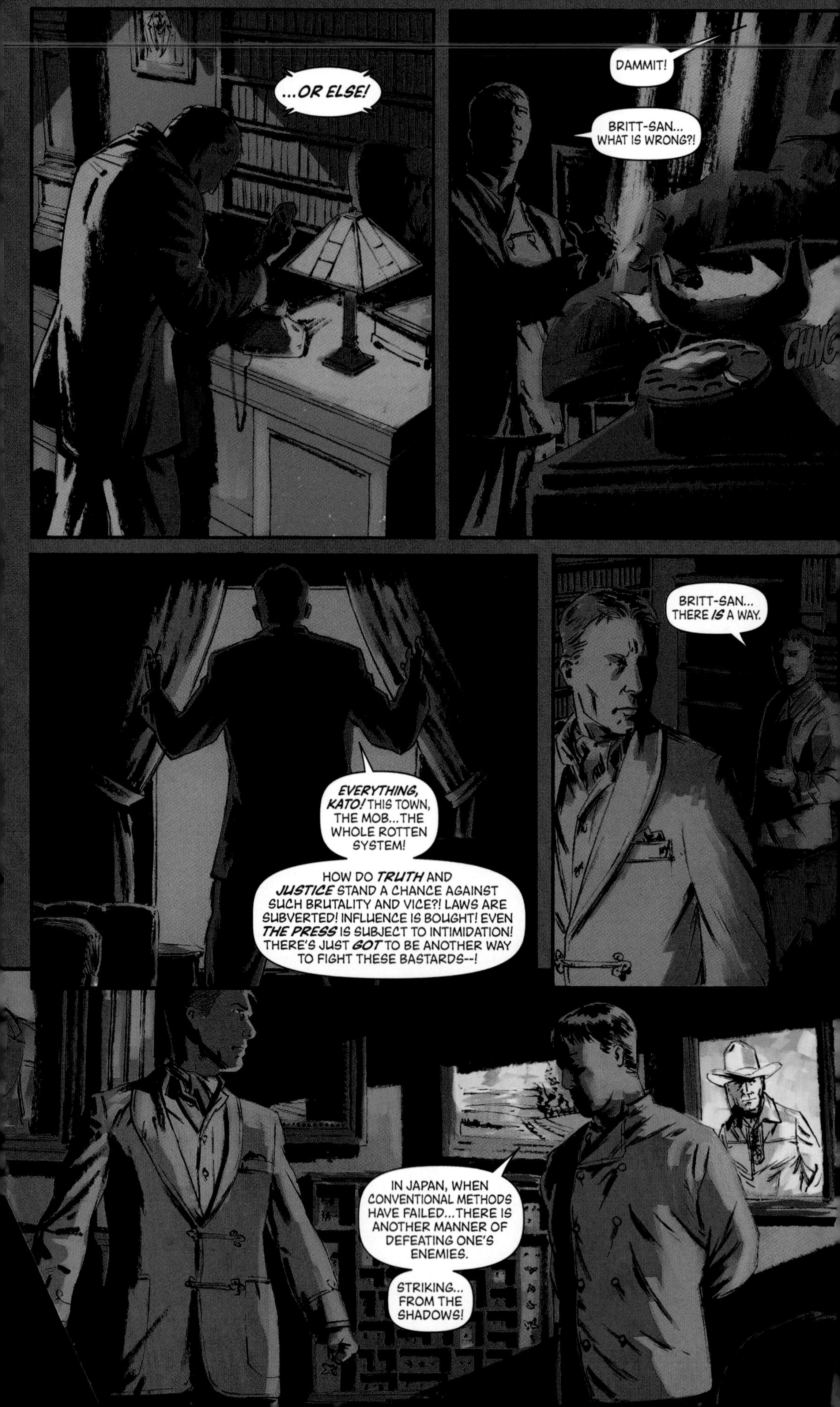
...OR ELSE!
DAMMIT!
BRITT-SAN... WHAT IS WRONG?!
CHNG
EVERYTHING, KATO! THIS TOWN, THE MOB...THE WHOLE ROTTEN SYSTEM!
HOW DO TRUTH AND JUSTICE STAND A CHANCE AGAINST SUCH BRUTALITY AND VICE?! LAWS ARE SUBVERTED! INFLUENCE IS BOUGHT! EVEN THE PRESS IS SUBJECT TO INTIMIDATION! THERE'S JUST GOT TO BE ANOTHER WAY TO FIGHT THESE BASTARDS--!
BRITT-SAN... THERE IS A WAY.
IN JAPAN, WHEN CONVENTIONAL METHODS HAVE FAILED...THERE IS ANOTHER MANNER OF DEFEATING ONE'S ENEMIES.
STRIKING... FROM THE SHADOWS!

ISSUE SIX

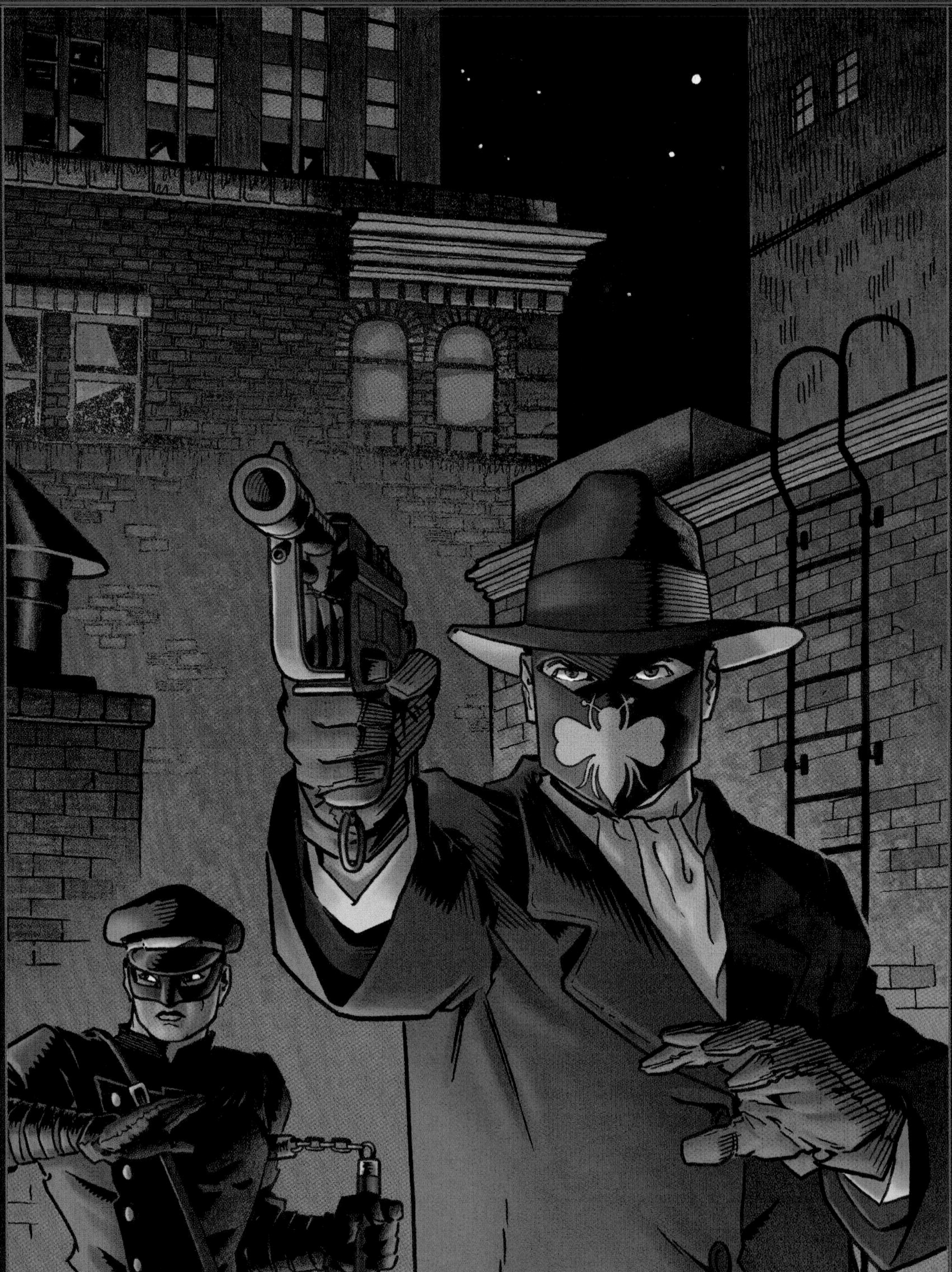

six cover by MATT WAGNER

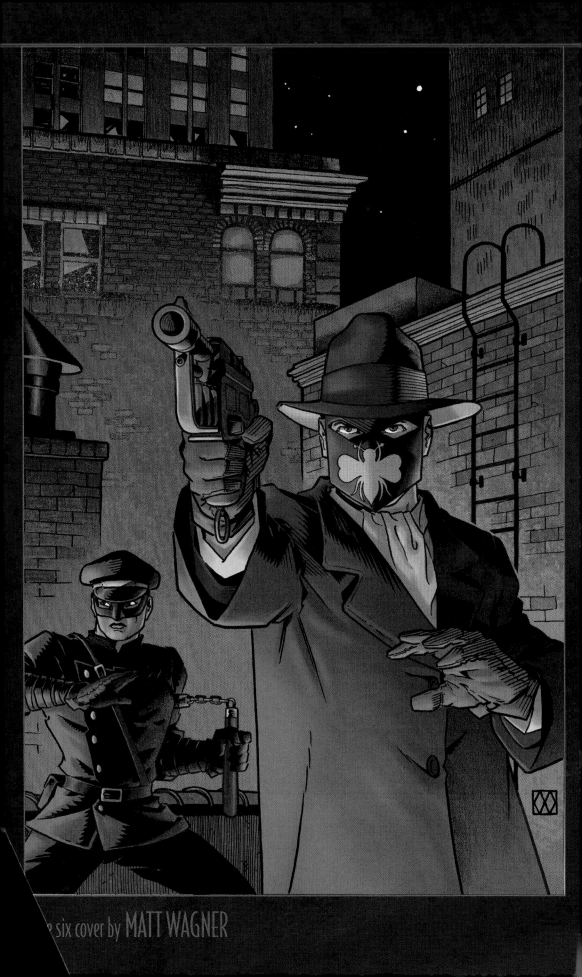

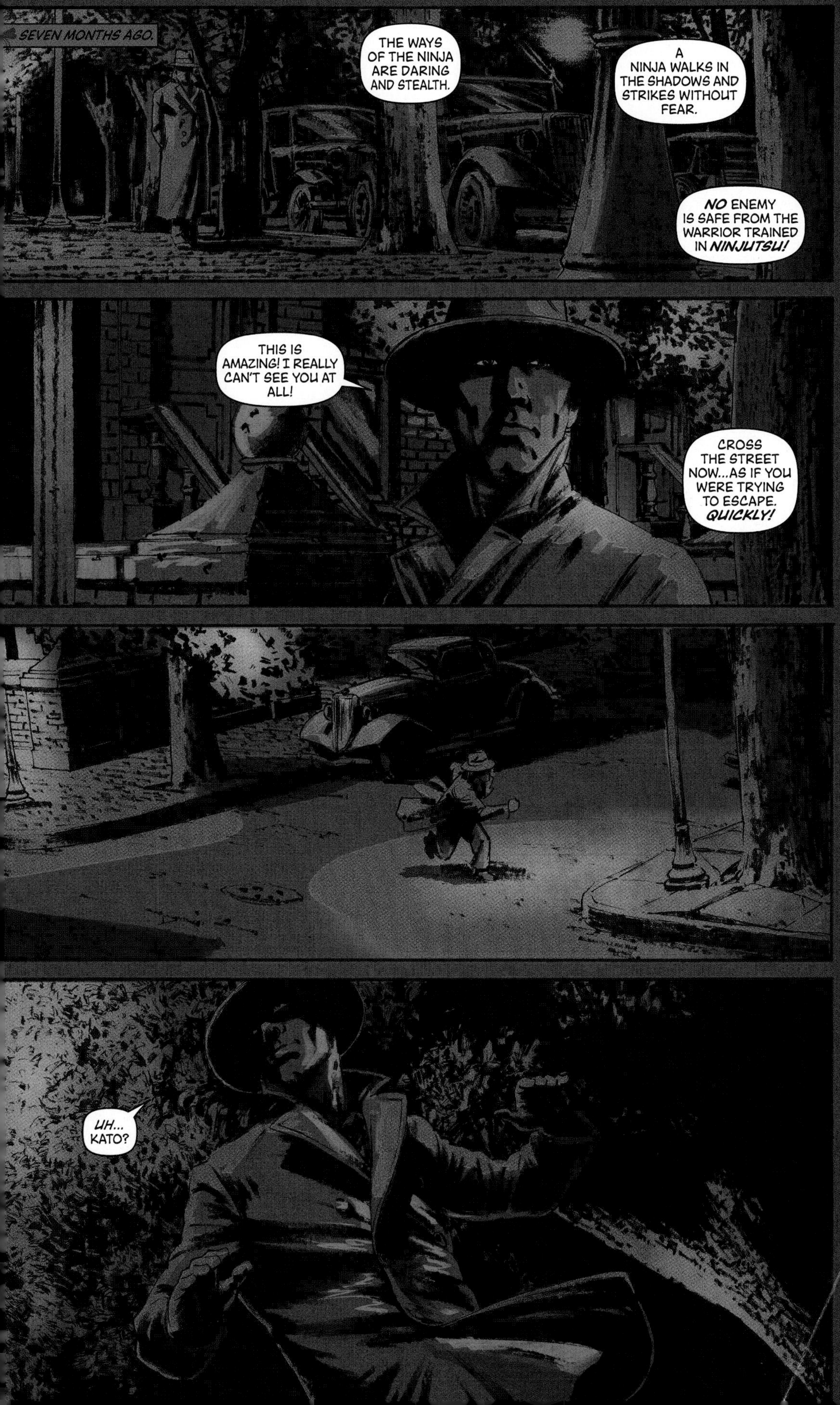
SEVEN MONTHS AGO.
THE WAYS OF THE NINJA ARE DARING AND STEALTH.
A NINJA WALKS IN THE SHADOWS AND STRIKES WITHOUT FEAR.
NO ENEMY IS SAFE FROM THE WARRIOR TRAINED IN NINJUTSU!
THIS IS AMAZING! I REALLY CAN'T SEE YOU AT ALL!
CROSS THE STREET NOW...AS IF YOU WERE TRYING TO ESCAPE. QUICKLY!
UH... KATO?

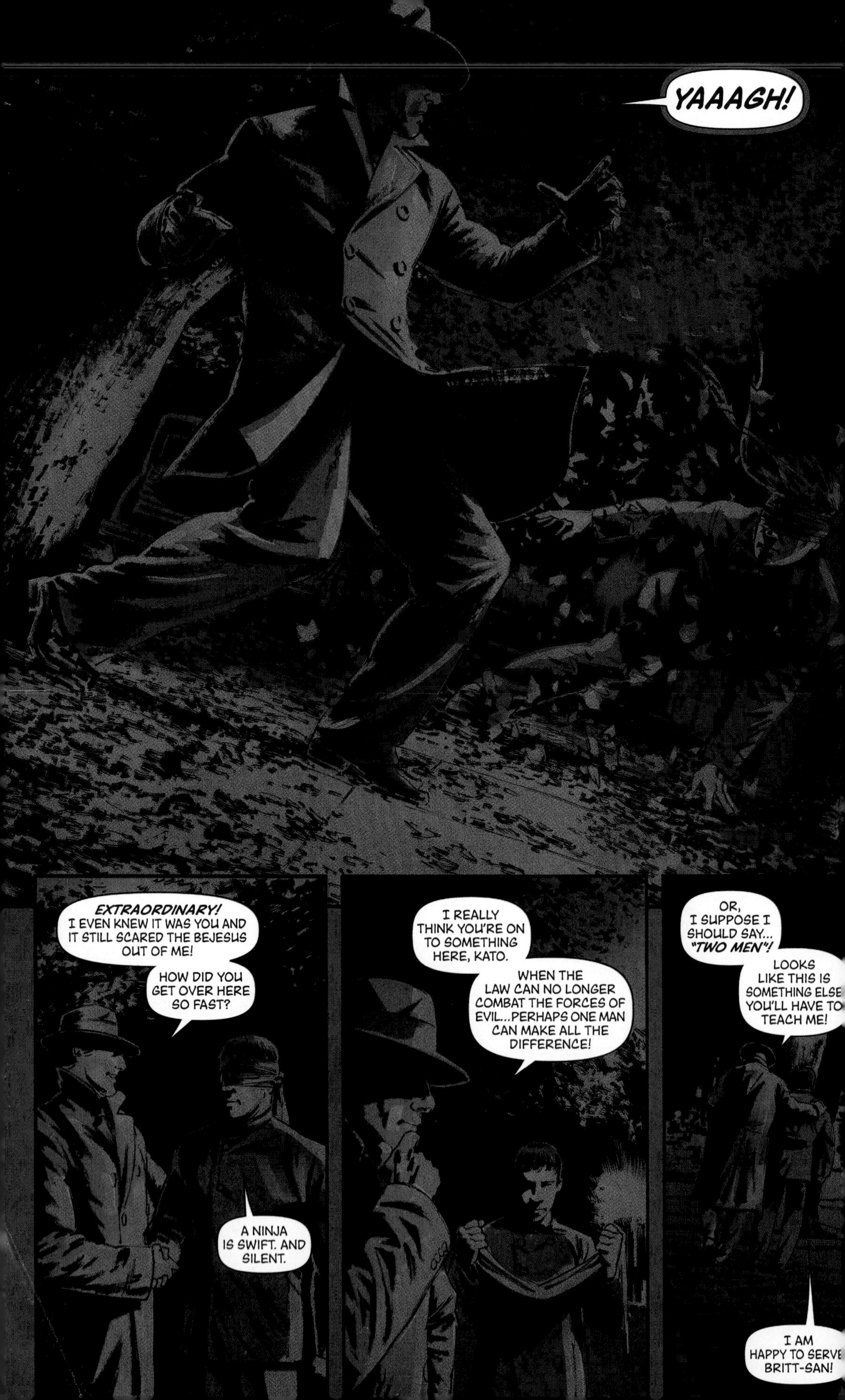
YAAAGH!
EXTRAORDINARY! I EVEN KNEW IT WAS YOU AND IT STILL SCARED THE BEJESUS OUT OF ME!
HOW DID YOU GET OVER HERE SO FAST?
A NINJA IS SWIFT. AND SILENT.
I REALLY THINK YOU'RE ON TO SOMETHING HERE, KATO.
WHEN THE LAW CAN NO LONGER COMBAT THE FORCES OF EVIL...PERHAPS ONE MAN CAN MAKE ALL THE DIFFERENCE!
OR, I SUPPOSE I SHOULD SAY... "TWO MEN"!
LOOKS LIKE THIS IS SOMETHING ELSE YOU'LL HAVE TO TEACH ME!
I AM HAPPY TO SERVE BRITT-SAN!

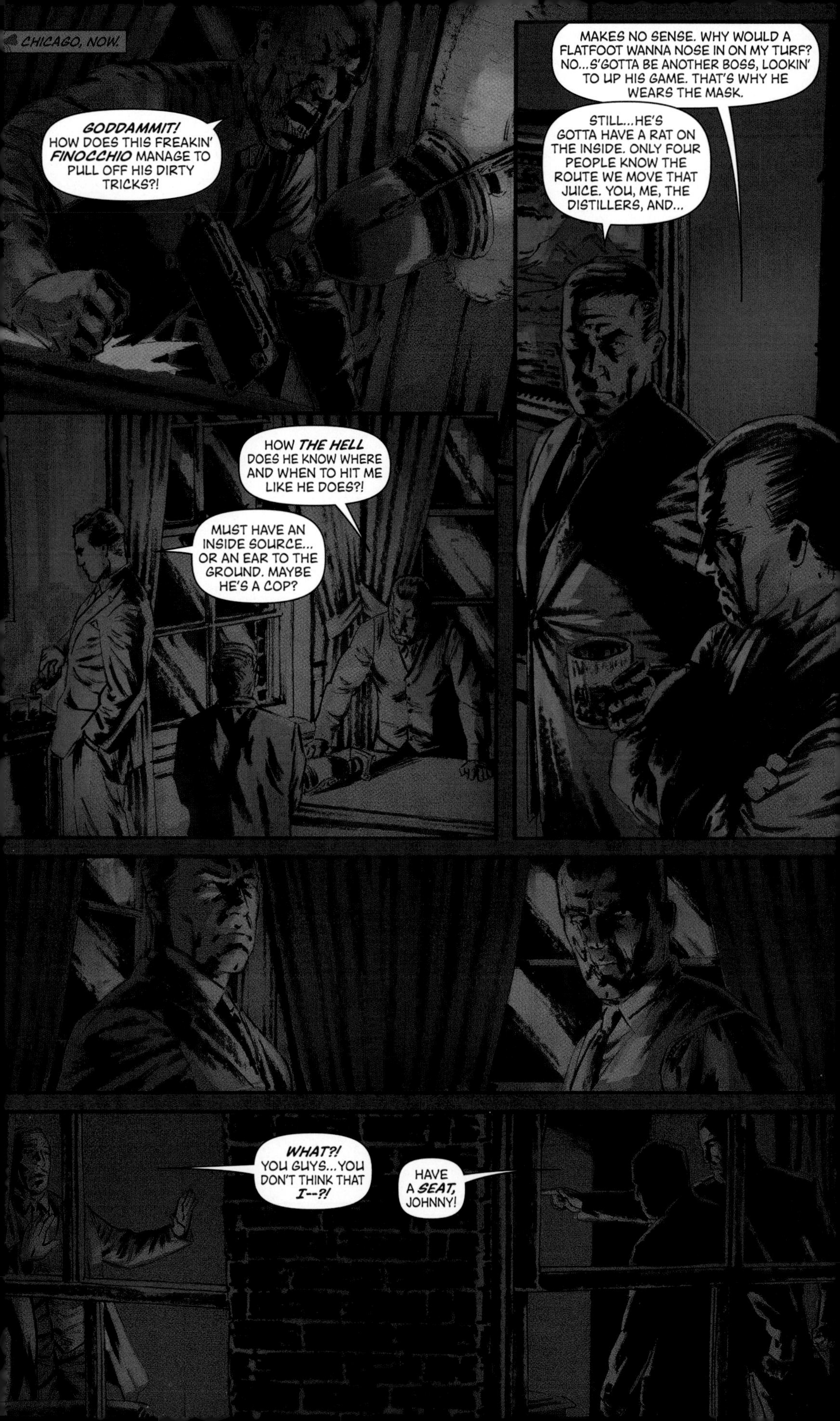
CHICAGO, NOW.
GODDAMMIT! HOW DOES THIS FREAKIN' FINOCCHIO MANAGE TO PULL OFF HIS DIRTY TRICKS?!
HOW THE HELL DOES HE KNOW WHERE AND WHEN TO HIT ME LIKE HE DOES?!
MUST HAVE AN INSIDE SOURCE... OR AN EAR TO THE GROUND. MAYBE HE'S A COP?
MAKES NO SENSE. WHY WOULD A FLATFOOT WANNA NOSE IN ON MY TURF? NO...S'GOTTA BE ANOTHER BOSS, LOOKIN' TO UP HIS GAME. THAT'S WHY HE WEARS THE MASK.
STILL...HE'S GOTTA HAVE A RAT ON THE INSIDE. ONLY FOUR PEOPLE KNOW THE ROUTE WE MOVE THAT JUICE. YOU, ME, THE DISTILLERS, AND...
WHAT?! YOU GUYS...YOU DON'T THINK THAT I--?!
HAVE A SEAT, JOHNNY!

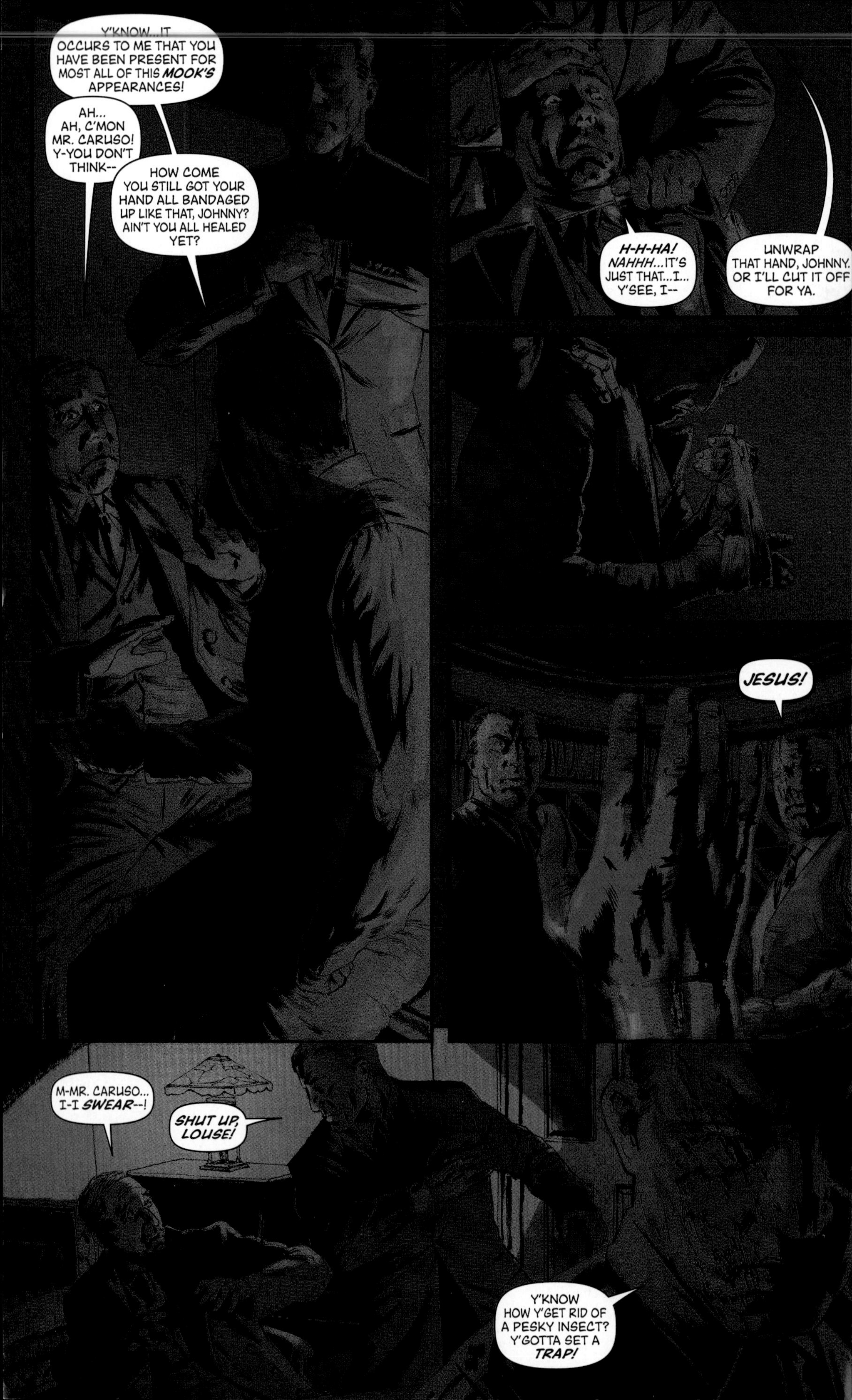
Y'KNOW...IT OCCURS TO ME THAT YOU HAVE BEEN PRESENT FOR MOST ALL OF THIS MOOK'S APPEARANCES!
AH... AH, C'MON MR. CARUSO! Y-YOU DON'T THINK--
HOW COME YOU STILL GOT YOUR HAND ALL BANDAGED UP LIKE THAT, JOHNNY? AIN'T YOU ALL HEALED YET?
H-H-HA! NAHHH...IT'S JUST THAT...I... Y'SEE, I--
UNWRAP THAT HAND, JOHNNY. OR I'LL CUT IT OFF FOR YA.
JESUS!
M-MR. CARUSO... I-I SWEAR--!
SHUT UP, LOUSE!
Y'KNOW HOW Y'GET RID OF A PESKY INSECT? Y'GOTTA SET A TRAP!

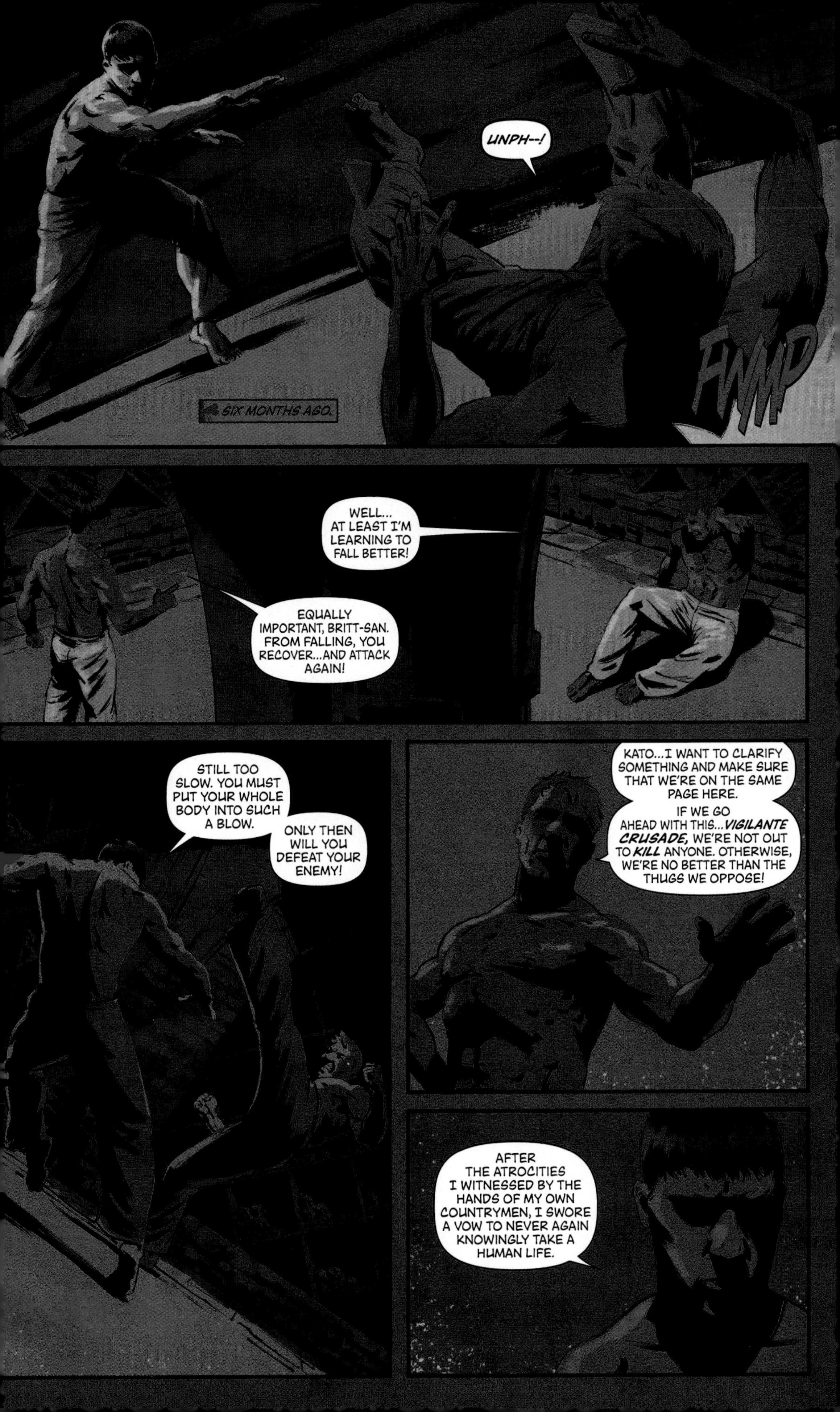

UNPH--!
FWMP
SIX MONTHS AGO.
WELL... AT LEAST I'M LEARNING TO FALL BETTER!
EQUALLY IMPORTANT, BRITT-SAN. FROM FALLING, YOU RECOVER...AND ATTACK AGAIN!
STILL TOO SLOW. YOU MUST PUT YOUR WHOLE BODY INTO SUCH A BLOW.
ONLY THEN WILL YOU DEFEAT YOUR ENEMY!
KATO...I WANT TO CLARIFY SOMETHING AND MAKE SURE THAT WE'RE ON THE SAME PAGE HERE.
IF WE GO AHEAD WITH THIS...VIGILANTE CRUSADE, WE'RE NOT OUT TO KILL ANYONE. OTHERWISE, WE'RE NO BETTER THAN THE THUGS WE OPPOSE!
AFTER THE ATROCITIES I WITNESSED BY THE HANDS OF MY OWN COUNTRYMEN, I SWORE A VOW TO NEVER AGAIN KNOWINGLY TAKE A HUMAN LIFE.

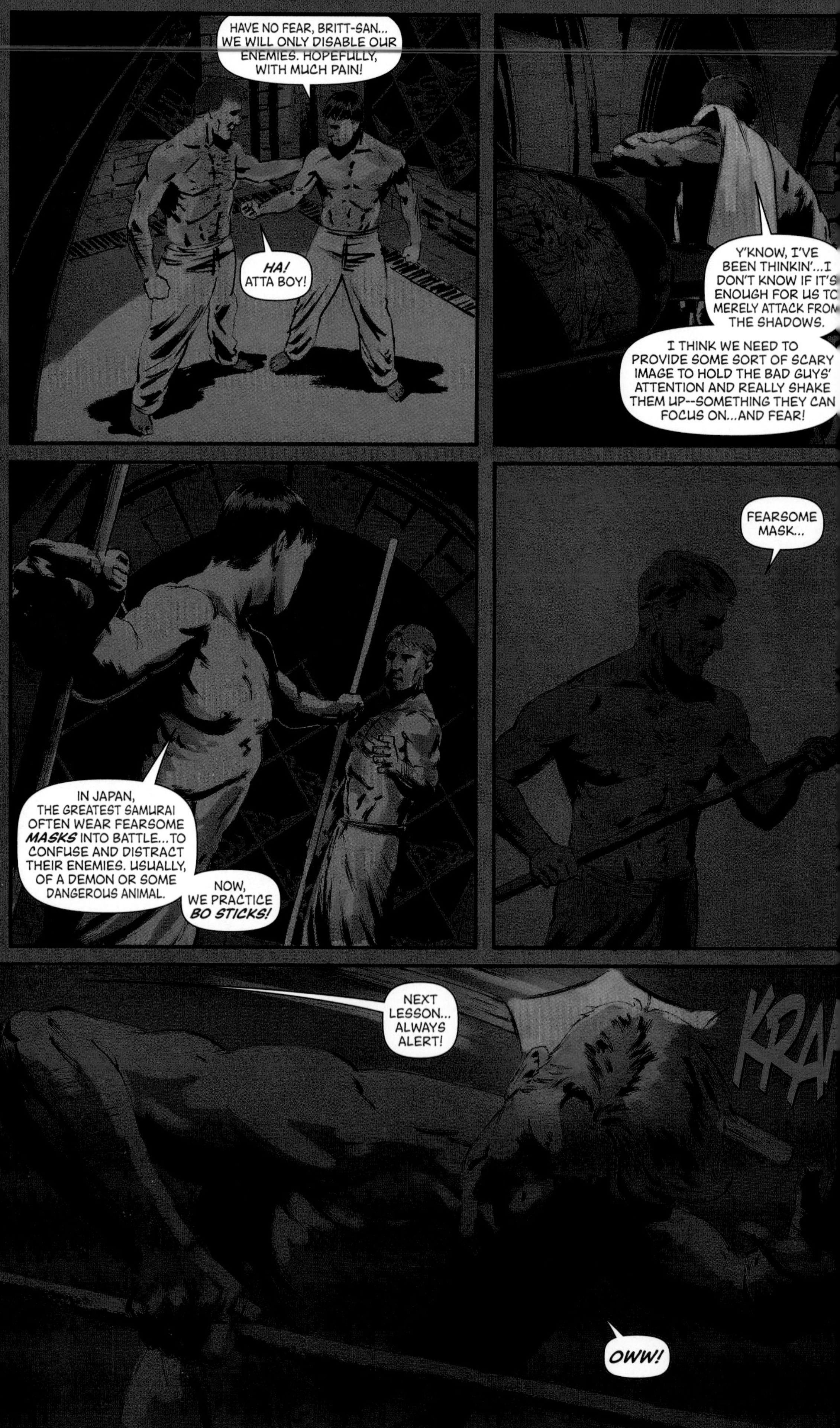
HAVE NO FEAR, BRITT-SAN... WE WILL ONLY DISABLE OUR ENEMIES. HOPEFULLY, WITH MUCH PAIN!
HA! ATTA BOY!
Y'KNOW, I'VE BEEN THINKIN'...I DON'T KNOW IF IT'S ENOUGH FOR US TO MERELY ATTACK FROM THE SHADOWS.
I THINK WE NEED TO PROVIDE SOME SORT OF SCARY IMAGE TO HOLD THE BAD GUYS' ATTENTION AND REALLY SHAKE THEM UP--SOMETHING THEY CAN FOCUS ON...AND FEAR!
IN JAPAN, THE GREATEST SAMURAI OFTEN WEAR FEARSOME MASKS INTO BATTLE...TO CONFUSE AND DISTRACT THEIR ENEMIES. USUALLY, OF A DEMON OR SOME DANGEROUS ANIMAL.
NOW, WE PRACTICE BO STICKS!
FEARSOME MASK...
NEXT LESSON... ALWAYS ALERT!
OWW!

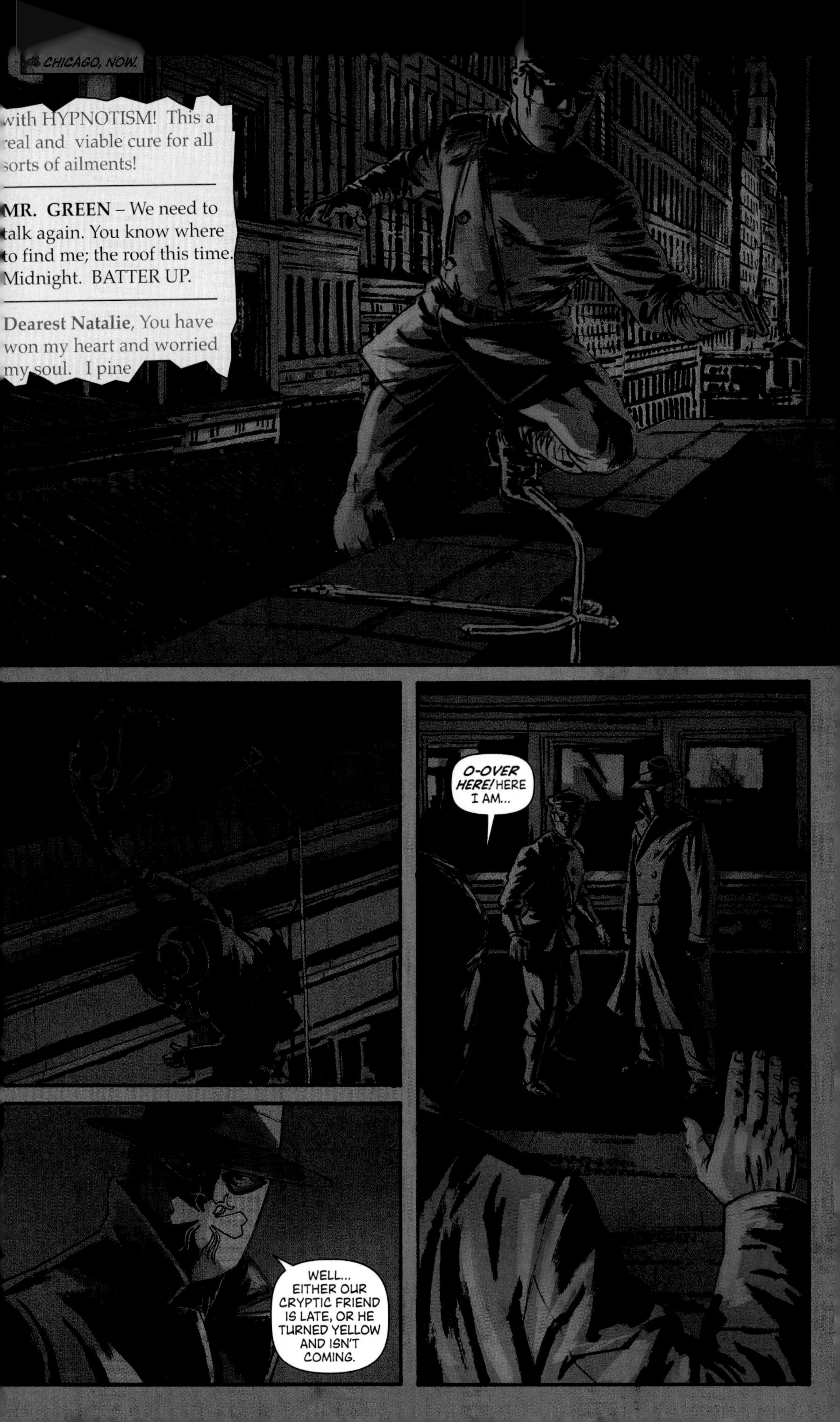
CHICAGO, NOW.
with HYPNOTISM! This a real and viable cure for all sorts of ailments!
MR. GREEN – We need to talk again. You know where to find me; the roof this time. Midnight. BATTER UP.
Dearest Natalie, You have won my heart and worried my soul. I pine
O-OVER HERE! HERE I AM...
WELL... EITHER OUR CRYPTIC FRIEND IS LATE, OR HE TURNED YELLOW AND ISN'T COMING.

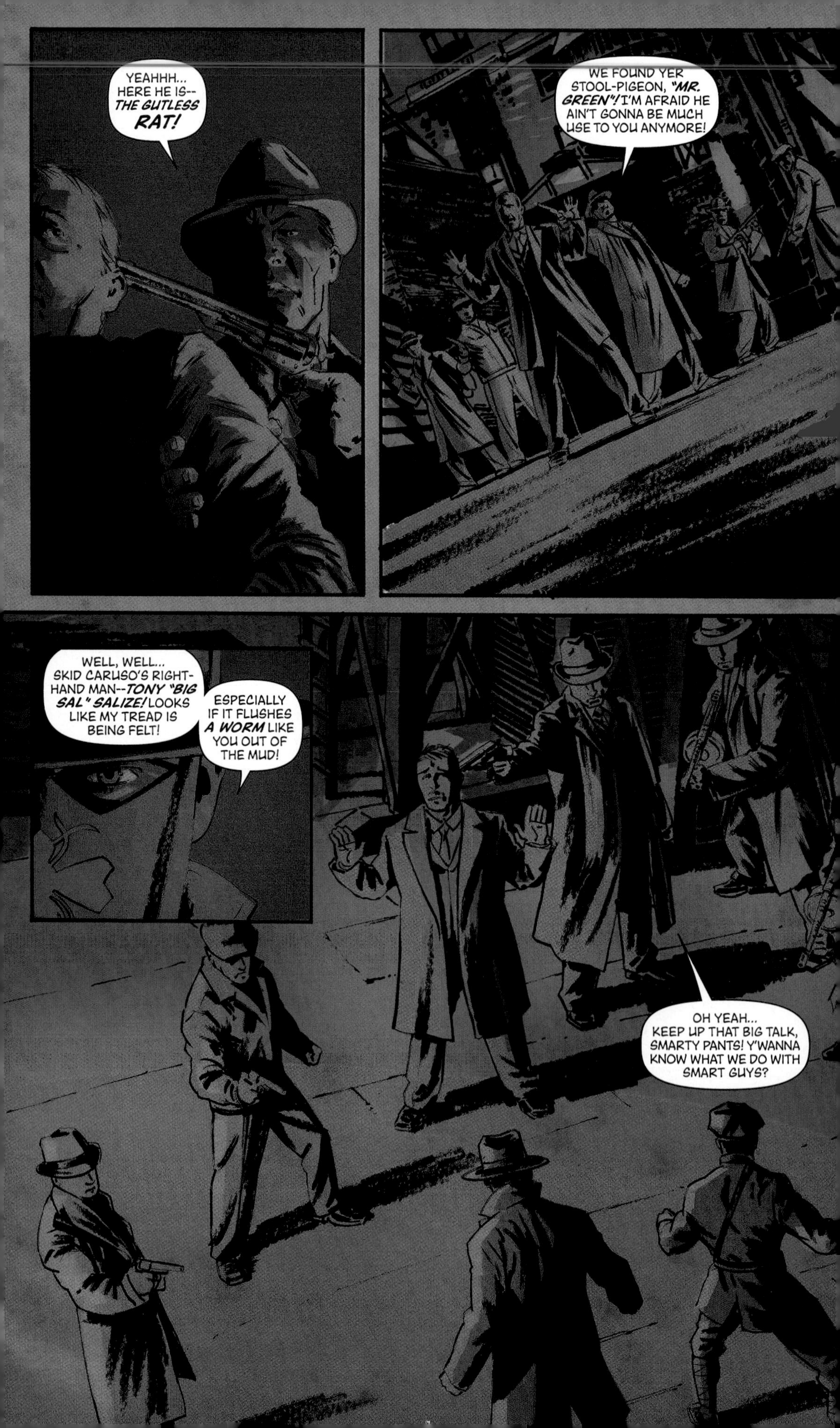
YEAHHH... HERE HE IS-- THE GUTLESS RAT!
WE FOUND YER STOOL-PIGEON, "MR. GREEN"! I'M AFRAID HE AIN'T GONNA BE MUCH USE TO YOU ANYMORE!
WELL, WELL... SKID CARUSO'S RIGHT-HAND MAN--TONY "BIG SAL" SALIZE! LOOKS LIKE MY TREAD IS BEING FELT!
ESPECIALLY IF IT FLUSHES A WORM LIKE YOU OUT OF THE MUD!
OH YEAH... KEEP UP THAT BIG TALK, SMARTY PANTS! Y'WANNA KNOW WHAT WE DO WITH SMART GUYS?

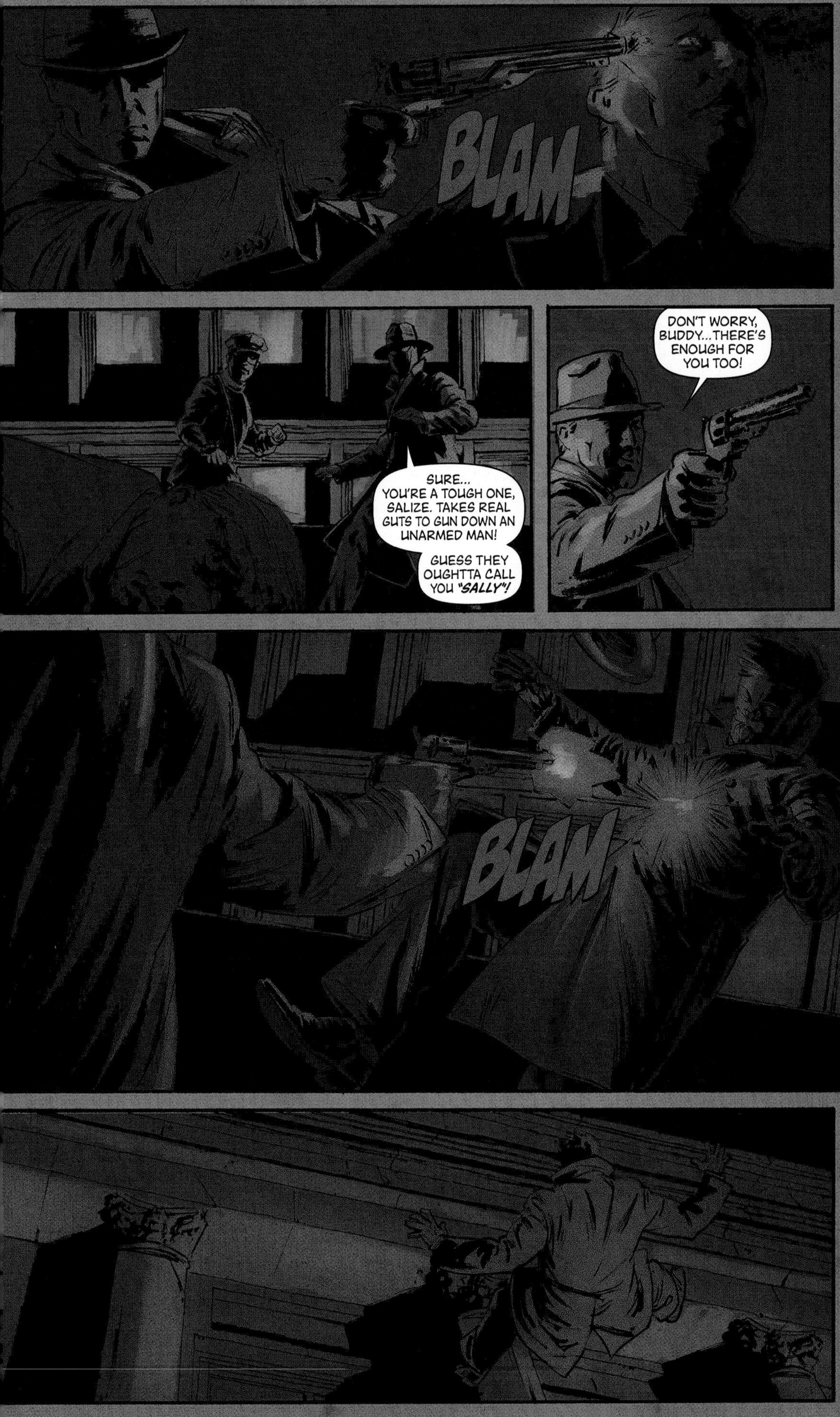
BLAM
SURE... YOU'RE A TOUGH ONE, SALIZE. TAKES REAL GUTS TO GUN DOWN AN UNARMED MAN!
GUESS THEY OUGHTTA CALL YOU "SALLY"!
DON'T WORRY, BUDDY...THERE'S ENOUGH FOR YOU TOO!
BLAM

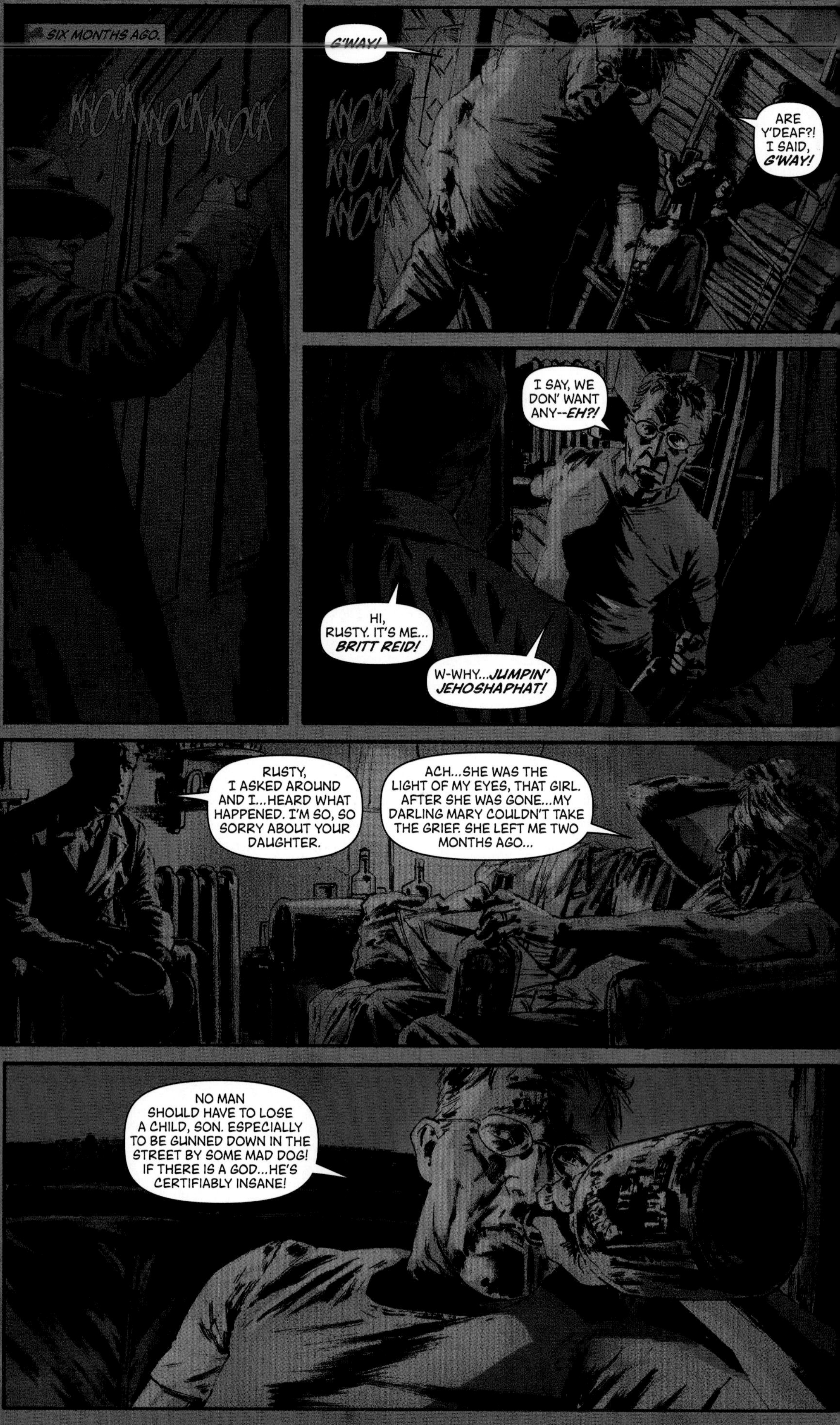
SIX MONTHS AGO.
KNOCK KNOCK KNOCK
G'WAY!
KNOCK KNOCK KNOCK
ARE Y'DEAF?! I SAID, G'WAY!
I SAY, WE DON' WANT ANY--EH?!
HI, RUSTY. IT'S ME... BRITT REID!
W-WHY...JUMPIN' JEHOSHAPHAT!
RUSTY, I ASKED AROUND AND I...HEARD WHAT HAPPENED. I'M SO, SO SORRY ABOUT YOUR DAUGHTER.
ACH...SHE WAS THE LIGHT OF MY EYES, THAT GIRL. AFTER SHE WAS GONE...MY DARLING MARY COULDN'T TAKE THE GRIEF. SHE LEFT ME TWO MONTHS AGO...
NO MAN SHOULD HAVE TO LOSE A CHILD, SON. ESPECIALLY TO BE GUNNED DOWN IN THE STREET BY SOME MAD DOG! IF THERE IS A GOD...HE'S CERTIFIABLY INSANE!

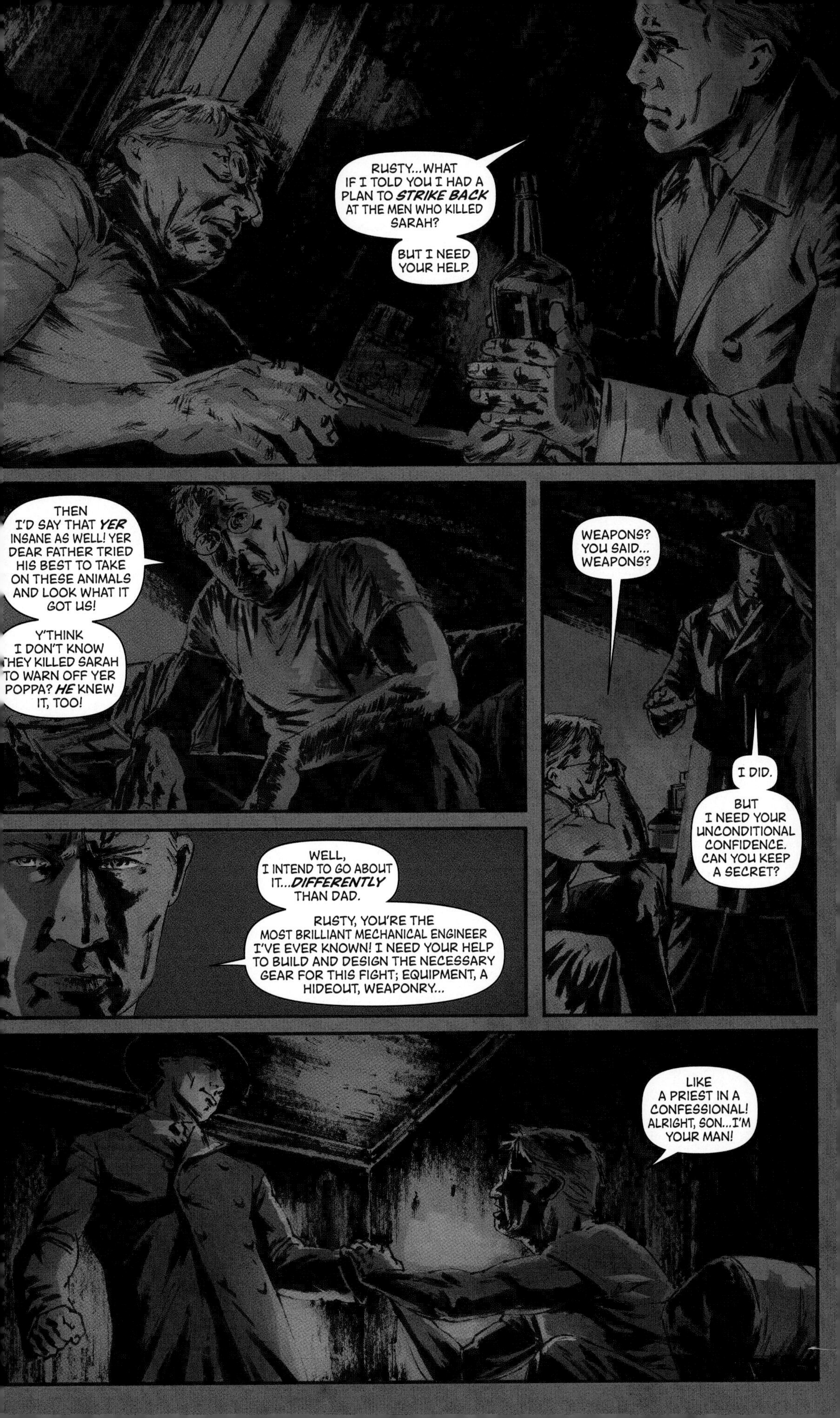
RUSTY...WHAT IF I TOLD YOU I HAD A PLAN TO *STRIKE BACK* AT THE MEN WHO KILLED SARAH?
BUT I NEED YOUR HELP.
THEN I'D SAY THAT *YER* INSANE AS WELL! YER DEAR FATHER TRIED HIS BEST TO TAKE ON THESE ANIMALS AND LOOK WHAT IT GOT US!
Y'THINK I DON'T KNOW THEY KILLED SARAH TO WARN OFF YER POPPA? *HE* KNEW IT, TOO!
WELL, I INTEND TO GO ABOUT IT...*DIFFERENTLY* THAN DAD.
RUSTY, YOU'RE THE MOST BRILLIANT MECHANICAL ENGINEER I'VE EVER KNOWN! I NEED YOUR HELP TO BUILD AND DESIGN THE NECESSARY GEAR FOR THIS FIGHT; EQUIPMENT, A HIDEOUT, WEAPONRY...
WEAPONS? YOU SAID... WEAPONS?
I DID.
BUT I NEED YOUR UNCONDITIONAL CONFIDENCE. CAN YOU KEEP A SECRET?
LIKE A PRIEST IN A CONFESSIONAL! ALRIGHT, SON...I'M YOUR MAN!

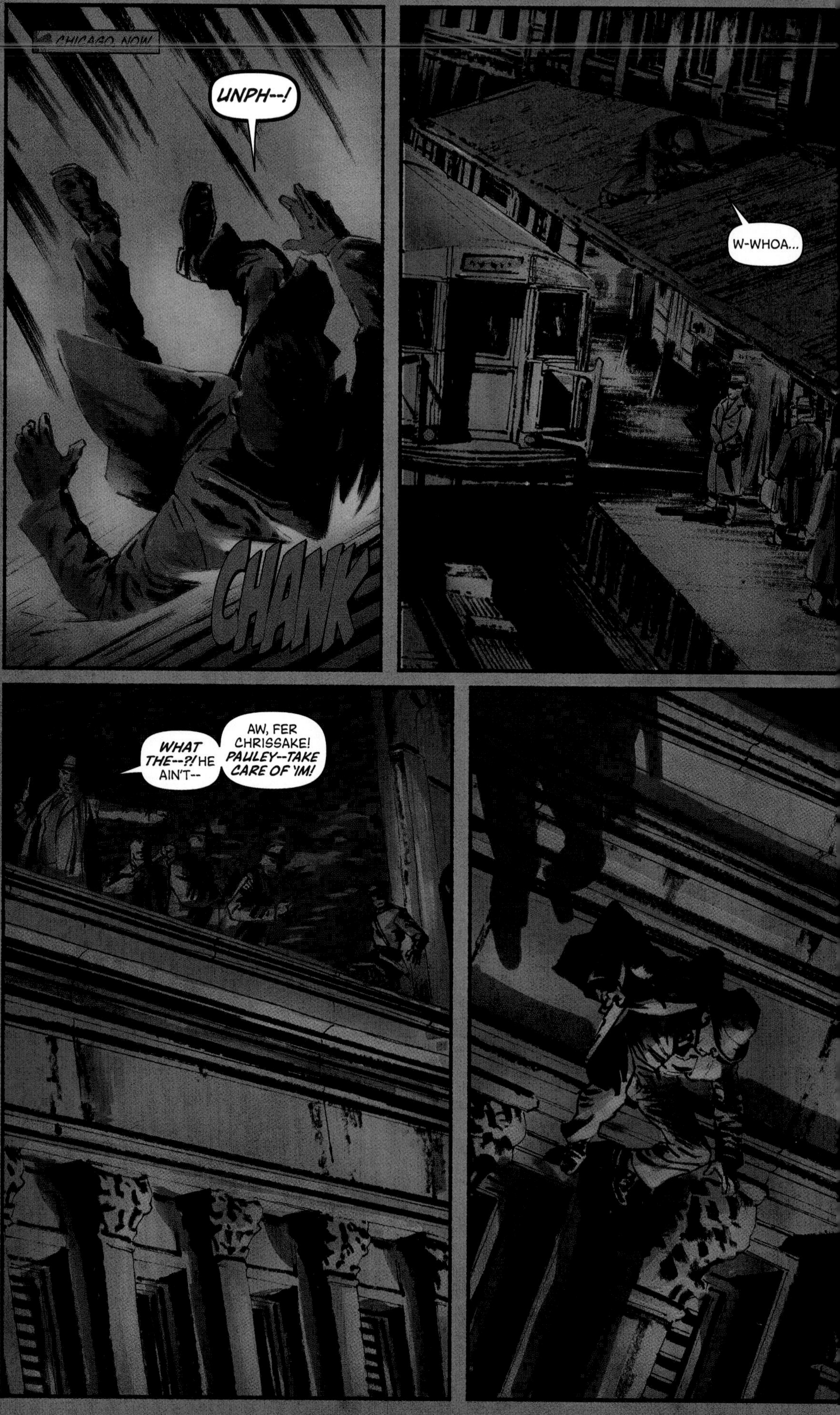
CHICAGO NOW
UNPH--!
CHANK
W-WHOA...
WHAT THE--?! HE AIN'T--
AW, FER CHRISSAKE! PAULEY--TAKE CARE OF 'IM!

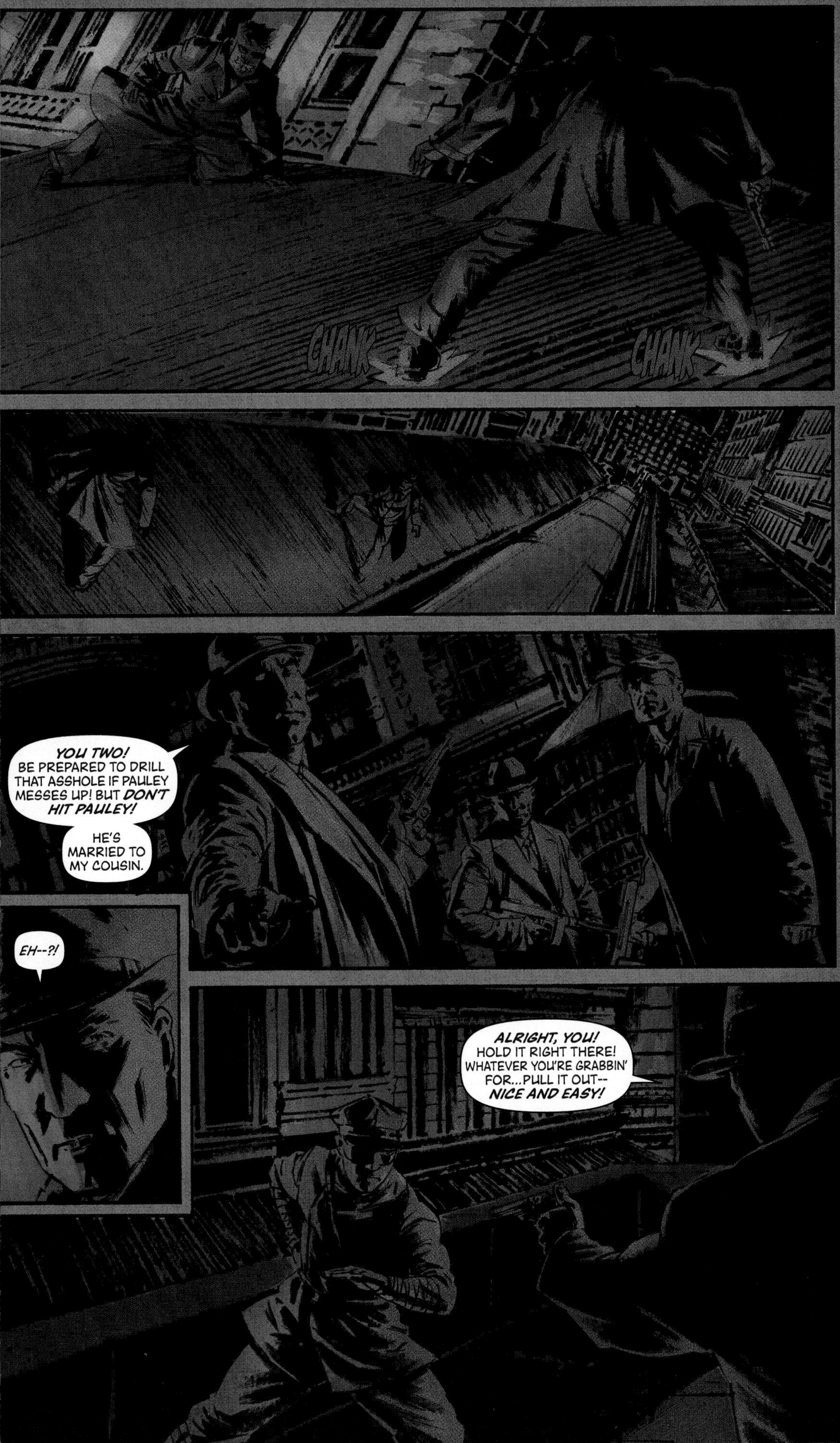
CHANK
CHANK
YOU TWO! BE PREPARED TO DRILL THAT ASSHOLE IF PAULEY MESSES UP! BUT DON'T HIT PAULEY!
HE'S MARRIED TO MY COUSIN.
EH--?!
ALRIGHT, YOU! HOLD IT RIGHT THERE! WHATEVER YOU'RE GRABBIN' FOR...PULL IT OUT-- NICE AND EASY!

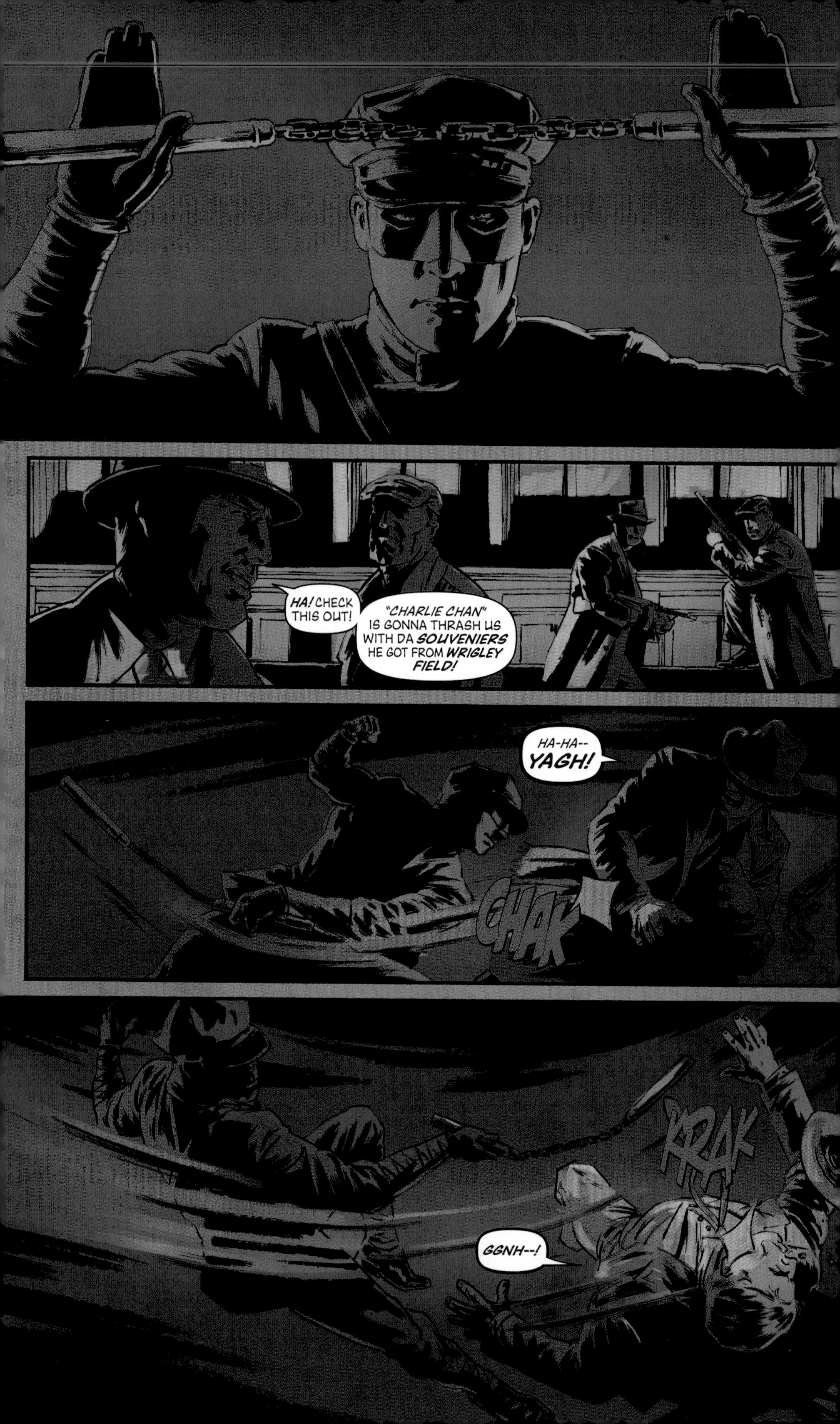
HA! CHECK THIS OUT!
"CHARLIE CHAN" IS GONNA THRASH US WITH DA SOUVENIERS HE GOT FROM WRIGLEY FIELD!
HA-HA-- YAGH!
CHAK
KRAK
GGNH--!

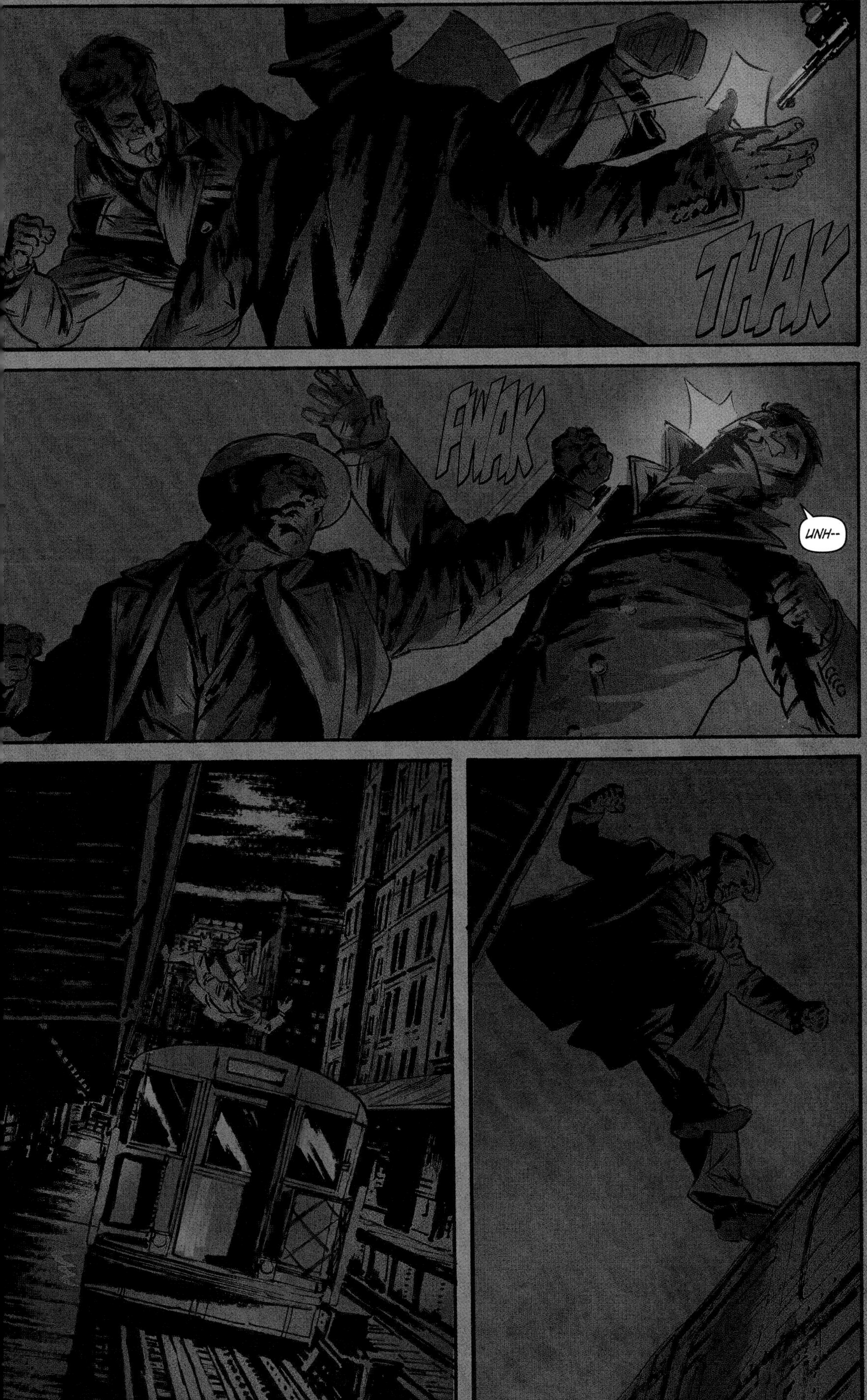
THAK
FWAK
UNH--

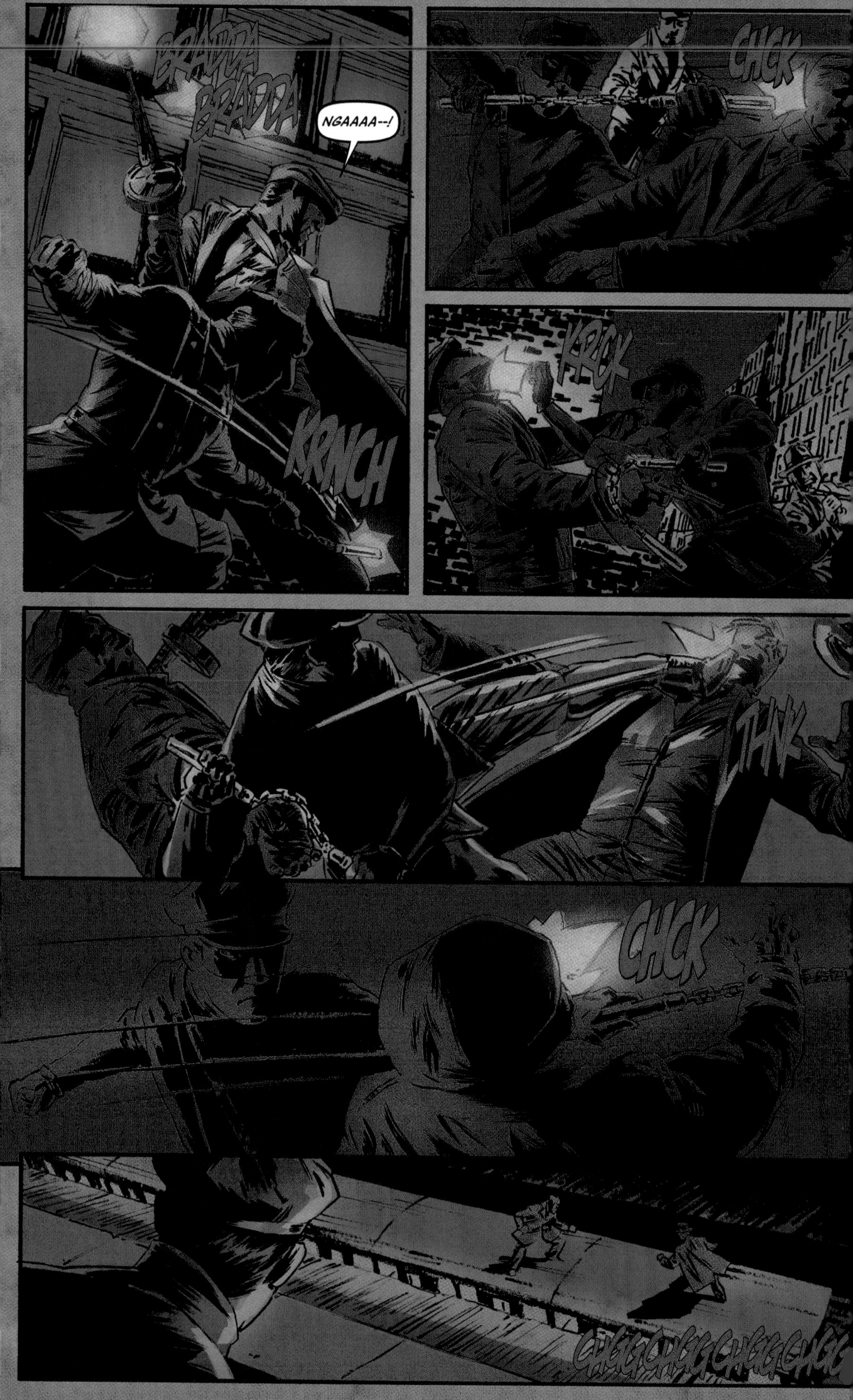
BRADDA
BRADDA
NGAAAA--!
KRNCH
CHCK
KRCK
THNK
CHCK
CHGGCHGGCHGGCHGG

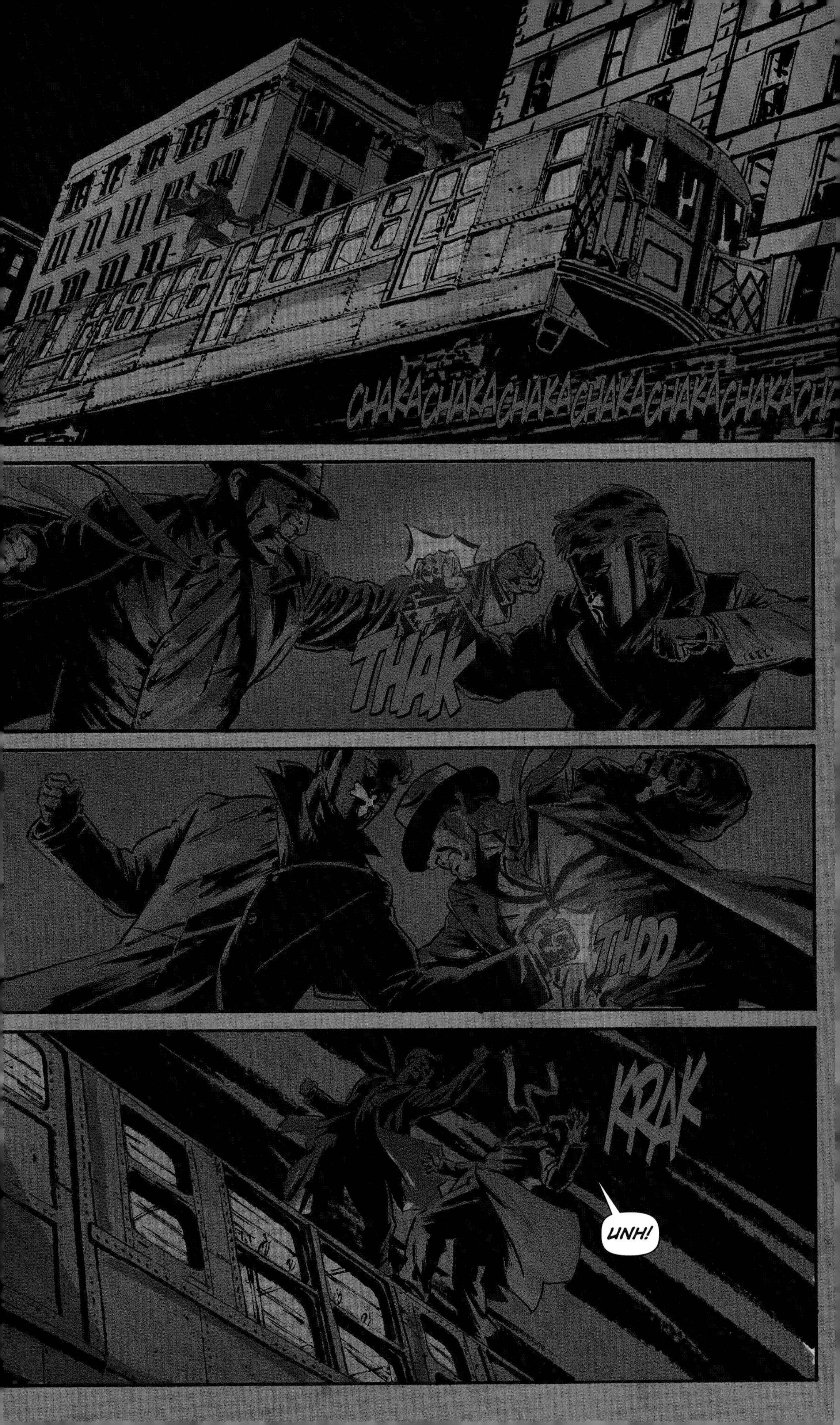
CHAKA CHAKA CHAKA CHAKA CHAKA CHAKA CHA
THAK
THDD
KRAK
UNH!

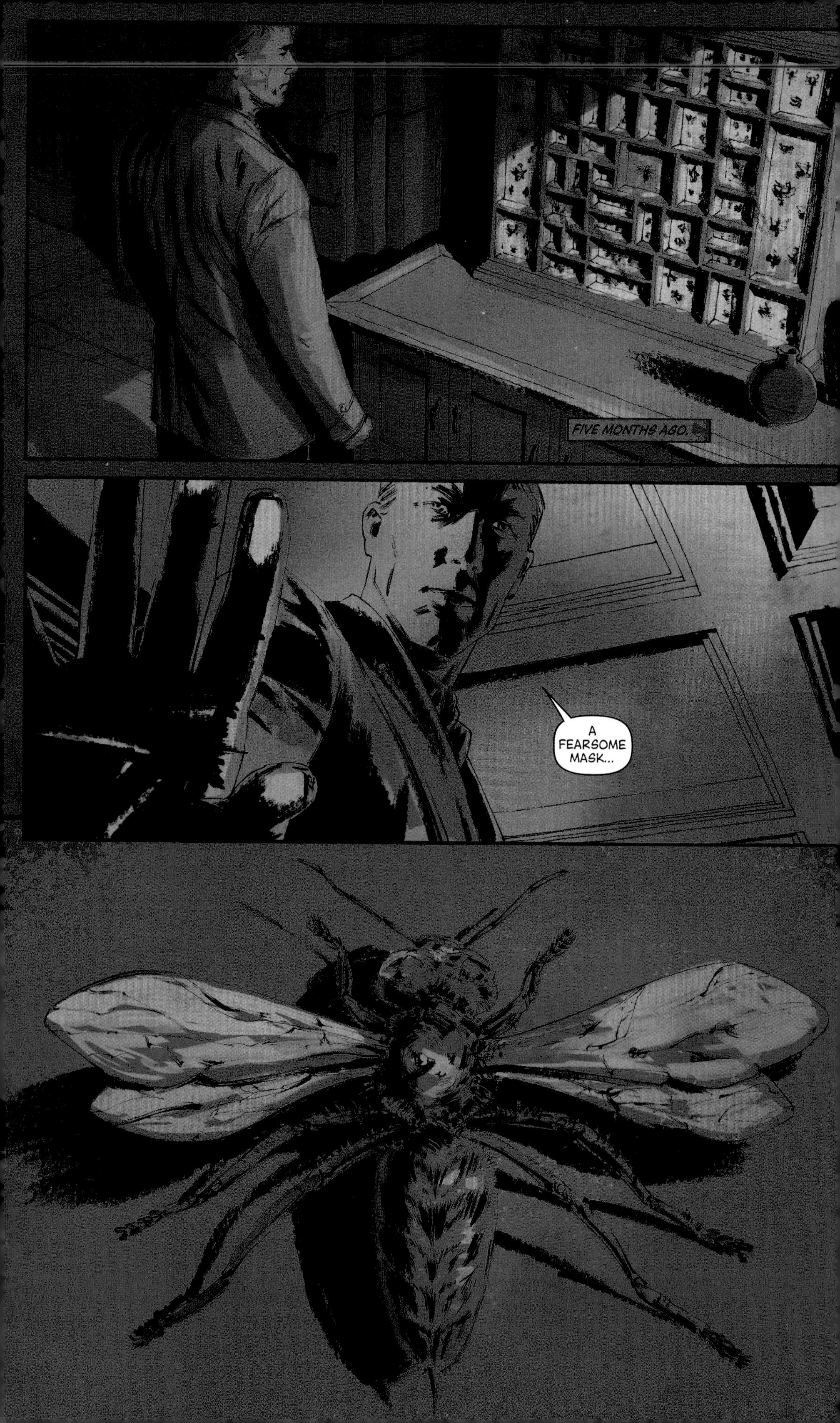
FIVE MONTHS AGO.
A FEARSOME MASK...

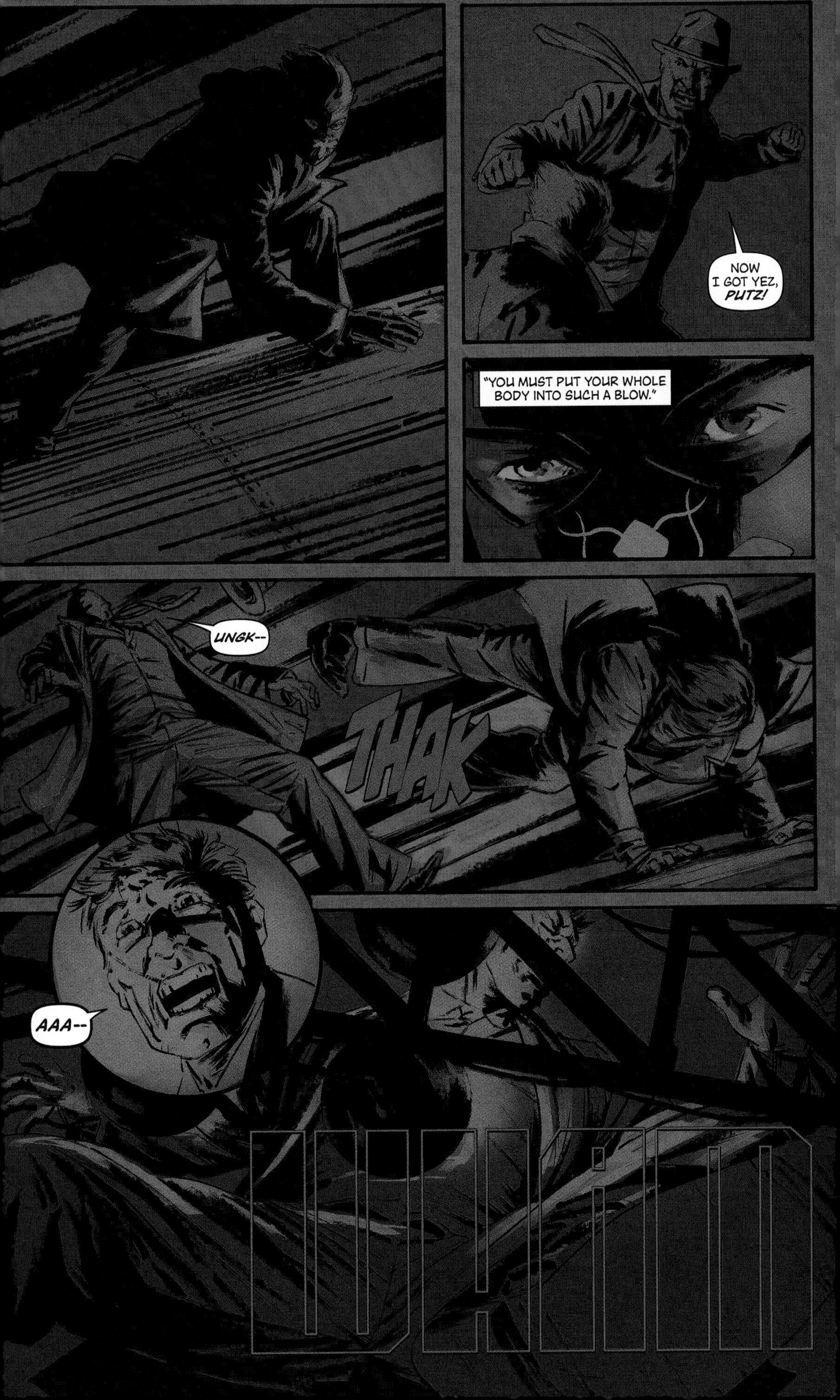
NOW I GOT YEZ, *PUTZ!*
"YOU MUST PUT YOUR WHOLE BODY INTO SUCH A BLOW."
UNGK--
THAK
AAA--

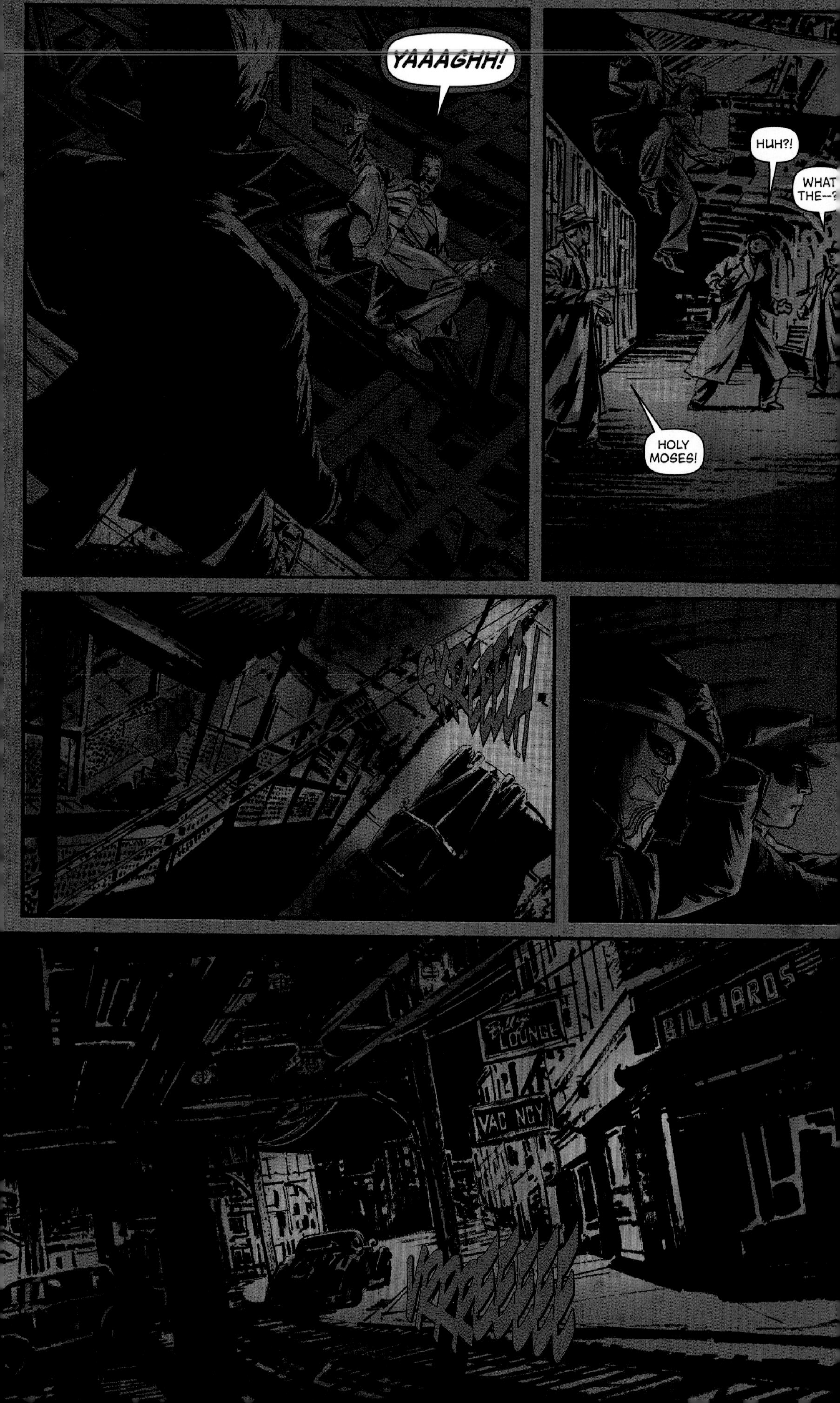
YAAAGHH!
HUH?!
WHAT THE--?
HOLY MOSES!
SKREEECH
LOUNGE
VAC NCY
BILLIARDS
VRRREEEEE

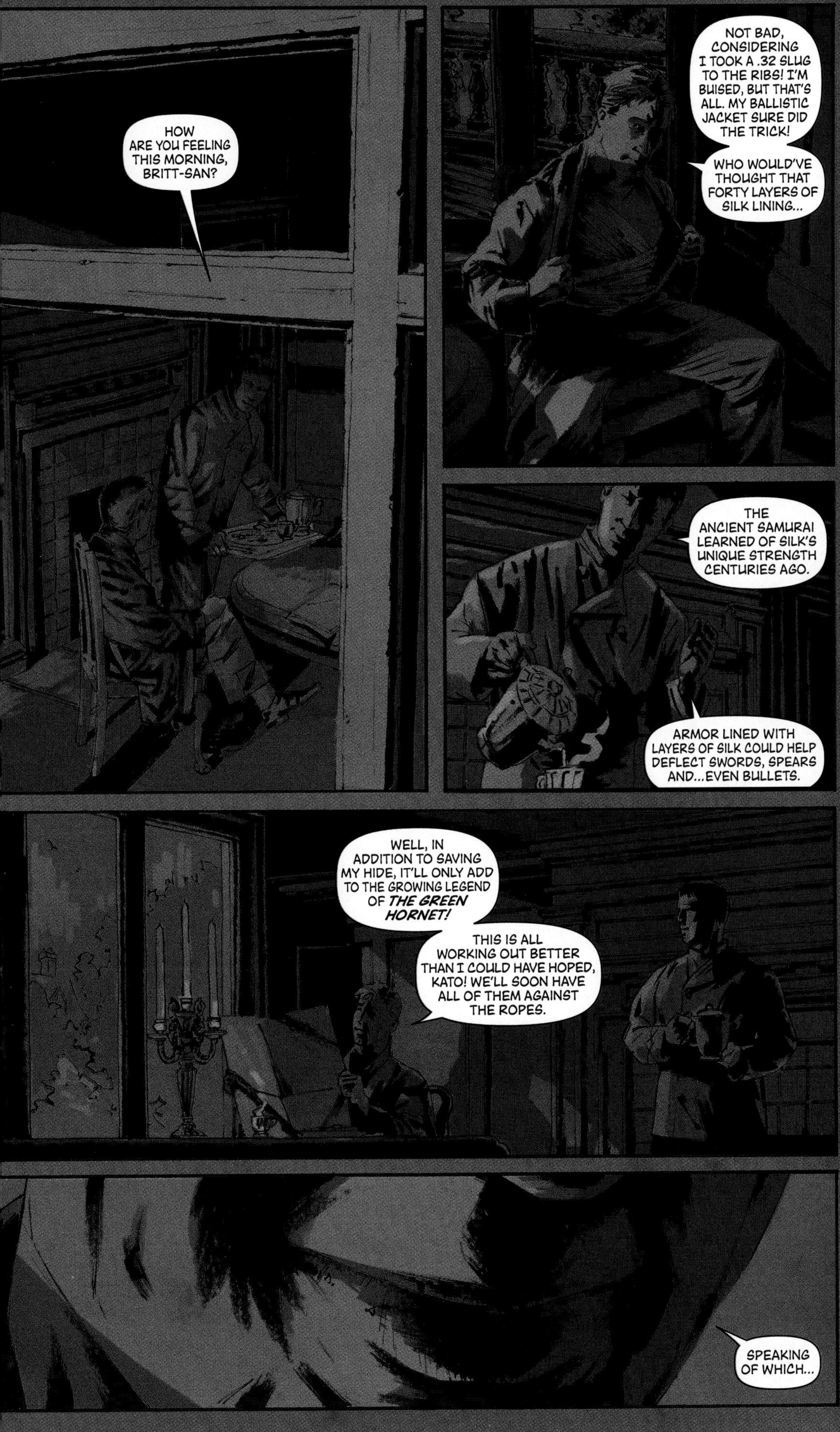
HOW ARE YOU FEELING THIS MORNING, BRITT-SAN?
NOT BAD, CONSIDERING I TOOK A .32 SLUG TO THE RIBS! I'M BUISED, BUT THAT'S ALL. MY BALLISTIC JACKET SURE DID THE TRICK!
WHO WOULD'VE THOUGHT THAT FORTY LAYERS OF SILK LINING...
THE ANCIENT SAMURAI LEARNED OF SILK'S UNIQUE STRENGTH CENTURIES AGO.
ARMOR LINED WITH LAYERS OF SILK COULD HELP DEFLECT SWORDS, SPEARS AND...EVEN BULLETS.
WELL, IN ADDITION TO SAVING MY HIDE, IT'LL ONLY ADD TO THE GROWING LEGEND OF *THE GREEN HORNET!*
THIS IS ALL WORKING OUT BETTER THAN I COULD HAVE HOPED, KATO! WE'LL SOON HAVE ALL OF THEM AGAINST THE ROPES.
SPEAKING OF WHICH...

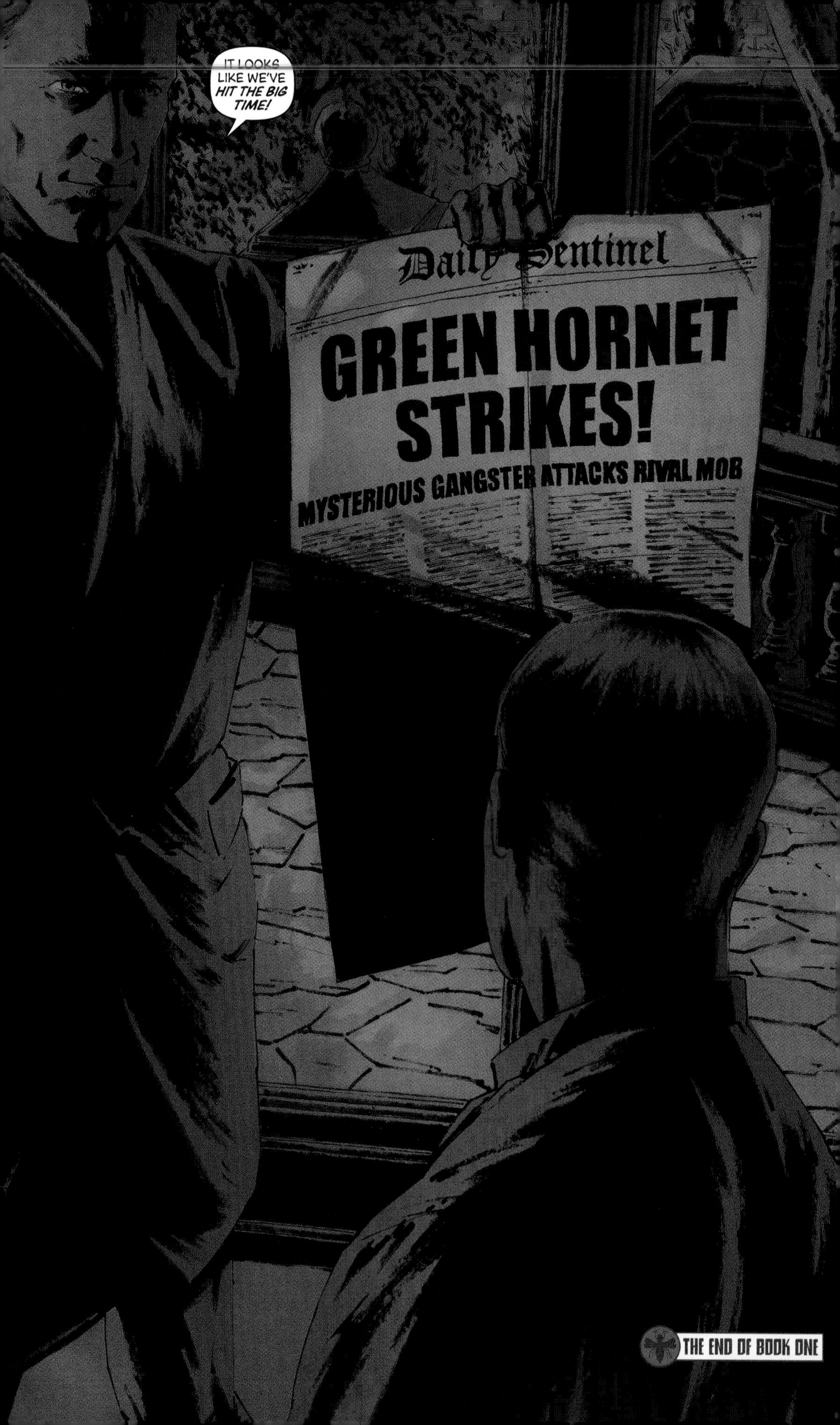
IT LOOKS LIKE WE'VE *HIT THE BIG TIME!*
Daily Sentinel
GREEN HORNET STRIKES!
MYSTERIOUS GANGSTER ATTACKS RIVAL MOB
THE END OF BOOK ONE

ALTERNATE COVERS

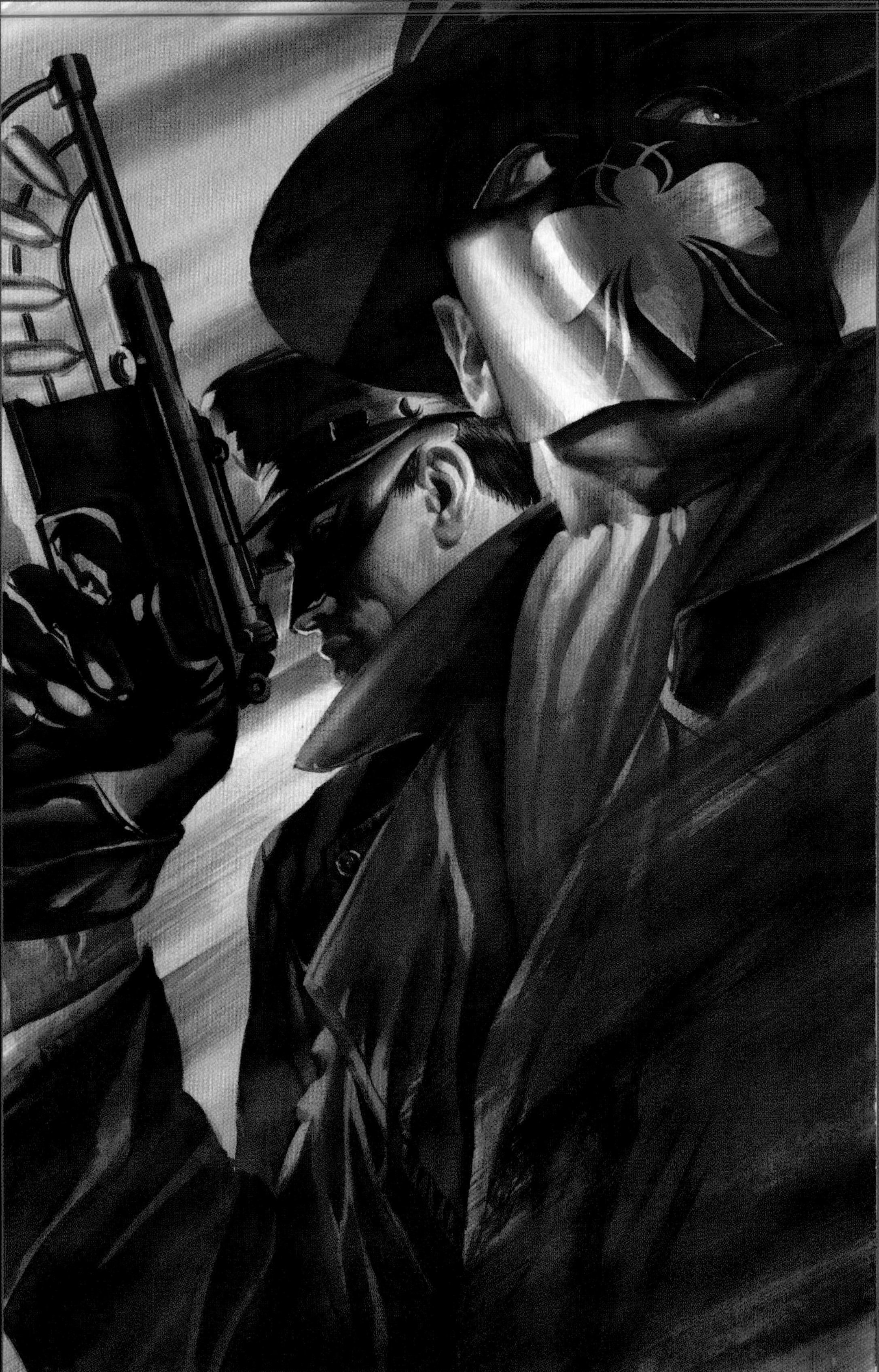

Issue one cover by ALEX ROSS

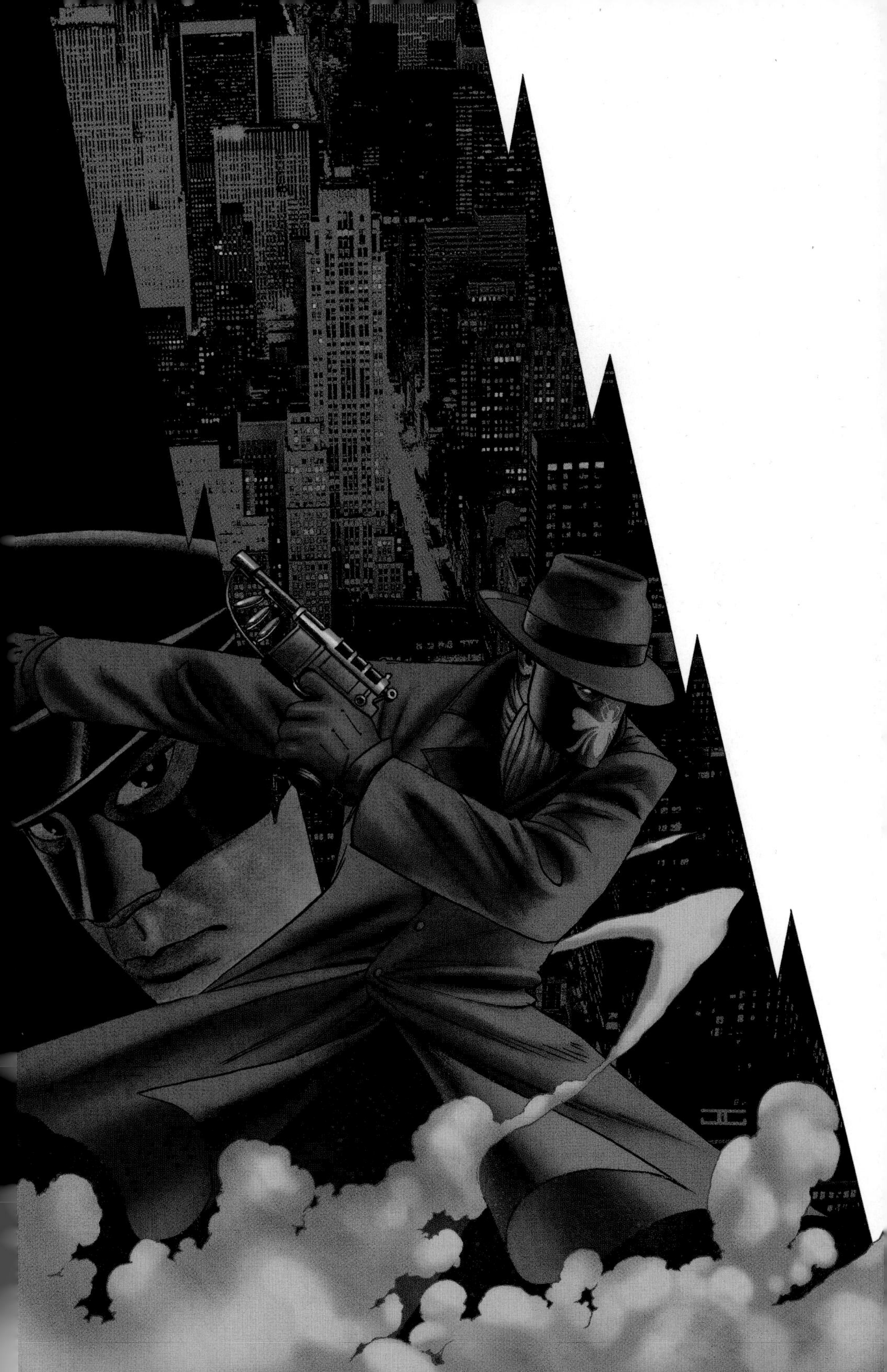

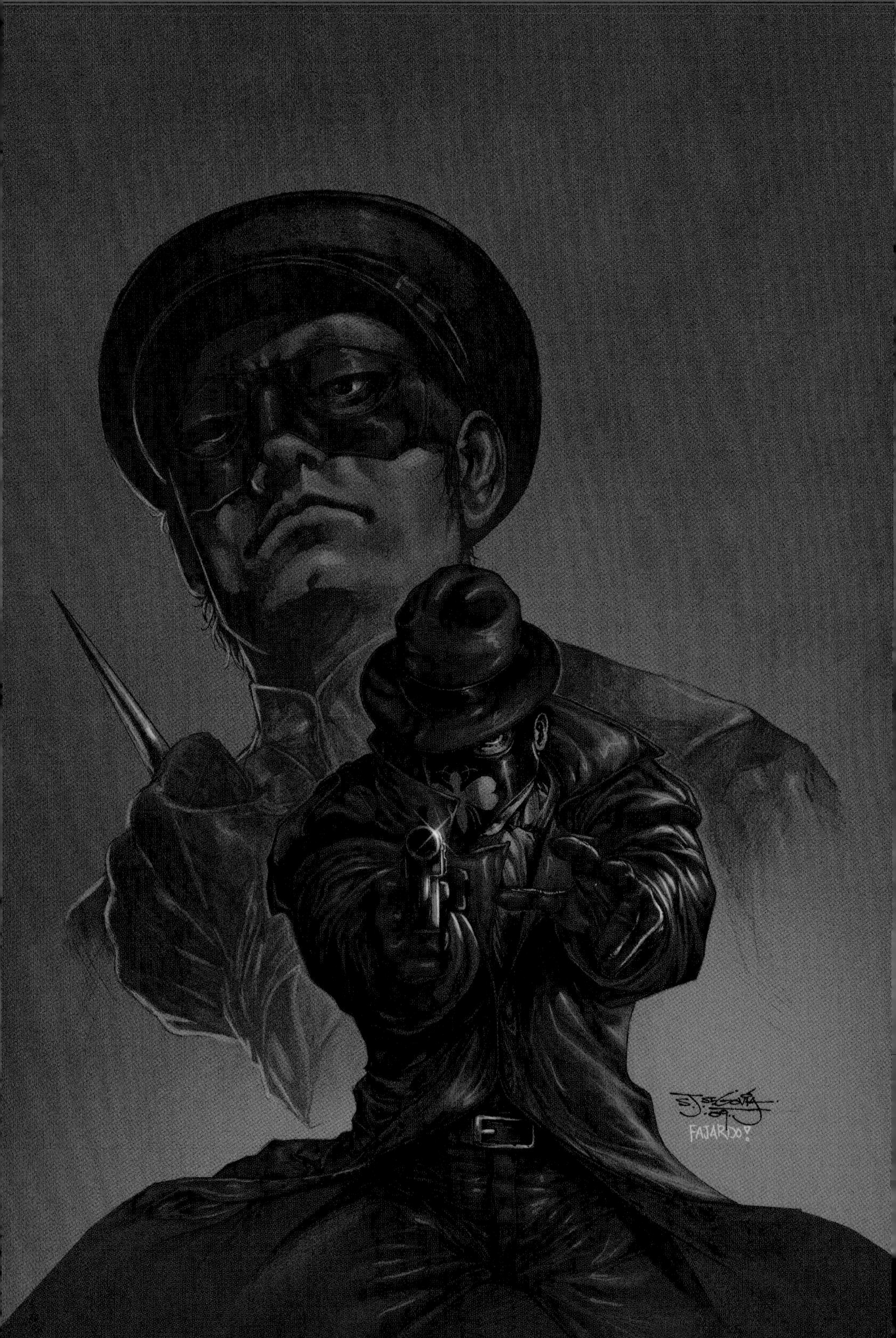
FAJARDO!

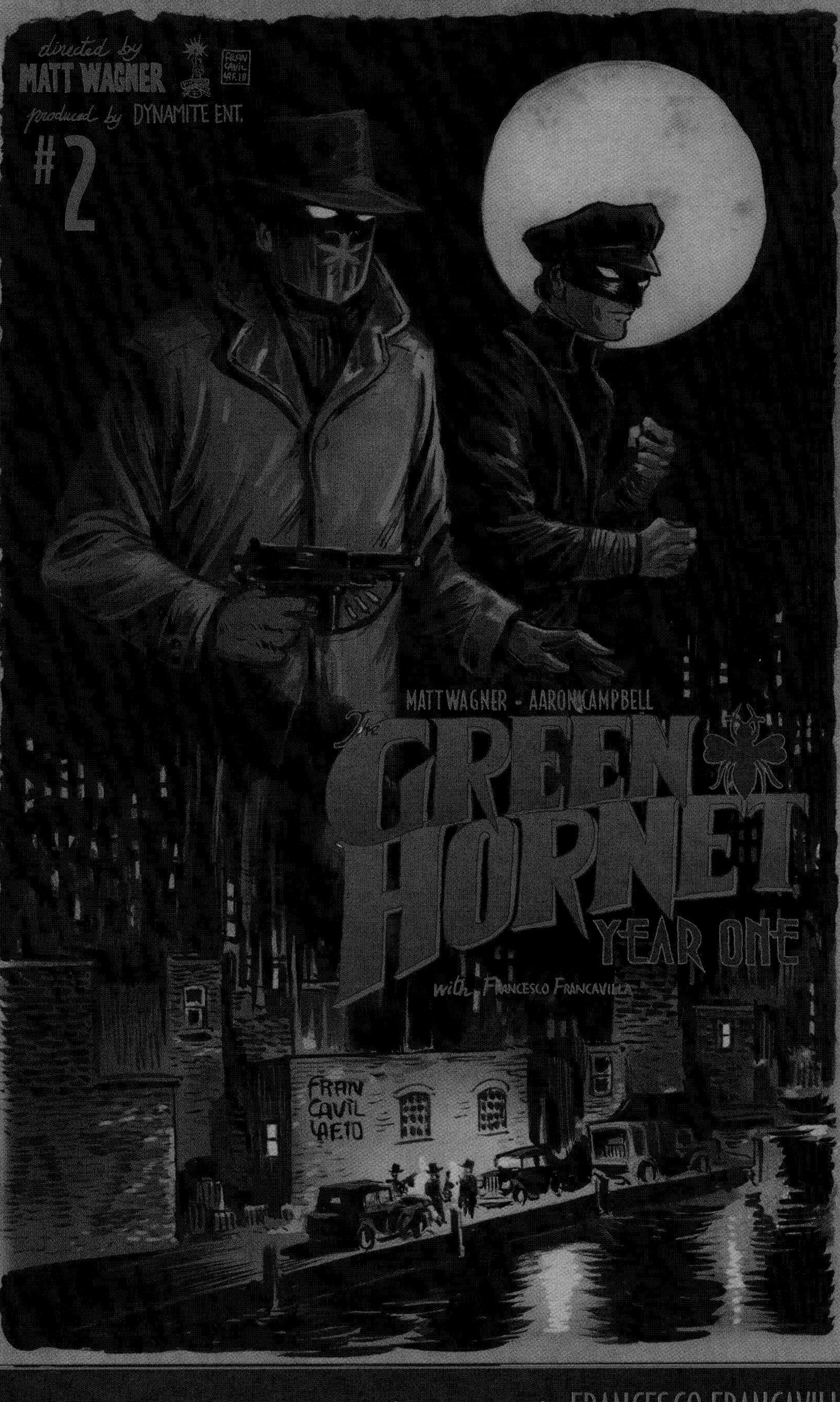
directed by
MATT WAGNER
produced by DYNAMITE ENT.
#2
FRAN CAVIL LAF.10
MATT WAGNER - AARON CAMPBELL
The
GREEN
HORNET
YEAR ONE
with FRANCESCO FRANCAVILLA
FRAN CAVIL LAF.10

Issue two cover by FRANCESCO FRANCAVILLA

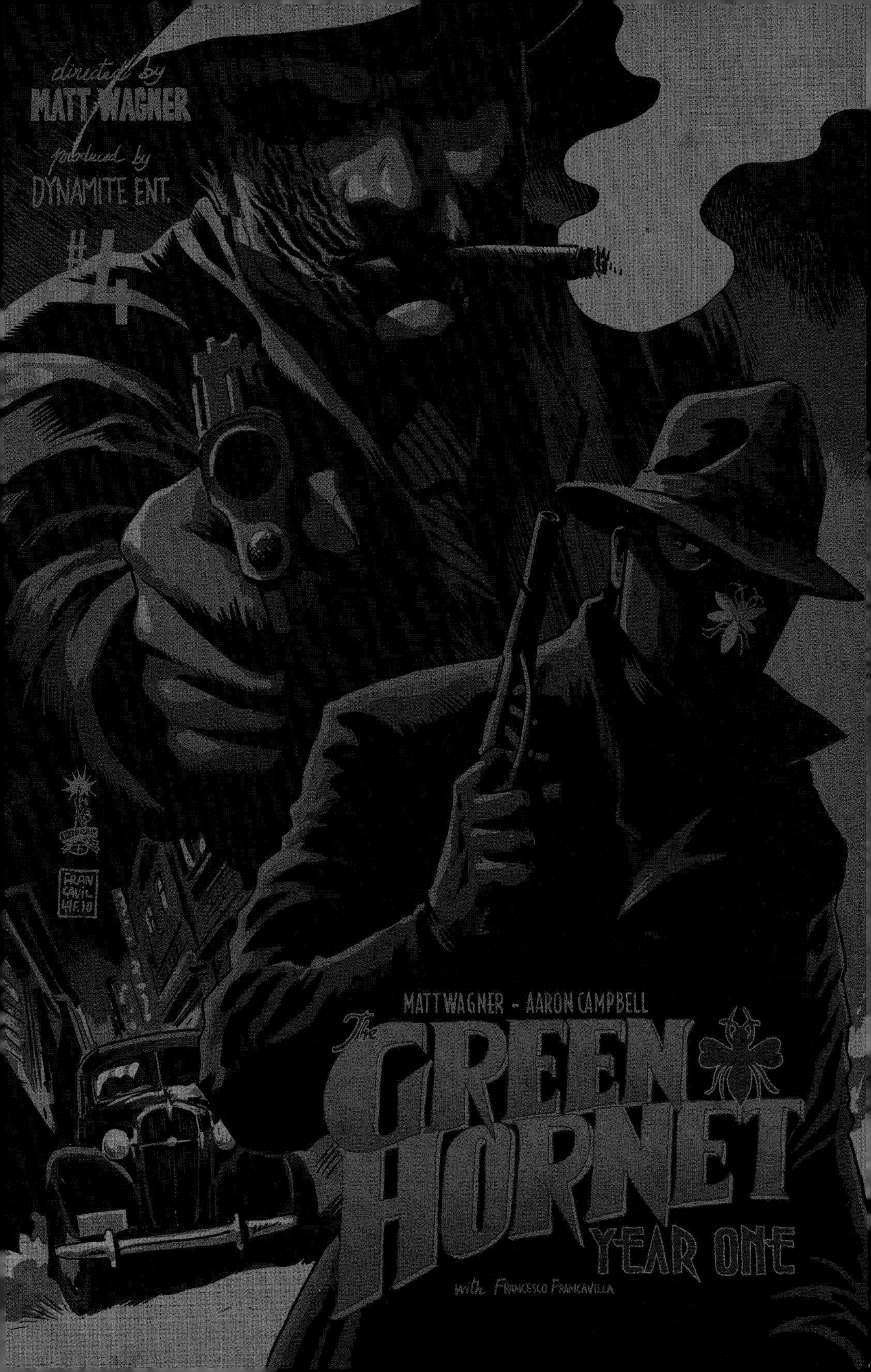
directed by
MATT WAGNER
produced by
DYNAMITE ENT.
#4
MATT WAGNER - AARON CAMPBELL
The GREEN HORNET
YEAR ONE
with FRANCESCO FRANCAVILLA

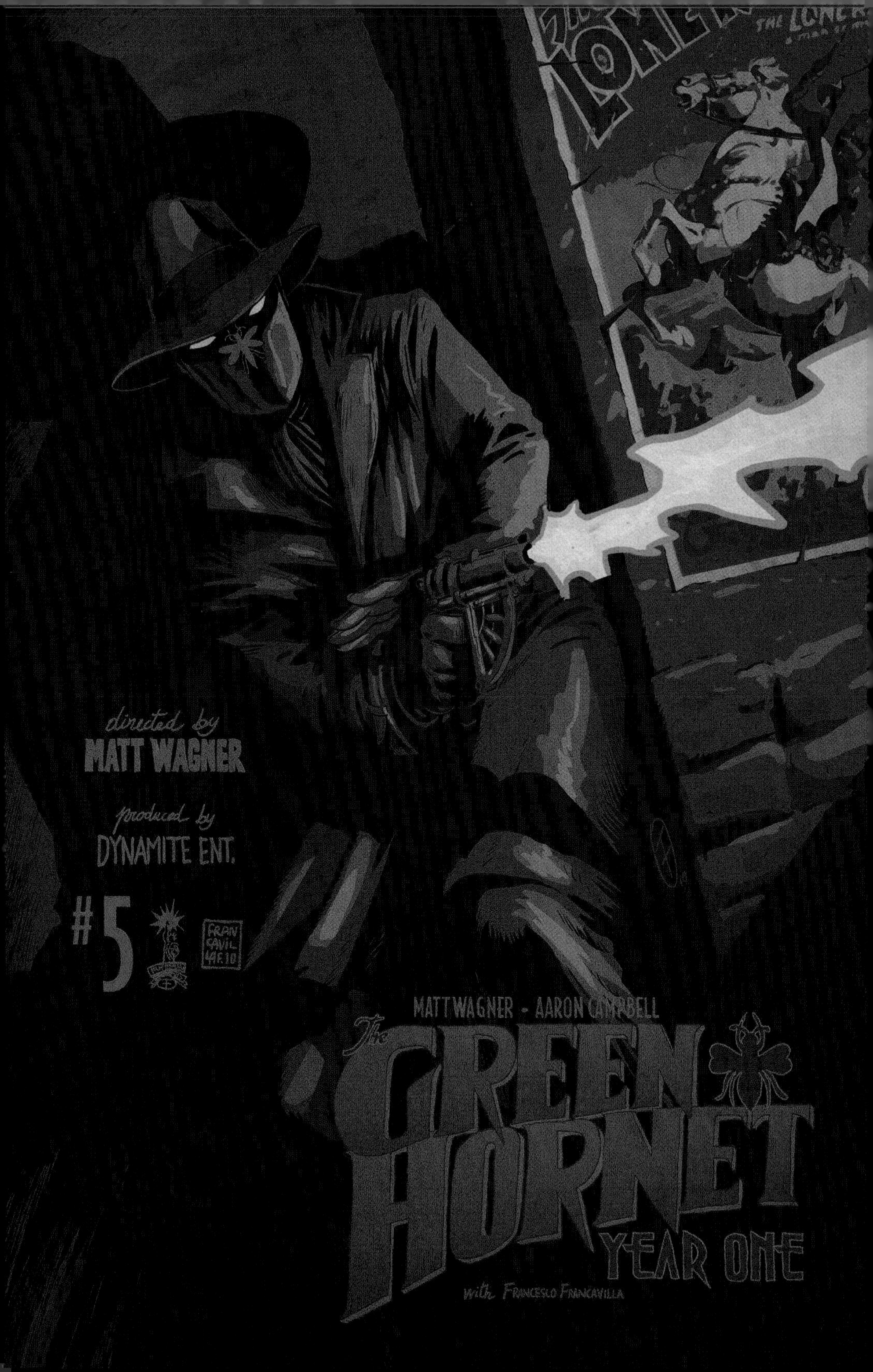
directed by
MATT WAGNER
produced by
DYNAMITE ENT.
#5
MATT WAGNER - AARON CAMPBELL
The GREEN HORNET
YEAR ONE
with FRANCESCO FRANCAVILLA

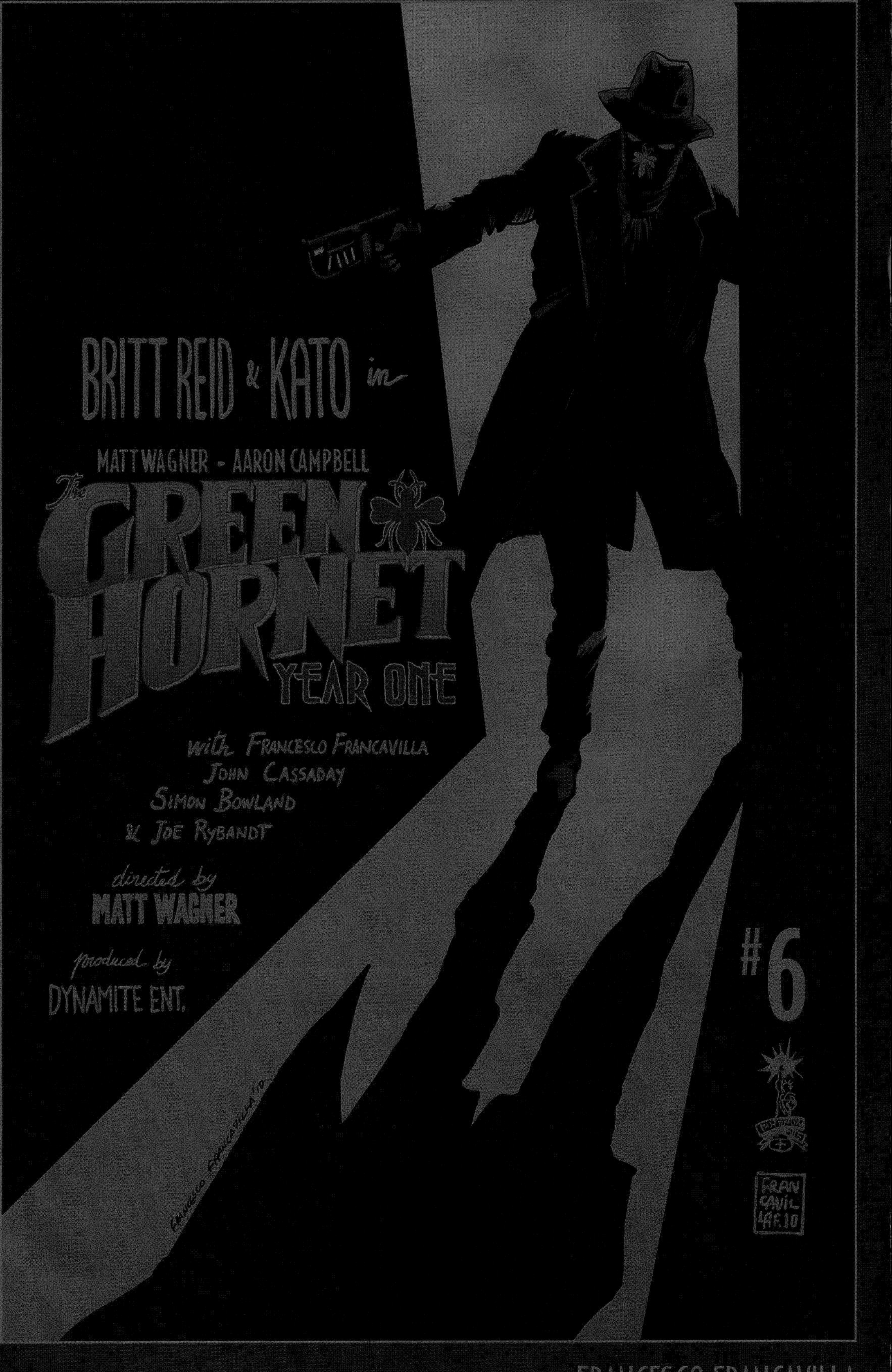
BRITT REID & KATO in
MATT WAGNER - AARON CAMPBELL
The GREEN HORNET
YEAR ONE
with FRANCESCO FRANCAVILLA
JOHN CASSADAY
SIMON BOWLAND
& JOE RYBANDT
directed by
MATT WAGNER
produced by
DYNAMITE ENT.
#6

Issue six cover by FRANCESCO FRANCAVILLA

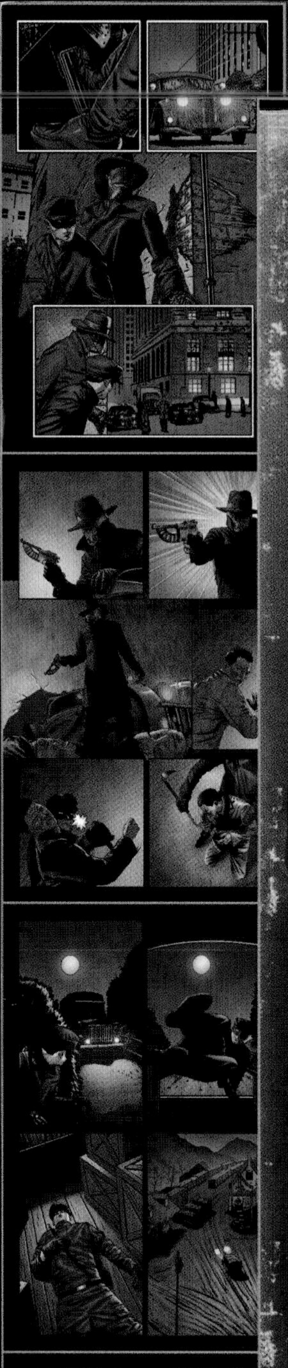

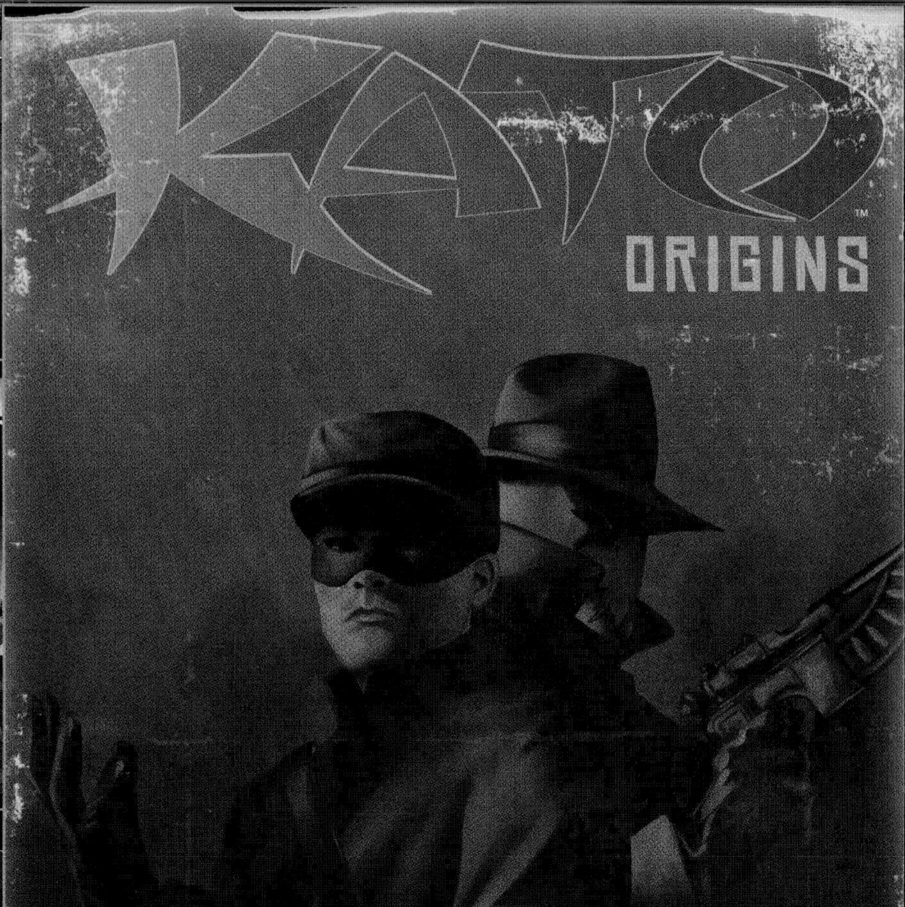
KATO
ORIGINS
FROM THE PAGES OF MATT WAGNER'S
GREEN HORNET

KEVIN SMITH presents THE GREEN HORNET!

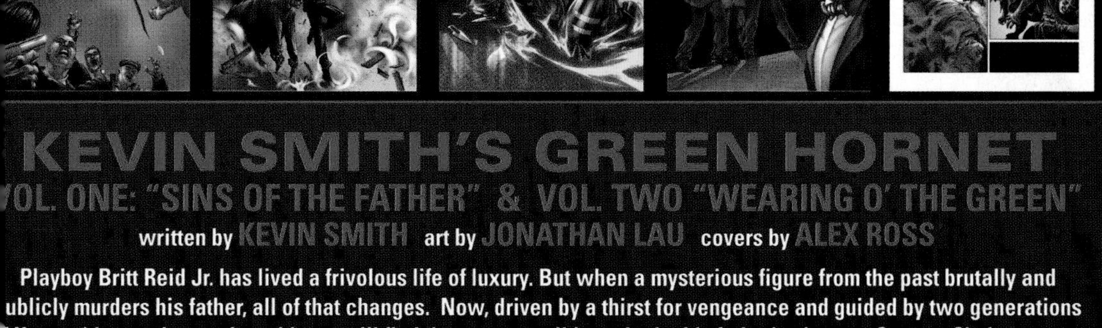

KEVIN SMITH'S GREEN HORNET
VOL. ONE: "SINS OF THE FATHER" & VOL. TWO "WEARING O' THE GREEN"
written by KEVIN SMITH   art by JONATHAN LAU   covers by ALEX ROSS

Playboy Britt Reid Jr. has lived a frivolous life of luxury. But when a mysterious figure from the past brutally and publicly murders his father, all of that changes. Now, driven by a thirst for vengeance and guided by two generations of Katos, this one time underachiever will find those responsible and take his father's place as Century City's greatest protector – The Green Hornet!

Volume 1 • In Stores Now!   Volume 1 • Coming Soon!

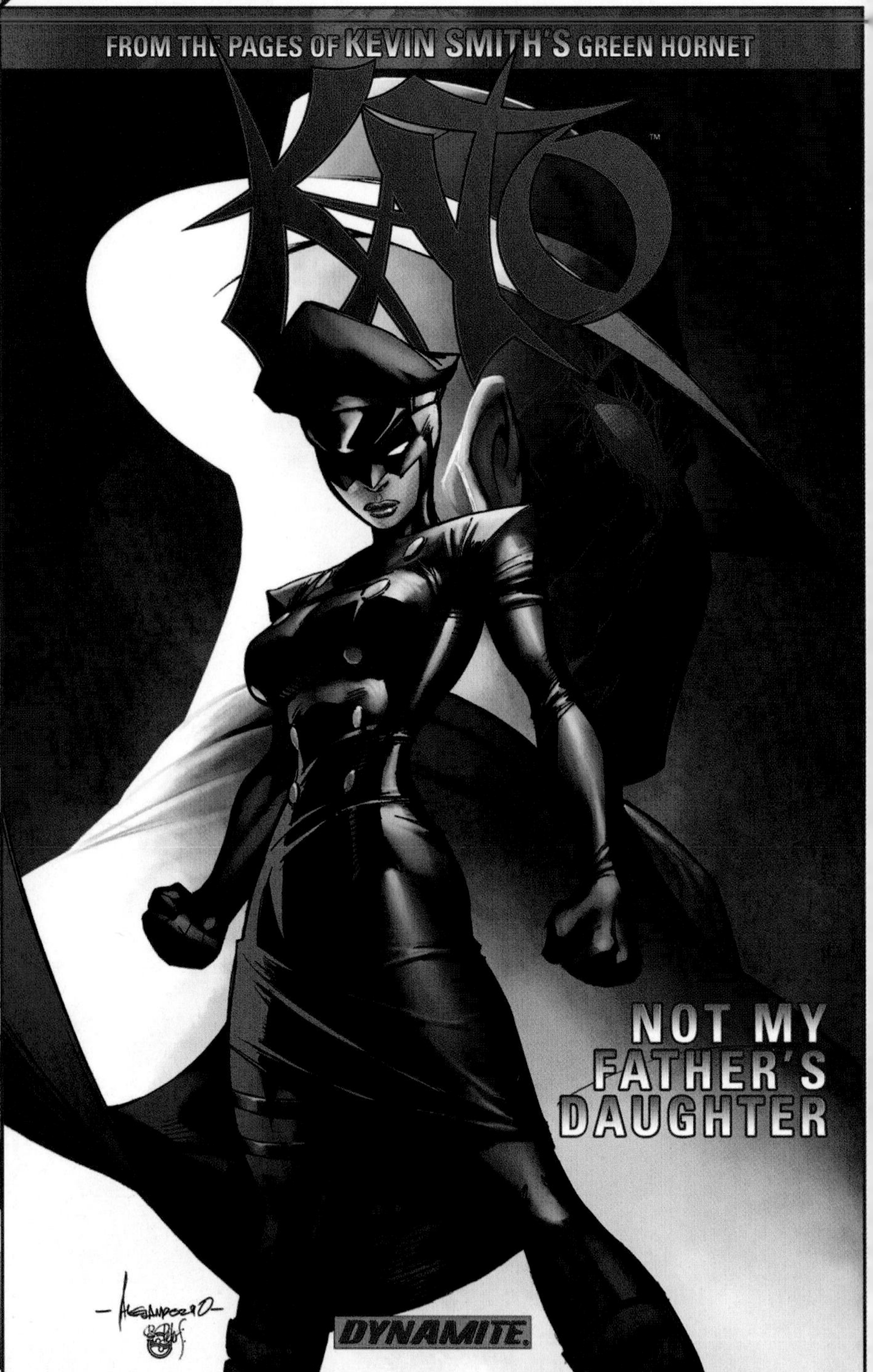

FROM THE PAGES OF KEVIN SMITH'S GREEN HORNET

NOT MY FATHER'S DAUGHTER

KEVIN SMITH'S KATO VOL. 1: NOT MY FATHER'S DAUGHTER

story by ANDE PARKS cover art by ALÉ GARZA
interior art by DIEGO BERNARD & ALÉ GARZA

From the pages of Kevin Smith's Green Hornet comes this thrilling lead-in story, starring Mulan Kato, daughter of the Green Hornet's faithful companion, Kato! Learn the secrets of Kato, his daughter, his wife's murder and the mysterious Black Hornet!

Collecting issues 1-5 of the prequel to Kevin Smith's Green Hornet • In stores November 201

ZORRO Vol. 1: YEAR ONE TRAIL OF THE FOX
Written by and cover by **MATT WAGNER**   Illustrated by **FRANCESCO FRANCAVILLA**
Reprints issues 1-8, and features all of the covers by Matt Wagner, John Cassaday, Mike Mayhew and more!

ZORRO Vol. 2: CLASHING BLADES
Written by and cover by **MATT WAGNER**   Illustrated by **CEZAR RAZEK**
Reprints issues 9-14, and features all of the covers by Matt Wagner, Ryan Sook and Francesco Francavilla!